D1415187

Joseph

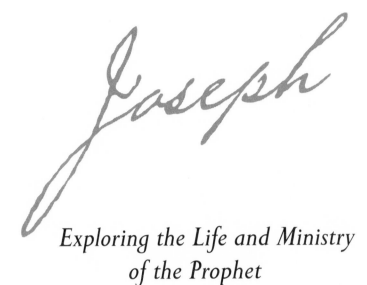

Exploring the Life and Ministry of the Prophet

Edited by

SUSAN EASTON BLACK AND ANDREW C. SKINNER

DESERET
BOOK

SALT LAKE CITY, UTAH

Library of Congress Cataloging-in-Publication Data

Joseph : Exploring the life and ministry of the prophet / edited by Susan Easton Black, Andrew C. Skinner.
    p. cm.
    Includes bibliographical references and index.
    ISBN 1-59038-471-7 (hardbound : alk. paper)
    1. Smith, Joseph, 1805–1844. I. Black, Susan Easton. II. Skinner, Andrew C., 1951–
    BX8695.S6J66   2005
    289.3'092—dc22   2005010663

Printed in Canada   29359
Friesens, Manitoba, Canada

10 9   8   7   6   5   4   3   2   1

JOSEPH SMITH,

the Prophet and Seer of the Lord,

has done more, save Jesus only,

for the salvation of men in this world,

than any other man that ever lived in it.

DOCTRINE AND COVENANTS 135:3

CONTENTS

Contents

Contents

ILLUSTRATIONS

Illustrations

Acknowledgments

As editors and contributors of this volume, we feel a deep gratitude for Joseph Smith. Together, we testify as disciple scholars that Joseph was the Lord's anointed, called to bring forth the truths of the gospel of Jesus Christ. We are deeply grateful for his life and his conviction of eternal truths. We know that Joseph Smith was indeed a prophet, and we take seriously our membership in The Church of Jesus Christ of Latter-day Saints.

We express appreciation to Cory Maxwell and others at Deseret Book who have helped to make this book/DVD a reality. To the donors to Brigham Young University who shared our vision of what this book could become and generously supported it, we express our gratitude. We extend special thanks to Christina Smith, a BYU student majoring in history, for her timely and valued research and editing skills. To Michael Hunter, producer of the companion BYU Television production, we express heartfelt appreciation for a job well done. To those associated with Michael at BYU Broadcasting, including John Reim, Sterling VanWagenen, Rob Sibley, Jordan Ormond and Diena Simmons, we express thanks for impressive expertise.

It is our hope that readers and listeners of *Joseph* will find answers to their questions about the life of this nineteenth-century Latter-day Saint leader and discover a spirit of testimony that will strengthen their own conviction that Joseph was a prophet of God.

INTRODUCTION

*I*n nineteenth-century western New York, contending religious revivalists claimed to represent Jesus Christ. Young Joseph Smith, confused by their contradicting Christian doctrines, sought clarity through prayer. The divine answer he received and the vision he saw of "two Personages, whose brightness and glory defy all description" filled his soul with eternal truths (Joseph Smith–History 1:17). Surprisingly, the sharing of truth in his small community of Palmyra, New York, led to open contempt and mockery of the young boy by his neighbors. Rather than succumb to the harassment, Joseph declared, "I had actually seen a light, and in the midst of that light I saw two Personages, and they did in reality speak to me. . . . I knew it, and I knew that God knew it, and I could not deny it" (Joseph Smith–History 1:25).

Three and a half years after Joseph's first divine manifestation, Moroni, an ancient prophet who had lived in the Americas in A.D. 400, appeared to him as a resurrected being. The angel told the seventeen-year-old Joseph of sacred engravings "written upon gold plates, giving an account of the former inhabitants of this continent" (Joseph Smith–History 1:34). In 1829 Joseph, by the gift and power of God, translated the ancient writings which became known as the Book of Mormon, Another Testament of Jesus Christ.

The book was shared with family, friends, and seekers of truth from the farthest frontiers of the United States to the British Isles. "From the first time I read this volume of volumes, even till now," wrote convert William W. Phelps, "I have been struck with a kind of

1

sacred joy at its title page. . . . What a wonderful volume! What a glorious treasure! By that book I learned the right way to God; by that book I received the fulness of the everlasting gospel; . . . and I was made glad."[1]

➤ As believers like Phelps embraced the truths of the Book of Mormon, disbelievers shunned their choice and rallied in angry mobs to overthrow what they perceived as the evil encroachment of Mormonism upon contemporary Christianity. "Hell may pour forth its rage like the burning lava of Mount Vesuvius, or of Etna," declared Joseph, "yet shall 'Mormonism' stand. . . . Truth is 'Mormonism.' God is the author of it."[2] His firm testimony made him a target of persecution and mobocracy. Believers, who testified that he was a prophet and the Book of Mormon was the word of God, also suffered.

When Father Smith was told to burn up those copies of the Book of Mormon and then his indebtedness of a small delinquent note would be forgiven, he refused, knowing that his refusal would mean his imprisonment. "I was not the first man who had been imprisoned for the truth's sake; and when I should meet Paul in the Paradise of God, I could tell him that I, too, had been in bonds for the Gospel which he had preached."[3] When Mother Smith was accosted by a Presbyterian pastor who said, "And you . . . are the mother of that poor, foolish, silly boy, Joe Smith, who pretended to translate the Book of Mormon," Lucy was unruffled. "Why do you apply to him such epithets as those?" she asked. The reverend scoffed, "Because . . . he should imagine he was going to break down all other churches with that simple 'Mormon' book." Lucy countered, "Let me tell you boldly, that that book contains the everlasting gospel. . . . mark my words—as true as God lives, before three years [Mormonism] will have more than one-third of your church."[4] The minister's hearty laugh diminished when Mormon elder Jared Carter baptized a third of his congregation.

Unswerving conviction was also the chosen lot of thousands of Latter-day Saint converts in the 1830s in New York, Ohio, and Missouri. Even though they were the objects of mockery and persecution, they did not deny their beliefs or the truth of Mormonism.

With resolute faithfulness, they followed their prophetic leader, Joseph Smith, in pioneering communities and establishing schools in the Midwest. At great personal sacrifice, they constructed a temple, a house of the Lord, in Kirtland, Ohio, contrary to the predictions of jeering critics.

A great trial of their faith came in the form of a state-sanctioned extermination order issued in 1838 by Governor Lilburn Boggs of Missouri. In the winter of 1838–39, the Latter-day Saints were driven by force from their Missouri homes. They trekked across the state and forded the icy Mississippi River, seeking refuge and safety from the injustice. One refugee, Parley P. Pratt, recalled his first reaction upon reaching Illinois: "I immediately stepped a few paces into the woods, and, kneeling down, kissed the ground as a land of liberty, and then poured out my soul in thanks to God."[5]

Residents of the small town of Quincy, Illinois, welcomed the exiled Latter-day Saints. Quincy lawyer O. H. Browning exclaimed, "Great God! have I not seen it? Yes, my eyes have beheld the blood-stained traces of innocent women and children, in the drear winter, who had traveled hundreds of miles barefoot, through frost and snow, to seek a refuge from their savage pursuers."[6] He and other town leaders advised the citizenry "to be careful not to say anything calculated to wound the feelings of the strangers thrown into their midst."[7] The local Democratic Association resolved that the Mormon exiles were "entitled to our sympathy and kindest regard, and that we recommend to the citizens of Quincy to extend all the kindness in their power to bestow on the persons who are in affliction."[8]

The Mormons were grateful for this outpouring of kindness but longed for a home of their own—a city on a hill, a city in which to worship God in peace. Near an unlikely bluff overlooking a bend in the Mississippi River their longings were fulfilled but not without additional suffering and sacrifice. In just six years the Latter-day Saints created from the marshy lowlands a city beautiful—Nauvoo. Although Mormon leader Heber C. Kimball helped drain the swampland, build homes, cultivate farms, and set up shops in the fledgling community, the Spirit whispered to him that this city was only a temporary refuge. Church leader Sidney Rigdon was enraged at Heber's seemingly pessimistic view and denounced his colleague: "I should suppose that Elder Kimball has passed through sufferings and privations and mobbings and drivings enough to learn to prophesy good concerning Israel."[9]

Heber was correct, however. Nauvoo was only a stopping point, a temporary refuge from the storm. "We ware . . . glad of a restingplace out of the reach of those that had sought our lives," wrote Sarah Rich. "We ware truely a thankfull and humble people."[10] Although they knew Nauvoo would flourish for a moment, their industrious labors led neighbors to believe they would be permanent residents. By the early 1840s, settlers along the Mississippi and river boat passengers were applauding Nauvoo as "the Jewel of the Mississippi." J. H. Buckingham, a gentleman from Boston, recorded:

> No one can visit Nauvoo, and come away without a conviction that . . . the body of the Mormons were an industrious, hard-working, and frugal people. In the history of the whole world there cannot be found such another instance of so rapid a rise of a city out of the wilderness—a city so well built, a territory so well cultivated.[11]

Visitors and converts daily swelled the population of the emerging community. They often sought audience with the town's leading citizen, Joseph Smith. "I have had the pleasure of welcoming about one hundred brethren [today]," wrote the Prophet.[12] Among those he greeted was English convert Jane Robinson, who mused, "It was a severe trial to me, in my feelings to leave my native land and the pleasing associations that I had formed there; but my heart was fixed. I knew in whom I had trusted and with the fire of Israel's God burning in my bosom, I forsook my home."[13] Another of the most distinguished visitors to Nauvoo was Josiah Quincy, formerly mayor of Boston. He wrote of Joseph Smith:

> It is by no means improbable that some future textbook . . . will contain a question something like this: What historical American of the nineteenth century has exerted the most powerful influence upon the destinies of his countrymen? And it is by no means impossible that the

answer to the interrogatory may be thus written: Joseph Smith, the Mormon Prophet.[14]

That is our conviction. Within these pages and through the lens of a camera in the capable hands of BYU Broadcasting personnel, learn of Joseph Smith, the Prophet of the Restoration. Read of his love for the Lord and for the Latter-day Saints. Learn of Nauvoo as it struggled to reach sacred heights and then in a moment of jealous avarice and plunder, fell to obscurity. Learn of the murder of the Smith brothers who "in life . . . were not divided, and in death they were not separated" (D&C 135:3).

NOTES

1. Phelps, in *Latter Day Saints' Messenger and Advocate* 1 (September 1835): 177–79.
2. Smith, *Teachings of the Prophet Joseph Smith,* 139.
3. Smith, *History of Joseph Smith by His Mother,* ed. Nibley, 185.
4. Smith, *History of Joseph Smith by His Mother,* ed. Nibley, 215–16.
5. Pratt, *Autobiography of Parley P. Pratt,* 278.
6. Smith, *History of the Church,* 4:370.
7. Ebenezer Robinson, *Return* 2 (1890): 243.
8. Smith, *History of the Church,* 3:268.
9. Whitney, *Life of Heber C. Kimball,* 256.
10. Autobiography of Sarah D. Rich, 1:57; cited in Arrington, *Charles C. Rich,* 69.
11. Cited in Kimball, "Nauvoo," *Improvement Era,* July 1962, 548.
12. Smith, *History of the Church,* 4:230.
13. "Jane C. Robinson Hindly Reminiscences and Diary"; cited in Holzapfel and Holzapfel, *Women of Nauvoo,* 14–15.
14. Roberts, *Comprehensive History,* 2:349–50.

CHAPTER ONE

JOSEPH SMITH FORETOLD

Andrew C. Skinner

The God of the universe does not leave anything to chance, especially when it comes to the salvation of his children. He knows all things and has prepared all things for the accomplishment of his grand designs and desires. "I am God," he said, "and there is none like me, declaring the end from the beginning, and from ancient times the things that are not yet done, saying, My counsel shall stand, and I will do all my pleasure" (Isaiah 46:9–10). Long before any of us were born into mortality, God planned, foresaw, and foreordained the events of the latter-day restoration of the gospel of Jesus Christ in this, the dispensation of the fulness of times. He tutored and prepared in premortality the man who would be the prophet-leader of the Restoration, the man the world knows as Joseph Smith Jr. Most impressive is the witness and testimony of Brigham Young, one who knew Joseph well and who knew for himself of Joseph Smith's divinely appointed destiny. Brigham Young declared:

> We are a people whose rise and progress from the beginning, has been the work of God our Heavenly Father . . .
>
> It was decreed in the counsels of eternity, long before the foundations of the earth were laid, that he, Joseph Smith, should be the man, in the last dispensation of this world, to bring forth the word of God to the people, and receive the fulness of the keys and power of the Priesthood of the Son of God. The Lord had his eyes upon him, and upon his father, and upon his father's father, and upon their progenitors clear back to Abraham, and from Abraham to the flood, from the flood to Enoch, and

Andrew C. Skinner serves as dean of Religous Education and is a professor of ancient scripture at Brigham Young University.

from Enoch to Adam. He has watched that family and that blood as it has circulated from its fountain to the birth of that man. He was fore-ordained in eternity to preside over this last dispensation.[1]

Neither the Restoration nor Joseph Smith's rise to greatness was accidental. Of that Brigham Young leaves no doubt. His personal witness of Joseph's premortal preparation affirms the scriptural record that tells of Joseph's foreknown and foretold mission and ministry on this earth. This scriptural record is both extensive and of ancient date. It includes the visions, revelations, and impressions of some of history's best known prophets and seers.

ADAM AND ENOCH

Though not mentioned explicitly, Joseph Smith surely must have been known to our first parents, Adam and Eve:

> Three years previous to the death of Adam, he called Seth, Enos, Cainan, Mahalaleel, Jared, Enoch, and Methuselah, who were all high priests, with the residue of his posterity who were righteous, into the valley of Adam-ondi-Ahman, and there bestowed upon them his last blessing. . . .
>
> And Adam stood up in the midst of the congregation; and, notwithstanding he was bowed down with age, being full of the Holy Ghost, predicted whatsoever should befall his posterity unto the latest generation. (D&C 107:53, 56)

Adam's panoramic revelation of all things that "should befall his posterity unto the latest generation" laid the foundation for Enoch's own vision. That seer conversed with God and witnessed in vision the mortal ministry of Jesus Christ, his crucifixion, resurrection, and ascension. Enoch asked about the second coming of our Lord and received this reply:

> And righteousness will I send down out of heaven; and truth will I send forth out of the earth, to bear testimony of mine Only Begotten; his resurrection from the dead; yea, and also the resurrection of all men; and righteousness and truth will I cause to sweep the earth as with a flood, to gather out mine elect from the four quarters of the earth, unto a place which I shall prepare, an Holy City, that my people may gird up their

Joseph Smith among the Prophets, *by Paul Mann*

loins, and be looking forth for the time of my coming; for there shall be my tabernacle, and it shall be called Zion, a New Jerusalem. (Moses 7:62)

Thousands of years before the actual events took place, Enoch was taught that before the second coming of Jesus Christ, righteousness would come down out of heaven and truth would be sent forth out of the earth. Stunningly, in our time, President Ezra Taft Benson declared the fulfillment of Enoch's prophecy:

We have seen the marvelous fulfillment of that prophecy in our generation. The Book of Mormon has come forth out of the earth, filled with truth. . . . God has also sent down righteousness from heaven. The Father Himself appeared with His Son to the Prophet Joseph Smith. The angel Moroni, John the Baptist, Peter, James, and numerous other angels were directed by heaven to restore the necessary powers to the kingdom.[2]

Enoch knew of the man we call Joseph Smith and the record we know as the Book of Mormon.

JOSEPH AND MOSES

With all that was shown to Abraham, we cannot help but suppose that he saw in vision that one of his innumerable posterity would be the latter-day instrument in God's hands through whom all families of the earth would be blessed (Abraham 2:9–11). We know with absolute certainty that almost four millennia before Joseph Smith was born, Abraham's great-grandson Joseph of Egypt spoke specifically about his latter-day namesake (JST Genesis 50; 2 Nephi 3). These lost prophecies were restored by Joseph Smith himself as he translated the Book of Mormon and then revised the Bible. It must have been a somewhat arresting and humbling experience for him to translate and restore sacred texts that he quickly realized were spoken about him thousands of years before. Through Joseph of old, the Lord declared his future intentions:

> And again, a seer will I raise up out of the fruit of thy loins, and unto him will I give power to bring forth my word unto the seed of thy loins; and not to the bringing forth of my word only, saith the Lord, but to the convincing them of my word, which shall have already gone forth among them in the last days. . . .
>
> And that seer will I bless, and they that seek to destroy him shall be confounded; for this promise I give unto you; for I will remember you from generation to generation; and his name shall be called Joseph, and it shall be after the name of his father; and he shall be like unto you, for the thing which the Lord shall bring forth by his hand shall bring my people unto salvation. (JST Genesis 50:30, 33)

This very prophecy is one that Father Lehi quoted to his own son Joseph (2 Nephi 3:5–22). It seems more than likely that Lehi knew of the prophecy (lost from the Massoretic text that was ultimately translated into the King James Version) because he had read it on the plates of brass, which his sons went back to Jerusalem to retrieve. Thus, the version of Joseph of Egypt's prophecy (JST Genesis 50) repeated by Lehi and now preserved in 2 Nephi 3 discusses four men named Joseph: Joseph, son of Lehi (2 Nephi 3:1–3); Joseph who was sold into Egypt (2 Nephi 3:4–5); Joseph Smith Jr. (2 Nephi 3:6–19); and Joseph Smith Sr. (2 Nephi 3:15). In this vein, it is interesting to note that the Hebrew name *Joseph* means "added to" or "increased." Indeed, the name and fame of Abraham's great-grandson Joseph was "added to" and "increased" by the great prophets who bore his name after him.

No less profound than ancient Joseph's knowledge of the latter-day prophet to be named Joseph was Moses' prophetic understanding of the same prophet. In another revelation given through Joseph Smith, now comprising the once-missing introduction to the book of Genesis, the prophet Moses was shown the latter days and one who would be raised up to restore the great Lawgiver's testimony: "And in a day when the children of men shall esteem my words as naught and take many of them from the book which thou shalt write, behold, I will raise up another like unto thee; and they shall be had again among the children of men—among as many as shall believe" (Moses 1:41).

Joseph Smith was the fulfillment of the Lord's promise to Moses. As the Lord told Oliver Cowdery, "No one shall be appointed to receive commandments and revelations in this church excepting my servant Joseph Smith, Jun., for he receiveth them even as Moses" (D&C 28:2). An interesting parallel can be seen. The Lord said to Joseph of old that the latter-day prophet named Joseph would be like him. The Lord said to Moses that the same latter-day prophet would be like him. Thus, Joseph Smith, it would seem, was prophesied to possess every gift, power, responsibility, and symbolic likeness of the ancient prophets. Moreover, it was foretold that the latter-day Joseph would be like Jesus Christ.

ISAIAH AND JESUS CHRIST

The Old Testament seer who prophesied the most about Christ's coming was Isaiah. He is the prophet most quoted in scripture, being referenced by Jesus, Paul, Peter, and John more frequently than any other Old Testament seer. Isaiah focused his attention not only on the first and second comings of the Messiah but also on the seminal doctrines and events of the kingdom of God—the gathering of Israel, the restoration of the latter days, and the Millennium.

Nephite prophets appreciated and quoted from the writings of Isaiah, who had announced a servant who would come forward in the future, possessing and fulfilling several significant, singular characteristics. Originally listed in Isaiah 49, these characteristics were quoted by Nephi, as recorded in 1 Nephi 21. This future servant would be—

- Someone whom "the Lord hath called . . . from the womb" (v. 1);
- Someone who would say that the Lord "formed me from the womb" to do a special work, or, in other words, someone who *knew* he had been foreordained (v. 5);
- Someone whose "mouth [was] like a sharp sword," or, in other words, someone who spoke with authority (v. 2);
- Someone who was hidden "in the shadow of [the Lord's] hand" (v. 2);
- Someone who was "made . . . a polished shaft; in his quiver hath he [the Lord] hid [him]" (v. 2);
- Someone who would say, "I have labored in vain" (v. 4);
- Someone who would authoritatively say, "And now, saith the Lord" (v. 5);
- Someone whose life's work would be "to bring Jacob again to [the Lord]—though Israel be not gathered" (v. 5);
- Someone who would be the Lord's "servant to raise up the tribes of Jacob, and to restore the preserved of Israel" (v. 6);
- Someone whom the Lord would "give . . . for a light to the Gentiles" (v. 6);
- Someone "whom man despiseth," but, at the same time,

11

someone whom "kings shall see and arise, princes also . . . worship" (v. 7); and

• Someone who will be given to Israel "for a covenant of the people, to establish the earth, to cause to inherit the desolate heritages," who will free the prisoners and enlighten those who sit in darkness, and who will shepherd the chosen people (vv. 8–9).

Though various specific aspects of Isaiah's prophetic list could probably fit a number of individuals, taken all together this list of qualifications applies to only two beings—one is Jesus Christ; the other, Joseph Smith.

• Joseph Smith was indeed called "from the womb," or foreordained (1 Nephi 21:1).

• He knew through revelation, now recorded as Doctrine and Covenants 127:2, that he had been chosen to be the Prophet of the Restoration. On another occasion, he said: "Every man who has a calling to minister to the inhabitants of the world was ordained to that very purpose in the Grand Council of heaven before this world was. I suppose I was ordained to this very office in that Grand Council. It is the testimony that I want that I am God's servant, and this people His people."[3]

• Joseph Smith spoke as a "sharp sword" because he spoke the words of the Lord (D&C 21:5; 18:35–36), which are described in modern revelation as "quick and powerful, sharper than a two-edged sword, to the dividing asunder of both joints and marrow" (D&C 6:2).

• Joseph Smith was "hid" by the Lord (D&C 86:9).

• Joseph Smith became a "polished shaft" in the quiver of the Almighty, as his self-characterization testifies:

I am like a huge, rough stone rolling down from a high mountain; and the only polishing I get is when some corner gets rubbed off by coming in contact with something else, striking with accelerated force against religious bigotry, priestcraft, lawyer-craft, doctor-craft, lying editors, suborned judges and jurors, and the authority of perjured

executives, backed by mobs, blasphemers, licentious and corrupt men
and women—all hell knocking off a corner here and a corner there. Thus
I will become a smooth and *polished shaft in the quiver of the Almighty*,
who will give me dominion over all and every one of them, when their
refuge of lies shall fail, and their hiding place shall be destroyed, while
these smooth-polished stones with which I come in contact become
marred.[4]

- Joseph Smith, in the harsh conditions of Liberty Jail, seems to
  have felt that his labors were in vain (D&C 121:2).
- Joseph Smith not only had the authority to speak for God but
  on numerous occasions validated his messages by uttering the
  very words Isaiah predicted he would: "Thus saith the Lord"
  (for example, D&C 52:1; 54:1; 60:1; 87:1).
- Joseph Smith's life work was to bring the house of Israel again to
  the Lord (Mormon 8:16; D&C 5:9–10; 6:6; 109:67).
- Joseph Smith was commissioned to raise up the tribes of Jacob
  and restore them by overseeing the latter-day gathering of Israel
  (D&C 110:11).
- Joseph Smith is spoken of in the scriptures as "a light unto the
  Gentiles" (D&C 86:11). Only one other person can claim that
  distinction—the Lord himself (Isaiah 42:6).
- Joseph Smith was both despised and revered, just as the Lord
  had foretold (Joseph Smith–History 1:33). Joseph was also
  promised that the gospel he restored would be preached before
  "kings and rulers" (D&C 1:23).
- Joseph Smith was the servant through whom the eternal gospel
  covenant was reestablished (D&C 1:17–22). Surely it is not just
  coincidence that the first section of the Doctrine and
  Covenants, the revelation by which the Lord introduces Joseph
  Smith to the world, begins with the same language as Isaiah
  49:1: "Hearken, ye people, from far." Just as Isaiah had foretold,
  Joseph was also commanded to "proclaim the acceptable year
  of the Lord, and the gospel of salvation" (D&C 93:51; compare
  Isaiah 61:2).

Indeed, we are justified in saying that not only was Joseph Smith foreseen by Isaiah but Joseph Smith was a type and similitude of the Messiah, our Savior.

The resurrected Savior himself endorsed and described the fore-ordained, prophetic, future leadership of Joseph Smith when He appeared to the Nephites:

> For in that day, for my sake shall the Father work a work, which shall be a great and a marvelous work among them; and there shall be among them those who will not believe it, although a man shall declare it unto them.
>
> But behold, the life of my servant shall be in my hand; therefore they shall not hurt him, although he shall be marred because of them. Yet I will heal him, for I will show unto them that my wisdom is greater than the cunning of the devil. (3 Nephi 21:9–10)

The Lord went on to declare in no uncertain terms that whoso-ever would not believe in his words, which the Father would cause to be brought forth by Joseph Smith, would be "cut off from among my people who are of the covenant" (3 Nephi 21:11).

Thus, the Lord made it clear that Joseph Smith and his mission were foreknown long before the latter-day seer was born into mortal-ity. Those who ignore him or his foreordained message do so at the peril of their very salvation.

SPECIAL TUTORS

God and his many prophets have, from the beginning of time, known of and declared the coming of Joseph Smith to inaugurate the dispensation of the fulness of times. Therefore, it is not surprising, though wondrous to contemplate, that Joseph Smith was personally tutored by many of those prophets, as well as the Lord, who knew of him before he was born. It can be said without exaggeration that just as they knew him, so he came to know them. Many of the ancient prophet-leaders and dispensation heads laid their hands upon Joseph's head and bestowed keys, powers, and knowledge they them-selves had gained from Deity. Who else among all the world's leaders and so-called power brokers have stood in the presence of God the Eternal Father, his Son Jesus Christ, Adam, Noah, Peter, James, John,

Paul, Moroni, and many, many more, including even Lucifer, the enemy of all righteousness? (D&C 128:20–21). President John Taylor, beloved friend and trusted associate of the Prophet Joseph Smith, summed up the matter in these words:

> Joseph Smith in the first place was set apart by the Almighty according to the counsels of the gods in the eternal worlds, to introduce the principles of life among the people, of which the Gospel is the grand power and influence, and through which salvation can extend to all peoples, all nations, all kindreds, all tongues and all worlds. It is the principle that brings life and immortality to light, and places us in communication with God. God selected him for that purpose, and he fulfilled his mission and lived honorably and died honorably. I know of what I speak for I was very well acquainted with him and was with him a great deal during his life, and was with him when he died. The principles which he had, placed him in communication with the Lord, and not only with the Lord, but with the ancient apostles and prophets; such men, for instance, as Abraham, Isaac, Jacob, Noah, Adam, Seth, Enoch, and Jesus and the Father, and the apostles that lived on this continent as well as those who lived on the Asiatic continent. He seemed to be as familiar with these people as we are with one another. Why? Because he had to introduce a dispensation which was called the dispensation of the fulness of times, and it was known as such by the ancient servants of God.[5]

ALL THINGS PREPARED

Just as Joseph Smith was foreknown, foreordained, and prepared in the eternities to be the founding Prophet of the Restoration, so, too, all other components necessary for the Restoration to succeed were foreknown and put in place by God. As early as the Middle Ages, the Lord "began to prepare those social, educational, religious, economic, and governmental conditions under which he could more easily restore the gospel for the last time among men."[6]

During the Renaissance and the Reformation, the religious landscape of Europe changed, owing to the work of such reformers as Wycliffe, Huss, Luther, Zwingli, Calvin, and Knox, upon whom the spirit of inspiration rested.[7] These men rebelled against the religious evils of their time and released Christendom from the stranglehold of the Roman church. The Lord raised up these good souls, said

President Joseph Fielding Smith, and "gave them power to break the shackles which bound the people" in order to prepare the world for the Restoration.[8]

Another monumental step toward the restoration of the fulness of the gospel of Jesus Christ was the discovery, colonization, and establishment of America by individuals and groups prepared, raised up, and inspired by God. President Joseph F. Smith testified:

> This great American nation the Almighty raised up by the power of his omnipotent hand, that it might be possible in the latter days for the kingdom of God to be established in the earth. If the Lord had not prepared the way by laying the foundations of this glorious nation, it would have been impossible (under the stringent laws and bigotry of the monarchical governments of the world) to have laid the foundations for the coming of his great kingdom. The Lord has done this.[9]

Last, but not least, the family into which Joseph Smith was born was foreknown and prepared by the Lord. Hard work, love of liberty, and personal religion were hallmarks of Joseph's New England heritage. But more than that, Joseph Smith's family provided the optimal environment in which to rear, tutor, and support a chosen prophet of God. The family seems to have anticipated some great change of the Lord's making—and they were not wrong. Joseph's grandfather Asael Smith felt moved upon to predict that "God was going to raise up some branch of his family to be a great benefit to mankind."[10] He lived long enough to know that his grandson Joseph was the fulfillment of his prescient feeling.

The God of the universe does not deal in chance. All things regarding the accomplishment of his purposes were foreknown, prepared, and foretold. As Brigham Young said, God had his eye on Joseph Smith from the beginning, and many others have come to understand that great truth.[11]

NOTES

1. Young, *Discourses of Brigham Young*, 108.
2. Benson, *Witness and a Warning*, 26.
3. Smith, *Teachings of the Prophet Joseph Smith*, 365.
4. Smith, *Teachings of the Prophet Joseph Smith*, 304; emphasis added.

5. Taylor, *Journal of Discourses,* 21:94.
6. McConkie, *Mormon Doctrine,* 717.
7. See McConkie, *Mormon Doctrine,* 717.
8. Smith, *Doctrines of Salvation,* 1:174.
9. Smith, *Gospel Doctrine,* 409.
10. Anderson, *Joseph Smith's New England Heritage,* 112.
11. See Young, *Discourses of Brigham Young,* 108.

CHAPTER TWO

THE SMITH FAMILY MOVES TO PALMYRA

Lawrence Flake

he first European inhabitants of what is now Palmyra, Wayne County, New York, were six men who traveled there in 1789 from the Wyoming River Valley in Pennsylvania.[1] The leader of the group, Captain John Swift, was the man historians consider the founder of Palmyra. Swift was a speculator, meaning that he purchased land at a low price and hoped to sell it for a profit. Of great interest to Latter-day Saints was land he purchased in western New York. This tract was blessed with twin waterways and had the promise of becoming excellent farmland. It attracted the attention not only of Swift but of many others who followed.

In 1791, four families lived in the area, a total of eleven men and three women. By 1792, the place that would become Palmyra was home to seventeen families; however, one town historian reports that "an alarming scarcity of food made some settlers return to Long Island, leaving nine families alone to face the rigors of the season."[2] The hardy settlers who remained, still under the direction of John Swift, built log homes and laid out Main and Canandaigua Streets, the latter being opened in 1793. The settlement was first called Swift or Swift's Landing. Later it was known as the District of Tolland, but in January 1796 townsfolk decided upon the name Palmyra, after the famous ancient city in Syria.[3] Captain Swift established the first gristmill in Palmyra in 1794 and began training a militia there. He also donated land for the first church, schoolhouse, and cemetery, which

Lawrence Flake is a professor of Church history and doctrine at Brigham Young University.

later became the resting place of Alvin, the oldest of Joseph Smith Sr.'s children. Asa Swift, the son of John, was the first male child of European ancestry born in the town.[4] "John Swift was a man of tremendous energy, diverse activities, and humanitarian spirit"; he is buried "in the cemetery which he had donated to the citizens of Palmyra."[5]

GROWTH OF PALMYRA

The fledgling town of Palmyra had the good fortune of being located along the proposed route of the Erie Canal. When Joseph Smith Sr. and his family moved to Palmyra in 1816, the canal was only one year away from the beginning of its construction. The canal put Palmyra on the map, making it an important city in early New York history rather than a small, unknown village. The Erie Canal was forty feet wide and four feet deep, with a series of locks that raised the water level 565 feet over its 363-mile course between Lake Erie and the Hudson River. This remarkable waterway provided inexpensive transportation to passengers as well as an excellent channel for economical transport of freight. Unfortunately, it also became a focus for unsavory elements of American life. It was sometimes called "the Big Ditch of Iniquity" because of prostitution, drinking, and gambling that inevitably thrived along its shores.[6]

As might be expected, many early residents of western New York did not belong to any particular church. Only 7 percent of the American population was considered active in an organized religion in 1800, and only 11 or 12 percent belonged to a Christian denomination in the Palmyra area by 1820, the year of Joseph's first vision.[7] The Presbyterian Church established a congregation in Palmyra as early as 1797. The Quakers (or Society of Friends) built a meetinghouse very near the Smith farm in 1816, the year of the Smiths' arrival. This small structure, though it has been moved from its original site, is the only meetinghouse in the area that was used in Joseph Smith's time and is still in existence today. By 1820, several denominations had arrived in the area—Baptists, Episcopalians,

A Year After the Eruption, *by Greg Harlin*

Methodists, and so forth. "Many churches were in Palmyra during the
period when Joseph Smith was 'inquiring after religion.' Churches
and revival meetings in neighboring towns would also have caught his
attention. Clearly religion was an integral part of life in Palmyra."[8]

By 1816, when the Joseph Smith Sr. family appeared on the
scene, Palmyra was a thriving town of 2,500 settlers with a number
of "cloth-making establishments, ten grist mills, two carding
machines, iron works, and a famous rope walk that existed until
1828."[9] There were also manufacturers of sleighs, wagons, boots, and
barrels.[10] By 1820, goods and services had expanded immensely, due
in part to commerce stimulated by the building of the Erie Canal:

> The people had a wide variety of services available to them, including
> lawyers, doctors, dentists, pharmacists, and bankers. Typical early
> American businesses were also found in Palmyra: asheries, tanneries,
> cooper shops, wagon and sleigh shops, breweries, foundries, sawmills, tin
> smith shops, blacksmith shops, grist mills, livery stables, lumber yards,
> tailors, shoe shops, bakeries, saddle and harness shops, and sign
> painters.[11]

Palmyra also had a larger proportion of newspapers than most towns its size, with about twenty papers circulated within a radius of thirty miles.[12]

THE MOVE FROM NORWICH, VERMONT, TO PALMYRA, NEW YORK

In 1814, the Joseph Smith Sr. family moved to Norwich, Vermont, from West Lebanon, New Hampshire, where they had suffered financial reverses resulting from the family's medical bills accrued during a devastating bout with typhoid fever. The fever left young Joseph, only seven years old, with a raging infection in his leg bone. It was in West Lebanon that he underwent an excruciatingly painful operation on his leg.

Desperate to make a living, the Smiths rented a hundred-acre farm across the Connecticut River from Lebanon in Norwich, and there they struggled to survive until they could sell the crops they planted in the spring of 1814. Unfortunately, in their new home, they suffered yet another setback. For three straight years their crops failed. The third year, 1816, was the worst of all. Between 6 June and 30 August, four killing frosts occurred. That year became known as "the year without a summer" or "1800 and froze to death." A record snowstorm fell on 8 June, destroying the crops and driving thousands of inhabitants out of Vermont and other areas of northern New England to more moderate climates in New York, Pennsylvania, and Ohio.[13]

Scientific studies attempting to explain this unseasonably cold weather have led to a fascinating conclusion. Weather experts have tracked the phenomenon to the massive explosion in 1815 of the volcano Tambora, about 10,000 miles away in Indonesia on the island of Sumbawa. According to available data, this huge explosion triggered a series of weather abnormalities that caused hardship in many parts of the world. The eruption displaced twenty-five cubic miles of matter, reducing the height of the mountain by 4,200 feet.[14] The following describes the effect on New England:

> As the dust in the upper atmosphere circled the earth after the eruption of Tambora, it gradually shadowed the high latitudes. The first two

months of 1816 were not exceptionally cold in New England, but by May observers had begun to comment on the lateness of the spring. June began auspiciously, and crops that had survived the unwonted frosts of mid-May started to progress. The first of three unseasonable cold waves moved eastward into New England early on June 6. The cold and wind lasted until June 11, leaving from three to six inches of snow on the ground in northern New England. A second killing frost struck the same areas on July 9 and a third and fourth on August 12 and 30, just as the harvest of twice-ravaged crops was about to begin. The repeated summer frosts destroyed all but the hardiest grains and vegetables.[15]

The Smith family was faced with the same difficult decision many of their neighbors had already made. Leaving Norwich at that time would not be easy. Lucy had just given birth to her eighth child, a son, Don Carlos, in March, and she would be subjected to the added difficulty of making the journey with a nursing infant. Also, as was usual for the times, the family had incurred many debts and had parties owing them money as well. The economy was based on trading goods and services, and many of these transactions were still pending for the Smith family.

At this challenging time, Joseph Sr. came across favorable reports concerning land in Palmyra, in western New York State. One such advertisement claimed that the land was "well-timbered, well-watered, easily accessible and undeniably fertile—all to be had on long-term payments for only two or three dollars an acre."[16] Father Smith decided to travel the three hundred miles to see for himself what the prospects were for establishing his family in that area. One of his acquaintances, a Mr. Howard, was also traveling there from Norwich. Accompanying him seemed a wise decision. Lucy assured her husband that she could manage their affairs in Norwich and make preparations for the family to join him when he sent for them. She suggested that he gather his debtors and creditors together and make arrangements for them to pay each other, thus freeing the family from their financial obligations. He did so, and in the summer of 1816 departed for the unknown territory to the west.[17]

Father Smith must have found immediate satisfaction and promise in the Palmyra area, for soon after his arrival, he sent for his family. Caleb Howard, a cousin of Father Smith's traveling companion, agreed to drive the Smiths' team and wagon back to Vermont and transport Lucy and the family of eight children to Palmyra. Lucy and her older sons made extensive preparations for the journey. Just before their departure, some of Joseph Sr.'s creditors appeared on the scene. They had purposely failed to present their claims at the time of his meeting with his debtors and creditors. They apparently planned to press Lucy for funds at the time of her vulnerability when she would have no recourse but to meet their demands. Two friends in Norwich told her she should take her case to court, but instead of facing such proceedings and the inevitable delays they would cause, she paid her creditors 150 dollars from the funds she had gathered for her family's journey and left with only a fraction of what she sorely needed to get herself and her children to Palmyra.[18]

More difficulties ensued. The family first traveled to Royalton, Vermont, to deliver Lucy's mother, Lydia Mack, who had been living with them for some years, to the home of Daniel Mack, with whom she now planned to live. The sleigh they were riding in overturned, seriously injuring the aged Lydia. She apparently never fully recovered from the effects of this accident, as the family blamed these injuries for her death two years later.[19]

At Royalton, amid much sorrow, Lucy parted from her dear mother. Both of them feared they would never see each other again in this life. Lucy wrote:

> My mother wept over me, long and bitterly. She told me that it was not probable she should ever behold my face again; "But, my dear child," said she, "I have lived long—my days are nearly numbered—I must soon exchange the things of this world for those which pertain to another state of existence, where I hope to enjoy the society of the blessed; and now as my last admonition, I beseech you to continue faithful in the service of God to the end of your days, that I may have the pleasure of embracing you in another and fairer world above."[20]

The driver, Caleb Howard, proved to be the source of their next difficulties. This unscrupulous man wasted in drunkenness the funds that Father Smith had given him to transport the family to Palmyra.

Joseph Jr., age ten, was still recovering from his leg operation and had difficulty walking. The Smiths, traveling by wagon, had joined with another family, the Gates, who were also on their way to Palmyra. Caleb forced Joseph off the wagon in deference to two young ladies of the Gates family, whose company he enjoyed a great deal more. Joseph wrote:

> Howard drove me from the wagon & made me travel in my weak state through the snow, 40 miles per day for several days, during which time I suffered the most excrutiating weariness & pain, & all this that Mr. Howard might enjoy the society of two of Mr. Gates' Daughters which he took on the wagon where I should hive rode, & this he continued to do day after day through the Journey, & when my brothers remonstrated with Mr. Howard, for his treatment to me, he would knock them down with the butt of his whip.[21]

And so under these adverse circumstances, especially for young Joseph, the family doggedly pursued their difficult journey across two states toward their new home, completely unaware of their extraordinary destiny.

Near Utica, yet another of the vexatious incidents with Mr. Howard occurred. Mother Smith gave an account of his rascality in her history:

> We bore patiently with his [Caleb Howard's] abuse, until we got about twenty miles west of Utica, when one morning, as we were getting ready to continue our journey, my oldest son came to me and said, "Mother, Mr. Howard has thrown the goods out of the wagon, and is about starting off with the team." Upon hearing this, I told him to call the man in. I met him in the bar-room, in the presence of a large company of travelers, both male and female, and I demanded his reason for the course which he was taking. He told me the money which I had given him was all expended, and he could go no further.
>
> I then turned to those present and said, "Gentlemen and ladies, please give your attention for a moment. Now, as sure as there is a God in heaven, that team, as well as the goods, belong to my husband, and this man intends to take them from me . . . leaving me with eight children, without the means of proceeding on my journey." Then turning to Mr. Howard, I said, "Sir, I now forbid you touching the team, or driving it one step further. You can go about your own business; I have no use

for you. I shall take charge of the team myself, and hereafter attend to my own affairs."[22]

Lucy's courage and resolve, and no doubt public pressure, dissuaded Caleb from his evil plan, and he departed from their company.

Continuing without him, Lucy made the mistake of trusting the Gates family to give Joseph a place in their sleigh. Joseph wrote that one of the sons in that family knocked him down as he tried to climb into the sleigh. He said that he was "left to wallow in my blood until a stranger came along, picked me up, and carried me to the Town of Palmyra."[23]

Because Lucy had no money left, she financed the last portion of their arduous journey by selling some of their belongings, including clothing and fabric. The last things she expended were the "eardrops," which her thirteen-year-old daughter, Sophronia, was wearing at the time. The beleaguered party of travelers arrived in Palmyra with only a few cents left to their names.[24] The long-anticipated meeting with their husband and father was sanguine. Lucy recorded:

> The joy I felt in throwing myself and My children upon the care and affection of a tender Husband and Father doubly paid me for all I had suffered. The children surrounded their Father clinging to his neck, covering his face with tears and kisses that were heartily reciprocated by him. . . . We all now sat down, and counselled together relative to the course which was best for us to adopt in our destitute circumstances.[25]

GETTING ESTABLISHED IN PALMYRA

The Smith family's dream of buying a farm in the Palmyra area had to be deferred for a year and a half. Mother Smith used her talent for painting oil tablecloths to keep food on the table while other family members engaged in various enterprises including running a small concessions shop and cart from which they sold refreshments at public gatherings. The men of the family—Joseph Sr., Alvin (age eighteen in 1816) and Hyrum (age sixteen)—took whatever manual labor jobs they could find, such as harvesting crops (mostly hay and wheat), gardening, digging wells, and so forth. The building of the Erie

Canal may have been a boon to them. They apparently did not work on it themselves—construction had not yet reached Palmyra—but other local men were drawn away from the area, attracted by wages of fifty cents per day. Their departure opened up additional jobs in the Palmyra area and kept wages relatively high.[26]

Money not absolutely required to provide bare necessities for the family of ten was put aside to purchase land. The family's dream was realized in 1818 when they contracted for some acreage about two miles from Palmyra. There they built a small two-story cabin, to which they later added a room.[27] Clearing and working the land proved very challenging. The farm did not immediately produce enough to sustain the family and meet the annual mortgage payment, but between family members working on the farm and at other jobs, they managed to remain on the land. Though they struggled to make the yearly mortgage payments of one hundred dollars, the family had a measure of satisfaction at what they had accomplished. Lucy wrote, "Again we began to rejoice in our prosperity, and our hearts glowed with gratitude to God for the manifestations of his favor that surrounded us."[28]

NOTES

1. Benjamin, "History of Palmyra," 1.
2. Benjamin, "History of Palmyra," 1.
3. Wayne County Guide to Historical Sites, www.waynecountyny.org, 1.
4. Wayne County Guide to Historical Sites, www.waynecountyny.org, 1
5. Backman, *Joseph Smith's First Vision*, 35.
6. Donald Q. Cannon, "Palmyra, New York: 1820–1830," in Porter, Backman, and Black, *New York*, 4.
7. Backman, *Joseph Smith's First Vision*, 54, 78.
8. Cannon, "Palmyra, New York: 1820–1830," 10.
9. Benjamin, "History of Palmyra," 2.
10. Benjamin, "History of Palmyra," 2.
11. Cannon, "Palmyra, New York: 1820–1830," 8.
12. Cannon, "Palmyra, New York: 1820–1830," 6.
13. Bushman, *Joseph Smith and the Beginnings of Mormonism*, 40.
14. Henry Stommel and Elizabeth Stommel, "The Year without a Summer," *Scientific American* 240, no. 6 (June 1979): 134.
15. Stommel and Stommel, "Year without a Summer," 134.
16. Rothman, *Unauthorized Biography of Joseph Smith*, 40.

17. Smith, *History of Joseph Smith by His Mother,* ed. Smith and Smith, 68.
18. Smith, *History of Joseph Smith by His Mother,* ed. Smith and Smith, 68.
19. Smith, *History of Joseph Smith by His Mother,* ed. Smith and Smith, 69.
20. Smith, *History of Joseph Smith by His Mother,* ed. Smith and Smith, 69.
21. Porter, "Study of the Origins of the Church," 32–33.
22. Smith, *History of Joseph Smith by His Mother,* ed. Smith and Smith, 70.
23. Bushman, *Joseph Smith and the Beginnings of Mormonism,* 42.
24. Bushman, *Joseph Smith and the Beginnings of Mormonism,* 42.
25. Bushman, *Joseph Smith and the Beginnings of Mormonism,* 42.
26. Bushman, *Joseph Smith and the Beginnings of Mormonism,* 47.
27. Bushman, *Joseph Smith and the Beginnings of Mormonism,* 48.
28. Bushman, *Joseph Smith and the Beginnings of Mormonism,* 49.

CHAPTER THREE

ON THE EVE OF THE FIRST VISION

Steven C. Harper

*T*he American Revolution reshaped the world into which Joseph Smith was born and in which he matured. Land on the New York frontier became available, markets became more accessible, and churches multiplied in every sense. Joseph came of age in an environment that was beginning to be transformed from an agrarian economy to an industrialized, capitalistic marketplace. For many that meant opportunity and wealth. For the Smith family it meant one setback after another. Like the markets, churches became more free and open, competing for converts with aggressive techniques, much as shoemakers and distillers competed for consumers. Ministers grew concerned that frontiers and economic forces pulled Americans away from established churches, both geographically and spiritually, and determined to curb "the tide of infidelity which was setting in with so strong a current."[1]

Beginning in 1799, periodic and scattered religious revivals marked the inauguration of a period some historians call the Second Great Awakening. A new nation with enlarged boundaries, untamed frontiers, and untried ways of tapping its resources fostered spiritual needs that none of the old approaches could quite satisfy. New ministers with new methods made salvation an individual quest and put responsibility for "experiencing religion" on the shoulders of every American. The response to their message was phenomenal, especially in western New York. Presbyterianism prospered: 6,500 Americans joined in 1820,

Steven C. Harper is an assistant professor of Church history and doctrine at Brigham Young University.

more than one-fourth of them in western New York.[2] "Baptists experienced similarly explosive growth."[3] Most impressively, Methodists went from a token presence in America at the end of the Revolution to the largest American denomination by the 1830s.[4] At an 1803 revival in Kirkwood, New York, a Mrs. Moore "experienced religion and joined the Methodist Episcopal Church." The local schoolteacher, nineteen-year-old George Lane, experienced religion himself that winter. "He was absent from school a few days, and when he returned he told his scholars that he had experienced religion, and exhorted them and prayed with them, and a great revival broke out immediately."[5] Lane left his school in 1804 and began to climb the ranks of the Methodist ministry, carrying out long preaching tours and proving himself both diligent and gifted, until, physically weakened, he opted for an easier mercantile career near Wilkes-Barre, Pennsylvania.

Meanwhile the Smith family improved opportunities offered by the new republic and bore its hardships. Often their prospects appeared promising. Still, they could never quite get ahead financially or settle on which church to join. The Smith family experienced frustration, confusion, and anxiety as often as they did prosperity, security, and liberty. These pressures sent the Smiths, along with many others, to seek both temporal and spiritual salvation—twin themes that pervade Lucy Mack Smith's narrative of her family's history.

Leaving New England for Palmyra's bustling economic and religious scene in 1816, the destitute Smith family found a religious revival firing the souls of their new neighbors. The number of local Baptists had jumped in revival-inspired spurts. The number of Palmyra's Presbyterians doubled, and a new congregation formed between the time the Smiths arrived in 1816 and moved south of town about two years later. In 1819 there were more local Presbyterian converts than in any previous year. "Methodists kept no records for individual congregations, but in 1821 they built a new meetinghouse in town."[6]

The Smiths had more than religious concerns at that time. Prosperity had eluded them too long. They "counseled together as to what course it was best to take." According to Lucy Mack Smith, they

agreed that able family members would "apply all our energies together
and endeavor to obtain a piece of land."[7] High wages drew Joseph Sr.
and his two eldest sons, Alvin and Hyrum, to odd jobs until they had
enough to pursue the increasingly American dream of owning the
means of their own prosperity. Lucy plied her skills, painting tablecloths to supply the family's daily needs. Joseph Jr. wrote of this period:
"Being in indigent circumstances [we] were obliged to labour hard for
the support of a large Family."[8] Historian Richard Bushman wrote:

> The combination of Palmyra's flourishing economy, the added con-
> tribution of Alvin and Hyrum, and their own industry put the Smiths in
> a better position by 1818 than they had occupied for fifteen years. For
> the first time they were able to contract for a farm and begin payments
> on land they hoped to make their own. . . . a wooded tract less than two
> miles south of Palmyra village on Stafford Street.[9]

The Smiths agreed to purchase a hundred acres from a New York
City speculator named Nicholas Evertson with an annual cash payment
of one hundred dollars. They built a small cabin, planted an orchard,
tapped the maple trees and made about a thousand pounds of sugar,
and began clearing the land to accommodate a cash crop. Lucy said it
was "not long until we had thirty acres ready for cultivation," a remarkable feat.[10] Joseph worked along with the rest of his family.

Meanwhile economic anxieties were complicated by spiritual
ones. Though sincere believers in God, neither Lucy nor Joseph Sr.
could find salvation among what LDS scholar Terryl Givens calls the
"embarrassment of denominational riches," including nearby congregations of Presbyterians, Methodists, Quakers, and Baptists.[11] Lucy
dreamed of finding temporal and spiritual security. A few years earlier, in New England, she had suffered with her children through a
typhoid epidemic. A decade before that she had faced her own death
fearfully as she suffered a severe fever. Doctors resigned her to the
grave, and when a Methodist exhorter visited her bedside, she
thought, "'I am not prepared to die, for I do not know the ways of
Christ,' and it seemed to me as though there was a dark and lonely
chasm between myself and Christ that I dared not attempt to cross."
Lucy pleaded and then "covenanted with God that if he would let me

Camp Meeting, *by Alexander Rider*

live, I would endeavor to get that religion that would enable me to serve him right, whether it was in the Bible or wherever it might be found." Thenceforth, she wrote, religion "occupied my mind entirely." Subsequent searching led her first to Presbyterianism, "but all was emptiness,"[12] and thence to Methodism, but Joseph Sr. had "little faith in the doctrine taught by them." This, together with pressure from her father-in-law to leave Methodism alone, left Lucy "very much hurt." She "retired to a grove of handsome wild cherry trees not far distant and prayed to the Lord" to soften her husband's heart. That night she dreamed of two trees, one of which was pliant and lively, the other unyielding. She was given to understand that the flexible tree represented her husband, who would hear and receive the "pure and undefiled gospel of the Son of God" later in life.[13]

Joseph Sr.'s quest for religious truth was likewise manifest in dreams, including three that occurred in the years leading up to the First Vision in the spring of 1820. In one dream he was sick, footsore, and weary. A guide showed him a beautiful flower garden, in which he was renewed. "I then asked my guide the meaning of all this," Lucy quoted him as saying, "but I awoke before I received an answer." In the second dream Joseph Sr. walked to what seemed like the final judgment. He arrived too late and found himself denied admission. Lucy quoted him as saying, "Presently I found that my flesh was perishing. I continued to pray, still my flesh withered upon my bones. I was in a state of almost total despair." At that point the doorkeeper questioned whether he had met all requirements for admission, to which he replied, "All that was in my power to do." The porter (or angel) said that mercy could take effect only after justice was satisfied, upon which Joseph Sr. "cried out in the agony of my soul" for forgiveness in the name of Jesus Christ. Father Smith dreamed that strength returned and the door opened, "but on entering, I awoke."[14] In a third dream Lucy dated to 1819, Joseph Sr. dreamed he met a peddler who promised to tell him the one thing he lacked to secure his salvation. He sprang to get some paper but awoke in the excitement.

Joseph Jr. thus matured under the care of what he called "goodly Parents who spared no pains" to teach him Christian principles. But no one in the Smith household could escape the tensions and anxieties inherent in their relentless quest for security in an insecure world. Joseph wrote that in the wake of the 1816–17 Palmyra-area revival, "at about the age of twelve years my mind became seriously imprest with regard to the all important concerns for the wellfare of my immortal Soul."[15] As Richard Bushman noted, "The recurrence of revivals meant that the urgent question, 'What must I do to be saved?' was on everyone's mind."[16] For the impressionable youth that question became inescapable and its answer elusive. "Being wrought up in my mind respecting the subject of Religion," Joseph explained, "and looking at the different systems . . . I knew not who was right or who was wrong, but I considered it of the first importance to me that I should be right, in matters of so such moment, matters involving eternal consequences."[17] Joseph wrote that he became

> excedingly distressed for I became convicted of my Sins and by Searching the Scriptures I found that mankind did not come unto the Lord but that they had apostatised from the true and liveing faith and there was no society or denomination that built upon the Gospel of Jesus

Christ as recorded in the new testament and I felt to mourn for my own Sins and for the Sins of the world.[18]

An 1818 impromptu camp meeting in the hills above Wilkes-Barre reminded George Lane of how exciting it felt to experience religion and how rewarding it was to lead willing souls to the same well. He "sold his stock at the Wilkes-Barre store in March 1819 and re-entered the itinerancy. On Thursday, 1 July 1819, he was in attendance as the annual Genesee Conference convened in Vienna (afterwards Phelps), Ontario County, New York," a half-day's walk from the Smith farm.[19] With more than a hundred ministers gathered from the region, the area pulsed with "unusual excitement on the subject of religion" (Joseph Smith–History 1:5). One participant in the week-long event remembered the 1819 Vienna conference as a "religious cyclone which swept over the whole region," and Joseph Smith may have been in the eye of the storm.[20] An acquaintance, Orsamus Turner, reported that Joseph caught a "spark of Methodism in the camp meeting, away down in the woods, on the Vienna road."[21] Reverend Lane may have espe-cially influenced Joseph in this setting. In 1883 Joseph's younger brother William recalled that Lane "preached a sermon on 'What church shall I join?' And the burden of his discourse was to ask God, using as a text, 'If any of you lack wisdom let him ask of God who giveth to all men liberally.'"[22] Whether in this setting or a similar one is uncer-tain, but Joseph later told friends that during one revival his mother and siblings "got Religion. He . . . wanted to feel and shout like the rest but could feel nothing."[23] Yet he was "greatly excited, the cry and tumult were so great and incessant" (Joseph Smith–History 1:9).

It was, Joseph wrote, "during this time of great excitement" that his religious concerns reached a peak. His parents used such words as *darkness, anxiety* and *despair* to describe their frustrated quest for salvation. To these Joseph added that he was *distressed, perplexed,* that it was a period of *confusion, extreme difficulties,* and *great uneasiness* exacerbated by interdenominational strife, which he described as a bewildering "war of words and tumult of opinions" (Joseph Smith–History 1:8, 10). The Bible was both the battleground of this war and its greatest casualty, "for the teachers of religion of the different sects understood the same passages of scripture so differently as to destroy all confidence in settling the question by an appeal to the Bible" (Joseph Smith–History 1:12).

Yet it was the Bible's God to whom Joseph successfully appealed. He had listened over and over as religious partisans wielded the Bible as a weapon, citing proof-texts, "endeavoring to establish their own tenets and disprove all others" (Joseph Smith–History 1:9). Now, perhaps prompted by Reverend Lane, Joseph approached the Bible privately, quietly, more as a living word than a dead law, and it spoke to his soul. "While thinking of this matter," Joseph said, "I opened the Testament promiscuously on these words, in James, Ask of the Lord who giveth to all men liberally and upbraideth not."[24] That invitation to receive revelation moved Joseph deeply. "Never did any passage of scripture come with more power to the heart of man than this did at this time to mine. It seemed to enter with great force into every feeling of my heart. I reflected on it again and again, knowing that if any person needed wisdom from God, I did" (Joseph Smith–History 1:12). Humbled by the demands of life, conscious of his own limitations and dependence upon the Almighty, desiring deeply to feel and shout and experience religion like the Methodists, Joseph Smith determined to take his question to the only remaining authority he had not consulted. Recalling the experience in 1843, Joseph said he "immediately went out into the woods."[25] There was no tumult, no "shouts of rejoicing," no anxious bench, no "deep tones of the preacher."[26] Instead Joseph had an unmediated, unquestionable experience (Joseph Smith–History 1: 15–20, 25–26). Afterwards he knew God. Though he was ridiculed, hounded, beaten, sued, threatened, and imprisoned, Joseph's experience rendered him unshakeable.[27]

NOTES

1. James H. Hotchkin, *A History of the Purchase and Settlement of Western New York, and the Rise, Progress, and Present State of the Presbyterian Church in That Section* (New York: M. W. Dodd, 1848), 74, as cited in Bushman, *Joseph Smith and the Beginnings of Mormonism*, 52.

2. Backman, "Awakenings in the Burned-Over District," *BYU Studies* 9, no. 3 (1969): 317.

3. Butler, *Awash in a Sea of Faith,* 269. See also Backman, "Awakenings in the Burned-Over District."

4. Wigger, *Taking Heaven by Storm,* 3–6.

5. George Peck, *Early Methodism* (New York, 1860), 492. Cited in Porter, "Reverend George Lane," 323.

6. Bushman, *Joseph Smith and the Beginnings of Mormonism,* 53.

7. Smith, *History of Joseph Smith by His Mother,* ed. Proctor and Proctor, 86.

8. Jessee, ed., "Early Accounts of Joseph Smith's First Vision," *BYU Studies* 18, no. 2 (1979): 279.

9. Bushman, *Joseph Smith and the Beginnings of Mormonism,* 47–48.

10. Smith, *History of Joseph Smith by His Mother,* ed. Proctor and Proctor, 86. See also Bushman, *Joseph Smith and the Beginnings of Mormonism,* 48.

11. Givens, *By the Hand of Mormon,* 8.

12. Smith, *History of Joseph Smith by His Mother,* ed. Proctor and Proctor, 47–49.

13. Smith, *History of Joseph Smith by His Mother,* ed. Proctor and Proctor, 59–60.

14. Smith, *History of Joseph Smith by His Mother,* ed. Proctor and Proctor, 89–90.

15. Backman, *Joseph Smith's First Vision,* 155–56.

16. Bushman, *Joseph Smith and the Beginnings of Mormonism,* 52.

17. Backman, *Joseph Smith's First Vision,* 158.

18. Backman, *Joseph Smith's First Vision,* 156.

19. Porter, "Reverend George Lane," 328.

20. Cited in Backman, "Awakenings in the Burned-Over District," 308.

21. Orsamus Turner, *History of the Pioneer Settlement of Phelps and Gorham's Purchase* (Rochester, 1852), 214. Cited in Richard L. Anderson, "Circumstantial Confirmation of the First Vision through Reminiscences," *BYU Studies* 9, no. 3 (Spring 1969): 379.

22. Cited in Porter, "Reverend George Lane," 338.

23. Backman, *Joseph Smith's First Vision,* 177.

24. Backman, *Joseph Smith's First Vision,* 176.

25. Backman, *Joseph Smith's First Vision,* 176.

26. *Minutes of the Annual Conferences,* 1860, 40, as cited in Porter, "Reverend George Lane," 325.

27. Richard L. Bushman develops this point about Joseph's confidence in "The Character of Joseph Smith," *BYU Studies* 42, no. 2 (2003): 29–30. Speaking of the period after the First Vision, Bushman wrote of Joseph, "He seems to have been perfectly sure of himself. Surely such confidence can arise only out of inner experiences so powerful they overwhelm everything else. Joseph could have acted so decisively and confidently only with the assurance that God was behind him."

CHAPTER FOUR

THE YOUTH OF THE GROVE AND THE PROPHET OF THE RESTORATION

Larry C. Porter

*I*n the spring of 1820 members of the Joseph Smith Sr. family were caught up in the midst of a "war of words and tumult of opinions" as expressed by the religionists of the day. Each denomination vied for converts to their particular persuasion. Members of the Smith household were left to determine their own course in the ensuing strife. Mother Lucy Mack Smith, along with her children Hyrum, Sophronia, and Samuel Harrison, elected to join with the Presbyterians[1] who were meeting at the Union Chapel on Church Street in the village of Palmyra.[2] William Smith confessed, "I attended the meetings with the rest, but being quite young and inconsiderate, did not take so much interest in the matter as the older ones did."[3] Father Smith and the eldest son, Alvin, remained "unchurch[ed]" and were not drawn to any particular persuasion. Joseph Sr.'s youthful son, Joseph Jr., now fourteen years of age, expressed some partiality toward the Methodist faith, although he had not joined with any sect (Joseph Smith–History 1:8).

Some two years before the events which were about to unfold in the 1820 revival period, Joseph recognized that his young spiritual life was not what he desired. Expressing his anxieties he recorded:

> At about the age of twelve years my mind become seriously imprest with regard to the all important concerns for the wellfare of my immortal Soul which led me to searching the scriptures believeing as I was taught, that they contained the word of God thus applying myself to them and my

Larry C. Porter is a professor emeritus of Church history and doctrine at Brigham Young University.

Joseph Smith's First Vision, *by Walter Rane*

intimate acquaintance with those of different denominations led me to marvel excedingly for I discovered that <they did not> . . . adorn their profession by a holy walk and Godly conversation agreeable to what I found contained in that sacred depository [the Bible] this was a grief to my Soul thus from the age of twelve years to fifteen I pondered many things in my heart concerning the sittuation of the world of mankind.[4]

William Smith also informs us that even before Joseph concluded to go to the grove in prayer he had "continued in secret to call upon the Lord for a full manifestation of his will, the assurance that he was accepted of him, and that he might have an understanding of the path of obedience."[5]

Young Joseph's mind was greatly excited by the diverse tenets presented by the various revivalistic preachers of the day, who cried, "We are right," "Come and Join us," "Walk with us and we will do you good."[6] The Prophet recorded that he had reached a point in searching the scriptures that he "felt to mourn for my own sins and for the sins of the world."[7] He later told John Taylor that "he was very ignorant of the ways, designs and purposes of God, and knew nothing about them; he was a youth unacquainted with religious matters or the systems and theories of the day," yet within his limited understanding he sought some means of reconciling himself with God.[8]

Joseph found that the one constant in the midst of this confusion was his reliance on the promise in James 1:5: "If any of you lack wisdom, let him ask of God, that giveth to all men liberally, and upbraideth not; and it shall be given him." The Prophet spoke with deep feeling concerning the impact of that meaningful text: "Never did any passage of scripture come with more power to the heart of man than this did at this time to mine. It seemed to enter with great force into every feeling of my heart. I reflected on it again and again, knowing that if any person needed wisdom from God, I did" (Joseph Smith–History 1:12). William Smith said that this scripture was indeed the driving force which led Joseph to the grove, affirming that his brother went "out in the woods with child like, simple trusting faith believing that God meant just what He said, he kneeled down and prayed."[9]

Acting on the powerful promise in James, Joseph chose a beautiful, clear day in the early spring of 1820 to make his heartfelt plea to the Lord for guidance in his personal dilemma. The Prophet seems not to have specified the exact location where he offered up his petition. Was it on the Palmyra side or the Farmington (later Manchester) side of the township line? The Smith log house was situated in Palmyra Township; the hundred acres for which his father and brother Alvin would article with a Canandaigua land agent that summer was in Farmington Township, just a few yards south of their Palmyra home.

The wood lot comprising what would later be termed the Sacred Grove spanned both townships; indeed, the whole area was a pristine wilderness in 1820. How far had he penetrated the "silent grove," or bush, when he knelt to pray? Orson Pratt recorded that whatever his course, it was "to a secret place, in a grove, but a short distance from his father's house."[10] Joseph supplied the additional insight that "I immediately went out into the woods where my father had a clearing, and went to the stump where I had stuck my axe when I had quit work, and I kneeled down, and prayed."[11]

Joseph had looked about himself to determine if he was alone and then commenced to offer up his heart's desire to God in what he termed his first attempt to pray vocally. He remembered that his "tongue seemed to be swoolen in [his] mouth"[12] so that he could not speak, and he was "siezed upon by some power which entirely overcame" him. He thought himself "doomed to sudden destruction . . . not to an imaginary ruin but to the power of some actual being from the unseen world who had such marvelous power as I had never before felt in any being."[13] The arch adversary of all mankind, even Satan, was present on this momentous occasion in an attempt to forestall this pivotal moment in the Lord's great plan of restoration. Joseph may not then have fully identified the source of this intrusion, but the enemy was soon to be unmasked with Moroni's open vision of Satan and his hosts shown to the Prophet at the Hill Cumorah just a few years hence.[14]

Young Joseph, exerting all his energies, called upon God for relief and was immediately enveloped in a pillar of light above the brightness of the sun, which delivered him from the enemy that had held him bound. He explained the astonishing circumstances of that moment:

> When the light rested upon me I saw two Personages, whose brightness and glory defy all description, standing above me in the air. One of them spake unto me, calling me by name and said, pointing to the other—*This is My Beloved Son. Hear him!*
>
> My object in going to inquire of the Lord was to know which of all the sects was right, that I might know which to join. No sooner, therefore, did I get possession of myself, so as to be able to speak, than I asked the Personages who stood above me in the light, which of all the sects was right (for at this time it had never entered into my heart that all were wrong)—and which I should join.
>
> I was answered that I must join none of them, for they were all wrong. . . . they teach for doctrines the commandments of men, having a form of godliness, but they deny the power thereof.
>
> He again forbade me to join with any of them; and many other things did he say unto me which I cannot write at this time. (Joseph Smith–History 1:17–20)[15]

An examination of the Prophet's accounts of his extraordinary vision reveals a twofold purpose to his inquiry of Deity: a knowledge of which sect was right and also a confirmation that his sins were forgiven of the Lord that he might be saved, for, Joseph said, "I become convicted of my sins."[16] Both desires were realized as Joseph affirmed, "I saw the Lord and he spake unto me saying Joseph <my son> thy sins are forgiven thee. go thy <way> walk in my statutes and keep my commandments behold I am the Lord of glory I was crucifyed for the world that all those who believe on my name may have Eternal life."[17] As the manifestation of the Father and the Son closed before him, Joseph once again became aware of his surroundings:

> I found myself lying on <my> back looking up into Heaven. When the light had departed I had no strength, but soon recovering in some degree. I went home. & as I leaned up to the firepiece. Mother Enquired what the matter was. I replied never mind all is well.—I am well enough off. I then told my mother I have learned for myself that Presbyterianism is not true.[18]

His singling out of this particular denomination was again in deference to his mother and some siblings having aligned themselves with the Western Presbyterian Church of Palmyra during this revivalistic period. His response would have been similar for any other sect, as he had been instructed to "join none of them."

Joseph said little to those about him concerning his woodland vision, perhaps judging it to be a highly personal matter. When he did try to share the wisdom he had gained, he found that the telling of his encounter with Deity caused immediate prejudgment and great persecution of himself. He observed, "It seems as though the adversary was aware at a very early period of my life that I was destined to prove a disturber & annoyer of his kingdom, or else why should the powers of Darkness combine against me, why the oppression & persecution that arose against me, almost in my infancy?"[19] He could only console himself with the affirmation: "I had actually seen a light, and in the midst of that light I saw two Personages, and they did in reality speak to me. . . . I knew it, and I knew that God knew it, and I could not deny it, neither dared I do it" (Joseph Smith–History 1:25).

Over a succession of years, the Prophet described to varied audiences the circumstances associated with the First Vision. These contemporary accounts were sometimes dictated to scribes, recorded by the press, or preserved in the writings of individuals who heard his recounting of the event. From their content we are able to assemble an invaluable array of details that help us to assess the immediate circumstances associated with the vision and the long-range significance of this singular moment. It is most doubtful that a young man in his fifteenth year could fully comprehend the meaning of what he had just seen, and it was likewise most improbable that he would have been able to analyze the ultimate implications of that which he had witnessed. With the passage of time, however, the Prophet attained an undeniable comprehension of the nature of God and his interaction with man. This understanding caused him to alter his own life in compliance to the will of the Master.

From the vision itself, it becomes evident that among the recognized truths revealed to the Prophet Joseph Smith were the following:

(1) God hears and answers prayers and intervenes in the affairs of men (2) the power of evil is real and strong (3) the power of God is stronger than the influence of evil (4) Joseph was enclosed in a pillar of light and filled with unspeakable joy—the spirit of God (5) Joseph beheld two personages who resembled each other in features and likeness (6) the two personages were distinctly identified as the Father and the Son (7) man was created in the image of God (8) Joseph's concern for the status of his immortal soul was recognized by Deity (9) he sought for and received forgiveness of his sins (10) God's true Church was not on the earth (11) the sectarian world held incorrect doctrines and denied the power of God (12) Jesus Christ was crucified for the world and all those who believe in Him will have eternal life (13) the apostasy, restoration, and Second Coming were announced (14) Joseph was called to restore the fulness of the gospel.[20]

Throughout the remaining years of his life, Joseph Smith's course of action was directed by the First Vision. In the waning moments of his life, just eleven days before his martyrdom at Carthage, Joseph addressed a large congregation on 16 June 1844 in a grove at Nauvoo. On that occasion he reiterated: "I have always declared God to be a distinct personage, Jesus Christ a separate and distinct personage from God the Father, and that the Holy Ghost was a distinct personage and a Spirit: and these three constitute three distinct personages and three Gods."[21]

Earlier that same year, 10 March 1844, he had spoken at the funeral of King Follett, who was accidentally crushed to death while digging a well in Nauvoo. The family and friends of Brother Follett approached the Prophet to say something of their loved one and address the subject of the dead at the annual conference of the Church on 7 April 1844. Joseph acknowledged his friend and the request but also used the occasion of the "King Follett Discourse" to speak of broader principles. Anxious to convey to the Saints key elements of his understanding, the Prophet Joseph Smith spent more than two hours unburdening himself on a variety of theological topics. On that occasion he expressed his great desire to lift the minds of the thousands who had gathered to hear his address "into a more lofty sphere and exalted standing than what the human mind generally understands."[22] Laying the groundwork for his remarks about the correct association existing between God and man, he stated:

> There are but very few beings in the world who understand rightly the character of God. If men do not comprehend the character of God, they do not comprehend their own character. They cannot comprehend anything that is past or that which is to come; they do not know—they do not understand their own relationship to God.[23]

Joseph explained to the congregation, "I want you all to know God and to be familiar with Him. If I can get you to know Him, I can bring you to Him."[24] He then related some of the crucial attributes of the Supreme Being that had been revealed to him:

> First, God Himself who sits enthroned in yonder heavens is a Man like unto one of yourselves—that is the great secret! If the veil were rent today and the great God that holds this world in its sphere and the planets in their orbit and who upholds all things by His power—if you were to see Him today, you would see Him in all the person, image, fashion, and very form of a man, like yourselves. For Adam was a man formed in his likeness and created in the very fashion and image of God. Adam received instruction, walked, talked, and conversed with Him as one man talks and communicates with another.[25]

The marvelous and illuminating doctrine which the Prophet taught the Saints on that singular occasion elevated their thoughts and practices. They joined with him as he revealed the mysteries of the kingdom and could readily assent to his declaration:

> This is good doctrine. It tastes good. You say honey is sweet and so do I. I can also taste the spirit and principles of eternal life, and so can you. I know it is good and that when I tell you of these words of eternal life that are given to me by the inspiration of the Holy Spirit and the revelations of Jesus Christ, you are bound to receive them as sweet. You taste them and I know you believe them.[26]

The awareness of our royal lineage from God changes the way that we look at and treat each other. It changes our perspective of how we relate to loved ones and friends who are of the same household of faith and enjoy the same kinship with our Heavenly Father. It is vital that we get to know God. As it is recorded in the scriptures, "And this is life eternal, that they might know thee the only true God, and Jesus Christ, whom thou hast sent" (John 17:3). Elder Bruce R. McConkie gave sharp focus to what it means to know God and the ultimate goal that the Father has for those who love and obey his precepts: "To know God is to think what he thinks, to feel what he feels, to have the power he possesses, to comprehend the truths he understands, and to do what he does. Those who know God become like him, and have his kind of life, which is eternal life."[27]

It seems far beyond the comprehension of mortal man, but the Prophet Joseph set the mark and has declared our lineage with Deity. God is indeed the "Father of Spirits," and "we are also his offspring."[28] As sons and daughters, he would claim us his and is prepared to teach us line upon line in this life and the next as we seek that perfection which he has designed for his children in the eternities. We can draw near to him in this life, heed his counsel, and eventually see his face through our faith and obedience to his earthly gospel. Even as Joseph Smith came to know God and his Son through prayer, we must cry unto the Lord for his support and pray for his guidance in all our undertakings. Let our thoughts be directed to the Lord and the afflictions of our hearts placed on him. Let us counsel with the Lord in all our doings. When we lie down at night, we should lie down unto the Lord, and when we rise in the morning may our hearts be filled with thanks to that God who answers our prayers.

President Wilford Woodruff addressed the unique role of the First Vision, recognizing it as the catalyst that was at the very core of our revelatory experience under the Prophet:

> I have never read anywhere, that I know of, of the same power manifested in any dispensation to the children of men, which was manifested to the Prophet of God in the organization of this Church, when the Father and the Son both appeared to the Prophet Joseph in answer to his prayer, and when the Father said, "This is my beloved Son; behold Him; hear ye Him." This was an important revelation, which has never been manifested in the same manner in any dispensation of the world, that God has given concerning His work. So in its organization, the Prophet of God was administered to by the angels of heaven. They were his teachers, they were his instructors, and all that he did, and all that he

performed from the commencement, from that day to the day of his martyrdom, was by the revelation of Jesus Christ.[29]

Acceptance of this miraculous event is based on our own personal faith. We are invited to call upon the Spirit of the Lord to bear witness to our souls that the words of the Prophet were spoken in truth: "For I had seen a vision; I knew it, and I knew that God knew it, and I could not deny it" (Joseph Smith–History 1:25). Each of us is the grand recipient of the First Vision legacy through Joseph Smith, the youth of the grove and the Prophet of the Restoration.

NOTES

1. Compare Jessee, *Papers of Joseph Smith,* 1:270. For a comprehensive background of this revivalistic period in New York and an itemization of the contemporary accounts of the First Vision, see Backman, *Joseph Smith's First Vision;* see also Dean C. Jessee, "The Early Accounts of Joseph Smith's First Vision," *BYU Studies* 9 (Spring 1969): 275–94; James B. Allen, "Eight Contemporary Accounts of Joseph Smith's First Vision: What Do We Learn from Them?" *Improvement Era,* April 1970, 4–13; and Richard Lloyd Anderson, "Joseph Smith's Testimony of the First Vision," *Ensign,* April 1996, 10–21.

2. Cook, *Palmyra and Vicinity,* 247.

3. Smith, *William Smith on Mormonism,* 6.

4. Jessee, *Papers of Joseph Smith,* 1:5.

5. Smith, *William Smith on Mormonism,* 8.

6. Smith, *William Smith on Mormonism,* 7.

7. Jessee, *Papers of Joseph Smith,* 1:5–6.

8. Taylor, *Journal of Discourses,* 21:161.

9. "Another Testimony," *Deseret Evening News,* January 20, 1894, 11.

10. Jessee, *Papers of Joseph Smith,* 1:390.

11. Jessee, *Papers of Joseph Smith,* 1:444.

12. Jessee, *Papers of Joseph Smith,* 1:127.

13. Jessee, *Papers of Joseph Smith,* 1:272.

14. Jessee, *Papers of Joseph Smith,* 1:87.

15. Compare Jessee, *Papers of Joseph Smith,* 2:72–73; also in the information conveyed to the Prophet during the vision was the illuminating promise later relayed by Orson Pratt that "the fullness of the gospel, should, at some future time, be made known to him." See Jessee, *Papers of Joseph Smith,* 1:391.

16. Jessee, *Papers of Joseph Smith,* 1:5.

17. Jessee, *Papers of Joseph Smith,* 1:6.

18. Jessee, *Papers of Joseph Smith,* 1:273 n. 1.

19. Jessee, *Papers of Joseph Smith,* 1:273 n. 1.

20. Backman, *Joseph Smith's First Vision,* 206–8; James B. Allen, "Eight Contemporary Accounts of Joseph Smith's First Vision," *Improvement Era,* April 1970, 12; see, especially, James E. Faust, Conference Report, April 1984, 92–93.

21. Smith, *History of the Church,* 6:474.

22. Cannon and Dahl, *Joseph Smith's King Follett Discourse,* 19; see also Donald Q. Cannon, "The King Follett Discourse: Joseph Smith's Greatest Sermon in Historical Perspective," *BYU Studies* 18 (Winter 1978): 179–92.

23. Cannon and Dahl, *Joseph Smith's King Follett Discourse,* 19.

24. Cannon and Dahl, *Joseph Smith's King Follett Discourse,* 25.

25. Cannon and Dahl, *Joseph Smith's King Follett Discourse,* 27.

26. Cannon and Dahl, *Joseph Smith's King Follett Discourse,* 53.

27. McConkie, *Doctrinal New Testament Commentary,* 1:762.

28. Hebrews 12:9 and Acts 17:28 in Cannon and Dahl, *Joseph Smith's King Follett Discourse,* 18.

29. Wilford Woodruff, *Millennial Star* 52 (April 28, 1890): 258.

INSIGHTS FROM MORONI'S
VISITS IN 1823

Clyde J. Williams

econd only to the visit of the Father and the Son, the visit of Moroni to young Joseph Smith marks the most wonderful fulfillment of latter-day prophecy. John the Revelator foresaw "another angel fly in the midst of heaven, having the everlasting gospel to preach unto them that dwell on the earth" (Revelation 14:6). In 1831 the Lord confirmed Moroni's fulfillment of this prophecy when he declared, "I have sent forth mine angel flying through the midst of heaven, having the everlasting gospel, who hath appeared unto some and hath committed it unto man" (D&C 133:36). There are twenty-two known appearances of Moroni in this dispensation.[1] The first five of those visits occurred on 21–22 September 1823. These experiences imparted rich lessons to Joseph and through him to millions of others since that time.[2]

MENTORING FROM MORONI

Although it had been more than three years since the First Vision, Moroni's visit was not unexpected. In Joseph's 1842 account of the First Vision, he indicated that he was given "a promise that the fulness of the gospel should at some future time be made known to me."[3] Furthermore, he wrote, "I had full confidence in obtaining a divine manifestation, as I previously had one" (Joseph Smith–History 1:29). On the evening of 21 September, he "retired to his bed in quite

---

Clyde J. Williams is an associate professor of ancient scripture at Brigham Young University.

a serious and contemplative state of mind."[4] That it was the Sabbath makes an interesting addition to the account. We do not know what happened earlier this particular Sabbath, but that may relate to Joseph's contemplative attitude and seems to add to the timeliness of Moroni's visit. It also seems important to mention that this visit came not as a result of necessity but as an answer to prayer. Joseph's previous experience with the Father and the Son did not preclude his need to overcome weaknesses and sins. Moreover, he received because he asked in faith. He knew that God answered prayers, and he desired to know his standing with the Lord (Joseph Smith–History 1:29).

From this experience we learn that great spiritual experiences come most often when we truly seek forgiveness by submitting to the Lord. Additionally, we learn that the first two great revelations of this dispensation came as a result of sincere, fervent prayer. Joseph had come to know the efficacy of repentance and prayer. Like prophets before him and after him, he felt "condemned for [his] weakness and imperfections" (Joseph Smith–History 1:29). The word of the Lord, recorded by Moroni so long before, would come to pass in Joseph's life and in the lives of many others:

> If men come unto me I will show unto them their weakness. I give unto men weakness that they may be humble; and my grace is sufficient for all men that humble themselves before me; for if they humble themselves before me, and have faith in me, then will I make weak things become strong unto them. (Ether 12:27)

Perhaps that is ultimately the process that began for Joseph with the appearance of Moroni. This passage was never more literally fulfilled than through the life of Joseph Smith. As he approached the Lord in prayer in 1820 and 1823, his desire was to come unto Christ. Indeed, Moroni's intent was to help mentor Joseph along the path towards perfection so that the Lord could use him as an instrument in his hands. Likewise, we must believe that the Lord can make our weaknesses become our strengths and so live as to see it fulfilled.

Several things were revealed or confirmed to Joseph concerning angels or heavenly beings. One was that they are "glorious beyond description," with clothing of a "whiteness beyond anything earthly

I had ever seen" (Joseph Smith–History 1:32, 31). Even though the angel's countenance was "truly like lightning," it did not consume or harm him (Joseph Smith–History 1:32). He realized that an angel could enter his room at will in a conduit of light and be suspended in the air, and his glory apparently did not disturb or affect others for whom the vision was not intended. Furthermore, Joseph's experience with Moroni reminds us that all are known to God. He knows us individually and can assist, direct, and sustain us if we are willing.

Some have wondered how Joseph remembered so clearly the things Moroni taught him that evening. Though it is within the Lord's capability to enhance our memory, it is also known that he has used more than once the pattern of repetition. Moroni repeated to Joseph three times over the course of the night and once again on the following day the message that he delivered.[5] This process was similar to the Lord's conveying to Peter in a repeated vision a significant procedural change for the Church (Acts 10:11–16).

A WITNESS AND A WARNING

Moroni had been directed to write a caution as well as a warning to Joseph concerning the value of the plates. Anciently, he had written "that no one shall have them to get gain" (Mormon 8:14). On the evening of 21 September, Joseph recorded that during his third appearance Moroni stated:

> Satan would try to tempt me (in consequence of the indigent circumstances of my father's family), to get the plates for the purpose of getting rich. This he forbade me, saying that I must have no other object in view in getting the plates but to glorify God, and must not be influenced by any other motive than that of building his kingdom; otherwise I could not get them. (Joseph Smith–History 1:46)

From this instruction we learn that the Lord has never intended that sacred things be used for personal gain or self-aggrandizement. Like Joseph, we too must work and give service in the Church with no "other motive than that of building [God's] kingdom" (Joseph Smith–History 1:46).

Joseph Smith Visited by Moroni in the Field, *by Gary Ernest Smith*

Another lesson Joseph was already learning was the blessing of being called of God. Many suppose that an important call from the Lord or even the calling to receive the gospel is a great blessing, which indeed it is. From Joseph's experience we learn that along with spiritual blessings opposition comes as we take any positive step toward forwarding or following the work of God. Moroni opened to Joseph's view both the "glory of God" and "the power of darkness." Moroni explained, "All this is shown, the good and the evil, the holy and impure, the glory of God and the power of darkness, that you may know hereafter the two powers and never be influenced or overcome by that wicked one."[6] A clear understanding of the power of these two forces that are vying for the souls of men can make a profound difference in the choices we make in mortality and in the destination we arrive at in eternity.

THE GREAT SIGN OF THE RESTORATION

The truth that the fulness of the gospel was not presently on the earth was made known to Joseph in the First Vision. Now, Moroni made it clear that the most important tool in helping correct this serious void was an ancient book written on gold plates. This record, he said, contained the fulness of the everlasting gospel as it had come from the Savior to ancient inhabitants of the American continent. Thus, Moroni announced the beginning of the fulfillment of the Savior's promise that the work of the Father would commence when his words, spoken to the Nephites, were made known (3 Nephi 21:1–7). The Book of Mormon, which was announced for the first time on this occasion, was the great sign of the commencement of the latter-day gathering and restoration, which had been foretold from Old Testament days.[7] Joseph learned that this record could come forth and be translated by the gift and power of God. Is it any wonder that the adversary would be preparing to mount serious opposition to this work and that Joseph needed to be forewarned? After all, the record he would bring forth, like the kingdom he would establish, "was destined to prove a disturber and an annoyer of [Satan's] kingdom" (Joseph Smith–History 1:20).

A FAMILY AFFAIR

On Monday morning Moroni visited Joseph again. This fourth visit occurred after Father Smith had sensed his son was not well and sent him home from the fields. Besides repeating the instruction that was spoken the previous night, Moroni commanded Joseph to return immediately and tell his father of the visions and instructions he had received. Although we cannot know all the reasons why this was to be done, it certainly emphasizes that Joseph needed the support and sustaining influence of his father. The burden must have been somewhat lighter once he shared with his father and later that evening shared what he could with other family members. Their acceptance and support were critical to Joseph's eventual success in obtaining the plates.

Much power comes to anyone who enjoys the support and encouragement of family members when undertaking a difficult calling from the Lord. That is true whether one is called as a full-time missionary, a bishop, or a general authority. We may never fully appreciate how much it must have meant to Joseph to have his older brother Alvin say, "Now, brother, let us go to bed, and rise early in the morning, in order to finish our day's work at an hour before sunset, then, if mother will get our suppers early, we will have a fine long evening, and we will all sit down for the purpose of listening to you while you tell us the great things which God has revealed to you."[8] Truly these were days never to be forgotten by Joseph or his family.

MORONI'S MESSAGE

When Moroni appeared on Sunday evening, he quoted passages of scripture. If Joseph had any questions as to why the Lord would have chosen him to be the messenger of the Restoration, Moroni's recitation of Paul's words shed significant light: "God hath chosen the weak things of the world to confound the things which are mighty" (1 Corinthians 1:27).[9] Moroni reaffirmed that it has ever been the Lord's pattern to choose the weak things of the earth to confound the wise. Moroni, too, had voiced his feelings of inadequacy: "When we write we behold our weakness, and stumble because of the placing of our words; and I fear lest the Gentiles shall mock at our words" (Ether 12:25).

On the evening of 21 September, as recorded by Joseph Smith and Oliver Cowdery, Moroni quoted or paraphrased more than thirty scriptural passages.[10] Perhaps the most concise statement summarizing all that Moroni taught that evening comes to us in the words of Oliver Cowdery. In one of his several letters to W. W. Phelps, he explained that Moroni outlined the "blessings, promises and covenants to Israel, and the great manifestations of favor to the world, in the ushering in of the fulness of the gospel, to prepare the way for the second advent of the Messiah, when he comes in the glory of the Father with the holy angels."[11] In light of the Savior's quoting all of Malachi 3–4 to the Nephites (3 Nephi 24–25) and then "expound[ing] all things, even from the beginning until the time that he should come in his glory" (3 Nephi 26:3), it is not surprising that Moroni begins with these significant passages.

Moroni unfolded at least seven major points through the recited scriptures. First, it was important that Joseph understand, at least in a fundamental way, that he was called of God to open this last dispensation (Malachi 3:1; Isaiah 11:1, 10; Joel 2:28–29).[12] Second, the work he was to undertake fulfilled prophecies of old (Malachi 3–4; Isaiah 2; 11; 29; Joel 2; Jeremiah 30–31). Third, the "marvellous work" about to come forth involved the restoration of the fulness of gospel, including all priesthood powers, keys, rights, covenants, and blessings (Isaiah 29:14; Malachi 4:5–6). Fourth, a key part of this restoration involved the coming forth of the Book of Mormon (Isaiah 29:11, 14). Fifth, the great latter-day work also involved a widespread and glorious gathering of scattered Israel and all the faithful who will come (Isaiah 2:1–4; 11:11–13; Psalm 107:1–7; Jeremiah 16:15–16; 31:6–9; 50:4–5). Sixth, if this marvelous work, its power, authority, ordinances, and covenants did not come forth, the whole earth would be utterly wasted or destroyed at the Savior's second coming (Malachi 4:5–6). Seventh, this work was in preparation for the second coming of the Lord Jesus Christ (Malachi 3:1–3; 4:1–3; Joel 2:30–31; Acts 3:22–23).

THE TIME TO PREPARE

About midday on Monday, 22 September, Moroni made his fifth appearance, this time at the Hill Cumorah. At that time Joseph was informed that he would not obtain the plates for four years. He had attempted to take the plates from the stone box three times that day and had been shocked. In each case his frustrated cry was, "Why can I not obtain this book?"[13] Joseph was not ready to translate the record. One might wonder why the Lord sent Moroni so soon. Was this visit a bit premature? Had the Lord overestimated Joseph's readiness? Did he not know Joseph would let desires for gain and relief of his family's economic woes overcome his feelings during his long walk to the hill that September day? Surely the Lord knew all these things and more.

The Lord often gives us premonitions or preparatory warnings of things we need to do to prepare ourselves for future callings or assignments in his kingdom. So it was with Joseph at this time. Oliver Cowdery explained:

> I discover wisdom in the dealings of the Lord: it was impossible for any man to translate the Book of Mormon by the gift of God, and endure the afflictions, and temptations, and devices of satan, without being overthrown, unless he had been previously benefited with a certain round of experience: and had our brother obtained the record the first time, not knowing how to detect the works of darkness, he might have been deprived of the blessing of sending forth the word of truth to this generation. Therefore, God knowing that satan would thus lead his mind astray, began at that early hour, that when the full time should arrive, he might have a servant prepared to fulfill his purpose.[14]

To help Joseph in his preparation, the Lord gave him a vision of the marvelous work that was about to unfold. He showed him his weakness and potential vulnerability if he did not prepare himself for such a great work. How many mortals have looked back with gratitude that the Lord gave them time to grow and prepare more fully for their present circumstances? The coming of Moroni in September 1823 was the beginning of a long mentoring process to prepare Joseph to be the prophet foreordained to prepare the way for the second coming of the Lord (Malachi 3:1).

THERE IS HOPE

That the Lord sent Moroni to a young boy, who had so much to learn, and weaknesses to overcome, should instill hope in everyone's heart. In the words of Elder Neal A. Maxwell: "One of the great messages that flows from the Lord's use of Joseph Smith as a 'choice seer' in the latter days is that there is indeed hope for each of us! The Lord can call us in our weaknesses and yet magnify us for his purposes."[15] Although few are called to be prophets, seers, and revelators, all who are willing to be tutored by the Lord and his servants can likewise overcome their weaknesses and play important individual roles in the Restoration and the gathering and preparing of a people for the second coming of the Lord. Such a course would surely further the mission that Moroni began 21 September 1823.

NOTES

1. See Alexander L. Baugh, "Parting the Veil: The Visions of Joseph Smith," *BYU Studies* 30, no. 1 (1999): 57–59.

2. This paper will not focus on a comparison of the various accounts of Moroni's visits on 21–22 September 1823. For a comparison, see Richard Lloyd Anderson, "Confirming Records of Moroni's Coming," *Improvement Era,* September 1970, 4–8, and Jackson, *From Apostasy to Restoration,* 89–100.

3. "Church History," *Times and Seasons* 3, no. 9 (March 1, 1842): 707.

4. Smith, *History of Joseph Smith by His Mother,* ed. Nibley, 74.

5. The four dictated accounts indicate Moroni came three times that first evening. The 1838 account clearly states that Moroni repeated all he had said the night before on the morning of 22 September 1823 (Joseph Smith–History 1:49).

6. Oliver Cowdery, "Letter VIII to W. W. Phelps," *Messenger and Advocate* 2, no. 13 (October 1835): 198.

7. For examples of these prophecies, see Isaiah 11:11–12; 29:14; Acts 3:20–21; Revelation 14:6–7.

8. Smith, *History of Joseph Smith by His Mother,* ed. Nibley, 81.

9. Oliver Cowdery, "Letter IV to W.W. Phelps," *Messenger and Advocate* 1, no. 5 (February 1835): 79.

10. For a more detailed treatment of the passages Moroni quoted, see Kent P. Jackson, "The Appearance of Moroni to Joseph Smith," *Studies in Scripture,* 2:339–66.

11. Oliver Cowdery, "Letter VII to W. W. Phelps," *Messenger and Advocate* 1, no. 10 (July 1835): 156.

12. The scriptures in parentheses after the seven points are passages Moroni quoted or paraphrased to Joseph on the evening of 21 September 1823 according to the Joseph Smith–History. Accounts written by Oliver Cowdery, particularly in letters no. 4 and no. 6, appear in the February and April issues of the *Messenger and Advocate*.
13. Oliver Cowdery, "Letter VIII to W. W. Phelps," 198.
14. Oliver Cowdery, "Letter VIII to W. W. Phelps," 199–200.
15. Neal A. Maxwell, "A Choice Seer," *BYU Speeches Online*, 30 March 1986, 9.

CHAPTER SIX

THE DEVELOPMENTAL YEARS, 1823–1827

Mary Jane Woodger

From 1823 to 1827, Joseph Smith's parents, siblings, and wife showed remarkable support of the eternal truths he had received from on high. Even when faced with opposition, they stood by Joseph and his claims of heavenly beings and of plates that had the appearance of gold. Their support during those crucial developmental years, years in which Joseph grew in understanding and line upon line in gospel knowledge, proved critical to his being able to endure verbal and physical persecution and his becoming worthy to receive the contents of the stone box.

FAMILY SUPPORT

Historian Richard Bushman asserts that the Joseph Smith Sr. family was not always perfectly united and had their share of flaws, as do most families. They "labored under a burden of serious poverty during all the years when Joseph was growing up; accumulating the necessities and a few of the simplest amenities was a struggle that engaged the family nearly every day of their lives. As if this were not enough, there were deep disagreements over religion." Young Joseph's visions became the impetus of the reconciliation of his father's "frustrated quest for visionary truth" and his "mother's desire for a Christian church."[1] After years of disagreement about religion, the family was united in support of Joseph's mission.

Mary Jane Woodger is an associate professor of Church history and doctrine at Brigham Young University.

With the first appearance of the angel Moroni, Joseph's ability to communicate to his family eternal truths proved exceptional. After a day's work, the family would gather to listen as the young Joseph described "the ancient inhabitants of this continent . . . as though he had spent his life with them." Because the angel had forbidden him to speak of these things to the world, he asked family members to guard the new information. They responded by holding sacred that which Moroni had revealed. Joseph's mother recalled her family listening "in breathless anxiety to the religious teachings of a boy eighteen years of age who had never read the Bible through by course in his life."[2] Showing her deep support, Mother Smith was convinced "that God was about to bring to light something that we might stay our minds upon, something that would give us a more perfect knowledge of the plan of salvation and the redemption of the human family than anything which had been taught us heretofore, and we rejoiced in it with exceeding great joy."[3] She added that the family experienced the "sweetest union and happiness" in their home.[4] Although it has been said that "Lucy, [in her writing,] consistently glosse[d] over whatever might seem to diminish the family status,"[5] her statement suggests that Joseph's position in the family was integral to family life.

Each family member showed great interest in hearing Joseph's "amusing recitals" but none more so than his oldest brother, Alvin, who "showed the most intense interest."[6] It is possible that Alvin may have had more than interest in the forthcoming record of antiquity because of an instruction from the angel Moroni. Joseph Knight wrote that Joseph Smith was told in 1823 that he could have the gold plates on 22 September 1824 if he brought the right person with him to the hill. When Joseph asked, "'Who is the right person?' The answer was, 'Your oldest brother' [Alvin Smith]."[7] Before September came, "Alvin was taken very sick with the bilious colic." When the family doctor was unavailable to help, "one Dr. Greenwood" was called, "who, when he came, immediately administered a heavy dose of calomel to the patient, although [Alvin] objected much against it." The mercury chloride solution, which was supposed to work as a laxative, lodged in his

Young Joseph Tells His Family of His Hill Cumorah Experience,
by Robert T. Barrett

stomach. Alvin's deathbed instructions to Hyrum and Sophronia were
to finish the frame house and take care of their parents. He implored
Joseph, "I want you to be a good boy and do everything that lies in
your power to obtain the record. Be faithful in receiving instruction
and in keeping every commandment that is given you."[8]

Hence, to the Smith family, the hidden record and Alvin's memory were intertwined. Lucy recites that thereafter, "the moment that Joseph spoke of the record it would immediately bring Alvin to our minds."⁹ Alvin's last wishes, no doubt, encouraged Joseph's pursuit to obtain, translate, and publish the record. It also solidified the family's support of that pursuit. At Alvin's funeral, Presbyterian minister Reverend Stockton "intimated very strongly that he had gone to hell, for Alvin was not a church member." Joseph Sr. did not accept his pronouncement, and neither did Lucy.¹⁰ Reverend Stockton's remarks solidified Joseph Sr.'s dislike of organized religions in Palmyra.

By the spring of 1824, a new preacher in town was teaching the need for religious denominations to agree and "worship God with one mind and one heart." Lucy "wished to join [this preacher's congregation], and [she] tried to persuade [her] husband to do so." He would not. Neither would young Joseph. Joseph told his mother that he could take his "Bible and go out into the woods and learn more in two hours than you could if you were to go to meeting for two years." His opinion as well as his divine gifts was respected by both parents. For instance, he once told his mother that it would not hurt her to join Presbyterianism but that within a year a man in the congregation, known for his piety and religious nature, Deacon Jessup, would take the last cow of a widowed mother of eight to satisfy a debt. Lucy stopped attending that church, though it seemed "impossible" that the man was capable of such an act. Her faith in her son's gifts was confirmed when Deacon Jessup fulfilled her son's prophecy.¹¹

According to his mother, Joseph was told on 22 September 1824 that he could try to obtain the plates. He described prying the stone that covered the plates, putting forth his hand, and lifting the plates out of the box. Of this experience, his mother wrote:

> In the excitement of the moment, he laid the record down in order to cover up the box. . . . When he turned again to take up the record, it was gone, but where he knew not, nor did he know by what means it had been taken away.
>
> He was much alarmed at this. He knelt down and asked the Lord why it was that the record was taken from him. The angel appeared to

him and told him that he had not done as he was commanded, for in a former revelation he had been commanded not to lay the plates down, or put them for a moment out of his hands. . . . After some further conversation, Joseph was permitted to raise the stone again, and there he beheld the plates, the same as before. He reached forth his hand to take them, but was hurled to the ground with great violence. When he recovered, the angel was gone, and he arose and returned to the house, weeping for grief and disappointment.[12]

Joseph was concerned that his family would not believe him when he returned home without the plates. His parents did believe him but feared that he might never qualify to obtain the plates. Mother Smith wrote that after this failure, the family "doubled [their] diligence in prayer and supplication to God."[13]

Nothing is recorded by Joseph Smith of the angel Moroni's visit on 22 September 1825. David Whitmer does write of Joseph going to the Hill Cumorah on that date in 1825, 1826, and 1827.[14] Joseph Knight's history also reports annual visits to the hill.[15] During those years, support of the Smith family for the young prophet was constant. The solidarity of the Smith family contrasts markedly with the behavior of the family of Lehi, the central family of the Book of Mormon.

THE COMMON VOCATIONS OF HIS DAY

Joseph "continued to pursue [his] common vocation," meaning that he farmed with his father and took odd jobs to supplement the family income (Joseph Smith–History 1:27). With Alvin's death and Hyrum's marriage, finishing the frame home and meeting the Smith's annual mortgage payment fell increasingly on the shoulders of young Joseph. Although the family worked hard in a variety of ways, the wheat crop provided their basic income. They contracted for its sale yearly with buyers such as Squire Josiah Stowell (sometimes spelled Stowel or Stoal) from South Bainbridge, New York.

It was the Smiths' connection with Stowell that brought about Joseph's first accusation in a court of law. Circumstances leading to the court action are steeped in "money digging, or treasure hunting," which "was a widespread practice" in the early 1800s in the eastern United States. A Palmyra newspaper in 1825 referred to such a practice: "We could name . . . at least five hundred respectable men who . . . believe that immense treasures lie concealed upon our green mountains, many of whom have been for a number of years industriously and perseveringly engaged in digging it up."[16] Elder Dallin H. Oaks of the Quorum of the Twelve Apostles relates:

> Some sources close to Joseph Smith claim that in his youth, during his spiritual immaturity prior to his being entrusted with the Book of Mormon plates, he sometimes used a stone in seeking for treasure. Whether this is so or not, we need to remember that no prophet is free from human frailties, especially before he is called to devote his life to the Lord's work. Line upon line, young Joseph Smith expanded his faith and understanding and his spiritual gifts matured until he stood with power and stature as the Prophet of the Restoration.[17]

Josiah Stowell heard that Joseph "'possessed certain keys, by which he could discern things invisible to the natural eye.'"[18] In the summer of 1825, Stowell approached Joseph and his father about digging for a lost Spanish silver mine in Harmony, Pennsylvania, located on the property of Isaac Hale. Joseph Sr. seems to have been excited about the money digging. Joseph endeavored to dissuade Stowell and his father from what he believed was a "vain pursuit,"[19] but Stowell was determined and offered such high wages that Joseph, his father, and several others agreed to dig for treasure. According to Martin Harris, after a short while "the angel told [Joseph] he must quit the company of the money-diggers. That there were wicked men among them. He must have no more to do with them."[20]

After the digging enterprise was abandoned, Father Smith returned to Palmyra. Stowell and Joseph Knight hired young Joseph to remain in the area and help on a farm and cut timber. Knight referred to Joseph as "the best hand he ever hired."[21] During the winter of 1826, while Joseph boarded with the Knight family, Stowell's nephew, Peter Bridgeman, accused Joseph Jr. of swindling his uncle and filed a complaint against him with a justice of the peace in South Bainbridge, New York. The complaint accused Joseph of being an imposter for claiming the ability to locate buried treasure. Appearing before Judge Albert Neely, Joseph admitted he "had been in the habit of looking through this stone to find lost property for three years, but of late had pretty much given it up."[22] No sentence was issued in return for Joseph's promise to quit seeking treasure.

MARRIAGE TO EMMA HALE

Emma Hale, the third daughter and seventh of nine children born to Isaac and Elizabeth Lewis Hale, was twenty-one years old when she first met Joseph. She was described as "well turned, of excellent form . . . with splendid physical development."[23] "She moved with slow precision but was capable of doing an amazing amount of work in little time."[24] Her lively and spirited communication and wit attracted Joseph's interest upon their first meeting. Buddy Youngreen described Joseph at the time as being

> six feet, two inches tall, fair-complexioned, and nearly twenty. He had penetrating blue eyes and light brown hair. Curiously, he combined a boyish shyness with a mannish self-confidence. His rough independence belied his awkwardness and lack of formal education and kept him from feeling inferior for lack of social experience. He would often say what was on his mind without regard for its appropriateness.[25]

The attraction Joseph felt toward Emma Hale that winter may have been more than incidental. Joseph Knight reports that the previous September in the annual angelic interview, Joseph was told that he could have the plates the following year "if he brought with him the right person." When Joseph asked, "'Who is the right person?' The answer was, 'You will know.'" Joseph then looked into his seer stone and found that the right person was Emma Hale.[26]

Joseph talked about his feelings for Emma with Martin Harris, the Knights, and his parents. Mother Smith recalled that Joseph said "that he had felt so lonely ever since Alvin's death, that he had come to the conclusion of getting married if we had no objections. He thought that no young woman that he ever was acquainted with was better calculated to render the man of her choice happy than Miss Emma Hale, a young lady whom he had been extremely fond of since his first introduction to her."[27]

Joseph sought Isaac Hales's approval on two different occasions for Emma's hand in marriage. Isaac was "bitterly opposed" to Joseph, whom he called a stranger, seeing little use for a man who was a money digger.[28] Although her father disapproved, Emma continued to see Joseph. On Thursday morning, 18 January 1827, Emma set off with Joseph to visit the Stowells. She recounted: "I had no intention of marrying when I left home; but during my visit at Mr. Stowell's, your father visited me there. My folks were bitterly opposed to him; and being importuned by your father, aided by Mr. Stowell, who urged me to marry him, and preferring to marry him to any other man I knew, I consented."[29] That evening Joseph and Emma took their marriage vows in the parlor of Esquire Zachariah Tarbell in South Bainbridge, New York.

After the ceremony, the newlyweds journeyed to Palmyra. There they found happiness in the Smith home. That summer Emma wrote to her father, asking if she could retrieve her clothes, cows, and furniture. When her father agreed, Joseph set out in August 1827 to acquire his wife's belongings. When he met his father-in-law, a teary Hale accused him of stealing his daughter. Joseph wept, too. Hale promised to help his son-in-law if Joseph would resolve "to give up his old habits of digging for money and looking into stones." Nevertheless, as history records, "gold and seer stones were still very much in his future," for the translation of the Book of Mormon still awaited him.[30]

In late winter or early spring of 1827, Joseph said to his father, "Father, I have had the severest chastisement that I ever had in my life." He then explained that "it was the angel of the Lord. He says I have been negligent, that the time has now come when the record should be brought forth, and that I must be up and doing, that I must set myself about the things which God has commanded me to do. But, Father, give yourself no uneasiness as to this reprimand, for I know what course I am to pursue, and all will be well."[31] On 22 September

1827 Joseph received the golden plates and began his life's work of restoring the gospel of Jesus Christ to the earth.

NOTES

1. Richard L. Bushman, "Joseph Smith's Family Background," in Porter and Black, *Prophet Joseph,* 14, 17.
2. Smith, *History of Joseph Smith by His Mother,* ed. Proctor and Proctor, 111–12.
3. Smith, *History of Joseph Smith by His Mother,* ed. Proctor and Proctor, 112.
4. Smith, *History of Joseph Smith by His Mother,* ed. Proctor and Proctor, 112.
5. Hill, *Joseph Smith, the First Mormon,* 60.
6. Smith, *History of Joseph Smith by His Mother,* ed. Proctor and Proctor, 112, 119; Smith, *History of the Church,* 1:126–27.
7. Hartley, *Stand by My Servant Joseph,* 26.
8. Smith, *History of Joseph Smith by His Mother,* ed. Proctor and Proctor, 115–16.
9. Smith, *History of Joseph Smith by His Mother,* ed. Proctor and Proctor, 119.
10. "William Smith," *Deseret Evening News,* January 20, 1894.
11. Smith, *History of Joseph Smith by His Mother,* ed. Proctor and Proctor, 121–22.
12. Smith, *History of Joseph Smith by His Mother,* ed. Proctor and Proctor, 122–23. See Joseph Knight's account of the 1824 meeting in Dean C. Jessee, ed., "Joseph Knight's Recollection of Early Mormon History," *BYU Studies* 17, no. 1 (Autumn 1976): 30–31.
13. Smith, *History of Joseph Smith by His Mother,* ed. Proctor and Proctor, 123–24.
14. See Cook, *David Whitmer Interviews,* 7.
15. Hartley, *Stand by My Servant Joseph,* 24.
16. Barnes Frisbie, *The History of Middletown, Vermont in Three Discourses* (Rutland, Vt.: Tuttle & Co., 1867), 44–46, as cited in Hill, *Joseph Smith,* 68.
17. Dallin H. Oaks, "Recent Events Involving Church History and Forged Documents," *Ensign,* October 1987, 68–69.
18. Bushman, "Joseph Smith's Family Background," 13.
19. Smith, *Biographical Sketches of Joseph Smith,* 6:92.
20. Martin Harris to Joel Tiffany, "Mormonism—No. II," *Tiffany's Monthly* 5, no. 4 (August 1859): 169, as cited in Bushman, *Joseph Smith and the Beginnings of Mormonism,* 74.
21. Knight, "Incidents of History," 1, as cited in Hartley, *Stand by My Servant Joseph,* 11.

22. Bushman, "Joseph Smith's Family Background," 13.

23. Inex K. Kennedy, *Recollections of Pioneers of Lee County,* 96.

24. Vesta C. Crawford, "Notes from Audentia."

25. Youngreen, *Reflections of Emma,* 4.

26. Hartley, *Stand by My Servant Joseph,* 26.

27. Smith, *History of Joseph Smith by His Mother,* ed. Proctor and Proctor, 126.

28. Smith, "Last Testimony of Sister Emma," *Saints Advocate* 2, no. 4 (October 1879): 49.

29. *Susquehanna Register,* 1 May 1834, as cited in Larry C. Porter, "Joseph Smith's Susquehanna Years," *Ensign,* February 2001, 42.

30. Givens, *By the Hand of Mormon,* 19.

31. Smith, *History of Joseph Smith by His Mother,* ed. Proctor and Proctor, 135.

CHAPTER SEVEN

OBTAINING AND PROTECTING
THE PLATES

H. Dean Garrett

*T*he angel Moroni warned the Prophet Joseph Smith when he received the plates on 22 September 1827:

> Now you have got the Record into your own hands, and you are but a man, therefore you will have to be watchful and faithful to your trust, or you will be overpowered by wicked men; for they will lay every plan and scheme that is possible to get it away from you, and if you do not take heed continually, they will succeed. While it was in my hands, I could keep it, and no man had power to take it away! but now I give it up to you. Beware, and look well to your ways, and you shall have power to retain it, until the time for it to be translated.[1]

This warning was important for Joseph to understand as he was schooled and prepared for the task of translating the Book of Mormon. From the time of the First Vision, Joseph's preparation and training were directed to this task. Some of that training focused on Joseph's need to seek spiritual blessings over his temporal needs and desires as well as on the importance of protecting the sacred gifts from Satan and others who would try to thwart the efforts to bring forth the Book of Mormon.

Before receiving the gold plates and almost two and half years after the Father and the Son had appeared to the Prophet in the Sacred Grove, Joseph, at the age of seventeen, was troubled by the lack of direction regarding his mission. He recorded his remorse over some of the "foolish errors and . . . weakness of youth, and the foibles

---

H. Dean Garrett is a professor of Church history and doctrine at Brigham Young University.

67

of human nature" that led him "into divers temptations, offensive in the sight of God." Joseph was not guilty of grievous sin, rather of "levity, and sometimes associated with jovial company, etc., not consistent with that character which ought to be maintained by one who was called of God as I had been" (Joseph Smith–History 1:28).

Consequently, on the night of 21 September 1823, as he retired to bed, Joseph poured out his heart to God, seeking forgiveness of his sins and pleading for direction as to what the Lord wanted him to do. As a result of this plea, the angel Moroni visited Joseph throughout the night, quoting Old and New Testament scriptures and teaching and directing the young prophet concerning his calling. He instructed Joseph that gold plates were buried in a hill not far from his home. During his final visit of the night, the angel warned Joseph "that Satan would try to tempt me (in consequence of the indigent circumstances of my father's family), to get the plates for the purpose of getting rich. This he forbade me, saying that I must have no other object in view in getting the plates but to glorify God, and must not be influenced by any other motive than that of building his kingdom; otherwise I could not get them" (Joseph Smith–History 1:46).

When Joseph viewed the plates the next morning, he struggled to keep focused on the purposes of God rather than the material opportunities the artifacts offered:

> I made an attempt to take them out, but was forbidden by the messenger, and was again informed that the time for bringing them forth had not yet arrived, neither would it, until four years from that time; but he told me that I should come to that place precisely in one year from that time; and that he would there meet with me, and that I should continue to do so until the time should come for obtaining the plates. (Joseph Smith–History 1:53)

The four intervening years before receiving the plates were challenging and life-changing for the Prophet—the sudden death of his beloved brother Alvin, his employment with Josiah Stowell, and his marriage to Emma Hale. Not until September 1827 did Joseph Smith receive the plates from the angel Moroni. Visitors at the Smith home on the evening of 21 September were Joseph Knight Sr. and Josiah

Stowell. Mother Smith was up late working on projects, and at about midnight Joseph went to her, asking for a chest with a lock and key. "I knew in an instant what he wanted it for, and not having one I was greatly alarmed, as I thought it might be a matter of considerable moment. But Joseph, discovering my anxiety, said, 'Never mind, I can do very well for the present without it—be calm—all is right.'"[2]

Soon after, Emma passed through the house dressed in traveling clothing. They left, taking Joseph Knight's horse and buggy. According to Mother Smith, they were gone the rest of the night, and Joseph was not at breakfast, which caused great agitation for Father Smith, who wanted to eat breakfast with Joseph, but Mother Smith was able to calm him by telling him that Joseph needed to be with his wife, Emma.[3] At about the same time, Joseph Knight discovered his horse missing, along with his wagon. The two Joseph seniors went looking for the missing horse and wagon, during which time the Prophet returned from the hill. Mother Smith recorded that because of her concerns, he told her things were well and informed her that he had the "key" and showed it to her. She later identified it as the Urim and Thummim.[4]

Protecting the plates proved no easy task for Joseph. Word had seeped into the community of the existence of the plates and that the time for obtaining them was soon. How this word got out is not clear. Mother Smith indicated that no one of the family discussed the existence of the plates with anyone except for Father Smith, who mentioned them to a trusted friend, Martin Harris.[5] Indications are that Father Smith also may have informed Mr. Willard Chase, a Methodist class leader and furniture maker, of the existence of the plates. The Smiths approached Mr. Chase twice to build a box for the plates, but he declined both times.[6]

Notwithstanding this secrecy, rumors abounded, and men attempted to obtain the plates from Joseph. The day after Joseph and Emma returned from the Hill Cumorah, Joseph, needing money to build a box for the plates, went to Macedon to help remove a wall from the well of a widow, Mrs. Wells. Joseph was on the job a short time when a neighbor of the Smiths approached Father Smith with

Joseph and Emma at the Hill Cumorah, *by Robert T. Barrett*

questions about the plates. Soon after, Father Smith gained intelligence that a group of men led by Mr. Willard Chase had obtained the service of a "conjonour" to use his divination to find the plates. Brigham Young indicated that this man rode "over sixty miles three times the same season," trying to find the plates. President Young described the man as "a fortune-teller, a necromancer, an astrologer, a soothsayer, and possessed as much talent as any man that walked on the American soil, and was one of the wickedest men I ever saw." He also declared that "when Joseph obtained the treasure, the priests, the deacons, and the religionists of every grade, went hand in hand with the fortune-teller, and with every wicked person, to get it out of his hands, and, to accomplish this, a part of them came out and persecuted him."[7]

Upon hearing of the effort to obtain the plates from Joseph, Father Smith sent Emma to warn him. Already informed of the danger through the Urim and Thummim, however, Joseph was out of the well and preparing to leave when Emma arrived. Giving notice to an unhappy Mrs. Wells, Joseph returned to the Smith home. He immediately went to a hollowed-out log about three miles away, where he had hidden the plates. Joseph took the plates from the log and "wrapping them in his linen frock, placed them under his arm and started for home. After proceeding a short distance, he thought it would be more safe to leave the road and go through the woods. Traveling some distance after he left the road, he came to a large windfall, and as he was jumping over a log, a man sprang up from behind it and gave him a heavy blow with a gun."[8] He was challenged two more times by individuals who attacked him, trying to get the plates. During the last attempt, Joseph struck the man, dislocating his thumb and badly bruising his hand.

With the plates secured in the Smith home, the Prophet sent his younger brother Don Carlos to get his brother Hyrum and have him bring the chest in which the plates and other items would be stored. It appears that before the plates were placed in the box, Josiah Stowell, Lucy Mack Smith, Katherine Smith, and perhaps others were allowed to handle them through the cloth. None, however, were allowed to see the plates.[9] But having the plates in the chest did not comfort the family. Martin Harris indicated that the "money-diggers claimed that they had as much right to the plates as Joseph had, as they were in company together. They claimed that Joseph had been [a] traitor, and had appropriated to himself that which belonged to them. For this reason Joseph was afraid of them, and continued concealing the plates."[10] This excitement caused much discussion as well as verbal and temporal abuse of the Smiths. Katherine Smith stated "that from the time the plates were brought into the house, the Smiths' premises were searched all around on a regular basis. Mobs of people even looked through the farm's field and its standing wheat stacks in hopes of finding the rumored treasure."[11]

Several other attempts to obtain the plates are noted in the historical record. For example, one day Joseph returned "to the house in great haste" and inquired if a company of men had come to the house. He indicated that a mob would be there before nighttime. The Smiths, with the help of a friend, Mr. Braman, took the brick hearth of the fireplace apart, placed the plates in the hearth, and reset the bricks. Soon, a well-armed mob came to the house. In an attempt to scare them away, the men of the Smith household crashed out of the doors hollering and yelling. The mob was struck with terror and "fled before the little Spartan band into the woods, where they dispersed themselves to their several homes."[12]

Soon after this experience, the Prophet learned of another attempt to steal the plates. He took the plates to the cooper's shop on his father's farm and concealed them in the floor of the shop. Being warned "by an angel," however, "he took them out and hid them up in the chamber of the cooper's shop among the flax. That night some one came, took up the floor, and dug up the earth, and would have found the plates had they not been removed."[13] Within a few days after this attempt, the Smith family learned that Sally, "the sister of Willard Chase[,] had led the mob to the barrel-making shop after looking through a piece of green glass and seeing the place where the Prophet had hidden the 'Gold Bible.' It is said that even after their failure to find the plates this mob still followed Chase's sister around to other places in a vain attempt to locate them."[14]

About this time, Martin Harris visited the Smith home, heard the story of how the plates were obtained, and hefted the covered plates, which he estimated were made of lead or gold. He was called to act as a scribe for Joseph as he began the translation process. After Harris lost 116 pages of the translated manuscript, however, he was not allowed to continue assisting in the translation process (D&C 3; 5; 10). During this experience, the external pressure of trying to obtain the plates mounted. Harris indicated: "The excitement in the village upon the subject had become such that some had threatened to mob Joseph, and also to tar and feather him. They said he should never leave until he had shown the plates. It was unsafe for him to remain, so I determined that he must go to his father-in-law's in Pennsylvania." Joseph wrote to his brother-in-law Alva Hale, asking for help in transporting him and Emma to the Hale farm. Martin then took upon himself the responsibility of paying all of Joseph's debts as well as giving him money for the journey. Martin advised him to take time enough to get ready, so that he might start a day or two in advance: for he would be mobbed if it was known when he started. We put the box of plates in a barrel about one-third full of beans and headed it up. I informed Mr. Hale of the matter, and advised them to cut each a good cudgel and put into the wagon with them, which they did. It was understood that they were to start on Monday; but they started on Saturday night and got through safe. This was the last of October, 1827. It might have been the first of November.[15]

Unfortunately, the move to Harmony was not without challenges. After learning that Joseph was leaving for Pennsylvania, "a mob of fifty men collected themselves together" and approached Dr. McIntyre, the physician whose absence had occasioned Dr. Greenwood's attending Alvin before he died. They tried to recruit the doctor to be their commander with the intentions of taking the gold bible from Joseph. The doctor did not go along with the request and told the men to go home and mind their own business. This led to a discussion and argument among them as to who would be the leader, and the mob dispersed for their homes.[16]

Orson Pratt recounted that as Joseph and Emma began their journey with Alva Hale for Harmony, they "had not gone far, before [they were] overtaken by an officer with a search-warrant, who flattered himself with the idea, that he should surely obtain the plates." When the search failed, the three were allowed to continue, only to be stopped a little later by another officer on the same business. After another failed search, they continued to the Hale farm.[17]

During their stay in Harmony, Oliver Cowdery joined Joseph as his scribe. The translation continued under mounting opposition from a Hale family member and others in the neighborhood. Joseph was told by revelation that "there are many that lie in wait to destroy thee from off the face of the earth" (D&C 5:33). Protection and assistance was given by the Knight family in Colesville, New York, and others in the area. In time, however, it became necessary for the Prophet to move back to New York. Joseph received a command through the Urim and Thummim to write a letter to David Whitmer, a friend of Oliver whom Joseph had never met. Upon receiving the letter, David traveled to Harmony to transport Joseph and Oliver back to Fayette so that they could continue the translation.[18] He recorded: "When I arrived at Harmony Joseph and Oliver were coming toward me, and met me some distance from the house. Oliver told me that Joseph had informed him . . . that I would be there that day before dinner, and this was why they had come out to meet me."[19]

Concerned for the safety of the plates during their journey to Fayette, Joseph "enquired of the Lord [to know] in what manner the plates should be conveyed to their point of destination. His answer was that he should give himself no trouble about [the matter] but hasten to [Fayette] and after he arrived [at] Mr. Whitmore's house if he would repair immediately to the garden he would receive the plates from the hand of an angel to whose charge they must be committed for their safety."[20] David Whitmer later recalled this experience:

> When I was returning to Fayette, with Joseph and Oliver . . . traveling along in a clear open place, a very pleasant, nice-looking old man suddenly appeared by the side of our wagon and saluted us with, "good morning, it is very warm," at the same time wiping his face or forehead with his hand. We returned the salutation, and, by a sign from Joseph, I invited him to ride if he was going our way. But he said very pleasantly, "No, I am going to Cumorah."

This was the first time David had heard the word *Cumorah* and did not know the meaning of the word. The old man instantly disappeared "so that I did not see him again."[21]

David and Oliver turned to Joseph, who was riding in the back of the wagon, and "asked the Prophet to inquire of the Lord who this stranger was. Soon David said they turned around and Joseph looked pale, almost transparent, and said that was one of the Nephites and he had the plates of the Book of Mormon in the knapsack."[22]

Arriving safely in Fayette about the first of June 1828, Joseph and Oliver continued the translation of the Book of Mormon. David Whitmer observed the availability of the plates from this point: "The plates were taken care of by a messenger of God, and when Joseph wanted to see the plates, this messenger was always at hand."[23]

Thus, through the persistent care of the Prophet, aided by family

and friends, and protected by God and angels, the plates were preserved until the translation was complete. Joseph was successful in
abiding by the commands given to him by the angel of the Lord in
protecting the plates. He mastered his own temporal desires as well
as overcame the challenges of Satan and others in their attempts to
obtain the plates and stop the translation of the Book of Mormon.
After the translation was finished, the Prophet declared of the plates
that "according to arrangements, the messenger called for them, I
delivered them up to him; and he has them in his charge until this
day."[24]

NOTES
1. Smith, *History of Joseph Smith by His Mother,* ed. Nibley, 110.
2. Smith, *History of Joseph Smith by His Mother,* ed. Nibley, 102.
3. Smith, *History of Joseph Smith by His Mother,* ed. Nibley, 102–3.
4. Smith, *History of Joseph Smith by His Mother,* ed. Nibley, 104 n. 1.
5. Smith, *History of Joseph Smith by His Mother,* ed. Nibley, 105.
6. Kirkham, *New Witness for Christ in America,* 1:134.
7. Young, *Journal of Discourses,* 2:180–81.
8. Smith, *History of Joseph Smith by His Mother,* ed. Nibley, 108.
9. See Brown, *Plates of Gold,* 48–49, for a discussion of these events.
10. Martin Harris, in *Tiffany's Monthly* 5, no. 4 (August 1859): 163.
11. *Kansas City Times,* 11 April 1895, as cited in Brown, *Plates of Gold,* 50.
12. Smith, *History of Joseph Smith by His Mother,* ed. Nibley, 112.
13. Martin Harris, in *Tiffany's Monthly,* 1859.
14. Brown, *Plates of Gold,* 51.
15. Martin Harris, in *Tiffany's Monthly,* 1859.
16. Smith, *History of Joseph Smith by His Mother,* ed. Nibley, 118–19.
17. Jessee, *Papers of Joseph Smith,* 1:400.
18. See Brown, *Plates of Gold,* 91, for a discussion of this preparation.
19. *Millennial Star* 40, no. 9 (December 1878): 772.
20. Anderson, *Lucy's Book,* 450.
21. *Millennial Star,* 40, no. 9 (December 1878): 772.
22. "Edward Stevenson Diary," January 2, 1886 as cited in Brown, *Plates of Gold,* 94.
23. *Kansas City Journal,* June 5, 1881, as cited in Cook, *David Whitmer Interviews,* 63.
24. Smith, *History of the Church,* 1:18.

CHAPTER EIGHT

THE BOOK OF LEHI

Grant Underwood

oseph Smith was too burdened to eat or sleep. Nearly forty-eight hours had passed since boarding the stagecoach in Harmony, Pennsylvania. As the stage approached the disembarking point for Palmyra, New York, the lone traveler sharing the coach with the Prophet, who throughout the journey had been observing Joseph's anxiety, was troubled. "You shall not go on foot 20 miles alone this night," declared the stranger, "for if you must and will go I will be your company." Joseph did not resist. The two trudged together for hours, arriving at the Smith family home just before dawn. Utterly exhausted and emotionally drained, the Prophet was soon under the tender care of his mother, Lucy Mack Smith.[1]

Two weeks previous, Joseph and Emma had lost their firstborn child just hours after his birth, a tragedy compounded by Emma's continuing ordeal. The difficult labor had brought her to death's door, where she lingered for days. "So uncertain seemed her faite for a season," recalled Lucy Mack Smith, "that in the space of 2 weeks her husband never slept one hour in undisturbed quiet."[2] Yet an even greater anxiety gnawed at him. The day before Emma's delivery, Martin Harris had taken home the first 116 manuscript pages of the Book of Mormon translation to show his family, and he had not yet returned the pages. Joseph had been reluctant to surrender them, but Harris was insistent. As the days wore on, the Prophet's worry increased. Finally, at Emma's urging, Joseph set off for Palmyra.

Grant Underwood is a professor of history at Brigham Young University.

Joseph Smith, Jr., Learns That the 116-Page Manuscript Is Lost, *by Clark Kelley Price.* © *Intellectual Reserve, Inc. Courtesy of the Museum of Church History and Art*

The Smith family had known Martin Harris, a prominent, well-to-do Palmyra farmer, from before the gold plates were discovered and considered him their "confidential friend." Harris's financial patronage had played a modest role in helping the Smiths make ends meet during the 1820s,[3] and it would play a major role in helping Joseph Smith translate and ultimately publish the Book of Mormon. Lucy remembered that when Joseph first pondered where to find the resources to launch the translation, he thought of Martin and sent his mother to the Harris home to arrange a meeting.[4] After Martin made his own careful investigation of the Smith family claims about the origin of the plates and after personally hefting the wooden box in which Joseph kept them, Martin said that he "prayed to God to show me concerning these things, and I covenanted that if it was his work and he would show me so, I would put forth my best ability to bring it before the world. He then showed me that it was his work . . . by the still small voice spoken in the soul. Then I was satisfied that it was the Lord's work, and I was under a covenant to bring it forth."[5]

When persecution in the Palmyra area compelled Joseph and

Emma to accept her parents' invitation to move to Harmony, Harris made good on his covenant of financial support. Prior to the Prophet's departure, he paid Joseph's local debts and "furnished him money for his journey."[6] The Prophet's mother recalled that while Joseph was "transacting some business" in a "public house" in Palmyra, Martin Harris entered, walked up to Joseph, "taking him by the hand, said, 'How do you do, Mr. Smith.' After which, he took a bag of silver from his pocket, and said again, 'Here, Mr. Smith, is fifty dollars [more than a thousand dollars today]; I give this to you to do the Lord's work with; no, I give it to the Lord for his own work.'"[7] Joseph wrote that as a result of Martin's "faith and this righteous deed the Lord appeared unto him in a vision and shewed unto him his marvilous work which he was about to do."[8] And now most recently, leaving family and farm, Harris had worked steadily for two months as the Prophet's scribe. Without such assistance, the first 116 pages of the Book of Mormon simply could not have been produced.

All of this Joseph knew as he waited that summer morning for Martin to join the family for breakfast. Joseph also would have recalled how insistent his patron and scribe had been in wanting to take the manuscript home. Three times Martin had pressed the Prophet to approach the Lord. Finally, Joseph recalled, "the Lord said unto me let him go with them only he shall covenant with me that he will not shew them to only but four persons" in his immediate family.[9] Now, several weeks later with the security of the manuscript in question, Joseph was fearful that

> the hot displeasure of the Almighty would be kindled against him for turning aside from the injunctions which was laid upon him and calling upon his heavenly Father to grant him an indulgence that was not according to instructions of the Angel of the Lord. for it now appeared to him upon reflection that he had acted hastily & in an inconsiderate manner and that he had regarded man more than his maker.[10]

Lucy's recollections of what happened next are vivid and dramatic:

> At eight o'clock we set the victuals on the table, as we were expecting him every moment. We waited till nine, and he came not—till ten, and

he was not there—till eleven, still he did not make his appearance. But at half-past twelve we saw him walking with a slow and measured tread towards the house, his eyes fixed thoughtfully upon the ground. On coming to the gate, he stopped, instead of passing through, and got upon the fence, and sat there some time with his hat drawn over his eyes. At length he entered the house. Soon after which we sat down to the table, Mr. Harris with the rest. He took up his knife and fork as if he were going to use them, but immediately dropped them. Hyrum, observing this, said "Martin, why do you not eat; are you sick?" Upon which Mr. Harris pressed his hands upon his temples, and cried out in a tone of deep anguish, "Oh, I have lost my soul! I have lost my soul!"

Joseph, who had not expressed his fears till now, sprang from the table, exclaiming, "Martin, have you lost that manuscript? have you broken your oath, and brought down condemnation upon my head, as well as your own?"

"Yes, it is gone," replied Martin, "and I know not where."

"Oh, my God!" said Joseph, clinching his hands. "All is lost! all is lost! What shall I do? I have sinned—it is I who tempted the wrath of God. I should have been satisfied with the first answer which I received from the Lord; for he told me that it was not safe to let the writing go out of my possession." He wept and groaned, and walked the floor continually.

At length he told Martin to go back and search again.

"No," said Martin, "it is all in vain; for I have ripped open beds and pillows, and I know it is not there."

"Then must I," said Joseph, "return to my wife with such a tale as this? . . . And how shall I appear before the Lord? Of what rebuke am I not worthy from the angel of the Most High?" . . . And he continued pacing back and forth, meantime weeping and grieving, until about sunset, when, by persuasion, he took a little nourishment.[11]

Sensing the futility of further searches in Palmyra, a frustrated Joseph Smith returned to Harmony to his recuperating wife. It was a low point for the Prophet and his family. "I well remember that day of darkness," his mother later remarked, "both within and without. To us, at least, the heavens seemed clothed with blackness, and the earth shrouded with gloom."[12] Shortly after returning home, however, "the former heavenly messenger appeared and handed to [Joseph] the Urim and Thummin again." The Prophet "enquired of the Lord through them and obtained" what is now Doctrine and Covenants, section three, the earliest recorded revelation to have survived.[13] In that revelation, which future Book of Mormon witness David Whitmer later characterized as "the stormiest kind of chastisement from the Lord,"[14] Joseph was warned that "although a man may have many revelations, and have power to do many mighty works, yet if he . . . sets at naught the counsels of God, and follows after the dictates of his own will and carnal desires, he must fall and incur the vengeance of a just God upon him" (D&C 3:4).

Joseph must have winced when the Lord declared, "Thou hast suffered the counsel of thy director to be trampled upon from the beginning" (D&C 3:15). More gently, he was reminded that he "should not have feared man more than God. Although men set at naught the counsels of God, and despise his words—Yet you should have been faithful; and he would have extended his arm and supported you against all the fiery darts of the adversary; and he would have been with you in every time of trouble" (D&C 3:7–8). Fortunately, the revelation also contained an explicit promise of forgiveness and restoration to divine calling: "But remember God is merciful: Therefore, repent of that which thou hast done, and he will only cause thee to be afflicted for a season, and thou art still chosen, and wilt again be called to the work."[15]

Following that requisite season of "much humility and affliction of soul,"[16] the plates and Urim and Thummim were returned to Joseph for the duration of the translation. With them came a revelation exhorting him to be "faithful and go on unto the finishing of the remainder of the work as you have begun," as well as explaining what had happened to the 116 pages. Joseph reported in the preface to the original edition of the Book of Mormon that "some person or persons have stolen and kept [them] from me, notwithstanding my utmost exertions to recover" them (Book of Mormon, Preface, 1830 publication). Later accounts finger Martin's wife. The Episcopal minister, John Clark, for instance, wrote:

> When the manuscript was discovered to be missing, suspicion immediately fastened upon Mrs. Harris. She, however, refused to give any information in relation to the matter, but simply replied: "If this be a divine

communication, the same being who revealed it to you can easily replace it." Mrs. H. believed the whole thing to be a gross deception, and she had formed a plan to expose the deception . . . she intended to keep the manuscript until the book was published, and then put these one hundred and sixteen pages into the hands of some one who would publish them, and show how they varied from those published in the Book of Mormon.[17]

Whether or not Lucy Harris was involved, the Lord did disclose to Joseph Smith that the individuals in possession of the stolen manuscript were planning such a scheme:

Satan hath put it into their hearts to alter the words which you have caused to be written . . .

Behold, they say and think in their hearts—We will see if God has given him power to translate; if so, he will also give him power again;

And if God giveth him power again, or if he translates again, or, in other words, if he bringeth forth the same words, behold, we have the same with us, and we have altered them;

Therefore they will not agree, and we will say that he has lied in his words, and that he has no gift, and that he has no power;

Therefore we will destroy him, and also the work. (D&C 10:10, 16–19)

Unbeknownst to the conspirators, however, a divine "contingency plan" had been in place for centuries. After abridging the "larger" plates of Nephi (Jacob 3:13) down to the reign of King Benjamin, Mormon wrote:

I searched among the records which had been delivered into my hands, and I found these plates, which contained this small account of the prophets, from Jacob down to the reign of this king Benjamin, and also many of the words of Nephi.

And the things which are upon these plates pleasing me, because of the prophecies of the coming of Christ . . .

Wherefore, I chose these things, to finish my record upon them. . . .

. . . behold, I shall take these plates, which contain these prophesyings and revelations, and put them with the remainder of my record, for they are choice unto me; and I know they will be choice unto my brethren.

And I do this for a wise purpose; for thus it whispereth me, according to the workings of the Spirit of the Lord which is in me. (Words of Mormon 1:3–7)

Nephi had made *two* sets of plates. The first contained "a more history part" (2 Nephi 4:14) of the Nephite experience, but Nephi also "received a commandment that the ministry and the prophecies, the more plain and precious parts of them, should be written upon [a second set of] plates." This he was directed to do for "wise purposes, which purposes are known unto the Lord" (1 Nephi 19:3). One purpose appears to have been to provide a replacement for the lost manuscript. As it turned out, the replacement would be doctrinally superior to the lost 116 pages. The Lord told Joseph Smith, "There are many things engraven upon the plates of Nephi which do throw greater views upon my gospel" (D&C 10:45). This unabridged, historically parallel account was published as the first six books of the Book of Mormon: 1 Nephi, 2 Nephi, Jacob, Enos, Jarom, and Omni.

The account that had been stolen and altered was known as the Book of Lehi. Joseph Smith said he took the 116 pages "from the Book of Lehi, which was an account abridged from the plates of Lehi, by the hand of Mormon" (Book of Mormon, Preface, 1830 publication). The plates of Lehi are to be understood not as a separate record abridged by Mormon apart from the large plates of Nephi, but rather as a part of it. Joseph's description parallels the way in which a portion of the small plates of Nephi were called the "plates of Jacob." Jacob explained that the plates on which he was engraving his record were "called the plates of Jacob" even though "they were made by the hand of Nephi" (Jacob 3:14), and today are known as the small plates of Nephi. Therefore, that the first portion of the large plates of Nephi should be called the "plates of Lehi" and Mormon's abridgment of them the "Book of Lehi" is similar to how the present Book of Jacob was taken from the "plates of Jacob," though they were actually part of the small plates of Nephi.

Moreover, from what can be gleaned from the Book of Mormon, the Book of Lehi is a wholly appropriate title for Mormon's abridgment of the first part of the large plates of Nephi. Regarding the early portion of the large plates, Nephi wrote, "I did engraven the record of my father . . . and the genealogy of his fathers, and the more part of all our proceedings in the wilderness" (1 Nephi 19:1–2). This large-plates emphasis on Lehi and the "proceedings" of his family seems to make the "Book of Lehi" more than an honorific title for Mormon's abridgment.

Extant records do not allow a precise determination of where Joseph Smith restarted his translation of the Book of Mormon. Most scholars believe that he picked up where he had previously left off—with Mormon's abridgment of the large plates, near the beginning of the Book of Mosiah. The small plates of Nephi are usually believed to be the last part of the Book of Mormon to be translated, even though they appear first in the published volume.[18] In any case, Joseph got off to a slow start. The historical record makes clear that the Prophet translated very little before April 1829 when Oliver Cowdery arrived to serve as his full-time scribe. Brother Cowdery later recalled, "I wrote with my own pen the entire Book of Mormon (save a few pages) as it fell from the lips of the prophet."[19]

Joseph Smith learned much from the traumatic experience of losing the Book of Lehi. He learned about human nature, about "friends," and about the absolute importance of relying on the Lord. He also learned practical lessons as well. Upon completing the translation of the Book of Mormon a year after losing the 116 pages, he directed Oliver Cowdery to copy the entire manuscript in case any manuscript pages were damaged or "lost" in transit to or from the printer's office, or while there, so that the original would be preserved. The Prophet was not about to make the same tragic mistake twice. Through it all, however, Joseph learned pointedly and poignantly that "the works, and the designs, and the purposes of God cannot be frustrated, neither can they come to naught" (D&C 3:1).

NOTES

1. Anderson, *Lucy's Book,* 416.

2. Anderson, *Lucy's Book,* 412.

3. Anderson, *Lucy's Book,* 394. Harris, who lived into his nineties, reminisced late in life about "often" giving teenaged Joseph Smith work on his farm and about them "hoe[ing] corn together many a day"; cited in Edward Stevenson, "The Three Witnesses to the Book of Mormon," *Millennial Star* 48 (June 21, 1886): 389.

4. Anderson, *Lucy's Book,* 394.

5. Kirkham, *New Witness for Christ in America,* 2:382.

6. Kirkham, *New Witness for Christ in America,* 2:382.

7. Anderson, *Lucy's Book,* 400.

8. Jessee, *Papers of Joseph Smith,* 1:9.

9. Jessee, *Papers of Joseph Smith,* 1:10.

10. Anderson, *Lucy's Book,* 414–15.

11. Anderson, *Lucy's Book,* 417–19.

12. Anderson, *Lucy's Book,* 423.

13. Jessee, *Papers of Joseph Smith,* 1:287.

14. Cook, *David Whitmer Interviews,* 200.

15. Book of Commandments, chapter 2, page 8.

16. Jessee, *Papers of Joseph Smith,* 1:10.

17. Clark, *Gleanings by the Way,* 247–48.

18. Backman, "Book of Mormon, Translation of," in Largey, *Book of Mormon Reference Companion,* 159–60.

19. Reuben Miller, Diary, 21 October 1848, as cited in Dean C. Jessee, "The Original Book of Mormon Manuscript," *BYU Studies* 10, no. 3 (Spring 1970): 276.

CHAPTER NINE

OLIVER COWDERY, BOOK OF MORMON SCRIBE

Scott H. Faulring

O n 21 October 1848, after more than a decade's absence from the fellowship of the Saints, Oliver Cowdery[1] arrived at Council Bluffs, Iowa, during an outdoor Church conference. He had come to the "Bluffs" to reconcile himself with the Church he helped found in 1830. Apostle Orson Hyde, the presiding official there, was giving a discourse when he noticed the arrival of Oliver. Elder Hyde immediately stopped speaking, stepped from the stand, went to Oliver, and embraced his former leader. Taking him by the arm, Elder Hyde led the former Second Elder up to the stand for all the Saints to see. After introducing Oliver, he invited him to give an impromptu speech to the 2,500 assembled Saints:

> Friends and brethren my name is Cowdery, Oliver Cowdery. In the early history of this church, I stood identified with her. And one in her councils . . . I wrote with my own pen the entire Book of Mormon (save a few pages) as it fell from the lips of the Prophet [Joseph Smith]. As he translated it by the gift and power of God, by means of the urim and thummim, or as it is called by that book holy Interpreters . . . I wrote it myself as it fell from the lips of the Prophet. It contains the everlasting gospel, and came in fulfillment of the revelations of John where he says he seen an angel come with the everlasting gospel to preach to every nation, tongue and people. It contains principles of salvation.[2]

Once again Oliver Cowdery was fellowshipping with the Saints of God and testifying to his sacred witness of and contribution to the coming forth of the Book of Mormon. This chapter will document the

Scott H. Faulring is a research historian at the Joseph Fielding Smith Institute for Latter-day Saint History, Brigham Young University.

activities of Oliver when he acted as the main scribe of the Book of Mormon translation from April through late June or early July 1829.

WESTERN NEW YORK INTRODUCTIONS

Oliver moved from Vermont to western New York in 1825 or 1826. He worked as a clerk in a mercantile store, perhaps keeping the account books and thereby developing skills essential to a scribe.[3] During the autumn of 1828, possibly in November, twenty-two-year-old Oliver had a chance meeting with twenty-three-year-old David Whitmer[4] in Palmyra, Wayne County, New York. David, a farmer from Fayette Township, Seneca County, New York, was in town on business. Shortly after they met, their conversation turned to the latest rumors about twenty-two-year-old Joseph Smith Jr. and the gold plates he had discovered in a drumlin three miles south of Palmyra village. David later said, "A great many people in the neighborhood were talking about the finding of certain golden plates by one Joseph Smith, jr., a young man of that neighborhood. Cowdery and I, as well as others, talked about the matter." Oliver told David that he knew the Smith family and "believed there must be some truth in the story of the plates." Intending to investigate the story further, Oliver promised to write to David with any additional information about Joseph Smith and his plates.[5]

About the same time, Lyman Cowdery, Oliver's older brother and a self-educated lawyer, applied to the Manchester School District Examiners, which included board trustee Hyrum Smith, to teach in the district school.[6] After being questioned about his moral and academic qualifications, Lyman was accepted as the Manchester District 11 schoolmaster. The next day, however, he declined the position, indicating that an unexpected business commitment had arisen. In his place, he presented his brother Oliver as a suitable replacement. School examiners interviewed Oliver and found him acceptable; thus he became the new district schoolmaster.[7]

Oliver's country schoolhouse, probably a wooden frame, one-room structure, was located on the west side of Stafford Road, a little less than two miles south of Joseph Smith Sr.'s one-hundred-acre farm.[8] The Smiths sent at least four of their children to the school as students. As part of the teacher's remuneration in those days, families with children in school took turns providing the schoolmaster with room and board. Since the Smith children attended the school on Stafford Road, Oliver came to live with the Smiths in late 1828. Mother Lucy Mack Smith, in her 1845 memoirs, recalled that Oliver

> board[ed] for the time being at our house. He had been in the school but a short time, when he began to hear from all quarters concerning the plates, and as soon began to importune [Father] Smith upon the subject, but for a considerable length of time did not succeed in eliciting any information. At last, however, he gained my husband's confidence, so far as to obtain a sketch of the facts relative to the plates.[9]

Hearing firsthand from Joseph Sr. about the angel Moroni, ancient plates, and the sublime work that Joseph Jr. was undertaking, greatly excited Oliver. He informed Father Smith that he was "highly delighted with what he had heard, that he had been in a deep study upon the subject all day, and that it was impressed upon his mind, that he should yet have the privilege of writing for Joseph. Furthermore, that he had determined to pay him a visit at the close of the school."[10] It is not known whether Father Smith mentioned to Oliver that Joseph was having difficulty translating without a dedicated scribe to write down the translation, but Oliver began to feel the Spirit prompting him to get involved.

As he learned more about this latter-day religious miracle, he began to ponder the truthfulness of the story. Oliver was encouraged by Father Smith to pray about the things he heard and determine for himself whether they were truly God's work. The thoughts of an angel being sent from God with ancient American scriptures yet to be translated and published to a modern world worked on his mind day and night, so much so that Oliver had difficulty thinking about much else. He confided in Mother Smith that the information was "working in my very bones." One evening, after all in the Smith home had retired, Oliver prayed for further information or a confirmation. In response, he received a vision of the plates and the Lord spoke "peace to [his]

Joseph Smith Translating the Book of Mormon, *by Del Parson.*
© *Intellectual Reserve, Inc. Courtesy of the Museum of*
Church History and Art

mind concerning the matter" (D&C 6:23). At this point, Oliver knew by the Spirit that what the Smiths had told him was true. In addition, he felt an overwhelming desire to meet Joseph and assist with the translation of the sacred record. He concluded that as soon as his teaching assignment was over in late March 1829, he would journey to Harmony, Pennsylvania, to assist Joseph Smith as a scribe.[11]

When the winter school term finished, Oliver, who had previously arranged with Hyrum Smith to collect his pay of $65.50 from the town and county funds, prepared to leave Palmyra. And true to his word, he set out in late March or early April for Harmony to meet Joseph. His traveling companion was Samuel Harrison Smith, Joseph's younger brother. The first night of their two-and-a-half day journey, they stayed at the Peter Whitmer Sr. farm in Fayette Township. Since the Whitmers had not met young Joseph, Samuel was probably asked many questions about his brother's prophetic calling and the ancient plates. It is not known what level of information Samuel was at liberty to share. David Whitmer was especially interested in Joseph's work.

ARRIVAL IN HARMONY, TRANSLATION RESUMES

Oliver and Samuel arrived in Harmony near sundown on Sunday, 5 April 1829. The next day, Oliver assisted Joseph Smith with a written legal agreement between Joseph and Isaac Hale.[12] According to the agreement, Joseph was purchasing 13.8 acres from his father-in-law. The property included a one-room clapboard house which served as the residence of Joseph and his wife, Emma. This residence proved significant to the translation. For it was in these close quarters that Joseph and Oliver worked from early April to late May 1829 on the Book of Mormon translation. Occasionally, they stopped their work to perform temporal labors to provide food and even writing paper for the translation process. A friend of the Smiths, Joseph Knight Sr., later recalled one of those occasions:

> In the spring of 1829, Oliver Cowdery, a young man from Palm[yra], went to see old [Father] Smith about the book that Joseph had found and he told him about it and advised him to go down to Pennsylvania and see for himself and to write for Joseph. He went down and [Joseph] received a Revelation [D&C 6] concerning the work and he was convinced of the truth of the work and he agreed to write for him [un]til it was done. Now Joseph and Oliver came up to [Colesville, New York, to] see me if I could help him to [get] some provisions, [they] having no way to buy any . . . I bought a barrel of mackerel and some lined paper for writing . . . I bought some nine or ten bushels of grain and five or six bushels of taters [potatoes] and a pound of tea and I went down to see him and they were in

want. Joseph and Oliver were gone to see if they could find a place to work for provisions, but found none. They returned home and found me there with provisions and they were glad, for they were out.[13]

With their worldly needs taken care of, Joseph was able to dictate each day between 8 and 10 manuscript foolscap pages.[14] According to noted linguistic scholar Royal Skousen, who has spent nearly twenty years producing a valuable critical text of the Book of Mormon, Joseph could see the English text of what he was translating. He worked with twenty to thirty words at a time and could see the spelling of names. Oliver would write down and read back the text to Joseph for verified correctness. If correctly transcribed, the process would continue.[15] Many witnesses of the translation testified that the Prophet would translate for lengthy periods of time and had neither paper nor a book to read from as he translated. Also, they indicated that Joseph knew exactly where to resume the translation after a break from the previous session. Neither Joseph nor Oliver ever gave a detailed description of the means and method used in translating the Book of Mormon. They only described the translation as having been accomplished by the "gift and power of God" using the Urim and Thummim.[16]

As promised in one of the revelations given to him through Joseph Smith (D&C 6:25), Oliver sought an opportunity to translate the Book of Mormon himself. A brief account of his efforts is written in the *History of the Church* (1:36–38) and Doctrine and Covenants 8 and 9. Oliver's role as second witness required him to understand the process of translation, but we do not know all the particulars of how that was accomplished. We do know that before late June 1829, Joseph was forbidden to show the plates to anyone unless the Lord commanded him to do so (D&C 5:3).[17] We know from the revelation given afterwards that Oliver "did not continue" to translate "as [he] commenced." Therefore, the Lord told him, "because you did not translate according to that which you desired of me, and did commence again to write for my servant, Joseph . . . I have taken away this privilege from you" (D&C 9:1, 5).

On 15 May 1829, inspired by a question from the translation of 3 Nephi 11, Joseph and Oliver retired to the nearby woods to pray.

There, near the banks of the Susquehannah River, they were visited by the resurrected John the Baptist (Joseph Smith–History 1:71–72, Cowdery endnote). From John the Baptist, Joseph and his scribe, Oliver, received the lesser priesthood, or Aaronic Priesthood, and were commanded to baptize each other. They immediately obeyed. Later that same month, Peter, James, and John, the Savior's apostles in the meridian of time, bestowed the Melchizedek Priesthood upon them.[18]

As news spread of Joseph's translation activities and the restoration of the priesthood, local townsmen in Harmony formed into a mob to protest such proceedings. The Prophet recorded:

> In the meantime we were forced to keep secret the circumstances of our having been baptized, and having received this priesthood; owing to a spirit of persecution which had already manifested itself in the neighborhood. We had been threatened with being mobbed, from time to time, and this too by professors of religion, and their intentions of mobbing us, were only counteracted by the influence of my wife's father's family (under Divine Providence) who had become very friendly to me and were opposed to mobs; and were willing that I should be allowed to continue the work of translation without interruption: And therefore offered and promised us protection from all unlawful proceedings as far as in them lay.[19]

By mid-May 1829, it had become quite clear that this was not enough to prevent harassment and persecution.

Joseph and Oliver were forced to seek a safe refuge in which to finish the translation. David Whitmer wrote that Joseph learned through revelation that the Whitmers could provide the needed safe haven for them. He penned, "I received another letter from Cowdery, telling me to come down into Pennsylvania and bring him and Joseph to my father's house, giving as a reason therefor that they had received a commandment from God to that effect." Mother Smith also recalled Joseph being commanded to solicit assistance from the Whitmers:

> As Joseph was translating by means of the Urim and Thummim, he received, instead of the words of the Book, a commandment to write a letter to a man by the name of David Whitmer, who lived in Waterloo,[20] requesting him to come immediately with his team, and convey himself and Oliver to his own residence, as an evil-designing people were seeking

to take away his (Joseph's) life, in order to prevent the work of God from going forth to the world.[21]

Sometime in late May or early June of 1829, David, with a team of horses and a buckboard wagon, set out from Fayette to get Joseph and Oliver and take them to his father's farm for refuge. Emma went up to Fayette some time later. At the Whitmers' farm, Joseph and Oliver, with the scribal assistance of at least the brothers John and Christian Whitmer, were busily completing the translation. On 11 June 1829, someone (likely Martin Harris, who had time and means to do so) filed the copyright for the Book of Mormon with the federal court clerk at Utica, New York.

CONCLUSION

Nearly the entire text of the current Book of Mormon was translated by the Prophet Joseph Smith from early April to the end of June 1829 with Oliver Cowdery as his primary scribe. To Oliver—

> [Those] were days never to be forgotten—to sit under the sound of a voice dictated by the *inspiration* of heaven, awakened the utmost gratitude of this bosom! Day after day I continued, uninterrupted, to write from [Joseph Smith's] mouth, as he translated, with the *Urim* and *Thummim,* or, as the Nephites whould have said, "Interpreters," the history, or record, called "The book of Mormon."
>
> To notice, in even a few words, the interesting account given by Mormon, and his faithful son Moroni, of a people once beloved and favored of heaven.[22]

NOTES
1. Oliver Cowdery, son of William Cowdery and Rebecca Fuller, was born on 3 October 1806 in Wells, Rutland, Vermont. One month before Oliver's third birthday, his mother died. William remarried about six months later to Keziah Pearce, herself a widow, and the couple had three daughters. See Mehling, *Cowdrey-Cowdery-Cowdray Genealogy,* 95–96.
2. Reuben Miller Journal, October 21, 1848, LDS Church Archives; spelling, punctuation, capitalization, and so forth in original manuscripts and contemporary published sources have been standardized for readability. The wording has not been changed.
3. Lucy Cowdery Young to Brigham H. Young, March 17, 1887, LDS Church Archives. Lucy (1814–1898) was Oliver's half-sister. According to her 1887

letter, Oliver moved from Vermont to New York when he was twenty years old. This would place the move after October 1826, but since Lucy incorrectly recalled that her older brother was born in 1805, versus the correct 1806, his move may have occurred in 1825.

4. David Whitmer (1805–1888) was one of five sons born to Peter Whitmer Sr. and Mary Musselman.

5. The details of Cowdery and Whitmer's first meeting are from an interview David Whitmer had with a reporter from the *Kansas City Journal;* the interview was published in the 5 June 1881 issue.

6. Stability of zoning is assumed. The former Smith farm appears in District 11 in Nichols, *Atlas of Ontario County,* 45.

7. See Smith, *Biographical Sketches of Joseph Smith,* 128.

8. Because the school was a combined-grade school, it is possible that sixteen-year-old William, fourteen-year-old Catherine, eleven-year-old Don Carlos, and six-year-old Lucy attended the same class, schoolmaster Cowdery working with each student individually and the class collectively. On the location of the original schoolhouse, see Berrett, *Sacred Places: New York and Pennsylvania,* 210–13.

9. Smith, *Biographical Sketches of Joseph Smith,* 128.

10. Smith, *Biographical Sketches of Joseph Smith,* 128–29.

11. In Mother Smith's history, Oliver is quoted as telling her, "I have made it a subject of prayer, and I firmly believe that it is the will of the Lord that I should go. If there is a work for me to do in this thing, I am determined to attend to it." Smith, *Biographical Sketches of Joseph Smith,* 129. In 1832, when the Prophet Joseph Smith prepared his earliest history, he said that the "Lord appeared unto a young man by the name of Oliver Cowdery and shewed unto him the plates in a vision and also the truth of the work and what the Lord was about to do through me his unworthy servant therefore he was desirous to come and write for me to translate." Joseph Smith's 1832 Autobiographical Sketch, Joseph Smith Letter Book 1, page 6 (earliest writing), Joseph Smith Collection, LDS Church Archives.

12. See Land Purchase Agreement between Isaac Hale and Joseph Smith Jr., 6 April 1829, Joseph Smith Collection, LDS Church Archives.

13. Dean C. Jessee, ed., "Joseph Knight's Recollections of Early Mormon History," *BYU Studies* 17, no. 1 (1976): 36.

14. So called due to a watermark of a fool's cap formerly applied to such paper.

15. See Royal Skousen, "Translating the Book of Mormon: Evidence from the Original Manuscript," in Reynolds, *Book of Mormon Authorship Revisited,* 61–93. See also Royal Skousen, ed., *The Original Manuscript of the Book of Mormon: Typographical Facsimile of the Extant Text,* Vol. 1 in Book of Mormon Critical Text Series (Provo, Utah: Foundation for Ancient Research and Mormon Studies, Brigham Young University, 2001).

16. For further information on the coming forth, translation, and printing of the Book of Mormon, see Dean C. Jessee, "The Original Book of Mormon Manuscript," *BYU Studies* 10 (Spring 1970): 259–78; Richard Lloyd

Anderson, "Gold Plates and Printer's Ink," *Ensign,* September 1976, 71–76; Richard Lloyd Anderson, "'By the Gift and Power of God,'" *Ensign,* September 1977, 78–85; John W. Welch and Tim Rathbone, "The Translation of the Book of Mormon: Basic Historical Information," part of FARMS Report WRR-86; Stephen Ricks, "Joseph Smith's Means and Methods of Translating the Book of Mormon," part of FARMS Report WRR-86; Royal Skousen, "Piecing Together the Original Manuscript," *BYU Today* 46 (May 1992): 18–24; Royal Skousen, "Translating the Book of Mormon: Evidence from the Original Manuscript," in Reynolds, *Book of Mormon Authorship Revisited,* 61–93; and Royal Skousen, "John Gilbert's 1892 Account of the 1830 Printing of the Book of Mormon," in Ricks, Parry, and Hedges, *Disciple as Witness,* 381–405.

17. To assist Oliver to translate, Joseph Smith appears to have copied seven lines of ancient Nephite characters from the plates. This "Caractors" manuscript artifact, presently in the Community of Christ (formerly the Reorganized Church of Jesus Christ of Latter Day Saints) was produced by the Prophet sometime between early 1828 and mid-1829. Contrary to Latter-day Saint tradition, this small sample of "Caractors" likely had nothing to do with Martin Harris and his trip to the eastern scholars in early 1828. Joseph Smith apparently gave the characters to his scribe Oliver Cowdery, who kept it in his possession until his death in 1850. The doctument was bequeathed to Oliver's friend and brother-in-law, David Whitmer. David treasured it with the other artifacts he had from the first decade of the Church. After David's death, the "Caractors" document eventually became the property of David's grandson George W. Schweich, who sold it to the RLDS Church in 1903.

18. Although neither the Prophet Joseph Smith nor Oliver Cowdery, his trusted assistant, ever revealed the exact date of the restoration of the Higher Priesthood, senior Mormon historian Larry C. Porter assembled all available contemporary historical evidence. His careful scholarly conclucion is that the Melchizedek Priesthood was restored before the end of May 1829 or before the move of Joseph and Oliver from Harmony to Fayette. See Larry C. Porter, "The Restoration of the Aaronic and Melchizedek Priesthoods," *Ensign,* December 1996, 30–47.

19. Manuscript History of the Church, Book A-1, 18; published in Jessee, *Papers of Joseph Smith,* 291–92.

20. Waterloo Village is three miles north of the Peter Whitmer farm. Mother Smith is probably referring to the closest village. See Berrett, *Sacred Places: New York and Pennsylvania,* 144.

21. Smith, *Biographical Sketches of Joseph Smith,* 135; parentheses in original.

22. *Messenger and Advocate* 1, no. 1 (October 1834): 14–15; see also Joseph Smith–History 1:71, Oliver Cowdery endnote.

CHAPTER TEN

THE THREE WITNESSES

Keith J. Wilson

Often observers of early Mormonism equate the entire movement as synonymous with the name of Joseph Smith. From this perspective, Joseph was both the nexus and wellspring of the religious movement. Even though others became involved, the movement survived principally because of this man's charismatic leadership. Sometimes Church members embrace this exclusivist perspective as well with statements such as "Mormonism must stand or fall solely on the story of Joseph Smith." What this interpretation overlooks is the vital contributions of those who assisted Joseph in the beginning days of Mormonism.

As the Book of Mormon translation was coming to a close, the Lord directed Joseph Smith to prepare Oliver Cowdery, David Whitmer, and Martin Harris for a manifestation of the plates. In that revelation, after admonishing the three to greater faith, the Lord promised that they would see the plates "with [their] eyes" and then "testify of them" (D&C 17:3). What is easily overlooked in that June 1829 revelation is that the Lord then explained why it was necessary for the three to add their witness to that of the Prophet: "And this you shall do that my servant Joseph Smith, Jun., may not be destroyed, that I may bring about my righteous purposes unto the children of men in this work" (D&C 17:4). Of particular note in this explanation was the idea that the witnesses were essential in preventing the young Prophet from being destroyed.

Keith J. Wilson is an associate professor of ancient scripture at Brigham Young University.

One facet of the revelation might illuminate Joseph Smith's human vulnerabilities. Were not the Three Witnesses summoned by the same revelation and then promised that because of their influence the Prophet would escape destruction? It stands to reason that collectively the Three Witnesses brought certain qualities and attributes that the Prophet desperately needed in order to survive. This line of reasoning invites a closer look at the Three Witnesses and what each contributed individually to Joseph Smith and his prophetic viability.

For the first five or six years following Joseph's singular vision, his followers in the Palmyra vicinity consisted mainly of his family members.[1] The one exception to this was Martin Harris. Mr. Harris had come to Palmyra in 1792 and had established himself in the bustling canal town as a respectable farmer. He was twenty-two years Joseph's senior, married with children, and the owner of a prosperous 240-acre farm. By the time he departed from Palmyra in 1831, Martin had served seven times as an overseer of highways. He voluntarily enlisted in the War of 1812 and upon his return continued his civic involvement. While he was never a high profile municipal leader, he certainly generated the respect of peers and was active in civic causes. Yet even with this widespread respect, Martin's fellow Palmyrans could never quite reconcile his irreproachable reputation with his persistent claims as a Book of Mormon witness. Four decades after Martin left Palmyra, James Reeves compiled a history of Palmyra in which he wrote extensively about the Harris family. He described Martin as "an industrious, hard-working farmer, shrewd in his business calculations, frugal in his habits, and what was termed a prosperous man in the world."[2] Mr. Reeves's only qualification in his praise of Martin was that these qualities existed *prior* to his devotion to Mormonism. A second affidavit for Martin's character also came from a "non believer" who was well acquainted with him. E. B. Grandin, printer of the Book of Mormon, wrote an editorial saluting Harris as he departed Palmyra in 1831. As the earliest account of Martin's character, this assessment seems especially relevant. "Mr. Harris was among the early settlers of this town, and has ever borne the character of an honorable and upright man, and an obliging and benevolent neighbor. He has secured to himself by

*David Whitmer (1805–1888), Martin Harris (1783–1875), and Oliver
Cowdery (1806–1850). © Intellectual Reserve, Inc. Courtesy of
the Museum of Church History and Art*

honest industry a respectable fortune—and he has left a large circle of
acquaintances and friends to pity his delusion."³ Invariably, the
Palmyrans who intimately knew Martin Harris attested to his impec-
cable character. Yet, their assessment was always followed by a comma
because he clung stubbornly to his golden plates story.

With Martin's character assessment in place, the question now
turns to his role in the life of Joseph Smith. Historians have documented the financial woes of the Joseph Sr. family.⁴ Driven from
Vermont by successive crop failures, Joseph Sr. and Lucy arrived in
Palmyra in 1816 with eight children and nine cents in Lucy's pocket.
In Palmyra, after securing a mortgage and with a nearly completed
frame home, their oldest son, Alvin, suddenly died. Once again, their
future clouded over. Within a short span, they lost both their farm
and frame house, not to mention Joseph Sr. being incarcerated on
account of an unpaid debt of fourteen dollars.⁵ To remain on their
farm as renters, the Smiths had to indenture their fourth son, Samuel,
for seven months in lieu of annual rent payments.⁶ The Smith family
struggled during their Palmyra years with one financial exigency after
another. Into this milieu came the prosperous Martin Harris. Mr.
Harris met Joseph Sr. prior to 1825 and was guardedly optimistic
about Joseph Jr.'s heavenly encounters.⁷ In the fall of 1827, Joseph Jr.
informed Martin that an angel had designated him as an assistant in

the translation project. To this, Martin replied, "If it is the devil's work, I will have nothing to do with it; but if it is the Lord's, you can have all the money necessary to bring it before the world."[8] Subsequently, Martin experienced a personal revelation confirming Joseph's authenticity. True to his word, he honored his pledge of monetary support to the Lord and the Prophet.

The first recorded instance of financial support from Martin occurred late in 1827 as opposition flared against Joseph. After numerous attempts to steal the plates and under the threat of physical violence, Joseph decided that he must relocate to Harmony, Pennsylvania. But first he had to settle his farming debts. Martin insisted on giving him fifty dollars to finance his journey and satisfy his remaining debts. With Martin's help, Joseph and Emma left Palmyra. The timeliness of Martin's assistance was remarkable. Joseph had few, if any, financial options, with the exception of generous Martin.

Two years later, Martin's sacrifice was considerably larger. On 11 June 1829, Joseph obtained the copyright for the Book of Mormon. The next step was to find a willing printer. The logical choice centered in Palmyra printer Egbert Grandin and his newly advertised book-printing services. However, when Martin and Joseph approached him, Grandin categorically refused based on his own religious preferences, the tenuous feasibility of a book that the community generally opposed, and the fear that Martin Harris was the victim of a cruel hoax.[9] Undaunted, Joseph and Martin located a willing printer in Rochester. Once again they approached Grandin, and this time he consented. Grandin proclaimed to all that it was simply a business transaction. As security, he received a lien on Martin Harris's farm for three thousand dollars. The printing commenced in late summer 1829. Less than two years later and with payment due, Martin was forced to relinquish about 150 acres of his farm on 7 April 1831.[10]

In a way, Martin Harris traded his financial status for 5,000 copies of the Book of Mormon. John Gilbert, typesetter for the Book of Mormon, later assessed Martin's contribution to Joseph Smith and early Mormonism with this summary: "Martin was the main spoke in the wheel of Mormonism in its start in Palmyra, and I may say, the only spoke."[11] Succinctly stated, Martin Harris was Joseph Smith's only bank account.

For Joseph, money was only one of his vulnerabilities. Following four probationary years, the angel Moroni in September 1827 entrusted him with the Book of Mormon plates. After relocating to Harmony, Pennsylvania, and eighteen months later, the work was hardly off the ground. Martin Harris had lost the 116 pages, and Joseph had to abandon him as a scribe. Joseph then turned to Emma for assistance. But according to Mother Smith, Emma "had so much of her time taken up with the care of her house, that she could write for him but a small portion of the time."[12] As the days turned into months, a frustrated Joseph in April 1829 petitioned the Lord for a capable scribe. The answer came three days later. His brother Samuel arrived in company with a stranger from Palmyra. This man, Oliver Cowdery, offered his services to Joseph and that night, as the two visited, the missing link was forged. It was a link of destiny.

Oliver was born in 1806 to a religious family in Wells, Vermont, the youngest of eight children. By 1829, he was clerking at his brother's store when an opening for a teacher surfaced in a rural school in Manchester, New York. His older brother Lyman received the school appointment but was unable to occupy it. He convinced school board members to accept Oliver in his stead. They were amenable. Oliver began teaching in the country school and boarding with the Smith family in lieu of tuition.[13] Meanwhile, Joseph Smith Jr. had left Palmyra and relocated in Harmony, Pennsylvania. News in the Manchester neighborhood reverberated with the events of Joseph, his vision, and the gold plates. Oliver's inquiries were slighted at first by the Smith family, owing to the derision that the Smiths faced whenever Joseph's story was told. At length, Oliver convinced them of his honest interest, and they explained the miraculous events. The information delighted Oliver, and he described the experience as "working in my very bones."[14] He commenced his own investigation. The Prophet Joseph later related that "the Lord appeared unto a young man by the name of Oliver Cowdery and shewed unto him the plates in a vision . . . and what the Lord was about to do through me, his unworthy servant therefore he was desirous to come and write for me to translate."[15] Oliver resolved to present himself to Joseph in Harmony as soon as he could fulfill his teaching obligations. Thus on 5 April 1829, after enduring 150 miles and terrible weather, Oliver Cowdery and Samuel Smith arrived in Harmony, Pennsylvania, to a young Prophet who had been praying for a scribe.

Little is known of Oliver's formal training and education excepting his position as a rural schoolteacher. But when he joined Joseph, the work shifted dramatically into high speed. They began translating somewhere near the beginning of the Book of Mosiah rather than backtracking on the lost 116 pages.[16] By 15 May they had reached 3 Nephi 11. In just 38 calendar days (assuming they worked Sundays), they translated over 55 percent of the book. As June approached, both violence and monetary concerns pressed upon Joseph and Oliver. In response to their request, David Whitmer offered them refuge at the Whitmer home in Fayette, New York. Here, as before, other scribes assisted with the work, but the bulk of the writing was from Oliver's pen. David Whitmer later recounted that the days were long and hot, and the two of them worked incessantly from morning until night. On 11 June, Joseph received the copyright for the book even though David Whitmer pinpointed the actual completion date as July.[17]

To put this in perspective, the translation process began in September 1827 and concluded 21 months later in June 1829. For 18 months, the work endured one setback after another with virtually no progress to speak of. Then entered Oliver and in the course of two or three months, the entire book of 588 pages was completed. The extant manuscripts verify that his handwriting comprises over 90 percent of the preserved text.[18] And his two-month presence attests to the birth of the Book of Mormon manuscript. This young schoolteacher came to the aid of both the translation work and the Prophet. Later he marveled at the process as he recounted, "Those were days never to be forgotten—to sit under the sound of a voice dictated by the inspiration of heaven, awakened the utmost gratitude of this bosom! Day after day I continued, uninterrupted, to write from his mouth, as he translated, with the Urim and Thummim."[19] It would be difficult to overstate Oliver's intellectual and emotional role in assisting the Prophet and bringing the Book of Mormon to light.

Still, there were other challenges facing the young Prophet in the spring of 1829. One of the most pressing was a safe environment. Repeating the pattern in Palmyra, opposition to the Prophet and his family in Harmony swelled to the point of boiling. Joseph, sensing his life was in danger, prayed. The Lord directed him to petition David Whitmer for safekeeping.[20] Although it was inopportune, David left his farm and swiftly came to Joseph and Oliver's aid. But why would David accept an unknown fugitive into his father's home?

The Whitmer family settled in Fayette in 1809 when young David was just four years old. In 1828, David (now twenty-three years old) made a business trip to Palmyra. There he encountered talk of Joseph and the golden plates. His casual curiosity turned into genuine interest as he met and experienced firsthand the enthusiasm of Oliver Cowdery. David's conversations with Oliver gave him much to ponder as he returned to Fayette.

Some months later, Oliver informed David that he was going to meet the Prophet in Harmony. En route, he stopped at Fayette and told David that he was determined to find the "truth or untruth" about Joseph. When he did, he would inform David of his conclusions.[21] Shortly thereafter, Oliver wrote David advising him that Joseph indeed had the plates and had asked Oliver to be his scribe. Not long after this first correspondence, a second letter arrived in which Oliver attested to the revealed knowledge of the ancient American inhabitants. Yet a third letter followed which included a request from Oliver to relocate to the Whitmer residence. His request was favorably received, and David made preparations to journey toward Harmony to provide assistance to Oliver and Joseph.

David recorded two miraculous events on this venture.[22] The first involved whether or not he should go. Spring planting was underway, and David knew he could not leave before plastering the fields. As he approached the arduous task, he found the five to seven acres already plowed and no one able to identify who had done the deed. The second miracle occurred as he neared Harmony. There Oliver shared with David the locations and schedule of his own trip to Harmony which Joseph had revealed through the seer stone. David recognized God's handiwork. He invited the Prophet to come to Fayette where he would be welcomed by both family and neighbors.[23] Joseph and Oliver gladly accepted. They arrived at Fayette on the first of June. The Book of Mormon translation resumed the following day. The translation was completed within the month, one account placing it as early as 11 June 1829.

In retrospect, how substantial was David's contribution to the Prophet and the translation? By one account, he only secured lodging for Joseph and Oliver some eleven days before the work was completed. Also the translators stayed at his parents' house and only received David's goodness indirectly. But consider these issues. David was the first of his family to investigate Mormonism. Upon hearing the story from Oliver, David questioned Palmyrans for further information. In his own words, he thought "over the matter for a long time."[24] In Fayette, he discussed it with his family. Later when Oliver sent David a few lines of translation, he again shared it with the Whitmers.[25] When Oliver and Joseph requested lodging with the family, Peter Whitmer Sr. placed the decision upon David's shoulders. Lucy Smith records that Father Whitmer told David that "he could not go [to Harmony], unless he could get a witness from God that it was absolutely necessary."[26] That night as David prayed, he was directed to go as soon as his fields were ready.

The following morning brought the next miracle, and David courageously took the next step. In the course of transporting the Prophet, additional miracles solidified his decision. By the time he delivered the translation team to Fayette, Joseph would observe, "We found Mr. Whitmer's family very anxious concerning the work, and very friendly toward ourselves."[27] David was the gatekeeper for a desperate Joseph, who had twice been driven out and now had few, if any, options remaining. Fortunately, Joseph found David through Oliver, and the work found a safe haven.

During the later stages of the translation, it became apparent that the Lord would commission special witnesses separate from Joseph to see the plates and add their testimonies to the record. Then as they translated 2 Nephi 27:12, it further specified "that three witnesses shall behold it, by the power of God." Meanwhile, back in Palmyra, word was conveyed to Father and Mother Smith as well as Martin Harris that the translation was finished. The next evening, these three anxiously joined the enclave at Fayette, reading scriptures and marveling over God's words. More particularly, Martin, Oliver, and David approached the Prophet about whether they might become the three prophesied witnesses. Their solicitations became so relentless that the Prophet later recorded, "They . . . teased me so much, that at length I complied."[28] Joseph's statement "that he complied" meant that he petitioned the Lord to know if Martin, Oliver, and David could be the designated witnesses, as prophesied in Ether 5:3. The Lord responded with the revelation now recorded as Doctrine and Covenants 17.

In this revelation, the Lord promised the three that if they relied upon the Lord "with full purpose of heart," they would view not only the plates but also the breastplate, the Urim and Thummim, the sword of Laban, and the Liahona. According to Joseph, a few days later the four of them went into a grove of trees not far from the house. There they knelt down and supplicated the Lord in vocal prayer, beginning with Joseph. After each had taken his turn, they repeated the sequence a second time. When no answer or manifestation came, Martin suggested that he might be the problem and excused himself. Shortly thereafter, the heavens opened for Joseph, Oliver, and David.

The manifestation began with a bright light, and then an angel stood before them with the plates. The messenger turned the leaves of the plates over one by one and admonished them to keep the commandments. At once, a voice from above was heard testifying that the plates were delivered and translated through the power of God. Joseph recalled that the vision concluded with the Savior's admonition, "And I command you to bear record of what you have seen and heard." Joseph then left Oliver and David and went in search of Martin. He found him in prayer pleading with the Lord. Together, as they importuned the Lord, the same vision seen by Oliver, David, and Joseph was repeated. As it unfolded, Joseph recorded that Martin cried out in total rapture, "'Tis enough; mine eyes have beheld. . . . Hosanna.'"[29]

The wooded area where the revelation took place was about 40 rods from the Whitmer farmhouse. As they returned, Joseph entered the Whitmer home and approached the bedroom where his parents and Mrs. Whitmer were sitting. Ecstatic, he threw himself upon the bed beside them. Lucy remembered that he declared, "Father!—mother!—said he, you do not know how happy I am; the Lord has caused the plates to be shown to 3 more besides me who have also seen an angel and will have to testify to the truth of what I have said for they know for themselves that I do not go about to deceive the people." Lucy remembered his unabashed relief: "I do feel as though I was relieved of a dreadful burden which was almost too much for me to endure but they will now have to bear a part . . . I am not any longer to be entirely alone in the world."[30] These remarkable exultations deserve further comment for they reveal some of the deeper emotions coursing through this nascent, twenty-three-year-old leader.

In reviewing the rejoicings of Joseph which underscore some of his deepest needs, note his expression, "I am not any longer to be *entirely* alone in the world [emphasis added]," and "I do not go about to deceive the people." Even though Emma and his family were right by his side physically, Joseph still carried a very lonely load. A sequel to his loneliness is echoed in his exclamation of relief: "3 more besides me . . . have also seen an angel and will have to testify to the truth of what I have said . . . [and] they will now have to bear a part." Finally, his heartfelt emotions all but overflowed as he expressed his euphoria, "Father!—mother! . . . you do not know how happy I am." Those were not idle words. They expressed the depths to which he had descended and the tremendous relief that followed.

In the final analysis, then, was Joseph Smith a vulnerable young man with a divine calling, or was he God's chosen servant, invincible from the onset? Beginning with Doctrine and Covenants 17, the voice of God declared that young Joseph, without the Three Witnesses, was indeed vulnerable. His vulnerabilities appear to have taken two forms. The first was his physical needs. Clearly, Joseph desperately needed Martin because he was a young adult without any money or resources. In 1829, it was so bad that Joseph had to stop the translation work and ask a friend for food, a pair of shoes, and three dollars in cash.[31] Money was a constant struggle for Joseph. Martin became his principal benefactor. How vital was Oliver to Joseph's survival? Emma once commented that Joseph was incapable of penning a coherent letter let alone a book.[32] Without Oliver, the translation floundered for eighteen months; with him, it took just two months. Oliver saved the work logistically. But certainly David was not as crucial to Joseph's survival as the other two witnesses. That is probably true unless consideration is given to the exigency of a fugitive without a place to go. In that case, David becomes the essential final piece to the puzzle of the Prophet's survival. In summary, Martin, Oliver, and David directly aided young Joseph and the Restoration.

Yet there was another Achilles' heel which might have destroyed the young Prophet if left unchecked. This was Joseph's emotional vulnerability. He was prophetically commissioned at age fourteen. In his own words, during those early years, he "frequently fell into many foolish errors, and displayed the weakness of youth and the foibles of human nature." Consequently, he lamented, "I often felt condemned for my weaknesses and imperfections" (Joseph Smith–History 1:28–29). As he worked tirelessly on the Book of Mormon, his weaknesses became painfully apparent. He had no money, no schooling, and not even a place to do his work. But the Lord met him in his extremities with three select individuals. After they had experienced their own manifestations, Joseph revealed the depth of his precarious situation. To his parents, he declared, "I do feel as though I was relieved of a dreadful burden which was almost too much for me to endure."[33] Joseph was human. He was vulnerable emotionally and physically. And because the Lord knew of these weaknesses, he sent three choice individuals to fortify this young and vulnerable prophet. The three were far from perfect, yet they were perfect for him at that moment in 1829.

NOTES

1. Anderson, *Investigating the Book of Mormon Witnesses*, 5.
2. *Palmyra Courier,* May 24, 1872, cited in Anderson, *Investigating the Book of Mormon Witnesses*, 97.

3. *Wayne Sentinel,* May 27, 1831, as cited in Anderson, *Investigating the Book of Mormon Witnesses,* 103.

4. Bushman, *Joseph Smith and the Beginnings of Mormonism,* 39–42, 64–68.

5. Porter, "Study of the Origins of the Church," 109.

6. Anderson, *Lucy's Book,* 373, 104n.

7. *Encyclopedia of Mormonism,* 2:574–75.

8. *Tiffany's Monthly,* 5:168–70, cited in Bushman, *Joseph Smith and the Beginnings of Mormonism,* 85.

9. Larry C. Porter, "The Book of Mormon: Historical Setting for Its Translation and Publication," in Black and Tate, *Joseph Smith: The Prophet, the Man,* 52.

10. Largey, *Book of Mormon Reference Companion,* 138.

11. *Memorandum,* 3, in Ricks, Parry, and Hedges, *Disciple as Witness,* 403.

12. Smith, *Joseph Smith and His Progenitors,* 154–55.

13. Gunn, *Oliver Cowdery,* 29.

14. Smith, *Joseph Smith and His Progenitors,* 152.

15. Jessee, *Papers of Joseph Smith,* 1:10.

16. Personal communication with Royal Skousen, author of Book of Mormon Critical Text Project at BYU, October 7, 2004.

17. Porter, "Study of the Origins of the Church," 161, 239; *Deseret Evening News,* 25 March 1884.

18. Personal communication with Royal Skousen, author of Book of Mormon Critical Text Project at BYU, October 7, 2004.

19. *Messenger and Advocate* 1 (October 1834): 14.

20. Smith, *Joseph Smith and His Progenitors,* 160.

21. Porter, "Study of the Origins of the Church," 235.

22. *Deseret Evening News,* March 25 1884; see Porter, "Study of the Origins of the Church," 23; Gunn, *Oliver Cowdery,* 54.

23. Smith, *History of the Church,* 1:49.

24. *Kansas City Journal,* June 5, 1881; see Porter, "Study of the Origins of the Church," 235.

25. Jenson, *Latter-day Saint Biographical Encyclopedia,* 1:264.

26. Smith, *Joseph Smith and His Progenitors,* 160–61.

27. Smith, *History of the Church,* 1:49.

28. *Times and Seasons* 3 (1842): 897; see also Smith, *History of the Church,* 1:51–52; Anderson, *Investigating the Book of Mormon Witnesses,* 10.

29. *Times and Seasons* 3 (1842): 898; Smith, *History of the Church,* 1:55.

30. Anderson, *Lucy's Book,* 453; see also *Times and Seasons* 3 (1842): 897; Smith, *History of the Church,* 1:51–52; Anderson, *Investigating the Book of Mormon Witnesses,* 11.

31. Bushman, *Joseph Smith and the Beginnings of Mormonism,* 95; Smith, *History of the Church,* 1:28.

32. Porter, "Study of the Origins of the Church," 151.

33. Anderson, *Lucy's Book,* 453.

CHAPTER ELEVEN

PUBLISHING THE BOOK OF MORMON

Kent P. Jackson

By the end of June 1829, Joseph Smith had completed the translation of the Book of Mormon into the English language. On 11 June he secured the copyright.[1] The Prophet now set out to hire a printer to publish the book. Printers were not hard to find in the state of New York in 1829. Most villages had local print establishments that brought forth newspapers and other print jobs, and many villages had printers who produced books. But by the time the translation of the Book of Mormon was finished, there was already much local sentiment against it. As in most cases today, publishers in the early nineteenth century bore the expenses of printing, binding, and marketing the volumes they produced. Their profits came only as the books were sold and their production and marketing costs were recovered.[2] As a result of the hostility against the "Gold Bible," printers in the Palmyra area were reluctant to take on the project for fear of sustaining financial loss and being associated with the religious movement that it represented. The Prophet finally struck a deal with a printer in Rochester, about twenty-five miles from Palmyra. The distance, however, would have limited the involvement of Joseph Smith and his associates in the book's production, and thus the Prophet opted instead to continue seeking a printer locally.[3]

Egbert B. Grandin was a Palmyra printer who published a village newspaper, the *Wayne Sentinel*.[4] In the summer of 1829, he was twenty-three years old and had printed only one small book.[5] Since

---

Kent P. Jackson is a professor of ancient scripture at Brigham Young University.

1827 he had been printing the *Sentinel* as well as miscellaneous documents and small jobs. In his newspaper, he advertised his services as "Job Printing" until the spring of 1829, after which his advertisement changed to "Book and Job Printer," announcing his intent to get into the book-publishing business more seriously.[6] It was soon thereafter that Joseph Smith needed a printer to produce the Book of Mormon. Grandin's print shop was located on Main Street in Palmyra, in a three-story building he rented from his brother and his brother's partners. It was a new building that reflected the growth of the village since the completion of the Erie Canal in 1825. Typical of printing establishments in the early nineteenth century, on the ground floor was a bookstore, where Grandin sold a wide variety of volumes, and upstairs were the presses and additional facilities, where the *Sentinel* and other jobs were typeset and printed.

When the Prophet first approached Grandin in June 1829, Grandin turned him down, but in August he finally was persuaded to take on the printing of the Book of Mormon. Grandin agreed to print the book on the condition that he would receive a guarantee for the money and not be dependent on sales to cover his expenses. The agreement was made to print five thousand copies at a cost of three thousand dollars.[7] That was an enormous sum of money—far beyond the resources of the Smith family and of most other families of the day. But the Lord had made preparations. By 1829, forty-six-year-old Martin Harris had enjoyed years of success as a farmer, and he was a prosperous man. As he had done earlier when Joseph Smith needed help to sustain him and his wife during the translation process, Martin used his resources to assist in the coming forth of the Book of Mormon. To pay the publishing expense, he took out an eighteen-month mortgage agreement with Grandin.[8] Money raised from the sale of the book would be used to pay Grandin his three thousand dollars within the specified time. If the book did not raise money, a portion of the Harris farm would be sold to pay the debt.

Joseph Smith now had the translation, a printer, and the financial resources to publish the book. But he also had the memory of what had happened the last time he let the translation out of his

Printing of the First Book of Mormon, *by Gary Ernest Smith.*
© *Intellectual Reserve, Inc. Courtesy of the Museum of*
Church History and Art

hands.[9] In order to assure that no part of the manuscript would be
lost, he instructed Oliver Cowdery to create a copy of it to take to the
printer; the Original Manuscript would remain in a secure place.
Oliver Cowdery (with some limited help from others) expended a
tremendous amount of effort to transcribe, by hand, a copy of the text
of the Book of Mormon. His doing so assured that the translation
would not be lost. The resulting document is called the Printer's
Manuscript. It was not made all at once but was written as needed
over the months of the typesetting, from August 1829 into the early
spring of 1830.[10] The Original Manuscript contained virtually no
punctuation, and the Printer's Manuscript contained very little.
Grandin's compositor, John H. Gilbert, reported that as he was setting the type for the book, he read through the manuscript pages and
inserted punctuation in pencil where he felt it was required.[11] In addition, he inserted much of the punctuation while he set the type in the

forms. In punctuating the text, Gilbert made a unique contribution to the coming forth of the Book of Mormon.[12]

Typesetting in the early nineteenth century was a slow and difficult process. It consisted of setting in place on the page, by hand, a small piece of metal type for each letter, each punctuation mark, each line, and each space. The type was kept in tall cabinets: capital letters in the upper cases and noncapital letters in the lower cases. In a typical print shop, after the printing of all the required copies of a signature—a sheet usually containing sixteen pages—each piece of type had to be redistributed into the appropriate slot in the case from which it had been taken. Then the next signature could be set, reusing the same pieces of type. A typical page of the 1830 Book of Mormon required more than twenty-five hundred pieces of metal.[13] Each piece was inserted into the printing forms by hand, upside-down and backwards so the pages would print properly. The work was done by John Gilbert and various assistants.[14] Not long before the printing of the Book of Mormon began, Grandin bought a new Smith Patented Improved press. It was a "single-pull" press, meaning that it was engineered in such a way that one pull of the handle would be sufficient to print the ink uniformly on the page. That was advanced technology for the day; earlier presses required more work and more time to print the same number of pages.[15] For the Book of Mormon, Grandin purchased five hundred pounds of type in a "Small Pica" font.[16] Ink was applied to the metal type by means of large leather balls with handles. They were rubbed in pasty ink on a smooth surface, and then the ink was pounded evenly onto the type in the forms.[17]

When the form for a page or signature was completed, a few copies were printed to serve as proof sheets. After the proofreading was complete, corrections were made where needed in the forms, and then the printing could begin.[18] John Gilbert recalled that Oliver Cowdery served as the main reader of the Book of Mormon proof sheets, with some help from Hyrum Smith and Martin Harris. According to Gilbert, Joseph Smith visited the shop only once during the work on the Book of Mormon.[19] During most of the time that it was in production, the Prophet was living at his home in Harmony, Pennsylvania.

Grandin and his associates employed a good system for typesetting the Book of Mormon. Each printed sheet consisted of sixteen pages on each side. After one side was printed, the sheets were turned over, and the same sixteen pages were printed on the back. The pages were aligned such that the large sheet would be cut in half, yielding two identical sixteen-page signatures with printing on both sides.[20] After the signatures were printed, they were hung on racks on the ceiling until they were dry enough to print the other side. When both sides were printed on all twenty-five hundred sheets of each signature necessary for the five thousand books (two copies of each signature on each sheet), they were stacked and stored until the binding began. The type could then be redistributed for subsequent use, but Grandin may have had enough type that the typesetting for the next signature could be under way while the printing was going on. Altogether, the printing of the 1830 Book of Mormon required 185 thousand pulls of the lever of Grandin's Smith Patented Improved press.[21]

When the printing was completed, the finished sheets were hoisted down from the third-floor print shop to the second floor, where the bindery was located. The bindery was run by a man named Luther Howard. When the title page of the Book of Mormon was typeset and printed in August 1829, the publication information was as follows: "Printed by E. B. Grandin, for the author." A few weeks later, Howard bought into the company, and he and Grandin became partners.[22] When the Book of Mormon was advertised for sale in March 1830, the publisher was listed as "Howard & Grandin."[23] In their partnership, Grandin ran the printing establishment and the bookstore, and Howard ran the bindery and the lending library.

As was the case with typesetting and printing, bookbinding was a difficult and time-consuming process. Each of the five thousand copies of the Book of Mormon was bound entirely by hand. The process included folding the signatures of printed text in a prescribed way that would ensure that each page would appear in the proper order and orientation. Each sixteen-page signature then needed to be placed in sequence with the other thirty-six signatures, after which they were placed in a vise to crease them tightly at the primary fold that would become the spine of the book. The signatures were stitched together through holes in the spine cut with a saw. Strings were run with a needle between the middle pages of each signature to tie each one not only together with its own pages but with adjacent signatures as well. The spines were glued and reinforced with a strip of cloth, and the remaining sides of each book were then shaved even with the sharp blade of a plane. Boards of cardboard were glued to a carefully sized piece of leather to create the cover, and then they were glued to the end pages, front and back, securing the book to its leather binding. Because the binding process required all thirty-seven signatures, it could not begin until some copies of the final signature were printed on both sides. It would take a long time before all the printed volumes were bound, and thus a typical book in the days of Joseph Smith would still be in production at the bindery months after the first copies were finished and sold.

In September 1829, while the Book of Mormon was being typeset and printed, Howard ran an advertisement for an assistant: "A GOOD Boy is wanted in the Book Bindery."[24] Two weeks later, he placed another advertisement: "SHEEP SKINS WANTED," in which he sought to purchase six hundred sheep skins "suitable for Book Binding to be delivered in the months of January, February and March."[25] The timing and the large quantity of sheep skins requested point to the Book of Mormon as the project for which the leather was needed. In the 1990s, scientists at Brigham Young University examined the DNA of the leather in some copies of the 1830 Book of Mormon. All proved to be bound in calfskin, suggesting that as a result either of cost issues or availability, Howard apparently used calfskin instead of sheepskin.[26]

As the printing progressed, Martin Harris became apprehensive. Even though he had already seen the plates and the angel Moroni, he still knew of the animosity against Joseph Smith, and he had reservations about whether the book would sell and whether he would lose his land if it did not. The Lord's message was clear: "Thou shalt not covet thine own property, but impart it freely to the printing of the Book of Mormon. . . . Impart a portion of thy property, yea, even part of thy lands, and all save the support of thy family. Pay the debt thou hast contracted with the printer. Release thyself from bondage" (D&C 19:26, 34–35). The blessings that would result from Martin's efforts would be of greater value than his farm or any other earthly things: "Pray always, and I will pour out my Spirit upon you, and great shall be your blessing—yea, even more than if you should obtain treasures of earth" (D&C 19:38). As it turned out, Martin's concerns were well-founded. The Book of Mormon did not sell well enough for him to pay off Grandin from its profits. Eventually he had to sell just over 150 acres of his farm to settle the debt.[27] That was a great sacrifice, and Martin rightly deserves to be honored for his contribution to this important part of the Restoration. It was a sacrifice that made the Book of Mormon possible.

On 26 March 1830, the *Wayne Sentinel* announced that the Book of Mormon was finally available for public sale.[28] The price was $1.75.[29] As the Lord told the Church, the book contained "a record of a fallen people, and the fulness of the gospel of Jesus Christ to the Gentiles and to the Jews also; Which was given by inspiration, and is confirmed to others by the ministering of angels, and is declared unto the world by them" (D&C 20:9–10). The publication of the Book of Mormon culminated a sanctified work of preparation that had started over two thousand years earlier when Nephi began his record. Now the work of ancient prophets, the protecting watch of Moroni, the committed service of Joseph and Emma Smith, and the varied contributions of Oliver Cowdery, Martin Harris, the Smith family, the Joseph Knight family, the Peter Whitmer family, and non–Latter-day Saints such as E. B. Grandin, John H. Gilbert, and Luther Howard had all come together to produce a great miracle—the first edition of the Book of Mormon.

Grandin and Howard remained partners only until 29 March 1830, three days after the publication of the Book of Mormon was announced. Howard immediately set up his bindery at a new location elsewhere in Palmyra,[30] and by June he was publishing his own newspaper there, seemingly in competition with Grandin's.[31] Howard took the ongoing Book of Mormon job with him to his new shop, under financial arrangements with Grandin that are not clear today. We do not know when he finished the binding of the Book of Mormon. Although enough copies were bound by March 1830 to warrant the announcement of the book's availability, most were bound in the ensuing months. In the summer of 1831, Howard became insolvent and moved away from Palmyra, leaving behind financial entanglements that were not sorted out for a considerable time. In July, Grandin transported Howard's inventory of "Gold Bibles" from Howard's shop to his own, and he later purchased some of Howard's other books at auctions. In September, he bought the equipment from Howard's bindery.[32]

In 1978, The Church of Jesus Christ of Latter-day Saints purchased the Palmyra building where the Howard and Grandin company published the first edition of the Book of Mormon. Some displays were set up on the ground floor, and the building became the Church's downtown Palmyra visitors' center. In the 1990s, it was decided to restore the building to look as it did when the Book of Mormon was published there. The result is a superb historical reconstruction of an entire print industry, with the print shop on the third floor, the bindery on the second, and the bookstore on the first. President Gordon B. Hinckley dedicated the building on 26 March 1998, the one hundred sixty-eighth anniversary of the publication of the Book of Mormon.

NOTES
1. Printed on the back of the Title Page in the 1830 Book of Mormon.
2. Many book publishers raised money in advance by selling "subscriptions" to forthcoming books, in effect selling the books in advance to cover printing and binding expenses.
3. See Gilbert, "Memorandum, made by John H. Gilbert Esq, Sept 8th. 1892," 1.
4. See Porter, "Grandin, Egbert Bratt," in Largey, *Book of Mormon Reference Companion,* 306–10.
5. Peter Crawley identifies the following as the only books Grandin printed in his publishing career: Tobias Ostrander, *The Mathematical Expositor;*

Containing Rules, Theorems, Lemmas, and Explanations; of Various Parts of the Mathematical Science (1828); the Book of Mormon (1830); *Notes on Title IV. Chapter II. of Part III. of the Revised statutes of the state of New York* (1830); David C. Bunnell, *The Travels and Adventures of David C. Bunnell . . . also Service among the Greeks, Imprisonment among the Turks, &c. &c.* (printed by Grandin; published by J. H. Bortles, 1831); and a revised edition of Ostrander, *Mathematical Expositor* (1832). See Crawley, *First Mormon Book,* 11.

6. Grandin's last "Job Printing" advertisement was published in the *Wayne Sentinel,* 13 March 1829; his first "Book and Job Printer" advertisement appeared 17 April 1829.

7. See Porter, "Book of Mormon, Printing and Publication of," in Largey, *Book of Mormon Reference Companion,* 134–39.

8. The mortgage agreement is reproduced in Gunnell, "Martin Harris—Witness and Benefactor to the Book of Mormon," 97–98.

9. See Smith, *Biographical Sketches of Joseph Smith* (1853), 117–27.

10. The Original Manuscript is only about 28 percent extant; see Skousen, *Original Manuscript of the Book of Mormon,* 7. Most fragments are housed in the LDS Church Archives in Salt Lake City. The Printer's Manuscript is in an excellent state of preservation and is virtually intact. It is housed in the Community of Christ Library-Archives in Independence, Missouri. See Skousen, *Printer's Manuscript of the Book of Mormon.*

11. At first he did this in the shop, but after some time he was allowed to take pages of the manuscript home to work on in the evenings. See Gilbert, "Memorandum," 2–3; and Skousen, "John Gilbert's 1892 Account of the 1830 Printing of the Book of Mormon," in Ricks, Parry and Hedges, *Disciple as Witness,* 392–93.

12. See Skousen, *Original Manuscript of the Book of Mormon,* 16–17. Seventy-two pages of the Original Manuscript were used by the typesetters, likely because the copying was outpaced for a while by the typesetting. See Skousen, "Piecing Together the Original Manuscript," *BYU Today* 46, no. 3 (1992): 23.

13. Counted on a randomly selected page in the book of Alma. Thus each sixteen-page form contained about forty thousand pieces of type.

14. Porter lists all those who are reported to have worked on the Book of Mormon; see Porter, "Book of Mormon, Printing and Publication of," in Largey, *Book of Mormon Reference Companion,* 135–36.

15. See Keith J. Wilson, "From Gutenberg to Grandin: Tracing the Development of the Printing Press," in Woods, Harper, and Hedges, *Prelude to the Restoration,* 269–85.

16. See Gilbert, "Memorandum," 2; Porter, "Book of Mormon, Printing and Publication of," in Largey, *Book of Mormon Reference Companion,* 135.

17. The press operator was called the puller, and the one who applied the ink to the type was called the beater.

18. See Skousen, "John Gilbert's 1892 Account," 388.

19. See Gilbert, "Memorandum," 4.

20. See Gilbert, "Memorandum," 3; and Draper, "Book of Mormon Editions," in Bradford and Coutts, *Uncovering the Original Text of the Book of Mormon,* 40–41.

21. Each pull printed one side (that is, half) of two signatures. Two pulls printed both sides of two signatures. Thus one pull equals one complete signature. Each signature was printed five thousand times, requiring five thousand pulls of the lever for each signature. There were thirty-seven signatures. Five thousand multiplied by thirty-seven yields one hundred eighty-five thousand total pulls of the lever to print the 1830 Book of Mormon (excluding proof sheets, misprints, etc.).

22. See *Wayne Sentinel,* 11 September 1829.

23. *Wayne Sentinel,* 26 March 1829.

24. *Wayne Sentinel,* 25 September 1829.

25. *Wayne Sentinel,* 9 October 1829.

26. Scott Woodward, personal communication. See Crawley, *A Descriptive Bibliography of the Mormon Church,* 1:31.

27. Porter discusses the financial arrangements in "Book of Mormon, Printing and Publication of," in Largey, *Book of Mormon Reference Companion,* 138. See also Gunnell, "Martin Harris—Witness and Benefactor to the Book of Mormon," 99–100.

28. *Wayne Sentinel,* 26 March 1830.

29. See Howe, *Mormonism Unvailed,* 13. Howe, a bitter critic of Mormonism, wrote: "The retail price of which they said was fixed by an Angel at $1.75, but afterwards reduced to $1.25, and from that down to any price they could obtain."

30. See *Wayne Sentinel,* 2 April 1830.

31. "Luther Howard, Proprieter and Publisher," *Western Spectator & Wayne Advertiser,* 9 June 1830.

32. See Egbert B. Grandin Diary, microfilm copy, Archives, The Church of Jesus Christ of Latter-day Saints, 12, 14 July; 6, 9 August; 5 September 1831.

CHAPTER TWELVE

THE ORGANIZATION OF THE CHURCH

W. Jeffrey Marsh

In our postmodern world, many people question the need for religion in their lives and membership in a particular religious organization. Some feel faith alone in the Lord Jesus Christ is sufficient for salvation. Earnest seekers of eternal truth, however, long to know God. To those seekers, we announce that on 6 April 1830 God established the Church of Jesus Christ and restored his everlasting covenant through the Prophet Joseph Smith. Jesus Christ stands at the head of this Church and invites all to come unto him and be saved (Moroni 10:32; D&C 20:59).

As Elder Bruce R. McConkie has explained, "Our Lord's true Church is the formal, official organization of believers who have taken upon themselves the name of Christ by baptism, thus covenanting to serve God and keep his commandments. (See D. & C. 10:67–69; 18:20–25.)"[1] The establishment of the true Church in these latter days was an important event of eternal significance. The Church was organized according to the pattern revealed by the Lord "for the perfecting of the saints . . . till we all come in the unity of the faith, and of the knowledge of the Son of God" (Ephesians 4:12–13). The restoration of the Church could not be accomplished by committees or creeds or by simple realignment of existing religions. It required revelation from on high (Jacob 4:8).

W. Jeffrey Marsh is an associate professor of ancient scripture at Brigham Young University.

Joseph Smith Presides over the Organization of the Church,
*by William Whitaker Jr. © Intellectual Reserve, Inc.
Courtesy of the Museum of Church History and Art*

REVEALED FROM HEAVEN

The divine pattern for organizing the Church was established at the time of Adam: "And thus the Gospel began to be preached, from the beginning, being declared by holy angels sent forth from the presence of God, and by his own voice, and by the gift of the Holy Ghost" (Moses 5:58). Unfortunately, no sooner had the gospel been established in the days of Adam than apostasy encroached upon its message. "Adam and Eve blessed the name of God, and they made all things known unto their sons and their daughters. And Satan came among them . . . and he commanded them, saying: Believe it not; and they believed it not, and they loved Satan more than God. And men began from that time forth to be carnal, sensual, and devilish" (Moses 5:12–13).

Throughout history, whenever such apostasy has occurred, of necessity the gospel and the saving ordinances have been revealed anew from heaven. This explains why there have been many gospel dispensations, each one "a period of time in which the Lord has at least one authorized servant on earth who bears the holy priesthood and the keys, and who has a divine commission to dispense the gospel to the inhabitants of the earth."[2] Leaders of such dispensations are named in holy writ—Adam, Enoch, Noah, Abraham, Moses, and most notably Jesus Christ.

The Church of Jesus Christ flourished in the apostolic era. "But as the centuries passed, the flame flickered and dimmed. Ordinances were changed or abandoned. The line was broken, and the authority to confer the Holy Ghost as a gift was gone. The Dark Ages of apostasy settled over the world."[3] As a result of this apostasy, it became necessary to restore once again the Church of Jesus Christ upon the earth (D&C 86:1–4).

THE FINAL RESTORATION

Joseph Smith was the prophet through whom the Lord restored his true gospel and priesthood keys. Joseph had the authority to act in the name of God to organize His Church. The Church was restored under the Savior's direction through a living prophet in harmony with the prophet Amos's inspired declaration, "Surely the Lord God will do nothing, until he revealeth his secret unto his servants the prophets" (JST Amos 3:7). In 1829 Joseph Smith and Oliver Cowdery "made [it] known to our brethren that we had received a commandment to organize the Church." They also said that they were told "the precise day upon which, according to [God's] will and commandment, we should proceed to organize His Church once more here upon the earth."[4] The date chosen by the Lord was 6 April 1830.

Accordingly, on that April day in 1830, about fifty believers in the prophetic calling of Joseph Smith met in the log home of Peter and Mary Whitmer in Fayette, New York. With Joseph presiding, the Church was "regularly organized and established agreeable to the laws of our country, by the will and commandments of God" (D&C 20:1). The laws referred to are printed in a 1784 New York statute regulating the creation of new churches within the state. The statute required that "three to nine trustees . . . take charge of church property and transact business affairs. Two elders of the congregation were to be selected to preside over the election. Fifteen days' notice, given for two successive Sabbaths, was required. A certificate establishing a name for the church and evidencing completion of the organizational events was to be recorded in the county or counties where the church was located."[5]

About noon on 6 April the foundational meeting of the Church convened. Six men were named to transact the affairs of the new religious organization—Joseph Smith (age twenty-four), Oliver Cowdery (age twenty-three), Hyrum Smith (age thirty), Peter Whitmer Jr. (age twenty), David Whitmer (age twenty-five), and Samuel H. Smith (age twenty-two).[6] These men constituted the official membership of the Church, which, according to David Whitmer, was called the Church of Christ, "being the same as [God] gave the Nephites."[7]

After Joseph explained to those assembled that the meeting was held according to the instructions he had received by revelation, he asked all to kneel with him in solemn prayer. When the prayer ended, Joseph arose and invited those present to express their willingness to accept him and Oliver Cowdery as "teachers in the things of the Kingdom of God." All concurred. Joseph then asked "whether they were satisfied that we should proceed and be organized as a Church according to said commandment." They again "consented by a unanimous vote."[8] In accordance with their approval, the Prophet ordained Oliver Cowdery an elder in the Church of Jesus Christ. Oliver then laid his hands upon the head of Joseph Smith and ordained him an elder in Christ's church.

The sacrament of the Lord's Supper was next administered. Joseph and Oliver blessed and passed the emblems—bread and wine (D&C 20:75–79). They then confirmed, by the laying on of hands, those who had previously been baptized. Through this ordinance, they bestowed upon the newly baptized members the gift of the Holy Ghost. The effect of the ordinance was immediate: "The Holy Ghost was poured out upon us to a very great degree—some prophesied, whilst we all praised the Lord, and rejoiced exceedingly," wrote Joseph. "We now proceeded to call out and ordain some others of the brethren to different offices of the Priesthood, according as the Spirit manifested unto us."[9]

Then to the amazement of those present, the Prophet Joseph received a revelation from God (D&C 21). In the revelation, the Lord admonished that a record be kept in which Joseph was called to be "a seer, a translator, a prophet, an apostle of Jesus Christ, an elder" (D&C 21:1). Members were commanded to

> give heed unto all his words and commandments which he shall give unto you as he receiveth them, walking in all holiness before me;
>
> For his word ye shall receive, as if from mine own mouth, in all patience and faith.
>
> For by doing these things the gates of hell shall not prevail against you; yea, and the Lord God will disperse the powers of darkness from before you, and cause the heavens to shake for your good, and his name's glory. (D&C 21:4–6)

Oliver Cowdery was called to be the first preacher (D&C 21:12), and the congregation was called upon to ratify a document called the

Articles and Covenants of the Church, later recorded as Doctrine and Covenants 20.[10] The organizational meeting was then adjourned.

Many present at the foundational meeting in Fayette desired to be baptized. "Several persons who had attended the above meeting, became convinced of the truth and came forward shortly after, and were received into the Church," penned Joseph. "Among the rest, my own father and mother were baptized, to my great joy and consolation."[11] Mother Smith wrote of that baptismal event: "Joseph stood upon the shore, and taking his father by the hand, he exclaimed, with tears of joy, 'Praise to my God! that I lived to see my own father baptized into the true Church of Jesus Christ!'"[12] Also baptized that first day were Martin Harris and seventeen-year-old Orrin Porter Rockwell.

GROWTH IN CHURCH ORGANIZATION

The Lord revealed the full organization of his Church line upon line to the Prophet Joseph Smith. Perhaps Professor Robert J. Matthews said it best:

> In June 1830 there were no wards, no stakes, no First Presidency, no Council of the Twelve, no patriarchs, no Seventies, no bishops, no Word of Wisdom, no revelation on the degrees of glory, no tithing, no welfare program, no law of consecration, no priesthood quorums of any kind, no temples, no endowments, no sealings, no marriages for eternity, no real understanding of the New Jerusalem, no baptisms for the dead, no Doctrine and Covenants, no Pearl of Great Price, and no Joseph Smith Translation [of the Bible]. How did these things, which today we recognize as vital to our spiritual life and as basic to the Church, come to be? They came when the time was right and in answer to prayer—the result of an earnest search. Each of these things was revealed at some particular time and place and in some particular situation; and each became, one by one, part of the doctrine and structure of the Church.[13]

As the early members waited upon the Lord for the doctrines of salvation, ordinances, and church government to be revealed, they enjoyed a spirit of anticipated hope. Sidney Rigdon recalled a meeting in which such hope predominated:

> I met the whole church of Christ in a little old log house about 20 feet

square, near Waterloo, N.Y. and we began to talk about the kingdom of God as if we had the world at our command; we talked with great confidence, and talked big things, although we were not many people, we had big feelings; . . . we were as big then, as we shall ever be; we began to talk like men in authority and power; . . . we saw by vision the church of God, a thousand times larger. . . . Many things were taught, believed, and preached, then, which have since come to pass; . . . if we had talked in public, we should have been ridiculed more than we were, the world being entirely ignorant of the testimony of the prophets and without knowledge of what God was about to do.[14]

CONCLUSION

The restoration and organization of the Lord's Church in April 1830 and its subsequent development was accomplished in harmony with five eternal, undergirding principles: (1) according to the will of God, (2) by divine directive, (3) with the authority of the holy priesthood, (4) by consent of the congregation, and (5) in agreement with the laws of the land. With these principles clearly in place, the Church, as prophesied by Daniel of old, began to roll forth to fill the earth (Daniel 2:34–35; see also Moses 7:62; 1 Nephi 14:12–14).

The "work" of God in restoring his Church has been accomplished. The Church of Jesus Christ of Latter-day Saints is now "sweep[ing] the earth as with a flood," carrying the "everlasting gospel" and the message of our resurrected Lord to every nation, kindred, tongue, and people (Matthew 24:14; Revelation 14:6).

NOTES
1. McConkie, *Mormon Doctrine*, 133.
2. "Dispensations," *LDS Bible Dictionary*, 657.
3. Boyd K. Packer, "The Cloven Tongues of Fire," *Ensign*, May 2000, 8.
4. Smith, *History of the Church*, 1:75, 64.
5. John K. Carmack, "Fayette: The Place Where the Church Was Organized," *Ensign*, February 1989, 16; see also John K. Carmack, "Organization of the Church, 1830," in *Encyclopedia of Mormonism*, 1049–50. The statute was updated on 5 April 1813 by the Thirty-sixth Session of the New York State Legislature. *Laws of the State of New York*, 212–19.
6. In an 1846 letter to Phineas Young, Oliver Cowdery described the feelings of hope that filled the hearts of these six members at the 1830

organizational meeting: "You say you are having a meeting on the 6th of April. Brother Phineas, [I wish] I could be with you, and tell you about the 6th of April 1830 when but six men then only belonged to the Church, and how we looked forward to a future." "I should gladly, but I cannot only in Spirit—but in spirit I shall be with you. And then in assembled kneel with those who are yet alive of that six. How many can you count?" Oliver Cowdery, letters, Oliver Cowdery to Phineas Young, 19 August 1842; as cited in Gunn, *Oliver Cowdery,* 251.

7. David Whitmer, *An Address to All Believers in Christ* (Richmond, Mo.: David Whitmer, 1887), 73 as cited in Larry C. Porter, "Organizational Origins of the Church of Jesus Christ, 6 April 1830," in Porter, Backman, and Black, *New York,* 160. This name sufficed until Joseph Smith received a revelation from God on 26 April 1838 at Far West announcing that the official name was to be The Church of Jesus Christ of Latter-day Saints (D&C 115:1–4).

8. Smith, *History of the Church,* 1:77.

9. Smith, *History of the Church,* 1:79.

10. Oliver Cowdery delivered the first public discourse in the Whitmer home on the following Sunday, 11 April 1830.

11. Smith, *History of the Church,* 1:79.

12. Smith, *History of Joseph Smith by His Mother,* ed. Nibley, 168.

13. Matthews, *A Bible! A Bible!* 149–50.

14. *Times and Seasons,* May 1, 1844, 522–23.

CHAPTER THIRTEEN

THE 1830 CONFERENCES

John P. Livingstone

hree conferences were held in western New York following the organization of the Church. The first conference was held in June 1830, the second in September 1830, and the third in January 1831, all at the Peter Whitmer Sr. farmhouse in Fayette. Of these three Church conferences, little is known of the 2 January 1831 meeting. "Conference convened according to adjournment but there were no minutes taken, save a commandment received, giving directions to the Saints" is unfortunately all that was recorded of that meeting.[1] Therefore, only the first two conferences of the fledgling Church can be discussed in any detail. Preserved minutes and journal entries from these conferences give clear evidence that despite increasing religious persecution, the work of the Lord rolled forth, and gospel truth and power were being restored to the earth.

THE FIRST 1830 CONFERENCE

In the revelation that set the date for the founding meeting of the Church, the Lord commanded "the several elders composing this church of Christ are to meet in conference once in three months, or from time to time as said conferences shall direct or appoint" (D&C 20:61). In accordance with the directive, a conference date was set for 9 June 1830. Saints traveled from South Bainbridge, Colesville, Palmyra, and Harmony to be present at the conference held in the

---

John P. Livingstone is an associate professor of Church history and doctrine at Brigham Young University.

Whitmer home at Fayette. Such a gathering was likely viewed as a welcome assembly where distant friends could meet and renew their faith and strengthen their acquaintances. Central to their purpose at this conference was to receive instruction and direction from the Prophet Joseph Smith.

As the meeting commenced, Oliver Cowdery was appointed to record the minutes. His minutes are included in their entirety:

> Minutes of the first Conference held in the Township of Fayette, Seneca County, State of New York. by the Elders of this Church, June 9th 1830. according to the Church Articles and Covenants [Sections 20 and 22 of the Doctrine and Covenants]
>
> Elders Present: Joseph Smith, junior Oliver Cowdery, Peter Whitmer, David Whitmer, John Whitmer, Ziba Peterson
>
> Ezekiel 14th read by Joseph Smith jr. and prayer by the same Articles and Covenants read by Joseph Smith jr. and received by unanimous voice of the whole congregation, which consisted of most of the male members of the Church. Samuel H. Smith was then ordained an Elder under the hand of Oliver Cowdery, & Joseph Smith seignior and Hyrum Smith were ordained Priests.
>
> The following persons were then seated repectively & received their licences, Viz:
>
> Elders of this church. David Whitmer John Whitmer Peter Whitmer Ziba Peterson Samuel H. Smith
>
> Priests of this Church Martin Harris Hyrum Smith Joseph Smith sen Teachers of this Church Hiram Page and Christian Whitmer.
>
> Exhortation by Joseph Smith jr. and Oliver Cowdery, conference adjourned to the 26th September 1830, to be held in the same place. Br. Oliver Cowdery appointed to keep the Church record and Conference minutes until the next conference. Prayer by all the Brethren present and dismissed by Br. Oliver Cowdery. The above minutes were taken at the time of this conference by Oliver Cowdery. Clerk.[2]

It is of particular interest to note that each Church officer is mentioned in the minutes, and "most" were in attendance. It may appear curious that there was no mention made of women being in attendance. It is presumed that women did attend but were not officially noted because of an early nineteenth century practice to include only males as official members of an organization.

As recorded by Oliver Cowdery, Joseph Smith opened the

Joseph Smith Preaching from the Book of Mormon, *by Robert T. Barrett*

conference by reading from the fourteenth chapter of Ezekiel. This chapter speaks of elders of Israel coming before the prophet to inquire of the Lord through him. Yet, Ezekiel notes that these elders have "set up their idols in their heart" and have "put the stumbling-block of their iniquity before their face" (Ezekiel 14:3). The Lord assures them that he will cut off the wicked, and "if the prophet be deceived when he hath spoken a thing, I the Lord have deceived that prophet, and I will stretch out my hand upon him, and will destroy him from the midst of my people" (Ezekiel 14:9).

Such words of warning surely were not lost on those in attendance. They were likely comforted with the egalitarian nature of the scripture which cautioned the prophet as well as the members. Ezekiel quotes the Lord as saying he is doing this "that the house of Israel may go no more astray from me, neither be polluted any more with all their transgressions; but that they may be my people, and I may be their God, saith the Lord God" (Ezekiel 14:11). The last phrase must have resonated with the new Church members. The final two verses of the chapter would undoubtedly have been understood in the context of the restoration of gospel truth and priesthood authority. The Prophet Joseph read:

> Yet, behold, therein shall be left a remnant that shall be brought forth, both sons and daughters: behold, they shall come forth unto you, and ye shall see their way and their doings: and ye shall be comforted concerning the evil that I have brought upon Jerusalem, even concerning all that I have brought upon it.
>
> And they shall comfort you, when ye see their ways and their doings: and ye shall know that I have not done without cause all that I have done in it, saith the Lord God. (Ezekiel 14:22–23)

One can only wonder if those at the conference saw themselves as the "remnant" whose behavior comforted ancient prophets.

The reading of Ezekiel and the reading and sustaining of the Articles and Covenants would not be unlike the format sometimes followed in today's Church leadership meetings, which may begin with a thought from the scriptures followed by a reading of the *Church Handbook of Instructions.* The same could be said of the three ordinations that followed. Each newly ordained priesthood officer received a "license" or piece of paper noting their office.

While the passing of the Lord's sacrament was not mentioned in the minutes taken by Oliver Cowdery, Joseph Smith and Newel Knight recorded that this ordinance was attended to during the conference as well as the confirmation of some who had been baptized previously:

> On the ninth day of June, 1830, we held our first conference as an organized Church. Our numbers were about thirty, besides whom many assembled with us, who were either believers or anxious to learn. Having opened by singing and prayer, we partook together of the emblems of the body and blood of our Lord Jesus Christ. We then proceeded to confirm several who had lately been baptized, after which we called out and ordained several to the various offices of the Priesthood.[3]

Talks were then given by Joseph and Oliver and the date for the next conference was set—26 September 1830. Oliver was designated to keep Church records until that conference. This action was followed by closing prayers, which may have featured each member present repeating the prayer in unison or perhaps each person in turn offering a prayer as the Three Witnesses did before seeing the plates.[4]

THE SECOND 1830 CONFERENCE

The second conference also convened at the Peter Whitmer Sr. home in Fayette, New York. Those wishing to attend this conference came early. Among the first to arrive were Joseph and Emma Smith from Harmony, Pennsylvania. They arrived the last week of August 1830. Others came to the Whitmer home the third week in September. The conference, which convened on the 26th, is remembered in the scriptures. At this meeting, Joseph received revelations that now form the last fourteen verses of Doctrine and Covenants, section 27 and all of sections 28 and 29.[5] In these revelations, keys of priesthood leadership, the order of revelation, and governing doctrines of the gospel are discussed.

The incident involving Hiram Page, who claimed to have received several revelations via a "seer stone" was resolved. It is recorded in the *History of the Church* that "at length our conference assembled. The subject of the stone previously mentioned was discussed, and after considerable investigation, Brother Page, as well as the whole Church who were present, renounced the said stone, and all things connected therewith, much to our mutual satisfaction and happiness." After this was solved, those present

> partook of the Sacrament, confirmed and ordained many, and attended to a great variety of Church business on the first and the two following days of the conference, during which time we had much of the power of God manifested amongst us; the Holy Ghost came upon us, and filled us with joy unspeakable; and peace, and faith, and hope, and charity abounded in our midst.[6]

Oliver Cowdery again recorded the official minutes of the conference. His note taking is included to show the brevity of the minutes as well as to give mention of those named as attending:

> Minutes of the second Conference held by the Elders of this Church according to adjournment, Sept. 26. 1830.
>
> Elders Joseph Smith jr. Oliver Cowdery David Whitmer John Whitmer Peter Whitmer Samuel H. Smith Thomas B. Marsh.
>
> Br. Joseph Smith jr. appointed leader of the Conference by vote.
>
> Brother Joseph Smith jr. was appointed by the voice of the Conference to receive and write Revelations & Commandments for this Church.
>
> The fifth chapter of Isaiah read by Br. Joseph Smith jr. & prayer by the same. Articles & Covenants read by br. Oliver Cowdery and remarks by Brother Joseph Smith jr.
>
> No. of the several members uniting to this Church since the last Conference, thirty-five, making in whole now belonging to this Church sixty-two. Br. Newel Knight ordained a priest under the hand of brother Oliver Cowdery and prayer by the same. Prayer by all present. Exhortation by all the Elders respectively. Singing and prayer in behalf of Br. Oliver Cowdery & Peter Whitmer jr. who were previously appointed to go to the Lamanites.
>
> Conference adjourned to January 1. 1831. to be held at this place. Br. David Whitmer appointed to keep the Church records until the next Conference. Prayer by br. Oliver Cowdery. The foregoing minutes were taken at the time of this Conference by Oliver Cowdery.[7]

The Prophet Joseph spoke of the fifth chapter of Isaiah, which tells of the apostasy of Israel and of a new ensign (banner or flag) that will be lifted up in the latter days before the nations to herald the restoration of the gospel to the earth. How fitting that the neophyte members in this official gathering of the Church would hear of the anger of the Lord towards those who treat lightly his revelations and his gospel. The harassment each had already felt as a new member must have been assuaged to some degree by the woes decreed by the Lord's condemnation of drunken persecutors. Surely, they could not miss the reference to "ensign" or the efficacy of the restoration of which they were founding members. Doubtless there was a measure of peace and assurance at this reading of Isaiah.

Oliver's reading of the Articles and Covenants must have sounded constitutional in nature to those who had attended the previous meetings at the Whitmer home. That the revelations of Hiram Page were disallowed made way for Joseph to be "appointed by the voice of the Conference to receive and write Revelations." The fact that Church membership increased by thirty-five converts inferred emphasis on missionary work that has continued until the present day, as has the practice of announcing membership growth during a conference. Some excitement must have been engendered by the reference to the missionary labors among the Lamanites to which Oliver Cowdery and Peter Whitmer Jr. had been called.

It was duly noted that a date for the next conference was determined and Oliver Cowdery relieved of his responsibility as recorder due to his mission call. David Whitmer was assigned to take his place in caring for Church records until the following January when the next conference would be held.

Once again, there was no mention in the official minutes of the passing of the sacrament or confirmations taking place during the conference. But as noted previously in the *History of the Church,* as well as in the journal of Newel Knight, "the sacrament was then administered, a number were confirmed, many were ordained."[8]

CONCLUSION

Conferences held in western New York in the early 1830s established a pattern that carries on today. They serve as the prototype for stake and general conferences. The gatherings were a precursor of worldwide satellite training meetings that carry the words of prophets to members and leaders gathered together in small and large groups everywhere. Instruction that feels impressively personal, yet is meant to influence the lives of God's children throughout the world, is given in comfortable settings over the continents as well as the isles of the sea. The miracle of it all is that it began with just a few dozen individuals who responded to the call of God given through his Prophet, even Joseph Smith. Notwithstanding the relative youthfulness of the Restoration, the gospel message continues to spread throughout the earth in a very personal way, yet reaches millions at once.

There can be no question that Joseph Smith received revelations from God and organized The Church of Jesus Christ of Latter-day Saints to publish these revelations to the world. While the revelations of today may not be so "foundation-building" as those in Joseph's day, they nevertheless continue and are broadcast to the world in conferences that trace their beginning to a humble setting in Fayette, New York.

NOTES

1. See Book of Commandments, 80; Far West Record Book, LDS Church Archives.
2. Cannon and Cook, *Far West Record*, 1–2.
3. Smith, *History of the Church*, 1:84. Newel Knight added: "Having opened the meeting by singing and prayer, we partook of the emblems of the body and blood of our Lord Jesus Christ. A number were confirmed who had lately been baptized, and several were called and ordained to various offices in the Priesthood." *Scraps of Biography*, 52.
4. "Martin Harris, David Whitmer, Oliver Cowdery and myself, agreed to retire into the woods, and try to obtain, by fervent and humble prayer, the fulfilment of the promises given in the above revelation—that they should have a view of the plates. We did not at the first trial, however, obtain any answer or manifestation of divine favor in our behalf. We again observed the same order of prayer, each calling on and praying fervently to God in rotation, but with the same result as before." Smith, *History of the Church*, 1:54.
5. Doctrine and Covenants 30 was received following the conference.
6. Smith, *History of the Church*, 1:115.
7. Cannon and Cook, *Far West Record*, 3.
8. *Scraps of Biography*, 65. "We now partook of the Sacrament, confirmed and ordained many." See Smith, *History of the Church*, 1:115.

"ASSEMBLE TOGETHER AT THE OHIO"

Steven C. Harper

*I*n December 1830 Joseph Smith received a revelation in New York: "A commandment I give unto the Church," the Lord spoke, "that it is expedient in me that they should assemble together at the Ohio." The rationale was terse: "because of the enemy and for your sakes." The New York Saints must "choose" to obey or disobey (D&C 37:1, 3, 4).[1] In the apocalyptic tradition of the prophets, Joseph preached in several locales, saying, "God is about to destroy this generation, and Christ will descend from heaven in power and great glory, with all the holy angels with him to take vengeance upon the wicked and they that know not God." A few hearkened, but most were either antagonistic or dead to his words. "The adversary of all righteousness," church historian John Whitmer explained, "beguiled the people, and stirred them up to anger, against the words spoken. . . . This generation abounds in . . . selfishness, idoletry." It was "hard" even "for those who receive the fulness of the gospel" to forsake "the traditions of their forefathers."[2] Their temporal and spiritual security was at stake.

In this challenging context, Joseph gathered the fledgling Church of Christ, not yet a year old, for general conference in Fayette, New York. It was January 1831. Newel Knight remembered that at this conference "the Lord commanded his people to move to Ohio so that they could 'be gathered . . . a righteous people, without spot and blameless.'"[3]"Joseph the seer addressed the congregation," Whitmer

---

Steven C. Harper is an assistant professor of Church history and doctrine at Brigham Young University.

Saints Move to Kirtland, *by Sam Lawlor*

wrote. Unsatisfied by the Lord's concise commandment to immigrate, the Saints "desired to know more concerning this matter. Therefore, the Seer enquired of the Lord in the presence of the whole congregation, and thus came the word of the Lord." This time the Lord elaborated a rationale for his unbelieving audience. He painted a vivid, apocalyptic picture of the different destinies awaiting those who believe and obey compared to the destiny of those "that will not hear my voice but harden their hearts, and wo, wo, wo, is their doom" (D&C 38:6). He empowered them with knowledge of his will, which enabled them to act for themselves, informed by the inevitable consequences. To survive impending spiritual destruction, the Saints must leave New York (D&C 38:10–13). Perhaps the enemy to which the Lord referred included the hostile persecutors well-known to Joseph Smith, or others with sinister, secret schemes. But the revelation suggests that the most dangerous "enemy" was the least expected. It was the mainstream culture, the things everyone thought and did. The Lord assessed the situation bleakly: "All flesh is corrupted," "the powers of darkness prevail," "eternity is pained" (D&C 38:11–12).

The French observer Alexis de Tocqueville arrived in America shortly after this revelation. His keen observations illustrate what the Lord loathed in American culture in 1831, which exalted the individual above the community. Such self-interestedness could be seen in the proliferation of churches and in the emphasis the new denominations put on the salvation of the individual and the role of the individual in opting for salvation. Methodism quickly became America's largest denomination, and other denominations became more like Methodism. This had strange effects. Whereas the Puritans of the 1630s were sure of their fallen nature, Methodists of the 1830s were confident in their perfectibility. A certain "pride of self" followed. Historian Andrew Delbanco asserted that by the time the Lord commanded the New York Saints to move to Ohio, individualism "was now not just a legitimate emotion but America's uncontested god. And since everyone had his own self, everyone had his own god."[4] Authority was vested in the people generally and the individual specifically. Many were sure their new institutions could perfect themselves and society.[5] God was everywhere acknowledged yet rendered dumb so as not to upset an unfettered "self-reliance," as Emerson called it, using the best possible term to describe the same thing the Lord decried in November 1831: "Every man walketh in his own way, and after the image of his own god, whose image is in the likeness of the world, and whose substance is that of an idol, which waxeth old and shall perish in Babylon, even Babylon the great, which shall fall" (D&C 1:16).[6]

"The true beginning of American democracy," wrote Tocqueville scholars Mansfield and Winthrop, "is the dogma of the sovereignty of the people, a dogma logically incompatible with the acceptance of *any* authority."[7] The commandment to gather, therefore, assumed an authority Americans were not very willing to grant in 1831. It compelled the Saints to decide whether to serve themselves or the Lord. The revelation provided them with a way out of this culture. It envisioned an alternative society. It came in the voice of the Lord who took "the Zion of Enoch into mine own bosom" (D&C 38:4). It pronounced the faithful and obedient "clean, but not all; and there is none else with whom I am well pleased" (D&C 38:10). It foretold evil designs to destroy the Saints "in process of time" (D&C 38:13). These were the same words recently revealed to Joseph to describe how Enoch's Zion made it safely out of this world (Moses 7:21). Their eerie corollary to the New York believers living in "Babylon" suggests that a creeping, cultural evil posed the greatest threat to the spiritual welfare of the Saints. They had to choose (for the revelations described an either/or proposition) to begin the "process" of becoming like Enoch's Zion or continue the "process" toward "destruction" (D&C 38:13). Through the Prophet Joseph, the Lord empowered the believers with all the information needed to choose wisely (D&C 37:4).

The choice to escape destruction required new converts to acknowledge the Lord as the source of authority, the maker of worlds as well as laws, and Joseph Smith as His spokesman (D&C 21:1–8). "Hear my voice and follow me," the Lord commanded unequivocally (D&C 38:22). The revelation required adherents to relieve poverty, esteem everyone equally, and to "be one" (D&C 38:27). It shouted contradictions to the cultural messages to be partisan, covetous, and to "possess that which is above another," "like the Nephites of old" (D&C 49:20; 38:39). It seemed calculated to test the integrity of covenant makers by compelling them to choose either "the things of this world" or the things of a better (D&C 25:10; see D&C 38:17–20, 25–26, 39). There was indifference if not disregard for the carnal security of the Saints: "They that have farms that cannot be sold, let them be left or rented as seemeth them good" (D&C 38:37). The irrelevance of property contrasted sharply with the revelation's emphasis on the welfare of souls: "That ye might escape the power of the enemy, and be gathered unto me a righteous people, without spot and blameless—wherefore, for this cause I gave unto you the commandment that ye should go to the Ohio" (D&C 38:31–32).

The revelation caused an initial shock. It created dissonance in believers conditioned to individualism. To get rid of their internal anxieties, fledgling converts could choose either to obey or reject the command and the Prophet Joseph. Initially there were some stirrings of rejection as some projected their own selfishness onto the Prophet. John Whitmer said the revelation caused "divisions among the congregation, some would not receive the above as the word of the Lord: but [held] that Joseph had invented it himself to deceive the people that in the end he might get gain. Now this was because, their hearts were not right in the sight of the Lord, for they wanted to serve God and man; but our Savior has declared that it was impossible to do so."[8]

Given the powerful pull of American culture in 1831, the remarkable fact is not that "one or two" chafed at the "monumental sacrifice" to gather but how the Saints aligned behind the authority of the command as the conference drew to a close.[9] Whitmer wrote that "the Lord had manifested his will to his people. Therefore they made preparations to Journey to the Ohio, with their wives, and children and all that they possessed, to obey the commandment of the Lord."[10] They were submitting to the process of becoming "less possessed" by temporal possessions.[11] The Saints quickly "started looking for buyers for their lands and homes and began packing."[12] By keeping the command to pull up telestial roots and forsake telestial concerns, the New York Saints were yielding up their *selves* to God.[13] They were, in other words, making a bold, counter-cultural declaration.[14] By so doing, they prepared themselves to receive the law of consecration the Lord promised. They were presenting themselves willing to be "endowed with power from on high" (D&C 38:32).

Newel Knight remembered that "the Saints manifested an unshaken confidence in the great work in which [they] were engaged."[15] Established families who were prospering in New York left for Ohio shortly after the January 1831 conference.[16] Expecting twins, Emma Smith went with Joseph "at the time of his going" in late January and never saw her parents again. She was cleaving to covenants and laying aside the things of this world for incorruptible treasures in a better one (D&C 25:10; 38:17–20). Polly and Joseph Knight fled from persecutors near Colesville, New York, and left their farms and mills to be sold. Along the way, they provided Emma and Joseph with means to travel to Ohio.[17] The remaining sixty-seven believers from Colesville helped each other prepare and determined "to travel together in one company" under the leadership of Newel

Knight. They left in April in a wagon train bound for Cayuga Lake and thence by canals to Lake Erie. On a journey toward Zion both geographical and metaphorical, they braved persecution, injuries, and seasickness together. Enemies subpoenaed Newel Knight, who had to return to Colesville. "The whole company," he wrote, "declined traveling until I should return." Meanwhile his aunt, Electa Peck, "fell and broke her shoulder in a most shocking manner." When Newel returned, she expressed her faith in the priesthood he held and bade him bless her: "O, Brother Newel, if you will lay your hands upon me, I shall be well and able to go on the journey with you." He did, and "the next morning she arose, dressed herself, and pursued the journey with us."[18] For two weeks the company was detained at Buffalo, New York, their boat to Fairport, Ohio, held hostage by the ice.

From Ohio, Joseph sent for his father and brother Hyrum. They came quickly in March. That left his capable mother, Lucy Mack Smith, to lead the rest of her family and others, numbering about fifty in all, from Waterloo, New York, as soon as "the brethren considered the spring sufficiently open for traveling on the water."[19] Having recently joined Saints in New York from his home in Boston, Thomas Marsh led a group of about thirty, including the Whitmers from Fayette. Martin Harris led perhaps fifty more from Palmyra to Kirtland in May. Converts from Colesville, Waterloo, and Fayette converged at Buffalo where the harbor was frozen. Places to stay while waiting for a sufficient thaw were at a premium. Prices were high, supplies low. Conditions were calculated to test the patience, faith, and will of covenantmakers.

Lucy Mack Smith had wanted the eldest man, a Brother Humphreys, to lead her group, but he declined and the whole company responded together, "We will do just as Mother Smith says." An Esquire Chamberlain provided funds for her to feed the sizeable group as the journey wore on. Lucy compared her little band to Lehi's. She was frustrated that some in her group did not seem to consider the revelation that they should help each other to be binding upon them (D&C 38:24–27). There was, for her taste, too much worldliness among them. She found "several of the brethren and sisters engaged in warm debate, others murmuring and grumbling, and a number of young ladies flirting, giggling, and laughing with gentlemen passengers who were entire strangers to them, whilst hundreds of people on shore and on other boats were witnessing this scene of clamor and vanity among our brethren." She reproved them: "We call ourselves Saints and profess to have come out from the world for the purpose of serving God at the expense of all earthly things; and will you, at the very onset, subject the cause of Christ to ridicule by your own unwise and improper conduct?"[20] While waiting for the ice to clear so the boat could move, Lucy went ashore in search of a room in which the women could rest and tend sick children. She found only selfishness, "human nature," she called it, until "a fine, cheerful old lady" gave her board in exchange for the message of the gospel. Lucy taught the good woman the restored truth until two o'clock in the morning. She considered herself an ambassador of the Lord Jesus Christ. She was frustrated by passive mothers and brethren who feared recrimination if they were discovered to be adherents of Mormonism.[21]

"You will be mobbed before morning," Thomas Marsh told Lucy when she refused to keep her faith secret. "Mob it is, then," she shot back, "for we shall sing and attend to prayers before sunset, mob or no mob." Lucy opened her mouth and it was filled with song, the good word of God, and reproof in season. She left boat captains and deck hands, the woman at the boarding house, and a man on the shore all wanting to hear more of the testimony that flowed freely from her. Over and over again Mother Smith acted in faith. She led and served her fellow Saints and extended glad tidings to those they passed on the way. Lucy seized her agency to obtain power over the telestial world, rather than letting it have power over her. She predicted that if her company would unite and call upon God to break the ice, "as sure as the Lord lives, it shall be done." It happened as she said, though the ice quickly "closed together again, and the Colesville brethren were left in Buffalo," she wrote, "unable to follow us." Neither death, hell, nor the devil could deter Mother Smith, who defied faithlessness and fear. Lucy Mack Smith's narrative demonstrates that she understood the principle and was intent on leaving temporal security and starting over. She was like Lehi. She was being born again in a new land. She would not be tethered to her old self or be afraid of completely forsaking a corrupt world.[22]

Less faithful and more fearful, perhaps, but still determined to act on the command to gather to Ohio, the Colesville Saints continued on their journey. Only one turned back. Having arrived in Buffalo a week earlier than Mother Smith's group, they followed her safely to Kirtland after an unpleasant voyage.[23] A local newspaper, the *Painesville Telegraph,* noted the May 1831 arrivals of "about two hundred men, women and children of the deluded followers of Jo Smith's Bible speculation."[24] The immigrants from New York were embraced by the Ohio Saints. Ann and Newel Whitney welcomed Emma and Joseph to their own hearth.

By fall 1831 antagonists ordered Joseph Smith and other Mormon families "immediately to depart the Township."[25] The Saints gathered in spite of the order. "Kirtland history is filled with examples of Saints who willingly sacrificed their worldly possessions to gather to Kirtland."[26] Jesus Christ was their "lawgiver," and Joseph, His spokesman (D&C 38:22). Brigham Young "had traveled and preached until I had nothing left to gather with; but Joseph said 'come up;' and I went up the best I could," a widower, with two young children. Amasa Lyman received baptism in New Hampshire in 1832 and walked most of the seven hundred miles to gather. Like her future husband Wilford Woodruff, Phoebe Carter left loved ones to gather in 1835. "I left the beloved home of my childhood to link my life with the saints of God," she later wrote. Caroline Crosby joined many others in foregoing comforts to house the immigrants. "The idea of accommodating friends," she wrote, "stimulated me to make the sacrifice."[27] Joseph Smith Sr. asked Oliver Huntington, a convert from upstate New York, to sell his farm and gather in 1835. He sold it for "much less than it was really worth for the sake of living with the church and obeying the word of God as given to Joseph Smith." When the Church's financial situation looked particularly bleak in the mid-1830s, Joseph and others joined in a solemn prayer meeting to ask the Lord to send a benefactor who could pay the mortgage on the Peter French farm. On Christmas day 1835, John Tanner, a wealthy hotel owner from eastern New York, arrived with the first of many generous gifts.

By 1832 the Mormons composed nearly 10 percent of the Kirtland Township residents. Two years later they were 27 percent of the populace. By 1835 they composed 32 percent of the residents and were evoking considerable anxiety in the local press, which imputed political motives to the gathering.[28] A year later the Saints made up nearly 50 percent of the township residents.[29] They were endowed with power in the temple that spring, fulfilling the last promise of the Ohio gathering (D&C 38:32).

A new revelation to Joseph Smith on 12 January 1838, similar in tone to the one commanding to gather to Ohio, commanded these Saints to move again. New enemies sought Joseph's life. Gathering to Kirtland had served its purpose. The promised blessings were fulfilled. The law had been revealed, and obedience to it had relieved poverty, sent missionaries far afield, and built several buildings, including the house of the Lord. There the promised endowment had been received. The Saints had gained invaluable "experience" and were "endowed with power from on high" (D&C 105:10; 38:32). They still needed to choose to be separate from the world, and thus the revelation sent them packing again: "Get out of this place," it said, "and gather . . . together unto Zion and be at peace among yourselves, O Ye inhabitants of Zion, or there shall be no safety for you."[30] The Saints overwhelmingly obeyed Joseph's revelations to gather, regardless of the "great sacrifices" required.[31] Those who knew Joseph best "accepted the voice in the revelations as the voice of God, investing in the revelations the highest authority, even above Joseph Smith's counsel."[32] He was "even as Moses" (D&C 28:2). And if, as Mother Smith wrote, his followers could be "even more unreasonable than the children of Israel," they were hardly deluded.[33]

NOTES

1. Richard L. Bushman, "The Little, Narrow Prison of Language," in Neilson and Woodworth, *Believing History,* 258.
2. Westergren, *From Historian to Dissident,* 8.

3. Hartley, *Stand by My Servant Joseph*, 103.

4. Delbanco, *Death of Satan*, 106.

5. Harvey C. Mansfield and Delba Winthrop, "Editor's Introduction," in Mansfield and Winthrop, *Democracy in America by Alexis de Tocqueville*, lxxxiii.

6. Robinson, *Spiritual Emerson*, 83.

7. Mansfield and Winthrop, "Editor's Introduction," lxxxiii.

8. Westergren, *From Historian to Dissident*, 12.

9. Hartley, *Stand by My Servant Joseph*, 103.

10. Westergren, *From Historian to Dissident*, 12–13.

11. "Increased consecration is not so much a demand for more hours of Church work as it is for more awareness of Whose work this really is! For now, consecration may not require giving up worldly possessions so much as being less possessed by them." Neal A. Maxwell, "Settle This in Your Hearts," *Ensign*, November 1992, 67.

12. Hartley, *Stand by My Servant Joseph*, 103.

13. "We tend to think of consecration only as yielding up, when divinely directed, our material possessions. But ultimate consecration is the yielding up of oneself to God." Neal A. Maxwell, "Consecrate Thy Performance," *Ensign*, May 2002, 36.

14. Elder Jeffrey R. Holland taught the same principle: "Pay your tithing as a declaration that possession of material goods and the accumulation of worldly wealth are *not* the uppermost goals of your existence. As one young husband and father, living on a student budget, recently told me, 'Perhaps our most pivotal moments as Latter-day Saints come when we have to swim directly against the current of the culture in which we live. Tithing provides just such a moment. Living in a world that emphasizes material acquisition and cultivates distrust for anyone or anything that has designs on our money, we shed that self-absorption to give freely, trustingly, and generously. By this act, we say—indeed—we are different, that we are God's peculiar people. In a society that tells us money is our most important asset, we declare emphatically it is not.'" Jeffrey R. Holland, "Like a Watered Garden," *Ensign*, November 2001, 34.

15. Hartley, *Stand by My Servant Joseph*, 102.

16. Hartley, *Stand by My Servant Joseph*, 20–21; Anderson, *Investigating the Book of Mormon Witnesses*, 124.

17. Hartley, *Stand by My Servant Joseph*, 105.

18. Hartley, *Stand by My Servant Joseph*, 110.

19. Smith, *History of Joseph Smith by His Mother*, ed. Proctor and Proctor, 259.

20. Smith, *History of Joseph Smith by His Mother*, ed. Proctor and Proctor, 260–68.

21. Smith, *History of Joseph Smith by His Mother*, ed. Proctor and Proctor, 266–67.

22. Smith, *History of Joseph Smith by His Mother,* ed. Proctor and Proctor, 264–65, 269–77.
23. Hartley, *Stand by My Servant Joseph,* 113.
24. Cited in Hartley, *Stand by My Servant Joseph,* 113.
25. Kirtland Township Trustees' Minutes and Poll Book, 1817–1838, Lake County Historical Society, Ohio.
26. See Anderson, *Joseph Smith's Kirtland,* 15; see also 11–19 for examples of the sacrifice.
27. "Caroline Burnes Crosby (1807–1844)" in Kenneth W. Godfrey, Audrey M. Godfrey, and Jill Mulvay Derr, *Women's Voices,* 52–53.
28. *Painesville Telegraph* 13:43, April 17, 1835, cited in Max H Parkin, "The Nature and Cause of Internal and External Conflict of the Mormons in Ohio Between 1830–1838" (M.A. thesis, Brigham Young University, 1966), 191.
29. These percentages were drawn from data in Backman, Perkins, and Black, *Profile of Latter-day Saints in Kirtland, Ohio,* Appendix A, 83.
30. Revelation of 12 January 1838. Archives of The Church of Jesus Christ of Latter-day Saints, Salt Lake City.
31. "Newel Knight Autobiography," 4:64.
32. Bushman, "Little, Narrow Prison of Language," 259.
33. Smith, *History of Joseph Smith by His Mother,* ed. Proctor and Proctor, 268; see Hartley, *Stand by My Servant Joseph,* 113.

CHAPTER FIFTEEN

THE MISSION TO THE LAMANITES

Grant Underwood

*I*n the fall of 1830, a series of revelations commissioned four elders to travel west to preach to the Native Americans, or Lamanites, as they were known to the Latter-day Saints. From the beginning, the Lamanites figured prominently in LDS doctrine. In his first visit from the angel Moroni in 1823, Joseph Smith was "informed concerning the aboriginal inhabitants of this country, and shown who they were, and from whence they came."[1] Subsequently, the Prophet received the metal plates upon which a portion of their history was recorded. The plates' title page declared that the record was "written to the Lamanites, which are a remnant of the House of Israel" and was designed to "show unto the remnant of the House of Israel how great things the Lord hath done for their fathers; and that they may know the covenants of the Lord, that they are not cast off forever" (Book of Mormon, Title Page). And in the earliest known recorded revelation, received when only part of the Book of Mormon had been translated, the Lord explained that "for this very purpose are these plates preserved . . . that the Lamanites might come to the knowledge of their fathers, and that they might know the promises of the Lord, and that they may believe the gospel and rely upon the merits of Jesus Christ" (D&C 3:19–20). Thereafter, in contrast to the often disparaging, even destructive, attitudes and actions of many contemporary Americans, the Latter-day Saints sought to help the Indians gain a sense of both their ancient identity and their prophetic destiny.

Grant Underwood is a professor of history at Brigham Young University.

What the Prophet and his associates may not have fully realized in the fall of 1830 was the timeliness of sending missionaries to the Lamanites. Only months before the revealed commission came, Congress passed the Indian Removal Act, which allowed any Indian tribe or nation residing in the states or organized territories of the United States to exchange their traditional lands for land in the unorganized territories west of the Mississippi. A number of tribes quickly agreed to do so and migrated to the territory west of the Missouri border in what is today eastern Kansas. This area, described in revelation as "the borders by the Lamanites" (D&C 28:9), was the ultimate destination of the missionaries, though along the way they also visited several Indian reservations within the states. As it turned out, the only baptismal success the missionaries experienced was when they preached to the white settlers of northeastern Ohio and in western Missouri.

The four men called on this mission, the first in Church history to single out a specific group of people, were Oliver Cowdery, Peter Whitmer Jr., Parley P. Pratt, and Ziba Peterson. Oliver Cowdery received his call in a revelation just before the Church convened its quarterly conference in late September: "Now, behold, I say unto you that you shall go unto the Lamanites and preach my gospel unto them . . . and cause my church to be established among them" (D&C 28:8). In the days that followed

> a great desire was manifest by several of the Elders respecting the remnants of the house of Joseph—the Lamanites residing in the west, knowing that the purposes of God were great to that people and hoping that the time had come when the promises of the Almighty in regard to that people were about to be accomplished . . . The desire being so great that it was agreed upon that we should enquire of the Lord.[2]

Several revelations resulted. Peter Whitmer Jr. was told:

> You shall take your journey with your brother Oliver; for the time has come that it is expedient in me that you shall open your mouth to declare my gospel; therefore, fear not, but give heed unto the words and advice of your brother, which he shall give you.
>
> And be you afflicted in all his afflictions, ever lifting up your heart

unto me in prayer and faith, for his and your deliverance; for I have
given unto him power to build up my church among the Lamanites.
(D&C 30:5–6)

Several days later it was revealed that Parley Pratt was to "go with my
servants, Oliver Cowdery and Peter Whitmer, Jun., into the wilderness among the Lamanites. And Ziba Peterson also shall go with
them; and I myself will go with them and be in their midst" (D&C
32:2–3).

After these revelations were received, the missionaries busied
themselves with getting ready for their journey to the West. One of
their most significant preparations was to sign a covenant committing
them to fulfill their mission. On Sunday, 17 October 1830, in the
presence of Joseph Smith and David Whitmer, mission leader Oliver
Cowdery signed this covenant:

> I, Oliver, being commanded of the Lord God, to go forth unto the
> Lamanites, to proclaim glad tidings of great joy unto them, by present-
> ing unto them the fulness of the Gospel, of the only begotten son of God;
> . . . and having certain brothers with me, who are called of God to assist
> me, whose names are Parley [Pratt], Peter [Whitmer] and Ziba
> [Peterson], do therefore most solemnly covenant before God, that I will
> walk humbly before him, and do this business, and this glorious work
> according as he shall direct me by the Holy Ghost; ever praying for mine
> and their prosperity, and deliverance from bonds, and from imprison-
> ments, and whatsoever may befal us, with all patience and faith.—Amen.

Next, his three companions affirmed:

> We, the undersigned, being called and commanded of the Lord God,
> to accompany our Brother Oliver Cowdery, to go to the Lamanites, and
> to assist in the above mentioned glorious work and business. We do,
> therefore, most solemnly covenant before God, that we will assist him
> faithfully in this thing, by giving heed unto all his words and advice,
> which is, or shall be given him by the spirit of truth, ever praying with
> all prayer and supplication, for our and his prosperity, and our deliver-
> ance from bonds, and imprisonments, and whatsoever may come upon
> us, with all patience and faith.—Amen.[3]

Not long after signing this covenant, the missionaries departed.
In a 12 November 1830 letter written from Kirtland, Ohio, Oliver

Go into the Wilderness, *by Robert T. Barrett.© Intellectual Reserve, Inc.*
Courtesy of the Museum of Church History and Art

Cowdery reported, "We arrived at this place two weeks this day [29 October]. On our journey we called at the Buffalo tribe, but stayed a few hours only but left two books with them."[4] What Cowdery called the "Buffalo tribe" was actually a group of the Seneca Nation of Indians (Iroquois Confederacy) living on Buffalo Creek Reservation a few miles southeast of downtown Buffalo. Parley P. Pratt described the visit in these words:

> We called on an Indian nation at or near Buffalo; and spent part of a day with them, instructing them in the knowledge of the record of their forefathers. We were kindly received, and much interest was manifested by them on hearing this news. We made a present of two copies of the Book of Mormon to certain of them who could read. . . . Thence we continued our journey.[5]

Following their brief interaction with the Seneca, the missionaries took passage on a Lake Erie boat bound for Fairport, Ohio, the port of entry for the Painesville-Kirtland area. Nearby, at Mentor, Ohio, the missionaries met with Parley Pratt's mentor, Sidney Rigdon, and taught and baptized him and many of his followers. The missionaries' next destination was Upper Sandusky on the Sandusky River south of Lake Erie. Whether or not Cowdery and company preached there is unknown, but Pratt later reported in his autobiography that "we were well received, and had an opportunity of laying before them [the Wyandot] the record of their forefathers." He remembered that the Indians "rejoiced in the tidings, bid us God speed, and desired us to write to them in relation to our success among the tribes further west, who had already removed to the Indian territory, where these expected soon to go. Taking an affectionate leave of this people, we continued our journey to Cincinnati."[6]

From Cincinnati, the missionaries traveled by boat down the Ohio River to its confluence with the Mississippi River. Normally, they would have then traveled upriver two hundred miles to St. Louis and then up the Missouri River another three hundred miles to the "borders by the Lamanites." Luck would have it, however, that they arrived in the midst of one of the coldest winters on record—the "winter of deep snow," it was called—and an arduous overland journey awaited them. Pratt described the Missouri portion:

> We travelled on foot for three hundred miles through vast prairies and through trackless wilds of snow—no beaten road; houses few and far between; and the bleak northwest wind always blowing in our faces with a keenness which would almost take the skin off the face. We travelled for whole days, from morning till night, without a house or fire, wading in snow to the knees at every step, and the cold so intense that the snow did not melt on the south side of the houses, even in the mid-day sun, for nearly six weeks. We carried on our backs our changes of clothing, several books, and corn bread and raw pork. We often ate our frozen bread and pork by the way, when the bread would be so frozen that we could not bite or penetrate any part of it but the outside crust.[7]

According to Peter Whitmer, the missionaries arrived in Independence, Missouri, near the western border of the United States, on 13 January 1831. "On the 14 daye of the month," he wrote, "I began to Labour with mine owne hands Brother[s] Oliver & Parly and Frederick started to see the deleware tribe[.] in a few dayes they came to see me and brother Ziba and they declared that the Lamanites recieved them with great joy."[8] Cowdery's 29 January 1831 letter to the Prophet confirms that the missionaries wasted no time in seeking out the Indians:

we arived at this place [Independence, Missouri,] a few days since which is about 25 miles from the Shawney indians on the south side of the Kansas River at its mouth & delewares on the north I have had two intervi<e>ws with the Chief of the delewares who is <a> very old & venerable looking man after laying before him & eighteen or twenty of the Council of that nation the truth he said that he and they were very glad for what I their Brother had told them and they had recived it in their hearts &c—But how the matter will go with this tribe to me is uncirtain nether Can I at presen<t> Conclude mutch about it.[9]

The principal Delaware chief at this time was Kik-Tha-We-Nund (William Anderson), a distinguished-looking man of Indian and white heritage in his mid-seventies. He had been the Delaware leader for more than a decade and only months before had negotiated their removal to land in present-day eastern Kansas where Cowdery, Pratt, and Williams visited them.[10] Like Cowdery, Pratt described the chief as

an aged and venerable looking man, who had long stood at the head of the Delawares, and been looked up to as the Great Grandfather, or Sachem of ten nations or tribes.

He was seated on a sofa of furs, skins and blankets, before a fire in the center of his lodge; which was a comfortable cabin, consisting of two large rooms.

His wives were neatly dressed, partly in calicoes and partly in skins; and wore a vast amount of silver ornaments. As we entered his cabin he took us by the hand with a hearty welcome, and then motioned us to be seated on a pleasant seat of blankets, or robes. His wives, at his bidding, set before us a tin pan full of beans and corn boiled up together, which proved to be good eating . . . There was an interpreter present and through him we commenced to make known our errand, and to tell him of the Book of Mormon.[11]

Pratt concurred that the initial reaction of Kik-Tha-We-Nund and his council was positive, but, the chief explained,

it is now winter, we are new settlers in this place; the snow is deep, our cattle and horses are dying, our wigwams are poor; we have much to do in the spring—to build houses, and fence and make farms; but we will build a council house, and meet together, and you shall read to us and teach us more concerning the Book of our fathers and the will of the Great Spirit.[12]

149

Such was not to be the case, however. Unbeknownst to the missionaries, they had arrived at the very time the Methodists and Baptists, prompted by the passage of the Indian Removal Act, were competing to establish missions and mission schools among the recently relocated Indians. Only two months before, both the Methodists and the Baptists had gained permission to start a mission school among the Shawnee, but the onset of winter had prevented either from formally launching their work by the time the Mormon missionaries arrived. Even more problematic than ministerial jealousy, however, was the fact that the elders did not possess formal governmental permission to begin their work. "To our sorrow," reported Peter Whitmer, "there came a man whose name was Cumons and told us [that] he was a man under authority[.] he told us that he would aprehend us up to the garoson."[13] Richard Cummins, the man so referred to, was head of the Shawnee Indian Agency and the ranking government official in the area. When he found that the missionaries lacked the necessary permit, he ordered them to desist and threatened to detain them at nearby Fort Leavenworth if they persisted. As he explained to his superior, St. Louis-based Superintendent of Indian Affairs William Clark, "I have refused to let them stay or, go among the Indians unless they first obtain permission from you or, some of the officers of the Genl. Government who I am bound to obey."[14] Cowdery responded promptly to his encounter with Cummins by writing to Superintendent Clark:

> While I address your honour by this communication I do it with much pleasure understanding it pleasing your honour to countenance every exertion made by the philanthropist for the instruction of the Indian in the arts of civilized life which is a sure productive of the Gospel of Christ.
>
> As I have been appointed by a society of Christians in the state of New York to superintend the establishing Missions among the Indians I doubt not but I shall have the approbation of your honour and a permit for myself and all who may be recommended to me by that Society to have free intercourse with the several tribes in establishing schools for the instruction of their children and also teaching them the Christian

religion without intruding or interfering with any other Mission now established."[15]

Cowdery's effort to capitalize on the Indian Removal Act's provision for the establishment of missions and mission schools, as well as his sensitivity to local mission politics, is striking. Parley Pratt was chosen to carry the letter to St. Louis. Unfortunately, Clark was absent when Pratt arrived and would be away for another month. After tarrying briefly in St. Louis, Pratt traveled on to Ohio. Meanwhile the missionaries worked as tailors or teachers to support themselves and waited patiently to continue their mission to the Lamanites. Nearly two months later, Cowdery wrote that Cummins

> is very strict with us and we think somewhat strenuous respecting our having liberty to visit our brethren the Lamanites but we trust that when our brother Parly returns we shall have a permit from General Clark who . . . must have a recommend or security before he can give a permit for any stranger or foreigner to go among them to teach or preach.[16]

It appears that part of Pratt's purpose in making the long journey back to Ohio was to obtain the necessary recommend. As it turned out, he would not return to Missouri until July when he arrived in company with Joseph Smith and a group of elders commissioned by revelation to visit the area. Significantly, the revelation contained an explicit command to bring a recommend for Oliver Cowdery (D&C 52:41).

Though weeks turned into months without the chance to preach to the Lamanites, Cowdery and his companions managed to keep their spirits up and hold out hope for a great work among the Indians. In Cowdery's April letter, he expressed his firm conviction that the Lord was "in very deed about to redeem his ancien[t] covenant people & lead them with the fulness of the Gentiles to springs yea fountain of living waters to his holy hill of Zion." He reported the encouraging news that

> this day heard from the deleware Nation of Lamanites by the man who is employed by [the] government [as] a smith for that Nation he believes the truth and says . . . that we have put more into the lamanites during the short time [we] were permited to be with them (which was but a few

days) then all the devels in the infernal pit [and] all the men on earth can get out of them in four generations.

James Pool, the government blacksmith referred to, also told Cowdery that Kik-Tha-We-Nund "the principle chief says he believes evry word of the Book and there are many <more> in the Nation who believes & we understand there are many among the Shawnees who also believe & we trust that when the Lord shall open <our> way we shall have glorious times."[17]

The missionaries' ongoing faith and patience in the face of difficulty are poignantly evident in another letter written by Oliver Cowdery in May: "We begin to expect our brother Parley soon we have heard from him only when he was at St Louis." Moreover, the missionaries' presence and preaching among local whites had managed to stir considerable opposition. "Almost the whole country," reported Cowdery, "which consists of Universalists Atheists Deists Presbyterians Methodists <Baptists> & professed Christian Priests & people with all the Devels from the infernel pit are united and foaming out ther own shame." That, however, did not prevent them from proselyting. Cowdery wrote that he and Ziba Peterson "went into the county East which is LaFayette about 40 miles and in the name of Jesus called on the people to repent many of whom <are I> believe earnestly searching for truth."[18] Cowdery and Peterson appear to have baptized a dozen or so in Lafayette and Jackson Counties in the months that followed, including Rebecca Hopper, whom Peterson married on 11 August 1831.[19]

As time passed, reports of belief among the Indians continued to be received. Johnston and Delilah Lykins, the recently arrived Baptist missionary couple to the Shawnee, wrote: "I think [the Mormons] will take in Shanes family." Shane, an Ottawa Indian, was serving as government interpreter for the Shawnee.[20] Still, because it was illegal for the missionaries to return to Indian territory, they were unable to baptize any of the reported believers. In July, Joseph and the others arrived, but the historical record is silent about further efforts to gain permission to work among the Indians. Whether they applied again at the time and were refused or whether they planned to apply in the future is simply unknown.

What is known is that that summer Church leaders considered several other ways to fulfill their mission to the Lamanites. Merchant-convert Sidney Gilbert, who had accompanied Joseph Smith to Missouri, was instructed by revelation to open a store in Independence and to obtain a license so that he could "send goods also unto the Lamanites [by] clerks employed in his service and thus the gospel may be preached unto them."[21] Yet another way of gaining entree to the Lamanites—intermarriage—also appears to have been contemplated. One of the visiting elders, W. W. Phelps, years later reported to Brigham Young that Joseph had received a revelation, the substance of which was that "it is my will, that, in time, ye should take unto you wives of the Lamanites and Nephites."[22] Though no contemporary account of this revelation survives in Latter-day Saint sources, Ezra Booth, who left the Church shortly after his trip to Missouri and who subsequently produced the first apostate attack on Mormonism, included in his allegations that while in Missouri, it was "made known by revelation, that it will be pleasing to the Lord, should [the elders] form a matrimonial alliance with the natives; and by this means . . . gain a residence in the Indian territory, independent of the agent."[23]

In the end, none of these initiatives materialized, and no official permit to establish a Latter-day Saint mission in Indian territory was ever received. Despite the missionaries' lack of success in establishing the Church among the Indians in 1831, however, throughout the remainder of the Prophet's life, he regularly promoted contacts with, and several subsequent missionary ventures to, various tribes.[24] Still very much alive was the March 1831 prophecy that "Jacob shall flourish in the wilderness, and the Lamanites shall blossom as the rose" (D&C 49:24).

NOTES

1. Jessee, *Papers of Joseph Smith,* 1:431.
2. Jessee, *Papers of Joseph Smith,* 1:324.
3. Reproduced in the *Ohio Star,* December 8, 1831.
4. Cited in Knight, "Autobiography," 207.

5. Pratt, *Autobiography of Parley P. Pratt,* 47. A decade later the Seneca Nation sold the Buffalo Creek reservation, and today it is the site of West Seneca, New York, a suburb of Buffalo. Since most Seneca living on the reservation moved some twenty miles southwest to the Cattaraugus Indian Reservation (situated along the Cattaraugus Creek and still owned by the Seneca Nation of Indians), nineteenth-century whites occasionally referred to them, as did Pratt elsewhere in his autobiography, as the "Catteraugus Indians" (see, for example, p. 57). His spelling of the word as "Catteraugus" has been widely perpetuated in Mormon sources.

6. Pratt, *Autobiography of Parley P. Pratt,* 51.

7. Pratt, *Autobiography of Parley P. Pratt,* 52. See Atkinson, "The Winter of Deep Snow," *Transactions of the Illinois State Historical Society* 13 (1909): 47–62.

8. Peter Whitmer Jr., "Journal," 1, Msd 5873, LDS Church Archives.

9. Copied into a letter from Joseph Smith Jr. to Hyrum Smith, 3 March 1831, MSS 155, Bx 2, Fd 3, LDS Church Archives.

10. See Weslager, *Delaware Indian Westward Migration,* 209–19; and Weslager, *Delaware Indians: A History,* 360–71.

11. Pratt, *Autobiography of Parley P. Pratt,* 53.

12. Pratt, *Autobiography of Parley P. Pratt,* 56.

13. Pratt, *Autobiography of Parley P. Pratt,* 52. See Atkinson, "The Winter of Deep Snow," *Transactions of the Illinois State Historical Society* 13 (1909): 47–62.

14. Richard W. Cummins to General William Clark, February 15, 1831, as cited in Gentry, "Light on the 'Mission to the Lamanites,'" *BYU Studies* 36 (1996–97): 234. The Intercourse Act of 1802 specified that permission was required before taking up residence among the Indians, but Cummins interpreted the Act more strictly by refusing to allow the missionaries even to "go among" the Indians.

15. Oliver Cowdery to Superintendent of Indian Affairs [William Clark], February 14, 1831, as cited in Gentry, "Light on the 'Mission to the Lamanites,'" 233.

16. Oliver Cowdery to Dearly Beloved Brethren & Sisters, April 8, 1831, Joseph Smith Letterbook 1:11–12, MSS 155, Bx 2, Fd 1, LDS Church Archives.

17. Cowdery to Brethren & Sisters, April 8, 1831, Joseph Smith Letterbook 1:10–11, MSS 155, Bx 2, Fd 1, LDS Church Archives.

18. Oliver Cowdery to Dearly Beloved Brethren, May 7, 1831, Joseph Smith Letterbook 1:12–13, MSS 155, Bx 2, Fd 1, LDS Church Archives.

19. See Romig, "The Lamanite Mission," in *John Whitmer Historical Association Journal* 14 (Spring 1994): 30–32.

20. Cited in Romig, "Lamanite Mission," 28 n. 22.

21. "Kirtland Revelation Book," 90, MS 4583, Fd 1, LDS Church Archives.

22. W. W. Phelps to Brigham Young, 12 August 1861, MS 4583, Fd 78, LDS Church Archives.

23. Booth to Ira Eddy, 6 December 1831, reproduced in *Painesville Telegraph*, 27 December 1831.

24. See Ronald W. Walker, "Seeking the 'Remnant'," *Journal of Mormon History* 19, no. 1 (Spring 1993): 1–33.

CHAPTER SIXTEEN

ESTABLISHING ZION IN MISSOURI

Matthew O. Richardson

oseph Smith reflected upon the concept of Zion on 2 May 1842 in an editorial in the *Times and Seasons:* "The building up of Zion is a cause that has interested the people of God in every age; it is a theme upon which prophets, priests, and kings have dwelt with peculiar delight."[1] Surely this statement was somewhat autobiographical for Joseph delighted to speak of Zion like the prophets of old. In many ways his perception of Zion, however, differed from the ancients. The Psalmist dreamily remembered Zion and its virtues. Joseph only looked back long enough to secure a vision for the future. Isaiah prophesied of a millennial city of God. Joseph spoke of Zion in tones of immediacy. While ancient prophets remembered Zion and Jerusalem in the same breath, Joseph spoke with urgency of establishing a New Jerusalem. It appears that all prophets shared a vision of Zion, yet none (save perhaps Enoch) did more to enlighten and establish Zion than the Prophet Joseph Smith.

His unique vision and unwavering passion for establishing Zion was not attributable to a single event as much as the developmental process that occurred with the passage of time. It is believed that his first encounter with the theme of establishing Zion began during the translation of the Book of Mormon in 1827. It is possible that concepts of Zion were found in the Book of Lehi, for such references are included in Nephi's comparative record.[2] It may have been as early as 1828, but surely by 1829, that he read Isaiah's prophecy that "the

Matthew O. Richardson is an associate professor of Church history and doctrine at Brigham Young University.

Lord shall bring again Zion" (Mosiah 12:22; 15:29). What is most interesting is that he was translating verses about Zion while, around the same time, receiving revelations that underscored Zion and its establishment. For example, in April 1829 Joseph asked the Lord for guidance and was told, "Now, as you have asked, behold, I say unto you, keep my commandments, and seek to bring forth and establish the cause of Zion" (D&C 6:6). This same charge was given the following month to Hyrum Smith and Joseph Knight Sr. (D&C 11:6; 12:6).

By June 1829 Joseph had completed translating 3 Nephi and had begun working on the small plates of Nephi. It was at this time he learned of "a city, which shall be called the New Jerusalem" (3 Nephi 21:23). Then, true to form, Joseph received a revelation admonishing David Whitmer to "bring forth and establish my Zion" (D&C 14:6).

While tangible evidence does not exist of efforts to establish Zion during the remainder of 1829 and early 1830, it would be a mistake to think that Zion was no longer important to Joseph. By April 1830, he was ready to "move the cause of Zion in mighty power for good" (D&C 21:7). But unlike times of old when prophets and Saints worked together for the *cause* of Zion, now there was the growing excitement about literally establishing a city of Zion. After all, the newly published Book of Mormon not only taught the concepts of Zion and a New Jerusalem, it spoke of the city of Zion being "built up upon this land" (Ether 13:6).

With a growing interest on the part of Latter-day Saints in establishing Zion came an increase in speculation and deception about the topic. In September 1830, for example, Hiram Page, a son-in-law to Peter and Mary Whitmer, professed to receive revelations through a stone about the "upbuilding of Zion"[3] and even the actual location of the city.[4] Naturally, his so-called revelation stirred speculative comments and heightened anticipation until Joseph was told by the Lord that "no man knoweth where the city Zion shall be built, but it shall be given hereafter" (D&C 28:9). It became clear that establishing Zion would be in accordance to a divine design and not hurried by personal motives (regardless of how sincere), frenzied anticipation, or even Satanic distraction. After all, how could the city of Zion be established save through God's direction and through his appointed prophet? (Amos 3:7) In this light, we can appreciate Joseph's understanding of his own mission. "I calculate to be one of the instruments of setting up the kingdom of Daniel by the word of the Lord, and I intend to lay a foundation that will revolutionize the whole world."[5] Joseph not only understood Zion and the influence it would have, he also understood his role in laying its foundation.

Even though the specific location for Zion had not been specified, the Lord informed Joseph of its general location and promised to give further details: "Behold, I say unto you that it [the city of Zion] shall be on the borders by the Lamanites" (D&C 28:9). In the same revelation, Oliver Cowdery was called on a mission to preach to the Lamanites (D&C 28:8). In compliance, Cowdery left on 18 October 1830 with Peter Whitmer Jr., Ziba Peterson, and Parley P. Pratt to serve the mission (D&C 30:5–6; 32:1–3). It is doubtful that these two events—clarifying the general location of Zion and sending missionaries to the Lamanites—were coincidental. Oliver Cowdery understood an apparent connection, for the *Painesville Telegraph* reported that he was "bound for the regions beyond the Mississippi, where he contemplates founding a 'City of Refuge' for his followers."[6]

Establishing Zion was once again impressed upon the Prophet Joseph in December 1830 while working with Sidney Rigdon on the Bible translation. While translating Genesis, for example, a mere handful of verses dealing with Enoch (Genesis 5:21–24) was expanded to over a hundred new verses (Moses 6:25–8:1) that became known as the "prophecy of Enoch."[7] It was in these verses that Zion was not only spoken of, but a conceptual description was given of how its City of Holiness was to be established. Zion was to become a sanctuary built upon the unity of disciples—all adhering to principles of righteousness. When the prophecy of Enoch was made known to the Saints, it was received "to the joy of the little flock."[8]

Another significant step towards establishing Zion came when Joseph instructed the Saints that it was "expedient" in the Lord "that they should assemble together at the Ohio" (D&C 37:3). Ohio was never meant to be construed as Zion itself but was to be a place where the Saints could escape from their enemies and have the freedom to exercise their beliefs, and, more importantly, become a righteous people (D&C 38:31–32). In practical terms, Ohio was also a step closer to "the border by the Lamanites," and it was here that Joseph Smith would receive important principles needed to build the city of Zion.

Shortly after his arrival in Kirtland in 1831, he received a revelation known as "the law of the church" (D&C 42). This revelation was an affirmation that Ohio was merely a staging ground for the establishment of Zion and that the time would come "when the city of the New Jerusalem shall be prepared" and the people be gathered in one (D&C 42:9). In March 1831, Joseph received yet another revelation which brought establishing Zion even closer. In this revelation, the eastern Saints were called to gather to a place called "the New Jerusalem, a land of peace, a city of refuge, a place of safety for the Saints of the Most High God . . . and it shall be called Zion" (D&C 45:66–67). The exact location of the New Jerusalem was "yet to be revealed," but one could sense that the timing for establishing Zion was near (D&C 48:5). After all, talk of "purchas[ing] the lands" and laying "the foundation of the city" was more common (D&C 48:6).

Not long after the June 1831 conference in Kirtland, Colesville Saints, who had settled in Thompson, Ohio, were instructed to "journey into the regions westward, unto the land of Missouri, unto the borders of the Lamanites" (D&C 54:8).[9] They were to gather in a place called the New Jerusalem (D&C 45:64–67). Soon after they left for Missouri, Joseph and a party of seven also left for that state on 19 June 1831.[10] After a "long and tedious" journey by wagons, canal boats, stages, steamers, and foot, they arrived in Missouri on 14 July.[11] Joseph described meeting the brethren who greeted their arrival as "a glorious one, and moistened with many tears." But within that greeting there were reasons for concern. Joseph wrote:

> Our reflections were many, coming as we had from a highly culti-
> vated state of society in the east, and standing now upon the confines
> or western limits of the United States, and looking into the vast wilder-
> ness of those that sat in darkness; how natural it was to observe the

159

degradation, leanness of intellect, ferocity, and jealousy of a people that were nearly a century behind the times.

As his initial observations collided with the concepts and visions of Zion that had percolated within him for years, is it little wonder that the Prophet mused: "When will the wilderness blossom as the rose? When will Zion be built up in her glory, and where will Thy temple stand, unto which all nations shall come in the last days?"[12]

Soon after Joseph arrived in Missouri, his anxiety over establishing Zion in the region was relieved. The Lord instructed that the land of Missouri is "the land which I have appointed and consecrated for the gathering of the saints" (D&C 57:1). Not only was the general location of Zion confirmed at this time, but the location for the City of Zion was also identified. "Wherefore, this is the land of promise, and the place for the city of Zion. . . . Behold, the place which is now called Independence is the center place" (D&C 57:2–3). Over the next twelve days, Latter-day Saints cut hay, cultivated the ground, sowed grain, and worked to provide shelter in the region.[13] In addition, several important events in establishing Zion took place. The first was a revelation received on 1 August 1831: "Give ear to my word," the Lord admonished, "and learn of me what I will concerning you, and also concerning this land unto which I have sent you" (D&C 58:1). This informational and even constitutional revelation was an important beginning to establishing Zion in Missouri for it made clear that Zion was not merely a prize waiting to be claimed. Zion required a union between God, his people, righteousness, and even geography. "And let the work of the gathering be not in haste," the Lord taught the Saints, "nor by flight; but let it be done as it shall be counseled by the elders of the church . . . according to the knowledge which they receive from time to time" (D&C 58:56). Thus, it was not only the land that was in need of preparation but also the Saints who needed preparation to receive the land.

On 2 August 1831, followers of Joseph Smith gathered in Kaw Township, Missouri. In ceremonious fashion, twelve men, symbolic of the twelve tribes of Israel, placed an oak log upon a cornerstone laid

Dedication of the Temple Lot in Independence, Missouri,
*by Dale Kilbourn.© Intellectual Reserve, Inc. Courtesy of the
Museum of Church History and Art*

by Oliver Cowdery.[14] This event symbolized laying the foundation of
the Zion city. Conceptually, Zion is also a people "of one heart and
one mind" (Moses 7:18). Thus, true to form, Sidney Rigdon asked the
gathered Saints, "Do you receive this land for the land of your inheritance with thankful hearts from the Lord?" Those present responded
in the affirmative. He then asked them to pledge to aid others and

keep the laws of God. After their affirmative response, he pronounced the land "consecrated and dedicated to the Lord for a possession and inheritance for the Saints."[15]

The following day (3 August), eleven men gathered a half mile west of the Independence courthouse to listen as Joseph Smith read the 87th Psalm and witness the dedication of a temple site.[16] A cornerstone marking the site was laid next to a sapling engraved with "ZOM," which stood for "Zomar." Ezra Booth reported that this was the "original word for Zion."[17] Thus, the foundation for the literal establishment of Zion in Missouri was in place. Before Joseph returned to Ohio, a conference was held on 4 August 1831 in the Joshua Lewis home in Kaw Township. Sidney Rigdon spoke to the congregation. Joseph followed and exhorted them to "acts of righteousness and keeping the commandments of the Lord."[18] They then partook of the sacrament, and Oliver Cowdery offered a benediction. A few days later, Joseph received a revelation reminding those whose "feet stand upon the land of Zion" that obedience was the key to their success (D&C 59:3).

After Joseph returned to Kirtland, Church membership in Missouri grew. In March 1832, the Prophet instructed those in Missouri to establish an organization that would regulate the affairs of the Saints so that they could be equal in earthly and heavenly matters (D&C 78:3–8). He then spoke of the necessity of sitting "in council with the saints which are in Zion" (D&C 78:9). As a result of this revelation, Joseph Smith, Sidney Rigdon, Newel K. Whitney, and Jesse Gause journeyed to Missouri in April 1832. The Prophet was happy to greet the Saints again and receive a "welcome only known by brethren and sisters united as one in the same faith, and by the same baptism, and supported by the same Lord." He concluded, "It is good to rejoice with the people of God."[19]

He understood that establishing Zion was more than deciding on borders, staking claims, and beautifying the land. It involved learning principles of consecration, equality, and common property. Such principles were necessary to establish Zion within the hearts, minds, and affairs of the Missouri Saints. After all, it was "the development of the attributes of godliness in this life and the attainment of eternal life in the world to come" that was essential.[20] After these teachings were received by the Saints, Joseph departed from Missouri on 6 May 1832 for Kirtland.

There were 810 Saints in Missouri and five established branches by November 1832 and Joseph was optimistic about Zion in Missouri. Unfortunately, pettiness, unbelief, and neglect surfaced within the communities of the Saints in that region (D&C 101:6–8). Such traits were the very antithesis of Zion. In spite of these difficulties, the establishment of Zion still burned within Joseph. He prepared a plat of Zion in June 1833 that showed a city that could accommodate 15,000 to 20,000 people and 24 temples.

Although his plat was inspired, it was never implemented. Mobs forced the Saints out of Missouri. The forced exile did not cause Joseph Smith to abandon the concept of establishing Zion. To him, Jackson County, Missouri, would always be the center of Zion. Yet his concept of Zion began to expand. "I have received instructions from the Lord," Joseph taught two months prior to his death, "that from henceforth wherever Elders of Israel shall build up churches and branches unto the Lord throughout the States, there shall be a stake of Zion."[21] He also taught that Zion would be established on a broader ground: "The whole of America is Zion itself from north to south."[22] To his dying day, Joseph spoke of Zion with unmitigated enthusiasm and hope. He remained true to his belief that "we ought to have the building up of Zion as our greatest object."[23]

NOTES

1. Smith, *Times and Seasons* 3 (2 May 1842): 776.
2. S. Kent Brown discusses Nephi's record in comparison with Lehi's writings in "Lehi's Personal Record: Quest for a Missing Source," *BYU Studies* 24, no. 1 (1984): 19–42.
3. Smith, *History of the Church*, 1:109.
4. Smith, *Doctrines of Salvation*, 3:75. There is no record of where Hiram Page said the city would be built.
5. Smith, *Teachings of the Prophet Joseph Smith*, 366.
6. "The Golden Bible," *Painesville Telegraph* 2, no. 22 (November 16, 1830).
7. Smith, *History of the Church*, 1:133.

8. Smith, *History of the Church,* 1:132.
9. This is the second time the Saints were called to gather to a new location. Most of the Saints living in Thompson, Ohio, had joined the Church in Colesville, New York.
10. The traveling party included Joseph Smith, Sidney Rigdon, Martin Harris, Edward Partridge, W. W. Phelps, Joseph Coe, Algernon S. Gilbert and his wife. Smith, *History of the Church,* 1:188.
11. Joseph Smith, "To the Elders of the Church of Latter Day Saints," *Messenger and Advocate* 1, no. 12 (September 1835): 179.
12. Smith, *History of the Church,* 1:189.
13. Pratt, *Autobiography of Parley P. Pratt,* 56.
14. Those carrying the oak beam included Joseph Smith, Oliver Cowdery, Sidney Rigdon, Hezekiah Peck, Ezekiel Peck, Joseph Knight Sr., Aaron Culver, Ezra Booth, Freeborn DeMille, William Stringham, and Ira Willis. Larry C. Porter, "The Colesville Branch in Kaw Township, Jackson County, Missouri, 1831–1833," in Garr and Johnson, *Missouri,* 287.
15. Whitmer, *Early Latter Day Saint History,* 79.
16. Joseph Smith, Oliver Cowdery, Sidney Rigdon, Edward Partridge, Peter Whitmer Jr., Frederick G. Williams, William W. Phelps, Martin Harris, Joseph Coe, Newel Knight, and Ezra Booth participated in this event. See Porter, "Colesville Branch," 289.
17. Ezra Booth, "Mormonism—No. VI," *Ohio Star,* November 17, 1831, in Porter, "Colesville Branch," 289.
18. Cannon and Cook, *Far West Record,* 9–10.
19. Smith, *History of the Church,* 1:269.
20. McConkie, *Mormon Doctrine,* 158.
21. Smith, *History of the Church,* 6:318–20.
22. Smith, *Teachings of the Prophet Joseph Smith,* 362.
23. Smith, *Teachings of the Prophet Joseph Smith,* 160.

CHAPTER SEVENTEEN

SCHOOL OF THE PROPHETS AND SCHOOL OF THE ELDERS

Milton V. Backman Jr.

oseph Smith was keenly interested in providing members with educational opportunities, and many Latter-day Saints were genuinely interested in various branches of learning. He actively supported a variety of educational programs in the 1830s in Kirtland, Ohio. The first school established under his direction was called the School of the Prophets. It was organized in Kirtland, Ohio, in January 1833 for priesthood leaders. Students met in the Newel K. Whitney store. One portion of the store was used for merchandising and post office needs. Another portion had been remodeled and had become the temporary home of Joseph Smith and his family. A small upstairs room in the northeast corner of the building served as a schoolroom. It was adjacent to the southeast room which was, in reality, the headquarters of the Church and sometimes called the revelation or translating room. In that southeast room, the Prophet worked on the translation of the Bible, dictated many revelations, and presided over conferences or meetings of Latter-day Saints.[1]

The School of the Prophets was organized in harmony with a revelation which Joseph Smith received in the "translating room" during a conference of high priests that continued for several days. Joseph said:

> To receive revelation and blessings of heaven it was necessary to have our minds on God and exercise faith and become of one heart and of one mind. therefore he recommended all present to pray separately and

---

Milton V. Backman Jr. is an emeritus professor of Church history and doctrine at Brigham Young University.

vocally to the Lord for [Him] to reveal his will unto us concerning the upbuilding of Zion & for the benifit of the saints and for the duty and employment of the Elders.[2]

Following these instructions, the high priests knelt in prayer and promised to keep the commandments. After which, Joseph received in their presence a revelation known as the Olive Leaf. The Prophet explained that the Olive Leaf, plucked from the tree of paradise, was the Lord's message of peace to them. Since the revelation was not finished on that day, the conference resumed the next, and Joseph continued to unfold many significant principles of the gospel.[3]

The Prophet was not only commanded to establish the school but received by revelation information concerning the operation of the school, curriculum, student body, and blessings to be given for obedience to the Lord's instructions. Although many of the rules and policies governing the School of the Prophets were similar to the general principles of the gospel which all members were encouraged to live, there were some procedures that were distinct and evident from the first session of the educational program. Students assembled early in the morning, about sunrise, in the spirit of fasting and prayer. They were admitted into the classroom by the instructor. After they had gathered, the instructor cited an oath which was repeated by the students. This oath included a promise to be brothers in the "bonds of love" and "to walk in all the commandments of God blameless, in thanksgiving, forever and ever. Amen" (D&C 88:133).

By revelation, members of the School of the Prophets were also told that they were to be received into the school by "partaking of bread and wine" (D&C 88:141). They were also instructed to participate in the "ordinance of washing of feet," patterned after the Savior's washing of the Apostles' feet during the Last Supper as described in the Gospel of John (D&C 88:139; see John 13:12–17).[4]

Many additional instructions in the Lord's message of peace applied not only to those in the School of the Prophets but to all Latter-day Saints. Members were told to "teach one another words of wisdom; yea, seek ye out of the best books words of wisdom; seek learning, even by study and also by faith." Members, including those

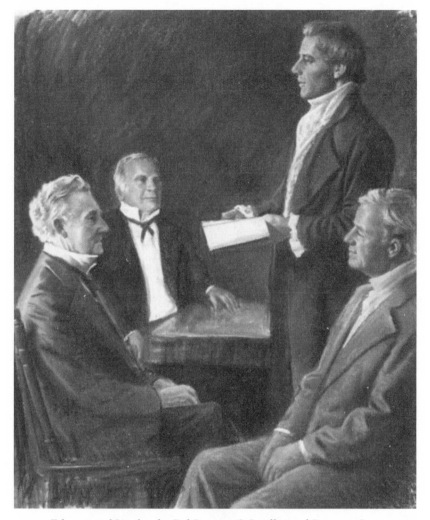

Educational Leader, *by Del Parson.* © *Intellectual Reserve, Inc.*
Courtesy of the Museum of Church History and Art

who participated in the school, were to cease from all their "wicked doings," including their "lustful desires," pride and "light-mindedness" (D&C 88:118, 121). They were to cease from idleness, fault-finding, and sleeping longer than needful so that their bodies and minds might be invigorated. They were also instructed to be clothed with the bonds of charity (D&C 88:124–25).

By revelation, those in the School of the Prophets were given instructions governing classroom procedures and curriculum. Although they were told to appoint a leader and instructor (who was Joseph Smith), they were informed that all should participate in order that all might edify one another (D&C 88:122). By revelation, members of the school and other Latter-day Saints were also told to "teach one another the doctrine of the kingdom" that they might be "instructed more perfectly in theory, in principle, in doctrine, in the law of the gospel, in all things that pertain unto the kingdom of God" that they should understand. They were also told to seek knowledge "of things both in heaven and in the earth, and under the earth; things which have been, things which are, things which must shortly come to pass; things which are at home, things which are abroad; the wars and perplexities of the nations, and the judgments which are on the land; and a knowledge also of countries and of kingdoms" (D&C 88:77–79). And they were told to seek wisdom out of the best books and "seek learning, even by study and also by faith" (D&C 88:118).

Joseph Smith summarized his principal activities during the winter of 1832–33, noting that he spent most of his time translating the Bible, attending meetings, and participating in the School of the Prophets.[5] The first session of the school began during the third week of January 1833. Fourteen men—twelve high priests and two elders— gathered to participate in the first organized missionary training program under the direction of the Prophet. This was a select group who were in Kirtland at that time. Others, including Orson Pratt, were later invited to participate. Many others, who may have wished to attend, were told to continue laboring in the vineyard for a season.[6]

The first sessions of the school were preceded by a meeting in which the gifts of the spirit were poured out as in ancient days. In preparation for the first day of class, Joseph Smith conducted a meeting on 22 January during which he spoke in tongues. After he had manifested that gift, Joseph testified that "the Lord poured out His Spirit in a miraculous manner, until all the Elders spake in tongues, and several members, both male and female, exercised the same gift." Members continued to sing and pray in tongues until a late hour of the night.[7]

The divine manifestations continued on 23 January, the day that the selected priesthood members gathered to participate in what was probably the first meeting of the School of the Prophets. Describing the first day of class, Joseph reported that "after much speaking, singing, praying, and praising God, all in tongues, we proceeded to the washing of feet" as described in the New Testament. They continued all day in fasting, prayer, and concluded by partaking of the Lord's Supper. According to Joseph, "I blessed the bread and wine in the name of the Lord, when we all ate and drank, and were filled; then we sang a hymn, and the meeting adjourned."[8]

One of the first revelations that Joseph Smith received after organizing the School of the Prophets was the Word of Wisdom, which was the Lord's law of health. Although the revelation, which was recorded on 27 February 1833, was directed to the council of high priests assembled in Kirtland, who were members of the School of the Prophets, this health code was applied to other members. It specified that herbs, fruits, meats, and grain were given by God for the use of man, but that same God prohibited the use of alcohol, tobacco, tea, and coffee. This revelation also included blessings and promises to the obedient.

Brigham Young later recalled that he was well-acquainted with the circumstances that led to the revelation known as the Word of Wisdom. He said that students traveled many miles to attend the school held in a small room, probably no larger than eleven by fourteen feet.

> When they assembled together in this room after breakfast, the first [thing] they did was to light their pipes, and, while smoking, talk about the great things of the kingdom, and spit all over the room, and as soon as the pipe was out of their mouths a large chew of tobacco would then be taken. Often when the Prophet entered the room to give the school instructions he would find himself in a cloud of tobacco smoke. This, and the complaints of his wife at having to clean so filthy a floor, made the Prophet think upon the matter, and he inquired of the Lord relating to the conduct of the elders in using tobacco, and the revelation known as the Word of Wisdom was the result of his inquiry.[9]

One of the participants in the school, Zebedee Coltrin, remembered that after Joseph Smith had received the Word of Wisdom revelation, the Prophet entered the schoolroom from the translating room and read the revelation to them. Immediately after the revelation was read, "twenty out of the twenty-one who used tobacco . . . immediately threw their tobacco and pipes into the fire."[10]

During these special meetings, participants were promised that through obedience they would gain an increased knowledge of the Savior. Joseph wrote to Church leaders in Missouri informing them that he was preparing the participants of the School of the Prophets to see unusual blessings, "even a visit from the heavens." This promise was realized. About two months after the school was organized, Joseph instructed the students to prepare themselves for a day of revelations and visions, with a promise that the pure in heart would behold a heavenly vision.[11]

On 18 March 1833, the heavens were opened. Members gathered in their classroom and while fasting and praying "the eyes of their understanding [were] opened by the Sprit of God, so as to behold many things." According to the minutes of this meeting, "many of the brethren saw a heavenly vision of the Savior, and concourses of angels, and many other things, of which each one has a record of what he saw."[12] Zebedee Coltrin testified that while he was praying with other members of the school, he saw a heavenly personage. "I saw him," he said, "and suppose others did [too]." Joseph informed him that the heavenly being was "Jesus, the Son of God, our elder brother." Shortly after Brother Coltrin beheld the Savior, he announced that he saw another personage who seemed to be surrounded with a flame of fire. He said that the personage was in the form of a perfect man. According to Coltrin, Joseph Smith told him that he had seen "the Father of our Lord Jesus Christ."[13]

John Murdock also testified that he saw the Savior during the period when the School of the Prophets was being held in the Newel K. Whitney store. He boarded temporarily in the home of the Prophet and recalled that he was invited to attend prayer meetings in the home. In describing one of those meetings, he declared:

> The prophet told us if we could humble ourselves before God, and exercise strong faith, we should see the face of the Lord. And about midday

the visions of my mind were opened, and the eyes of my understanding were enlightened, and I saw the form of a man, most lovely, the visage of his face was sound and fair as the sun. His hair a bright silver gray, curled in most majestic form, His eyes a keen penetrating blue, and the skin of his neck a most beautiful white and he was covered from the neck to the feet with a loose garment, pure white, whiter than any garment I have ever before seen. His countenance was most penetrating, and yet most lovely. And while I was endeavoring to comprehend the whole personage from head to feet it slipped from me, and the vision was closed up. But it left on my mind the impression of love, for months, that I never felt before to that degree.[14]

Records do not indicate how frequently the students gathered or how many days of schooling were included in that first term, but sometime in April 1833 the school closed with the intention of resuming the next winter. Following the last session, participants were instructed to return to their mission field or to continue serving in areas where they lived.

A number of major objectives of the School of the Prophets were accomplished that first term. After reflecting on their experiences, several students emphasized that one of the major thrusts of that missionary training program was to recognize and learn to listen to the Spirit. Orson Pratt recalled one reason the elders gathered was to learn "the operations of the Spirit upon the mind of man."[15] According to John Taylor, Joseph Smith instructed the students not to hesitate in expressing their thoughts for "it was very common for the Holy Spirit to reveal some things to obscure individuals" that might not be known by others.[16] The school was also established to sanctify the elders and prepare them for spiritual blessings, including heavenly visions, which they received (D&C 88:137). And Joseph declared that "great joy and satisfaction continually beamed in the countenances" of the Latter-day Saints who participated in the School of the Prophets "on account of the things revealed, and our progress in the knowledge of God."[17]

171

SCHOOL OF THE ELDERS

Eight months after the School of the Prophets adjourned, a new missionary training program began. This new school was called the School of the Elders. It functioned in Kirtland for three winters. In some respects, the new school was different from the School of the Prophets for apparently participants were not received by an oath or salutation or by the ordinance of washing of feet. Although this new school was different, sometimes contemporaries referred to the School of the Elders as the School of the Elders and the School of the Prophets. Classes were held during the winter months, often from November to March. A variety of subjects were taught. Students studied English grammar, writing, philosophy, government, literature, geography, and ancient and modern history. The major curriculum emphasis, however, was religion. Various religious themes were emphasized for the purpose of training priesthood bearers to be more effective missionaries and leaders. Another purpose was to prepare the priesthood to receive a special gift or endowment in the Kirtland Temple that was under construction.

Joseph Smith was one of many competent teachers who lectured and directed the education of the students. While Joseph taught and presided, other participants, including Sidney Rigdon, Frederick G. Williams, and William E. McLellin, assisted. During the second session of this school, participants met in a schoolroom located under the printing office constructed on a lot near the Kirtland Temple.[18] According to Joseph Smith's history, the Prophet was "busily engaged" in November 1834 in making "preparations for the school of the Elders, wherein they might be more perfectly instructed in the great things of God."[19] On 1 December the Prophet reported that the school was well attended and that students were absorbed in the study of lectures on theology, particularly the seven Lectures on Faith. Most attendees gave studious attention to qualifying themselves to become messengers of Jesus Christ.[20] With Joseph's approval, the seven Lectures on Faith were published in the first edition of the Doctrine and Covenants in 1835.[21]

On 22 December 1834 a Grammar School was opened in Kirtland with Sidney Rigdon and William E. McLellin as teachers. Joseph and other participants in the School of the Elders began meeting with the Grammar School. A Hebrew School was organized in January 1836. This school met daily in the west room on the third floor of the unfinished temple, a room also referred to as the "translating room."[22] On 18 January 1836, the School of the Elders was moved to a room in the temple that adjoined the room used by the Hebrew School.[23] Many leaders devoted much of their time to studying and attending these schools.

Although the School of the Prophets was not reconstituted, one of the ordinances introduced in that school was renewed in the temple as part of the preliminary endowment. On 29 March 1836, two days after the dedication of the Kirtland Temple, Joseph Smith and other members of the First Presidency met with bishops and their counselors and other leaders in the temple. Under the direction of Joseph, this group participated in the ordinances of washing of feet and partaking of the sacrament. Summarizing this meeting, Joseph wrote, "The Holy Spirit rested down upon us, and we continued in the Lord's House all night, prophesying and giving glory to God."[24]

The next morning, Wednesday, 30 March, about three hundred priesthood bearers met in the temple. They spent the day rejoicing as they partook of the bread and wine and participated in the ordinance of washing of feet and listened to the words of the Prophet. After they had participated in these ordinances, Joseph informed them of the need to be "endowed" with power from on high (D&C 38:32). This endowment would be a preliminary endowment, a special gift of power from God. Joseph informed those present that they had been endowed and told them to go forth in all meekness, in sobriety, and preach Jesus Christ and him crucified.[25]

Based on available records, the School of the Prophets was one of the most unusual schools organized under the direction of Joseph Smith. Although members of that school met for less than three months, they enjoyed a season of great spiritual experiences that helped prepare them to receive power from on high in the Kirtland

Temple. A school patterned after the initial School of the Prophets was not organized until 1869 in Utah. Meanwhile, Latter-day Saint leaders and members continued their genuine interest in education. Nearly all principles outlined in the Olive Leaf revelation have served as influential guidelines for Latter-day Saint educational programs. As Joseph Smith learned by revelation, "the glory of God is intelligence, or, in other words, light and truth. Light and truth forsake that evil one" (D&C 93:36–37).

NOTES

1. For approximately eighteen months, Joseph and his family lived in the east wing of the Newel K. Whitney store, and during that brief period (from about 3 December 1832 to 21 June 1833) Joseph received seventeen revelations that are in the current edition of the Doctrine and Covenants. Moreover, he organized the First Presidency and conducted at least eighteen meetings or conferences in that building. Anderson, *Joseph Smith's Kirtland,* 153.

2. Kirtland Council Minute Book, LDS Church Archives, 3–4. Also cited in McConkie and Ostler, *Revelations of the Restoration,* 626.

3. Smith, *History of the Church,* 1:316.

4. It is assumed that members of the School of the Prophets partook of the "bread and wine" during all or nearly all their meetings but only participated in the ordinance of foot washing when they were initiated into the school. It is further assumed that the ordinance of washing of feet performed in that school was the same as or part of the preliminary or partial endowment given in the Kirtland Temple in 1836. Peterson, "History of the Schools," 26–27. See also Minutes, Salt Lake City School of the Prophets, October 3, 1883; McConkie, *Mormon Doctrine,* 831.

5. Smith, *History of the Church,* 1:322.

6. Peterson, "History of the Schools," 15–17; Smith, *History of the Church,* 1:322–23.

7. Smith, *History of the Church,* 1:323.

8. Smith, *History of the Church,* 1:323–24.

9. Young, *Journal of Discourses,* 12:158.

10. Minutes, Salt Lake City School of the Prophets, October 3, 1883, 56.

11. Smith, *History of the Church,* 1:316, 334–35.

12. Smith, *History of the Church,* 1:334–35; see Backman, *Heavens Resound,* 266–67; Kirtland Council Minute Book, 17; *Times and Seasons* 5 (December 15, 1844): 738.

13. Minutes, Salt Lake City School of the Prophets, October 3, 1883, 56;

Backman, *Heavens Resound,* 267; see Zebedee Coltrin, Minutes, High Priest, Spanish Fork, February 5, 1870, 103.

14. John Murdock Journal, typescript, 13.
15. Minutes, School of the Prophets, November 12, 1870, as cited in Backman, *Heavens Resound,* 266.
16. Minutes, School of the Prophets, June 3, 1871, as cited in Backman, *Heavens Resound,* 266.
17. Smith, *History of the Church,* 1:334.
18. Smith, *History of the Church,* 2:169–70.
19. Smith, *History of the Church,* 2:169–70, 180.
20. Smith, *History of the Church,* 2:175–76.
21. See Dahl and Tate, *Lectures on Faith in Historical Perspective,* 269.
22. Smith, *History of the Church,* 2:355–56, 376.
23. Smith, *History of the Church,* 2:376.
24. Smith, *History of the Church,* 2:430. Joseph also noted in his history that on March 29 the last lectures by Professor (Joshua) Seixas (who was the Hebrew scholar hired as an instructor) were delivered. Smith, *History of the Church,* 2:429.
25. Smith, *History of the Church,* 2:430–33.

CHAPTER EIGHTEEN

THE NEW TRANSLATION
OF THE BIBLE

Robert J. Matthews

he Joseph Smith Translation of the Bible (JST) is an inspired revision or translation of the King James Version. Joseph Smith was divinely commissioned to make the translation and regarded it as a "branch of [his] calling."[1] Although not the official Bible of The Church of Jesus Christ of Latter-day Saints, the Joseph Smith Translation offers many informative doctrinal and historical insights about the biblical record. Using the Joseph Smith Translation is like having Joseph Smith as a study companion because it is such a fruitful source of material about biblical events and personalities that is not available elsewhere. The labor was its own reward, as it not only resulted in a better Bible but was a spiritual learning experience for the Prophet himself.

The greatest value of the Joseph Smith Translation is its strong witness for the sacred mission of the Lord Jesus Christ as the Son of God, Savior and Redeemer. It is also tangible testimony and evidence of the divine calling of the Prophet Joseph Smith.

WHAT IS THE JOSEPH SMITH
TRANSLATION OF THE BIBLE?

The Joseph Smith Translation of the Bible is a collection of sacred documents prepared by the Prophet Joseph Smith and his scribes, chiefly between June 1830 and July 1833. It has the literary style, vocabulary, and content of the King James Version, frequently

---

Robert J. Matthews is an emeritus professor of ancient scripture and former dean of Religious Education at Brigham Young University.

modified, clarified, and supplemented by Joseph Smith as he received divine inspiration pertaining to specific passages and topics. The work has been variously known as the New Translation (which was Joseph Smith's own term for it), the Inspired Version, and the Inspired Revision. Since 1979 The Church of Jesus Christ of Latter-day Saints has officially used the name Joseph Smith Translation for the work.

The Joseph Smith Translation is markedly different in procedure and in content from any other Bible because the Prophet did not make use of ancient manuscripts or a knowledge of biblical languages, but rather the wording was prompted by divine revelatory experiences through the study of the English text of the King James Version.

In the Joseph Smith Translation many new passages add information not found in any other Bible. Hundreds of other passages are rephrased in a manner to interpret and clarify existing material. This generally gives meaning to formerly vague or obscure passages and often removes contradictory statements. Some deletions also occur, the most notable being an explanation that one Old Testament book, the Song of Solomon, is "not Inspired writings."[2]

The most important corrections are doctrinal in substance and pertain to the nature of God, the nature of man, the reality of the devil, the mission of Jesus Christ, priesthood, ordinances, forgiveness, and explanations interpreting the parables of Jesus. Considerable emphasis is given to the antiquity of the plan of salvation, with unmistakable evidence that the gospel of Jesus Christ, with priesthood and all the ordinances, was known and obeyed by Adam, Enoch, Noah, Abraham, Moses, and their followers. Such information is incorporated into the text in such a way that it restores information once in the Bible but which has been lost to all presently known biblical manuscripts.

The Joseph Smith Translation encompasses both the Old and the New Testaments, with attention given to all of the sixty-six books. Genesis, Exodus, Psalms, Isaiah, Matthew, Luke, Romans, and 1, 2 Corinthians received the most corrections. No changes were made in the books of Ruth, Esther, Song of Solomon, Lamentations, Obadiah, Micah, Nahum, Habakkuk, Zephaniah, Haggai, Malachi, 2 and 3 John.

Translation of the Bible, *by Liz Lemon Swindle*

Even the books that have no textual corrections are cited in the Prophet's manuscript as "correct," meaning they needed no revision. Interestingly, the book of Ecclesiastes, for some reason, probably an oversight, is not mentioned in the Prophet's manuscript. The King James Version used by the Prophet as a base contained the fourteen books of Old Testament Apocrypha. The Lord told Joseph Smith that it was not needful for those books to be translated (D&C 91).

WHAT WAS THE METHOD OF TRANSLATION?

The Prophet Joseph Smith did not leave a detailed account explaining how the translation was made, however existing original documents give certain clues. A large edition of the King James Version of the Bible published by H. and E. Phinney of Cooperstown, New York, in 1828, was used. The assumption and likelihood is that the Prophet would read, perhaps aloud, and receive inspiration from the Holy Spirit and dictate to a scribe who would write on sheets of paper that were 14" x 17," folded so as to make 8½ " x 14" leaves.

At the commencement of the project, the entire biblical text was copied, even chapters having no corrections. Later a shorter method was devised by marking in Joseph Smith's Bible verses needing adjustment and recording on paper only the actual corrections. Parts of the Bible thus received many markings, some in pencil, others in ink. The actual words of the new text were written only on the manuscript pages.

WHO WERE THE SCRIBES?

Various scribes participated, beginning with Oliver Cowdery, probably at Harmony, Pennsylvania, in June 1830, and subsequently John Whitmer at Fayette, New York, beginning in October 1830, and Sidney Rigdon in Fayette, New York, Kirtland, Ohio, and Hiram, Ohio, from December 1830 throughout 1831 into early 1832. Frederick G. Williams served as scribe in 1832 and 1833. Emma Smith served briefly in December 1830, and one other scribe, writing in early 1832, has not yet been identified.

WHAT HAPPENED TO THE MANUSCRIPT?

For the Old Testament, the manuscript consists of a preliminary copy of Genesis through chapter 24 (Old Testament Manuscript 1), followed by a second manuscript, more polished, recopying the earlier draft and continuing through Malachi (Old Testament Manuscript 2). The New Testament follows a similar pattern, with a preliminary manuscript of Matthew, chapters 1 through 26 (New Testament Manuscript 1), and a more advanced manuscript recopying the earlier manuscript and continuing through Revelation (New Testament Manuscript 2). The pages have yellowed, and the ink, once black, is now a rich brown. A few unintentional ink splatters decorate the pages, and even some finger or thumbprints can be seen in the ink spots. Portions of the pages were sewn together at the fold to produce a folio-type collection. The total manuscript numbers approximately 450 pages, some being misnumbered.

The "marked Bible" and the manuscripts are still intact, although showing signs of age and wear, and are carefully preserved in the archives of the Community of Christ (formerly the Reorganized

Church of Jesus Christ of Latter Day Saints) in Independence, Missouri. The pages frequently show evidence of revisions after the original dictation, either because of additional revelation or error in the first draft. They also show the addition of punctuation, capitalization, and versification after the initial writing, evidently preparing the manuscript for publication. In about twenty places there was not enough room between the lines to insert the desired additions. In these cases, the final corrections were placed on scraps of paper and pinned onto the manuscript sheets at the appropriate places. Occasional explanatory notes, not intended to be actual text, were written in the margins of the manuscripts. I have handled and examined the marked Bible and the manuscripts on many occasions.

SPECIAL SIGNIFICANCE OF THE MANUSCRIPTS

It is of major significance that the manuscripts sometimes contain the date of writing, which enables us to reconstruct the sequence and to know precisely when particular Bible passages were being considered. Dates help correlate the translation with known events in Church history and also establish chronology. This chronology is especially rewarding by showing that in many instances specific doctrinal items were recorded in the Joseph Smith Translation manuscript at an earlier date than the same concepts appear in the Doctrine and Covenants. Such items confer a primal and foundational status on the Joseph Smith Translation. Among the topics of this category are the fall of Lucifer (Moses 4:1–4 and D&C 29:36–41), the sanctity of animal life (JST Genesis 9:11 and D&C 49:19–21), and the age of accountability of children (JST Genesis 17:1–12 and D&C 68:25–27). This relationship indicates the meaningful (but generally overlooked) role of the Joseph Smith Translation as a contributor to the content of the Doctrine and Covenants and also to the teachings of the Church. It also illustrates that making the translation was a learning experience for the Prophet, for it introduced him to some major doctrinal concepts not discussed earlier in the scriptures.

WHY WAS A NEW TRANSLATION OF THE BIBLE NECESSARY?

The Lord revealed to Nephi that many plain and precious parts of the Bible were deliberately taken away from the Bible at a very early date, before it was distributed throughout the world (1 Nephi 13:20–29). Since original manuscripts of the Bible are not available today, the problem is not one of language or of skill in translating; the real problem is lack of an adequate manuscript to translate from. The Apostasy not only left the world without an adequate church, it also left the world without an adequate Bible. Only by revelation could the true church and the true biblical record be restored to the earth. Such is the rationale undergirding the need for Joseph Smith to make a revelatory translation of the Bible, and why it was not necessary for him to have an ancient manuscript or a knowledge of biblical languages. The angel explained to Nephi that the Book of Mormon and "other books" in the last days would make known the material lost from the Bible (1 Nephi 13:38–40). The Joseph Smith Translation could be one of those "other books."

HOW IS THE JOSEPH SMITH TRANSLATION A "TRANSLATION"?

Some object to calling the Joseph Smith Translation a "translation" because it did not involve a change of language. Joseph Smith studied the English text of the King James Version and produced the English text of the Joseph Smith Translation as the Lord gave him the larger and original meaning. We might ask: "Who was in fact the actual translator?" The Holy Ghost was the translator, and Joseph Smith was the mortal instrument through whom the revealed restoration of meaning was made known. Joseph did not restore an original manuscript in an ancient language. He restored in an English text ancient information that was once recorded by biblical prophets in ancient languages. That is tantamount to a translation.

That Joseph Smith had the spiritual endowment to translate by the Spirit is illustrated in the following two examples. First, after being baptized and receiving the Holy Ghost, the Prophet wrote: "Our minds being now enlightened, we began to have the scriptures laid open to our understandings, and the true meaning and intention of their more mysterious passages revealed unto us in a manner which we never could attain to previously, nor ever before had thought of" (Joseph Smith–History 1:74). Second, the minutes of the School of the Prophets under the date of 14 January 1871 contain this information: "He [Elder Orson Pratt] mentioned that as Joseph used the Urim and Thummim in the translation of the Book of Mormon, he wondered why he did not use it in the translation of the New Testament. Joseph explained to him that the experience he had acquired while translating the Book of Mormon by the use of the Urim and Thummim had rendered him so well acquainted with the Spirit of Revelation and Prophecy, that in the translating of the New Testament he did not need the aid that was necessary in the 1st instance."[3] Acceptance of Joseph Smith as a prophet of God leaves no difficulty in also accepting the Joseph Smith Translation as a type of revealed translation.

THE QUESTION OF COMPLETENESS

Did Joseph Smith finish the Bible translation? In a letter written to W. W. Phelps on 2 July 1833, Sidney Rigdon said Joseph had finished,[4] and such a note is also given on the manuscript under that same date.[5] However, the Prophet subsequently made additional revisions. In public addresses he frequently cited corrections needed in various passages of the Bible but which are not included in the Joseph Smith Translation manuscript.[6] Even so, the Prophet endeavored to get the Joseph Smith Translation manuscript ready for publication in Nauvoo. These and other factors lead to the conclusion that the Prophet had completed what the Lord required of him at the time, but he did not make all the corrections that are needed and which probably will be made at some future time as part of the restoration of all things.

PUBLICATION OF THE
JOSEPH SMITH TRANSLATION

The Prophet Joseph Smith did not publish the entire Joseph Smith Translation material. However, parts of Genesis, including the "Prophecy of Enoch" (Moses 7), were published in *The Evening and the Morning Star* in Independence, Missouri, in August 1832, and March and April 1833. Lengthy portions of Genesis, chapters 1 through 5, were published in the *Lectures on Faith,*[7] lecture 2. Romans 10:14 was published in lecture 3. A broadside tract 8" x 12" containing Joseph Smith Translation Matthew 24 was published sometime between 1832 and 1837 in Kirtland, Ohio. The "Vision of Moses" (Moses 1) was published in the *Times and Seasons,* January 1843, on pages 71–73.

After the Prophet's death, some Genesis materials as well as Matthew 24 were published in the Pearl of Great Price in Liverpool, England, in July 1851, and in every subsequent edition. The Reorganized Church of Jesus Christ of Latter Day Saints published the entire translation in 1867 at Plano, Illinois, and has published many editions since. Beginning in 1979, The Church of Jesus Christ of Latter-day Saints published an edition of the King James Version, with hundreds of selections from the Joseph Smith Translation as footnotes and appendices. In 2004 the Religious Studies Center at Brigham Young University published a typographic transcription of all the original manuscript pages.[8]

CONCLUSION

Some LDS scholars regard the Joseph Smith Translation as the finest Bible now on earth and the best witness for the Lord Jesus Christ of any known Bible. Compared to other Bibles, it is more vivid, the doctrine is stronger, situations are more focused, the ancient patriarchs are more grand, the Jewish leaders are worse, and Jesus is greater. Furthermore, it was through the translation process that many fundamental doctrines now held by The Church of Jesus Christ of Latter-day Saints were revealed to the Prophet Joseph. It is therefore a major accomplishment of the Prophet Joseph Smith and a remarkable document of importance to the dispensation of the fulness of times.[9]

NOTES

1. Smith, *History of the Church,* 1:238.
2. Old Testament Manuscript 2, 97; see Scott H. Faulring, Kent P. Jackson, and Robert J. Matthews, eds., *Joseph Smith's New Translation of the Bible: Original Manuscripts* (Provo, Utah: Religious Studies Center, Brigham Young University, 2004), 785.
3. As cited in Matthews, *"A Plainer Translation,"* 40. The original is in the secure vault of the Archives, The Church of Jesus Christ of Latter-day Saints, Salt Lake City, Utah.
4. Smith, *History of the Church,* 1:368–69.
5. Old Testament Manuscript 2, 119; see Faulring, Jackson, and Matthews, *Joseph Smith's New Translation of the Bible,* 851.
6. Cited in Matthews, *"A Plainer Translation,"* 210–13.
7. These lectures, delivered in Kirtland, Ohio, in 1834–1835, were published in every edition of the Doctrine and Covenants from 1835 to 1921.
8. See Faulring, Jackson, and Matthews, *Joseph Smith's New Translation of the Bible.*
9. For further study, see Bible Dictionary, LDS edition of the Bible, s.v. "Joseph Smith Translation," 717; Robert J. Matthews, "Joseph Smith's Efforts to Publish His Bible Translation," *Ensign,* January 1983, 57–64.

CHAPTER NINETEEN

THE VISION: DOCTRINE AND COVENANTS 76

Randy L. Bott

ollowing the mission of Joseph Smith and Sidney Rigdon to counteract growing antagonistic feelings generated by the spread of apostates' lies, there was a short season of relative calm.[1] During this reprieve, Joseph commenced again his work on the Bible translation (D&C 73:3). While engaged in this rather demanding enterprise, he and Sidney experienced one of the most remarkable visions ever recorded by mortal men. During the experience, which lasted over one and a half hours, Joseph and Sidney sat enrapt in a six-part vision that was so illuminating that the Prophet would later say, "Could you gaze into heaven five minutes, you would know more than you would by reading all that ever was written on the subject."[2]

As to the comprehensiveness of the vision recorded in Doctrine and Covenants 76, Joseph said, "I could explain a hundred fold more than I ever have of the glories of the kingdoms manifested to me in the vision, were I permitted, and were the people prepared to receive them."[3] Although we have only a hundredth part of what was seen, what we do have leaves the mind reeling and fires the imagination far beyond any other recorded vision in scripture.

The sequence in which the six visions were recorded starts at the extremes and works toward the middle of the spectrum of eternity. First comes the vision of God and Christ (D&C 76:20–24). The account begins by explaining that the Father and the Son were seen and that Joseph and Sidney "received of his fulness" (D&C 76:20).

Randy L. Bott is a professor of Church history and doctrine at Brigham Young University.

Earlier in the translation of the book of St. John, the Lord informed Joseph of what it meant to receive this blessing: "For in the beginning was the Word, even the Son, who is made flesh, and sent unto us by the will of the Father. And as many as believe on his name shall receive of his fulness. And of his fulness have all we received, even immortality and eternal life, through his grace" (JST John 1:16). So we can rightly expect this vision covered extensively the variety of options available in eternal dwellings for humanity.

After seeing and conversing with the Savior, holy angels, and those who dwell with God eternally, Joseph and Sidney left a final testimony—appended to all those who had so testified before—that Christ is a real, living Being. Then Joseph expanded the scope of Christ's atonement beyond any recorded accounts penned before. The Prophet announced that the Atonement, worked out on this earth, was efficacious on countless other worlds (D&C 76:24).[4]

Immediately following this theophany comes one of the saddest but most illuminating visions given to man—the fall of Lucifer, son of the morning (D&C 76:25–29). Once an angel in authority, this spirit son of God chose to exercise his agency in opposition to God's "great plan of happiness" established for the salvation and exaltation of His spirit children (Alma 42:8–16). Open rebellion in the very presence of God and Christ resulted in his being thrust down to the earth, where he became Perdition, meaning ruined or utterly lost (Revelation 12:7–9). The fact that "the heavens wept over him" indicates that we knew him and loved him before his rebellion and descent.[5]

We learn from this vision that Lucifer's objective was to dethrone God and take over his kingdom (D&C 76:28). For this objective, he was cast out from the presence of God. After having been cast out, Satan was not satisfied with just one-third of God's spirit children (Revelation 12:4–9; D&C 29:36). He sought the misery of all mankind (2 Nephi 2:18, 27). It is instructive to know the intensity and difference between Satan's destructive efforts upon humanity in general contrasted with the Saints of God. In Doctrine and Covenants 29 we learn that "it must needs be that the devil should tempt the children

The Glories of Heaven, *by Gary Ernest Smith*

of men" (D&C 29:39). Section 76, verse 29, chillingly adds that "he [Satan] maketh war with the saints of God, and encompasseth them round about" (see also Revelation 12:17).

The third vision recorded in section 76 (vv. 30–49) continues with the plight of those who are overcome by the deceptive tactics of Satan after having embraced the gospel and having qualified through faithfulness to be called "Saints." Although relatively few, compared to the totality of humanity who have and will ever live, Joseph Smith stated that a terrible fate would be "the case with many apostates of the Church of Jesus Christ of Latter-day Saints."[6]

In addition to the steps recorded in the vision of what a person must do to become a son of perdition, which includes knowing the power of God, being partakers of that power, and then denying and defying God's power, Joseph recorded the following:

> What must a man do to commit the unpardonable sin? He must receive the Holy Ghost, have the heavens opened unto him, and know God, and then sin against Him. After a man has sinned against the Holy Ghost, there is no repentance for him. He has got to say that the sun does not shine while he sees it; he has got to deny Jesus Christ when the heavens have been opened unto him, and to deny the plan of salvation with his eyes open to the truth of it; and from that time he begins to be an enemy.[7]

Thankfully, the power of the adversary is limited to this earth life so that no man can commit the unpardonable sin after death. Joseph said, "I know the Scriptures and understand them. I said, no man can commit the unpardonable sin after the dissolution of the body, nor in this life, until he receives the Holy Ghost; but they must do it in this world."[8] Everyone, excepting the sons of perdition, will be saved in one of the kingdoms of glory. The fate of the sons of perdition, however, is not known to man, although some have seen it, but once seen the vision is "straightway shut . . . up again" (D&C 76:47).[9] Only those consigned to that awful fate will know the extent and intensity of the sufferings of outer darkness or hell forever.

The next vision turns from this darkness to the effulgent light of those who inherit exaltation in the celestial kingdom (D&C 76:50–70). Some have mistakenly assumed that very few will qualify for this supernal glory. God himself outlines the requirements and process for attaining this kingdom. Gratefully, they are within reach of everyone who is willing to comply. The steps include receiving a testimony of Jesus, believing and being baptized in his name by following his divine example, sufficiently keeping his commandments to activate the Atonement in cleansing former sins, receiving the Holy Ghost, and having the necessary faith to have the Holy Spirit seal ordinances and covenants made in the presence of God and his witnesses (D&C 76:51–53; 132:7).

The question is often asked, "Must one be perfect to qualify for the celestial kingdom?" In answer, the Lord revealed, "And they shall overcome all things" (D&C 76:60). The word "shall" describes a future event and leads one to understand that even those in the celestial kingdom are still in the process of perfecting themselves and will continue to do so until they are perfected in Christ. A few mistaken, overzealous Saints have misunderstood the phrase "the church of the Firstborn" as it relates to those who enter celestial glory (D&C 76:54). They do not realize that this means "they who dwell in his presence are the church of the Firstborn; and they see as they are seen, and know as they are known, having received of his fulness and of his grace" (D&C 76:94).

The vision reveals the incomprehensible blessing of celestial glory, that of dwelling in the presence of God and Christ forever (D&C 76:62). Those who may not understand God's grand objective for his children—to receive immortality and eternal lives—may view this doctrine as bordering on blasphemous to think that man could eventually become like God (Moses 1:39). But it is true. God revealed to Joseph and Sidney, "And he makes them equal in power, and in might, and in dominion" (D&C 76:95).

These consoling words prove a comfort to those who have lost loved ones to death. The mourners acknowledge the Lord's promise that their loved ones will rise in the first resurrection and participate in the glorious prophesied events that will accompany the second coming of the Savior before entering their eternal home in the celestial kingdom.[10] Their resurrected bodies will shine like the glory of the sun and have a never-ending eternity of eternal life with God and Christ. Whatever price is required to attain such glory will pale compared to the blessings which will come to the Saints who endure faithfully to the end (D&C 76:70).

When that vision closed, another glorious vision opened to Joseph's and Sidney's view—the terrestrial kingdom (D&C 76:71–80). Although this kingdom's glory exceeds man's ability to comprehend, it pales in comparison to the celestial kingdom, just as the moon's light is dwarfed by the brightness of the sun. Those who merit this kingdom show descriptors which explain elements of a single group rather than a number of separate groups. These are they who die outside the law—"without law"—suggesting that they had the option of embracing the law but would not (D&C 76:72). Included in this group are those who once lived in mortality but did not qualify for paradisiacal rest in the great world of spirits after their death. They did not receive a testimony of Jesus in mortality, suggesting that they had the chance to receive it, but refused. After their death, they did receive a testimony. One of the reasons they may not have received it in the flesh is because they, albeit being "honorable men," were deceived by the craftiness of the ungodly. If we stop at this point, then vicarious work for the dead would be meaningless. However, if we can understand that all of these verses are defining a single group, then the problem is solved as we consider verse 79 of this section. "These are they who are not valiant in the testimony of Jesus; wherefore, they obtain not the crown over the kingdom of our God" (D&C 76:79). They were deceived. Although they accepted the gospel in the spirit world, they still "are not valiant"—hence they do not qualify for celestial glory.

What if they were deceived so as not to receive the fulness of the gospel on the earth but afterwards received it and then are valiant? Would they not qualify for the celestial kingdom? Therefore, all of the vicarious work we do on this earth depends solely upon their accepting and being valiant in their testimony in the world of spirits. Every son or daughter of God from Adam to the last person born during the "little season" following the Millennium will have a full opportunity—either in mortality or in the spirit world—to accept or reject the gospel of Jesus Christ.

This understanding enables Latter-day Saints to see God as a just Being, not favoring one of his children over another because of time or location of birth or opportunities received or denied in the mortal existence. Having proven by right use of agency that they were not willing to abide the law of the celestial kingdom, these good and honorable people will be assigned to the terrestrial kingdom, where they will enjoy the "presence of the Son, but not of the fulness of the Father" (D&C 88:21–22; 76:77). Although they will receive of the glory of Christ, they are denied the fulness, which includes the power of procreation. They will not be allowed to live in a married state but will live "separately and singly" forever and ever (D&C 132:15–17).

Although this sounds like a harsh punishment, in truth it is where they will choose to be. God, who allowed one-third of his spirit children to go to hell forever rather than coerce them into doing something they chose not to do, is not going to reverse himself and force his somewhat faithful children to reside for eternity where they would not be comfortable. In actuality, they would be more miserable dwelling in the presence of God than they would be in their earned kingdom (Mormon 9:4).

With the closing of that vision, yet another glorious vision burst upon Joseph and Sidney. They saw the telestial kingdom.[11] Those in the telestial kingdom received neither the gospel nor the testimony of Jesus. They didn't deny the Holy Ghost—which would have qualified them as sons of perdition—because they never had it. After a mortal life of carnality, sensuality, and living far below their understanding of Divine expectations, these are "thrust down to hell" where they must pay for their own sins, as far as that is possible, because they would not take advantage of the atonement of Christ. They will suffer in hell—that portion of the spirit world where suffering for sins takes place—for the length of the Millennium, through the "little season" following the Millennium, and until the "end of the earth" (D&C 88:100–101). In hell, the devil will rule over them. In the deepest portion of that cursed place, the Spirit of God does not have its mitigating influence (Alma 34:35). After the eternal scales of justice are balanced and they have paid for their sins as far as it is possible, they will be prepared for a kingdom of glory which is far from being a place of punishment. In fact, the Lord revealed, "And thus we saw, in the heavenly vision, the glory of the telestial, which surpasses all understanding; and no man knows it except him to whom God has revealed it" (D&C 76:89–90).

In the telestial kingdom, however, they have limited access to the

Godhead. They can enjoy the presence of the Holy Spirit through the ministration of terrestrial kingdom inhabitants, but "where God and Christ dwell they cannot come, worlds without end" (D&C 76:112). Those who are "liars, and sorcerers, and adulterers, and whore-mongers, and whosoever loves and makes a lie" are heading for the hell part of the spirit world en route to an endless eternity in the telestial kingdom unless they repent (D&C 76:103). Those who, even in the spirit world, will not abandon their false beliefs in man-made churches will likewise forfeit their opportunities for celestial glory (D&C 76:99–102).

It is imperative that all mankind know and understand that they will be judged according to the works done in the flesh, and factored into their final judgment will be the desires of their hearts (D&C 76:111; 137:9). Anyone who has carefully and prayerfully read section 76 is constrained to admit that it came from God. But there is always that nagging desire to know more, to expand our vision, and to enlarge our understanding. Often one wishes that Joseph had been given heavenly permission to reveal more of what was seen in vision.

It is of more than passing interest that the Lord started the vision and ended it with a promise that shifts the burden of increased vision from Joseph and Sidney to each individual. For the Lord said:

> I, the Lord, am merciful and gracious unto those who fear me, and delight to honor those who serve me in righteousness and in truth unto the end.
>
> Great shall be their reward and eternal shall be their glory.
>
> And to them will I reveal all mysteries, yea, all the hidden mysteries of my kingdom from days of old, and for ages to come, will I make known unto them the good pleasure of my will concerning all things pertaining to my kingdom.
>
> Yea, even the wonders of eternity shall they know, and things to come will I show them, even the things of many generations.
>
> And their wisdom shall be great, and their understanding reach to heaven; and before them the wisdom of the wise shall perish, and the understanding of the prudent shall come to naught.
>
> For by my Spirit will I enlighten them, and by my power will I make known unto them the secrets of my will—yea, even those things which

eye has not seen, nor ear heard, nor yet entered into the heart of man. (D&C 76:5–10)

One suspects that many of the "wonders of eternity" were included in the ninety-nine parts of "The Vision" which Joseph Smith and Sidney Rigdon saw but were not authorized to record. So what must one do to qualify to see such a vision? Joseph Smith concluded the section by explaining:

> Great and marvelous are the works of the Lord, and the mysteries of his kingdom which he showed unto us, which surpass all understanding in glory, and in might, and in dominion;
>
> Which he commanded us we should not write while we were yet in the Spirit, and are not lawful for man to utter;
>
> Neither is man capable to make them known, for they are only to be seen and understood by the power of the Holy Spirit, which God bestows on those who love him, and purify themselves before him;
>
> To whom he grants this privilege of seeing and knowing for themselves;
>
> That through the power and manifestation of the Spirit, while in the flesh, they may be able to bear his presence in the world of glory. (D&C 76:114–18)

If we truly love him, we will keep his commandments (John 14:15; D&C 42:29). To purify and sanctify ourselves, we must be willing to yield our hearts unto God (Helaman 3:35). The challenge then becomes a personal one. How much of this world am I willing to give up to enjoy the same visions and revelations experienced by the Prophet Joseph Smith and Sidney Rigdon? The answer to that query and subsequent actions dictates when the eyes of our understanding will be opened and we will see what God has promised.

NOTES

1. From 4 December 1831 until the "8th or 10th of January, 1832," Joseph and Sidney preached in "Shalersville, Ravenna, and other places, setting forth the truth, . . . by which means we did much towards allaying the excited feelings which were growing out of the scandalous letters then being published in the *Ohio Star,* at Ravenna," by apostate Ezra Booth. Smith, *History of the Church,* 1:241; see D&C 71.

2. Smith, *Teachings of the Prophet Joseph Smith,* 324.

3. Smith, *Teachings of the Prophet Joseph Smith,* 305.

4. For example, Elder Bruce R. McConkie wrote of the universal Lordship of

Jesus: "Now our Lord's jurisdiction and power extend far beyond the limits of this one small earth on which we dwell . . . the resurrection is universal in scope. . . . the resurrection applies to and is going on in other worlds and other galaxies." McConkie, *Mormon Doctrine,* 65, 642.

5. "The heavens wept over him" refers to those in the premortal state who followed Christ.

6. Smith, *Teachings of the Prophet Joseph Smith,* 358.

7. Smith, *Teachings of the Prophet Joseph Smith,* 358.

8. Smith, *Teachings of the Prophet Joseph Smith,* 357.

9. See D&C 88:24; see also Smith, *Doctrines of Salvation,* 1:47–49.

10. For a clear statement on appearing with the Savior at his second coming, read D&C 88:96–98.

11. Although the narrative starts in verse 81 and proceeds to almost the end of the section, there are phrases interspersed within the verses that shed additional light on other kingdoms of glory. The careful reader should distinguish when the verse in question refers to the telestial kingdom or a higher kingdom.

CHAPTER TWENTY

HIRAM, OHIO

Milton V. Backman Jr.

he John Johnson home in Hiram, Portage County, Ohio, located about thirty miles southeast of Kirtland, was the home of Joseph Smith for approximately six months, from mid-September 1831 to late March 1832. During that brief period, this frame farmhouse became a temporary headquarters of the Church. Many Latter-day Saints traveled there to meet Joseph, to seek his counsel and attend meetings. At least eight conferences and many other meetings were held in the home. There the Prophet received sixteen revelations which are currently in our Doctrine and Covenants (1; 65; 67–69; 71; 73–74; 76–81; 99; 133).

In 1831, the year that Joseph Smith moved to Hiram, he was extremely busy traveling, teaching, recording revelations, and calling leaders to new positions in the Church. In February, he initiated a gathering to Kirtland. By early summer, most New York converts had moved to northeastern Ohio (D&C 37; 38:31–32). In June, Joseph instructed many of the New York Saints to relocate in western Missouri (D&C 54:8), and then in July, he led a group of missionaries to Independence, Jackson County, Missouri. After identifying Independence as "Zion" and a place of refuge and gathering, he participated in the dedication of a site designated for the building of a temple. From mid-August to early September, Joseph traveled back

Milton V. Backman Jr. is an emeritus professor of Church history and doctrine at Brigham Young University.

The Prophet Joseph Attacked by a Mob, *by Sam Lawlor*

to Ohio, but instead of relocating in Kirtland, he moved with his family to the John Johnson farmhouse in Hiram.[1]

Johnson and his wife, Alice, known as Elsa, became acquainted with Joseph shortly after he moved to northeastern Ohio. After receiving word that a latter-day prophet was teaching about a restored gospel, the Johnsons traveled to Kirtland to investigate. They listened as the Prophet Joseph Smith bore witness of the restoration of the gospel of Jesus Christ, which included the same spiritual gifts that were manifest during the days of the ancient apostles. When Joseph learned that Elsa Johnson had been afflicted for some time with a lame arm, he said, "Woman, in the name of the Lord Jesus Christ I command thee to be whole." Elsa was instantly healed and upon returning home washed her clothes without pain.[2]

One of Joseph Smith's principal activities while living with the Johnsons in Hiram was working with Sidney Rigdon, his scribe, on a new translation of the Bible. Sidney, a former Baptist preacher, followed Joseph to Hiram and lived with his family in a log home near the Johnson's residence. Day after day, these two men met in the Johnson home, and while they pondered and prayed, the Prophet dictated and Sidney wrote. Many of the revelations he received in Hiram were results of questions asked and answers given while these men were engaged in that work.[3]

An important early conference of the restored Church occurred in the Johnson home on 1 and 2 November 1831. The principal subject discussed at this conference was the compilation and publication of the revelations which Joseph had received. He did not record some of the earlier revelations received, but in July 1830, the Lord instructed him to continue "calling upon God in my name, and writing the things which shall be given thee" (D&C 24:5). Joseph immediately began "copying and arranging the revelations received up to that time, evidently with a view to their publication in book form."[4]

Parley P. Pratt, present when Joseph recorded a number of the revelations, recalled that on one occasion a question arose regarding spiritual manifestations, and the problem was presented to the Prophet. Elder Pratt wrote:

> After we had joined in prayer in his translating room, he dictated in our presence the following revelation:—[D&C 50] Each sentence was uttered slowly and very distinctly, and with a pause between each, sufficiently long for it to be recorded, by an ordinary writer, in long hand.
>
> This was the manner in which all his written revelations were dictated and written. There was never any hesitation, reviewing, or reading back, in order to keep the run of the subject; . . . I was present to witness the dictation of several communications of several pages each.[5]

William E. McLellin, another early convert who also witnessed the recording of a number of the revelations, declared:

> I, as scribe, have written revelations from the mouth of [the Prophet]. And I have been present many times when others wrote for Joseph; therefore I speak as one having experience. The scribe seats himself at a desk or table, with pen, ink, and paper. The subject of enquiry being understood, the Prophet and Revelator enquires of God. He spiritually sees, hears, and feels, and then speaks as he is moved upon by the Holy Ghost, the "thus saith the Lord," sentence after sentence, and waits for his amanuenses to write and then read aloud each sentence. Thus they proceed until the revelator says Amen, at the close of what is then communicated. I have known [Joseph], without premeditation, to thus

deliver off in broken sentences, some of the most sublime pieces of composition which I ever perused in any book.[6]

Many revelations were copied by hand and circulated. Because of their importance, the demand for copies increased. Since there was not a compilation of the revelations, many members did not have access to doctrines and policies that were being unfolded. Members also desired a copy of the revelations in an authoritative form. Prior to 1831, thirty-six revelations that are in our current edition of the Doctrine and Covenants had been recorded. In one year alone, 1831, another thirty-seven revelations were received. The combined total prior to 1832 composes half of all the revelations in the Doctrine and Covenants.

Therefore, during the November conference, members of the Church considered publishing more than sixty revelations under the title Book of Commandments. A committee was appointed to draft a preface for this work. After the committee made their report, the conference requested that Joseph enquire of the Lord regarding it. He responded by asking those in attendance to bow in prayer with him. They did and Joseph Smith prayed. According to one account,

> when they arose, Joseph dictated by the Spirit the preface found in the Book of Doctrine and Covenants while sitting by a window of the room [in the John Johnson home in Hiram, Ohio] in which the conference was sitting; and Sidney Rigdon wrote it down. Joseph would deliver a few sentences and Sidney [Rigdon] would write them down, then read them aloud, and if correct, then Joseph [Smith] would proceed and deliver more, and by this process the preface was given.[7]

After the Preface had been received by revelation, William E. McLellin expressed some concern regarding the language of the revelations. Joseph Smith responded to his concern by commenting that William E. McLellin considered himself to be the "wiset man," and McLellin "endeavored to write a commandment like unto one of the least of the Lord's, but failed." He also observed that all who witnessed McLellin's failure in imitating the language of Jesus Christ increased their faith in the truth of the commandments and revelations which the Lord had given to the Church through his instrumentality. Then he added, it was "an awful responsibility to write in the name of the Lord."[8]

After priesthood leaders agreed to print several thousand copies of the revelations, elders agreed to serve as witnesses of this work and provide a written testimony to the world of the Lord's commandments. In their testimony, they declared that the Lord, through the Holy Ghost, had borne record to them "that these commandments were given by inspiration of God, and are profitable for all men, and are verily true."[9]

Before the conference adjourned, Joseph Smith received yet another revelation—section 133 of the Doctrine and Covenants. This section was initially added as an appendix to the Book of Commandments.

Thus, in November 1831, Joseph conducted conferences in the Johnson home, worked on the Inspired Revision of the Bible (which is known in the Church as the Joseph Smith Translation), received at least six revelations, and reviewed the commandments for publication. As editor, he selected about sixty-five revelations for inclusion in the Book of Commandments. These revelations did not include all that he had received prior to November 1831. A few were published in later collections.

In mid-November, Oliver Cowdery and John Whitmer left Hiram, bound for Independence, Missouri, carrying approved copies of the revelations. After their arrival in Independence, with the assistance of William W. Phelps, the revelations were published in a Church periodical, *The Evening and the Morning Star.* Although most revelations in the Book of Commandments were published in the *Star,* just as the publication of the book was nearing completion in July 1833 a mob broke into the Phelps home and destroyed the press. Some copies of the printed revelations were saved and reprinted in a new edition of revelations in Kirtland called the Doctrine and Covenants (1835). The first sixty-four sections of that work nearly parallel chapters in the Book of Commandments.

Meanwhile, Joseph Smith continued to receive revelations and to send revelatory writings to Missouri for publication. The first published account of the Visions of Glories which Joseph received in the John Johnson farmhouse on 16 February 1832 is one example. This series of visions was published in *The Evening and the Morning Star* in the summer of 1832.

PERSECUTION IN HIRAM

Although the new nation was known as a land of liberty, ugly forces of persecution periodically erupted. Joseph Smith fled from serious mob threats in Harmony, Pennsylvania, and across the border in New York. After he moved to Kirtland, threats against Latter-day Saints increased. When he returned to Kirtland following his first journey to Missouri in 1831, he feared that if he again located there he and his family would be attacked. For six months Joseph lived in relative peace in Hiram, Portage County, but tranquillity was erased in March 1832 by the actions of an angry mob.

It is difficult for many today to imagine that mobs would beat and cover with tar and feathers peace-loving citizens and sometimes drive them from their communities or even kill them. Such actions, however, occurred in early nineteenth-century America. In Ohio in the 1830s, for example, abolitionists, considered a threat to the unity of the nation, were beaten and driven from their homes. During an anti-slavery convention in that state in 1836, delegates reported that the previous year abolitionists had been attacked in thirteen Ohio towns and about the same time settlers of Putnam had been attacked and ordered to leave their homes.[10]

Mobs, often under the influence of liquor, were aroused and excited to intolerant actions by vicious articles published in biased newspapers. Abolitionists, Masons, Mormons, Roman Catholics, and Indians became targets of attack and expulsion. Some reporters developed a list of derogatory terms which were applied to several groups, such as the Masons and Mormons. During the years that E. D. Howe was editor of the *Painesville Telegraph,* he published many articles denouncing Mormonism. A few of these articles were republished in newspapers in the Hiram area. Using some of the same terms applied to others, Howe characterized members of the restored Church as "fanatics," "deluded beings," "dregs of this community," "a gang of deluded mortals" and "profound believers in witchcraft, ghosts, [and] goblins." Joseph Smith's family was called a "gang of money diggers." Witnesses to the Book of Mormon were referred to as "pious reprobates" and the revelations of the Prophet as "volumes of . . . trash."[11] On 9 December 1830 the *Ohio Star* in Ravenna, Ohio, reported that Joseph Smith claimed to have been visited three times in a dream by the "spirit of the Almighty," which eventually led to the coming forth of the Book of Mormon.[12] After Joseph moved to Ohio, the *Painesville Telegraph* reported that he moved to Portage County so that he could manufacture additional revelations and remodel the New Testament by pretending to translate it through inspiration from heaven.[13] According to the Prophet, these and similar comments inflamed the minds of many readers, preventing them from gaining a correct understanding of the Restoration.[14]

Opposition to Mormonism in Hiram and vicinity was led by two early converts, Ezra Booth and Symonds Ryder. These men had joined the Church in May 1831, served short-term missions, and left the Church about the same time Joseph moved to Hiram. Without realizing that Joseph dictated revelations to his scribes, Symonds complained that his name was misspelled in one of the revelations. Ironically, his name was spelled differently in other records of that time, including the minute book in the church at Hiram where he served as the minister.

Meanwhile, Ezra Booth, a former Protestant minister who returned to that service, was the first dissident to publish articles against the Church. These articles were circulated locally, throughout northeastern Ohio, and in other parts of the country. Booth did not understand the role of a prophet. Joseph Smith was a man and a prophet. As a man he did not behave as Booth imagined a prophet should conduct himself. For example, Booth wrote that while he traveled west with the Prophet to Missouri, Joseph sat around a campfire and joked with others. Booth did not complain that the jokes themselves were inappropriate but reported that Joseph's behavior showed a lack of "sobriety, prudence, and stability," qualities that should be maintained by anointed prophets. He expressed concern over the authoritative nature of Joseph's calling. The Prophet unfolded revelations specifying that members should receive revelations within the bounds of their callings and that only one person, the head of the Church, had the right to receive revelation for the entire Church. Booth denounced such teachings. Such a practice, he said, would eventually lead men into "a state of servitude" and "despotism" and would result in "unqualified vassalage."[15] Booth also complained about the behavior of missionaries traveling to Missouri and said that some members of the Church were selfish and discontent. He announced that leaders urged others not to contract debts but secured Church property on credit. He also wrote that he was disappointed because during his mission he did not receive the spiritual gifts he had anticipated.

The newspaper publications of Joseph Smith's revelations on the law of consecration and stewardship also led to persecution (D&C 42). The laws were an economic program designed to maintain the capitalistic concept of independent ownership of property with the concept that people share their wealth to help another. They were also designed to help in the financial operations of the Church. For various reasons, including the shortage of members' property, the laws were never fully implemented in Ohio. Only a few leaders participated in the law of consecration and stewardship in Kirtland. In Hiram and vicinity, this economic program was advertised and greatly misunderstood. Some suggested that if they united with the Latter-day Saints, they would lose their farms. The fear of surrendering farms to leaders of the restored Church further ignited the flames of persecution.[16]

After Booth announced that he left the restored Church, in part, because of its authoritarianism, inconsistencies, and imperfections of leaders and members, Joseph Smith asserted that Booth failed to realize that "faith, humility, patience, and tribulation go before blessings and that God brings low before He exalts." Joseph also suggested that Booth's conversion had been based on witnessing a miracle. Joseph taught that faith should not be based on miracles but that miracles follow faith. He quoted the Gospel of John, where Jesus said, "Ye seek me, not because ye saw the miracles, but because ye did eat of the loaves, and were filled" (John 6:26). Joseph explained that Booth became disappointed with the restored gospel and because of his own weaknesses and wickedness wrote letters, which, by their "coloring, falsity, and vain calculations" were designed to overthrow the work of the Lord.[17] He also declared that his scandalous letters were causing others to reject the true light and be filled with "prejudice, blindness and darkness." He realized that these negative attitudes would lead to persecution of members of the Church.[18]

To allay the excited feelings which were developing in Hiram and vicinity, Joseph temporarily discontinued working on the inspired Bible revision, and he and others served short-term missions. For approximately one month, from mid-December 1831 to mid-January 1832, Joseph Smith, Sidney Rigdon, David Whitmer, Reynolds Cahoon, Thomas B. Marsh, and others preached in the area of Portage County, Ohio, responding to charges made by Ezra Booth.[19]

In an attempt to crush the expansion of Mormonism in Portage County, on the night of 24 March 1832 a mob of about fifty men launched an attack. They broke into the cabin where Sidney Rigdon and his family lived. They dragged Rigdon from the home by his heels so that his head was pulled along a rough, frozen field. His head was lacerated. One of the mob returned to Rigdon's home to secure feather pillows and was temporarily locked in a room. When the mobber escaped, he provided the mob with feathers to cover the bodies of Sidney and Joseph. The mob left Rigdon unconscious, his bleeding body covered with tar and feathers. When Joseph visited him the next day, Rigdon was delirious and his head highly inflamed. For many years, he suffered difficulties as a consequence of the mob actions that night.[20]

While Sidney Ridgon was lying unconscious, mobbers broke into the John Johnson farmhouse where Joseph, Emma, and their adopted twins were living. On the night of 24 March, the twins, Joseph and Julia, were sick. For some time they had been afflicted with measles, and on that fateful night, Joseph suggested that Emma retire with Julia and he would care for young Joseph. As the night hours waned, Emma suggested that Joseph lay down on the trundle bed. He did so until being awakened by Emma screaming, "Murder."

Joseph recalled:

> I found myself going out of the door, in the hands of about a dozen men; some of whose hands were in my hair, and some had hold of my shirt, drawers and limbs. . . .
>
> . . . they passed along with me, about thirty rods from the house, I saw Elder Rigdon stretched out on the ground, whither they had dragged him by his heels. I supposed he was dead. I began to plead with them, saying, "You will have mercy and spare my life, I hope." To which they replied, "G—d—ye, call on yer God for help, we'll show ye no mercy;" and the people began to show themselves in every direction; one coming from the orchard had a plank; and I expected they would kill me, and carry me off on the plank. . . . They held a council, and as I could occasionally overhear a word, I supposed it was to know whether or not it was best to kill me. They returned after a while, when I learned that they had concluded not to kill me, but to beat and scratch me well, tear off my shirt and drawers, and leave me naked. One cried, "Simonds, Simonds, where's the tar bucket?" "I don't know," answered one, "where 'tis, Eli's left it." They ran back and fetched the bucket of tar, when one exclaimed, with an oath, "Let us tar up his mouth"; and they tried to force the tar-paddle into my mouth; I twisted my head around, so that they could not; and they cried out, "G—d—ye, hold up yer head and let us giv ye some tar." They then tried to force a vial into my mouth, and broke it in my teeth. All my clothes were torn off me except my shirt collar; and one man fell on me and scratched my body with his nails like a mad cat, and then muttered out: "G—d—ye, that's the way the Holy Ghost falls on folks!"
>
> They then left me, and I attempted to rise, but fell again; I pulled the tar away from my lips, so that I could breathe more freely, and after a while I began to recover, and raised myself up, whereupon I saw two lights. I made my way towards one of them, and found it was Father Johnson's. When I came to the door I was naked, and the tar made me look as if I were covered with blood, and when my wife saw me she thought I was all crushed to pieces, and fainted. During the affray abroad, the sisters of the neighborhood had collected at my room. I called for a blanket, they threw me one and shut the door; I wrapped it around me and went in. . . . My friends spent the night in scraping and

removing the tar, and washing and cleansing my body; so that by morning I was ready to be clothed again. This being the Sabbath morning, the
people assembled for meeting at the usual hour of worship, and among
them came also the mobbers. . . . With my flesh all scarified and defaced,
I preached to the congregation as usual, and in the afternoon of the same
day baptized three individuals.[21]

During the mobbing on the 24th, one of the twins, Joseph Smith
Murdock, contracted a severe cold, which grew worse. On March 29
the eleven-month-old adopted son of Joseph and Emma died. Joseph's
son was one of the first to die as a result of the persecution of the
Latter-day Saints.

Mobs continued to molest and menace Father Johnson's house for
a long time.[22] Joseph was afraid to go immediately to Kirtland because
the spirit of mobocracy was prevalent there also. Subsequently, he
traveled to Missouri in April 1832 to instruct the Saints.[23] While he
was on this journey, his family and the family of Sidney Rigdon
returned to Kirtland. Although Joseph returned briefly to Hiram to
visit the Johnson family, following his second journey to Missouri, he
relocated in Kirtland. From the summer of 1832 to early 1838,
Kirtland served as the headquarters of the Church.

NOTES

1. For a discussion of the "Gathering to Ohio," see Backman, *Heavens Resound,* chapter 3.
2. Backman, *Heavens Resound,* 83; see Smith, *History of the Church,* 1:215–16; Philo Dibble, "Early Scenes in Church History,"in *Four Faith-Promoting Classics,* 79; George A. Smith, *Journal of Discourses,* 11:4–5.
3. See Matthews, *"A Plainer Translation,"* 32–36.
4. Backman and Cowan, *Joseph Smith and the Doctrine and Covenants,* 1.
5. Pratt, *Autobiography of Parley P. Pratt,* 48.
6. "The Ensign of Liberty of the Church of Christ . . . Kirtland, Lake County, Ohio," 1 (January 1848): 98–99, cited in Backman and Cowan, *Joseph Smith and the Doctrine and Covenants,* 1–2.
7. William Kelley letter dated January 16, 1882 in *Saints' Herald* 29 (1882), 67, cited in Backman and Cowan, *Joseph Smith and the Doctrine and Covenants,* 2.
8. Smith, *History of the Church,* 1:226.
9. Smith, *History of the Church,* 1:226.
10. Backman, *Heavens Resound,* 332–33.

11. Backman, *Heavens Resound,* 53–54.

12. Backman, *Heavens Resound,* 55.

13. Backman, *Heavens Resound,* 57–58.

14. Smith, *History of the Church,* 1:158.

15. Backman, *Heavens Resound,* 95.

16. Backman, *Heavens Resound,* 93.

17. Smith, *History of the Church,* 1:216–17.

18. Smith, *History of the Church,* 1:241; see Backman, *Heavens Resound,* 97.

19. Backman, *Heavens Resound,* 96–97.

20. Smith, *History of the Church,* 1:265.

21. Smith, *History of the Church,* 1:261–64.

22. Smith, *History of the Church,* 1:265.

23. Smith, *History of the Church,* 1:265–66.

MOBOCRACY IN JACKSON COUNTY

Andrew H. Hedges

*T*he Saints' efforts to settle in Jackson County, Missouri, begun with such optimism in the summer of 1831, quickly met with opposition from the Missourians already living there. Mormon settlers were the targets of petty acts of violence as early as the spring of 1832, and by the summer of 1833 antagonism against the Saints had taken the form of a mob bent on driving them from the county. Efforts to defend their rights through peaceful means only infuriated the Missourians further. Launching a fresh attack on the night of 31 October, the mob began driving the Saints from their homes and farms. The Mormons' weak attempts at defense proved useless, and by the middle of November the Jackson County Saints were no more. Zion had lasted just over two years.

The Missourians' animosity against the Mormons was rooted in a variety of factors. Perhaps most fundamental was the difference in ideology between the two groups. A slave state, Missouri as a whole took its cues from the South; most of her early settlers were southerners, and her political and economic sensibilities were clearly oriented toward the South both before and after obtaining statehood in 1821. Western Missouri, in addition, and specifically Jackson County, was *the* frontier of the United States in the early 1830s. Independence, the county's principal town and designated "center place" for Zion (D&C 57:3), was only four years old when the Mormons began arriving in 1831. More of an outfitting post for traders

Andrew H. Hedges is an associate professor of Church history and doctrine at Brigham Young University.

and trappers heading to Santa Fe and the Rocky Mountains than a town, Independence quickly became notorious as "a godless place, filled with . . . profane swearers, . . . suspicious characters," taverns, brothels, and other "centers of sin."[1] The Mormon settlers, of course, had a completely different orientation and world view. Hailing largely from the anti-slavery Northeast and Puritan New England and looking for a place to raise families and worship their God, they were a poor fit for Missouri in general and Jackson County society in particular.

Many Missourians also took exception to the Mormon's religious beliefs. Although considered by more genteel easterners to be "a sad lot of churchmen, untrained, uncouth, [and] given to imbibing spiritous liquors,"[2] the "Universalists, . . . Deists, Presbyterians, Methodists, Baptists, and other professed Christians"[3] in the West were nevertheless devout enough in their own faiths to be offended by the Saints' strange new doctrines about revelation, healing the sick, and speaking in tongues.[4] It is a telling point that many of the most notable and influential of the mob leaders, in fact, were ministers of other faiths.[5]

Missourians of all persuasions found other beliefs and practices of the Saints even more immediately sinister than a belief in miracles or direct revelation. Several reported being told by members of the Church that the Missourians of Jackson County were "to be cut off, and [their] lands appropriated by them for their inheritances"[6]—an indiscretion which, if true, represents a serious act of disobedience on the part of the Saints, who had been warned of the Lord against doing that very type of thing (D&C 45:72). Misreading an article in *The Evening and the Morning Star* (the Church's newspaper),[7] the edgy Missourians became convinced that "one of the means resorted to by them [the Mormons], in order to drive us to emigrate, is an indirect invitation to the free brethren of color in Illinois, to come up like the rest, to the land of Zion."[8] The Saints' alleged plan, conceded the Missourians, was "one of the surest means of driving us from the country" the Mormons could have devised, "for it would require none of the supernatural gifts that they pretend to, to see that the introduction of such a caste amongst us would corrupt our blacks,

Saints Driven from Jackson County, Missouri, *by C. C. A. Christensen.*
© *Intellectual Reserve, Inc. Courtesy BYU Museum of Art*

and instigate them to bloodshed."[9] The Saints hotly denied all such accusations but to no avail.[10]

These differences in ideology, orientation, and religion probably would not have appeared so acute to the Missourians had the Saints' population in Missouri not grown at such an alarming rate. Joseph's revelations had cautioned the Church against settling the area too quickly and stipulated that for the first several years at least, only those Saints who were specifically appointed by Church leaders to do so should make the move (D&C 58:44, 46, 55–56). Many Saints, however, rejected this counsel. Noting that "between three & four hundred" people had arrived in Jackson County by July 1832, Church leaders there advised members in the East to "come not up to Zion, until preparations can be made for them," and reminded them about the policy of receiving an official appointment to make the move.[11] By November, however, another three to four hundred had made the journey—apparently on their own recognizance—bringing the total number of Saints in the county to 810—an eightfold increase over the number of Church members there the previous November.[12] The exponential growth was not lost on the resident Missourians, who were quick to note the following summer, after yet another season of unabated immigration into Jackson County, how the "two or three" Mormons who had "made their appearance on the Upper Missouri" in 1831 had swelled to "some twelve hundred souls in this county," and how "each successive autumn and spring pours forth its swarms among us." Trembling to think on the "fate of [their] lives and property" in the hands of such deluded "jurors and witnesses" and realizing that if the Mormon population continued to grow, the "day is not far distant when the civil government of the county will be in [the Mormons'] hands; when the sheriff, the justices, and the county judges will be Mormons, or persons wishing to court their favor," the Missourians decided to take decisive action in the summer of 1833.[13]

Indeed, a few of the old settlers had violently expressed their disdain for the Saints a year earlier, stoning some homes belonging to members of the Church, shooting into others, and burning a stack of the Mormons' hay.[14] More irritating than destructive, these somewhat random, disjointed acts of violence in 1832 were followed by a far more organized response to the perceived Mormon threat in April 1833, when some three hundred Missourians met in Independence with the sole purpose of devising a plan that would eliminate the Church from Jackson County.[15] Following this first meeting, which reportedly ended in a drunken brawl without having decided anything, non-Mormon citizens of the county drew up the so-called "Manifesto of the Mob," a lengthy document wherein the Missourians—including several county officials and officers of the law—spelled out their grievances against the Saints, "pledge[d] to each other" to "use such means as may be sufficient" to remove the Mormons from the county and agreed to meet at the Independence courthouse the next Saturday, 20 July, "to consult on subsequent movements."[16]

"Between four and five hundred persons" from every part of the county attended this next meeting.[17] After unanimously resolving that "no Mormon shall in future move and settle in this county"; that those who were already in the county "give a definite pledge of their

intention, within a reasonable time to remove out of the county"; that
the Church printing office—run by W. W. Phelps—"forthwith . . . dis-
continue the business of printing in this county"; and that "all other
stores and shops belonging to the sect"—specifically, the Church
store run by Algernon Sidney Gilbert—immediately close their doors
to business, the meeting adjourned for two hours while a committee
of twelve men informed W. W. Phelps, Bishop Edward Partridge,
Algernon Sidney Gilbert, and a few others of its decisions.[18] "We asked
for three months for consideration," Partridge and others later wrote.
"They would not grant it—We asked for ten days—They would not
grant it but said fifteen minutes was the longest, and refused to hear
any reasons."[19] Reporting the Church leaders' response as "unreasonable," the reconvened meeting "unanimously resolved" to destroy the
Church printing office and take possession of the press.[20]

True to its word, "four or five hundred persons, as a *Mob*" immediately swarmed the two-story brick printing office, which also served
as a home for the family of W. W. Phelps. Driving the Phelps family
members, including a sick infant, out of the lower story and throwing
the press from the upper, the mob razed the building and destroyed
what it could of the unbound sheets of the Book of Commandments
then at press. Algernon Sidney Gilbert's willingness to immediately
close the Church store saved that building from a similar fate.
Turning its wrath on the Mormons themselves, mob members then
took Edward Partridge from his home, escorted him a half mile to the
public square near the courthouse, and tarred and feathered him.[21]
Charles Allen, another Church member, was similarly served; others
who had been taken by the mob for a similar purpose only managed
to escape "through the over anxiety of their keepers, who wished to
have sport of seeing those who were being tarred."[22] Lilburn W. Boggs,
Jackson County resident and lieutenant governor of Missouri, calmly
witnessed much of the day's excitement.[23]

Reporting in its minutes of the day's activities that the resolution
to destroy the Church's printing office "was, with the utmost order,
and the least noise and disturbance possible, forthwith carried into
execution, as also some other steps of a similar tendency," the

citizens' meeting adjourned for three days.[24] Early in the morning of 23 July, according to the previous appointment, an estimated five hundred men again assembled—bearing a red flag and armed with everything from rifles to whips—and began accosting Church members. Threatened with from fifty to five hundred lashes apiece, as well as with the destruction of their homes and crops, several Church leaders at this point "offered themselves a ransom for the church, willing to be scourged or die, if that would appease their anger toward the church."[25] The mob, intent on ridding the county of its Mormon inhabitants, rejected the proposal and renewed its threats against the Saints at large. In what was clearly more of an effort to buy time than a capitulation to the demands of the mob, Church leaders then entered into a written agreement with a mob committee stipulating the timing and conditions of the Saints' removal from the area: leaders, their families, and roughly one-half of the Church members then in the county would leave by 1 January 1834, to be followed by everyone else by 1 April.[26]

Secure, for the time being, in their lives and possessions, the Jackson County Saints immediately began looking for ways to defend themselves against the mob and retain their property. Oliver Cowdery was sent to Ohio to confer with Joseph Smith on the matter, while W. W. Phelps and Orson Hyde hand-delivered a petition for help to Daniel Dunklin, governor of Missouri.[27] Dunklin only recommended that Church members appeal to the courts for help and redress, in spite of the fact that many of Jackson County's legal officers had been members of the mob.[28] Attempting to follow the governor's instructions, the Saints, at the end of October, hired four lawyers from Clay County to represent them and publicly announced their intention to defend their lands and homes.[29]

Until now, the Missourians had apparently been under the impression that the Mormons were planning to honor the terms of the agreement they had been forced to sign in July. Realizing by the end of October that this was not the case, the mob reconvened and, on the night of 31 October, began driving the Saints from their homes. Attacking the Whitmer Settlement near the Big Blue River that first night, mob members partially destroyed several homes and whipped a number of men. Another small settlement outside Independence was attacked the following night, as well as several homes and the Church store in town. Leaving their homes to the mob, Saints living in Independence proper relocated together for their mutual defense, a short distance outside of town on 2 November; that night, in the meantime, a young Missourian was shot in the thigh during another attack on Saints living near the Big Blue. News of the wounded Missourian quickly spread throughout the county, in retaliation for which the mob planned an intensified campaign against the Saints on the 4th.[30]

Church members, taking advantage of the reprieve on 3 November, attempted to enlist the help of several peace officers, but to no avail. Monday morning, 4 November, found the mob back near the Big Blue and at least two small bands of Saints armed for defense. One of these, a group of thirty—only half of whom had guns—came across a group of some forty or fifty of the mob in the process of threatening Mormon women and children. A small firefight erupted, in which two Missourians were killed and several on both sides were wounded. One Mormon, Andrew Barber, died of his wounds early the next morning.[31]

Like the wounding of the young Missourian earlier, this show of resistance on the part of the Saints served more as a rallying cry than as a deterrent for the mob, which, on 5 November, began to organize under the auspices of the Jackson County militia. Their commanding officer, Colonel Thomas Pitcher, pledging both the honor and author-ity of the state, demanded the Saints hand over those who had been involved in the deadly battle the day previous, as well as surrender their guns.[32] The men involved in the earlier battle gave themselves up, while Lyman Wight, veteran of the War of 1812 and ad hoc leader of the Mormon resistance, agreed to hand over their guns but only on condition that Pitcher require the same of the militia—many of whom were erstwhile members of the mob. The colonel, according to Wight, "cheerfully agreed" to the proposition, at which point the Saints delivered forty-nine guns and a pistol into his custody and "returned home, resting assured on their honor, that we would not be farther molested." The militia-mob, however, retained its weapons, and the following day went "from house to house in gangs of from sixty to seventy in number, threatening the lives of women and children, if they did not leave forthwith."[33]

Unarmed and defenseless, and smarting from Pitcher's duplicity, the Saints had little choice but to flee—some under frightening circumstances. Pursued, fired upon, and whipped if they were captured, many Mormon men had to abandon their families for safety, leaving them to the mercy of the mob and the elements.[34] Neither was very kind; Lyman Wight, for example, recalled seeing a group of 190 women and children "driven thirty miles across the prairie" and found it easy to "follow on their trail by the *blood that flowed from their lacerated feet!!* on the stubble of the burnt prairie."[35] Parley P. Pratt recalled a similar group of 150 women and children who wandered about on the prairie "for several days, mostly without food; and nothing but the open firmament for shelter." Rain, sleet, and cold dogged the Saints in their flight, which for most was in the direction of the Missouri River. By 7 November, hundreds began arriving at the south bank of the river, to the point where, Parley P. Pratt recalled, the river bottoms "had much the appearance of a camp meeting."[36]

> Hundreds of people were seen in every direction, some in tents and some in the open air around their fires, while the rain descended in torrents. Husbands were inquiring for their wives, wives for their husbands; parents for children, and children for parents. Some had the good fortune to escape with their families, household goods, and some provisions; while others knew not the fate of their friends, and had lost all their goods. The scene was indescribable.[37]

More arrived the following day, which was spent erecting small, temporary cabins for the refugees. Through it all, the ferry was "constantly employed," shuttling Saints over the river to the relative safety of Clay County. Clearing weather made life easier for those waiting their turn, and within a matter of days the more part of the LDS population in Jackson County—some 1,200 men, women, and children—had made their way over the Missouri River.[38] The Church's effort to establish Zion in Jackson County, at least for the time being, was over.

Joseph Smith was not present during the Jackson County persecutions. He had, in the summer of 1831, helped settle the first Saints in the area and had visited them again in April 1832, but his permanent home during this period was in Kirtland, Ohio. It is clear from his revelations and correspondence, however, that Zion and the Missouri Saints were very much on his mind and that he was closely watching everything that transpired with them. It is clear, too, that he faulted the Saints for their part in the developing problems in the area. In November of 1832, having been informed that many of the Saints who had moved to Missouri that summer had done so without the proper authorization and were not living the law of consecration like they were supposed to (D&C 58:35–36), Joseph wrote to W. W. Phelps that such should be excommunicated from the Church.[39] Few, if any, such excommunications actually took place—in part, possibly, because several Church leaders in Missouri soon became highly critical of the Prophet. Having received several letters of a critical nature, Joseph wrote to Missouri Church leaders in January 1833, informing them that their attitude was "wasting the strength of Zion like a pestilence" and warning them that "if it is not detected and driven from you, it will ripen Zion for the threatened judgments of God." "This from your brother who trembles for Zion," Joseph's letter concluded, "and for the wrath of heaven, which awaits her if she repent not."[40]

Church leaders in Jackson County heeded the warning to a degree (D&C 90:34), but it was not enough. Learning of the destruction of the printing house and the mob violence in July 1833, Joseph wrote to Missouri resident Vienna Jacques in September 1833 that he was "not at all astonished at what has happened to you, neither to what has happened to Zion, and I could tell the whys and wherefores of all these calamities. But alas, it is in vain to warn and give precepts, for all men are naturally disposed to walk in their own paths."[41] And later that year, in December, having learned that the Saints had, in fact, been driven out of the county, he could only sadly conclude that the disobedience on the part of some had resulted in the affliction of all.[42] Zion, for Joseph, was something the Saints had lost, at least for the time being, not something that had been taken from them.

NOTES

1. T. Edgar Lyon, "Independence, Missouri, and the Mormons, 1827–1833," *BYU Studies* 13, no. 1 (1972): 16.
2. Lyon, "Independence, Missouri," 16.
3. Smith, *History of the Church*, 1:182.
4. See Smith, *History of the Church*, 1:375–76, 397.
5. Smith, *History of the Church*, 1:392.
6. Smith, *History of the Church*, 1:396.
7. See "Free People of Color," *Evening and the Morning Star* 2, no. 14 (July 1833): 109.
8. Smith, *History of the Church*, 1:397.
9. Smith, *History of the Church*, 1:375.
10. See Smith, *History of the Church*, 1:379.
11. "The Elders in the Land of Zion to The Church of Christ Scattered Abroad," *Evening and the Morning Star* 1, no. 2 (July 1832).
12. "The Gathering," *Evening and the Morning Star* 1, no. 6 (November 1832).
13. Smith, *History of the Church*, 1:396–97.
14. See "To His Excellency, Daniel Dunklin, Governor of the State of Missouri," *Evening and the Morning Star* 2, no. 15 (December 1833): 114.
15. See Smith, *History of the Church*, 1:342.
16. Smith, *History of the Church*, 1:374–76.
17. Smith, *History of the Church*, 1:395.
18. Smith, *History of the Church*, 1:398–99.
19. "To His Excellency, Daniel Dunklin," 114.
20. Smith, *History of the Church*, 1:399.
21. "To His Excellency, Daniel Dunklin," 114.
22. *Times and Seasons* 1, no. 2 (December 1839): 18.
23. See Smith, *History of the Church*, 1:391–92.
24. Smith, *History of the Church*, 1:399.
25. "To His Excellency, Daniel Dunklin," 114. Those who offered their lives were John Corrill, John Whitmer, W. W. Phelps, Algernon Sidney Gilbert, Edward Partridge, and Isaac Morley.
26. See "To His Excellency, Daniel Dunklin," 115.
27. See Smith, *History of the Church*, 1:410.
28. See "To His Excellency, Daniel Dunklin," 115.
29. See Smith, *History of the Church*, 1:424–25; Roberts, *Missouri Persecutions*, 77.
30. See Smith, *History of the Church*, 1:426–29.
31. See Smith, *History of the Church*, 1:429–31.

32. See Smith, *History of the Church,* 1:432–34.

33. The men who turned themselves in were released after a day; see Smith, *History of the Church,* 1:435–36. For the surrender of the Mormons' guns and subsequent action, see "Trial of Joseph Smith," *Times and Seasons* 4, no. 17 (15 July 1843): 263, and Roberts, *Missouri Persecutions,* 87. Quotations are from *Times and Seasons.*

34. See Pratt, *Autobiography of Parley P. Pratt,* 82.

35. "Trial of Joseph Smith," 264.

36. Pratt, *Autobiography of Parley P. Pratt,* 82.

37. Pratt, *Autobiography of Parley P. Pratt,* 82.

38. Pratt, *Autobiography of Parley P. Pratt,* 82–83.

39. Smith, *History of the Church,* 1:297–99; see also D&C 85:3–5.

40. See Smith, *History of the Church,* 1:317.

41. Smith, *History of the Church,* 1:408.

42. See Smith, *History of the Church,* 1:454.

CHAPTER TWENTY-TWO

ZION'S CAMP

Craig J. Ostler

In the fall of 1833 mobs mercilessly drove members of the Church from their properties in Jackson County, Missouri, which the Lord had designated as the center place of a latter-day Zion. These exiles crossed the Missouri River to the north in Clay County. In 1834 the Lord called upon the Prophet Joseph Smith to lead an expedition of Saints known as Zion's Camp, to help restore the Missouri Saints' property and to protect them from further attacks in occupying their homes and places of business (D&C 103). The Prophet's involvement in Zion's Camp might best be understood as a three-act play. First to be considered is the Prophet's preparation and travels to recruit brethren to journey with him on the trek to Missouri. Second is the actual expedition with those who volunteered to redeem Zion, and last are the outcomes of the experience.

PREPARATION AND RECRUITING
FOR ZION'S CAMP

It was with great difficulty that the Prophet Joseph Smith was able to fulfill the Lord's command to lead Zion's Camp. When the Lord gave the revelation to aid the Saints in Missouri on 24 February 1834, Joseph had reason to remain behind in Kirtland. First, he was busily engaged in directing the building of the Kirtland Temple. In addition, the theft and destruction of the Saints' property in Missouri

---

Craig J. Ostler is an associate professor of Church history and doctrine at Brigham Young University.

added to a financial crisis for Joseph as president of the Church. He had secured loans with creditors in New York City to stock Church-owned mercantile and printing businesses. With the loss of William W. Phelps's printing press and Sidney Gilbert's store, both income-producing properties in Missouri, Joseph needed to assure his creditors that their notes would be paid. Further, he was involved in a lawsuit with an adulterous apostate, Philastus Hurlburt, who sought to obtain Church-owned properties in Ohio and threatened him with physical harm.

Joseph felt that he could not leave Ohio until the problems associated with debts and lawsuits were resolved. However, he also realized that "if I do not go [to Missouri], it will be impossible to get my brethren in Kirtland, any of them, to go."[1] Thus, the success of Zion's Camp was connected to resolving the problems with Joseph's creditors and enemies. The way for the Prophet to direct his full attention to Zion's Camp was ultimately opened for him. He called Oliver Cowdery and Sidney Rigdon to oversee the work of the temple. The Lord promised to soften the hearts of the creditors in New York City (D&C 104:78–86) and eventually, legal relief was obtained when the courts ruled against Hurlburt. With these hindrances removed Joseph was free to travel among the branches of the Church to recruit members for the camp.

On 26 February 1834 he recorded, "I started from home to obtain volunteers for Zion."[2] For a little over one month, Joseph traveled through northeastern Ohio, western Pennsylvania, and New York, traversing approximately 550 miles—no small task in itself. In May the Prophet, and a few more than one hundred men, most of them young, gathered to march to Missouri. "On Sunday, May 4th," recorded George A. Smith, a camp participant,

> the Prophet Joseph preached to the Saints in Kirtland under the shade of the new school house, which was partially enclosed, many of those who were to form the "Camp of Zion" being present. . . . He bore testimony of the truth of the work which God had revealed through him, and promised the brethren that if they all should live as they should before the Lord, keeping his commandments, and not like the children of Israel,

Joseph Helps Pull a Wagon Out of the Swamps, *by Clark Kelley Price*

murmur against the Lord and his servants, they should all safely return and not one of them should fall upon the mission they were about to undertake, for if they were united and exercised faith, God would deliver them out of the hands of their enemies, but should they, like the Children of Israel, forget God and His promises and treat lightly His commandments, He would visit them in His wrath, and vex them in his sore displeasure.[3]

This set the tone for the camp and set it apart from other groups that might be traveling the same roads. The most important path that the camp members were to travel was not really the dusty or muddy trails but the path of righteousness.

THE JOURNEY TO JACKSON COUNTY, MISSOURI

During the initial journey and the return trip, Joseph traveled over two thousand miles and was absent from home for just four days shy of three months. This gave the Prophet time to instruct and be with the brethren in intimate circumstances and day-to-day events while away from their homes and familiar surroundings. Also noteworthy is that he was part of every experience, not an aloof observer of events but rather a primary participant. Much has been made by chroniclers of Zion's Camp regarding the mud, the heat, wigglers in the drinking water, etc., along the way and the trial of faith that Zion's Camp provided for those that were being forged into future leaders of the Church. One should not forget that Joseph walked the same muddy paths, trudged in the same heat, and had to strain the same water of wigglers. Indeed, on one occasion "the Prophet discovered that a part of his mess had been served with sour bread, while he had received good sweet bread from the same cook, whom he reproved for this partiality, saying, he wanted his brethren to fare as well as he did, and preferred to eat his portion of sour bread with them."[4] On another occasion Joseph and those in his tent were willing to eat mush and honey, while the rest of the camp feasted on hams procured earlier that day.[5] Thus, we must suppose that, like the other participants, Joseph also learned from the small things, such as sharing water, helping carry another's load, and always serving as a witness for God. Regarding the daily events of the journey, Joseph reported, "Every night before retiring to rest, at the sound of the trumpet, we bowed before the Lord in the several tents, and presented our thank-offerings with prayer and supplication; and at the sound of the morning trumpet every man was again on his knees before the Lord, imploring His blessing for the day."[6]

Although Joseph had taken two previous journeys to Jackson County, Missouri, one in the summer of 1831 and the other in the spring of 1832, he had never traveled leading such a large group. Further, on the earlier journeys Joseph traveled on the Ohio and Missouri Rivers. Members of Zion's Camp primarily walked the distance on foot next to the wagons, which were loaded with supplies to aid the desperate, exiled Saints. In a letter to his wife, Emma, written on 4 June 1834 on the banks of the Mississippi River, Joseph reported, "I have been able to endur[e] the fatigue of the journey far beyond my most sanguine expectations, except have been troubled some with lameness, have had my feet blistered, but are now well, and have also had a little touch of my side complaint."[7] In addition to the personal challenges of the journey's rigors, Joseph also had responsibility for the welfare of the camp members. The Lord revealed that he was to lead the company "like as Moses led the children of Israel" (D&C 103:16). For good order and safety, he organized the camp into companies of twelve, which included "two cooks, two firemen, two tent men, two watermen, one runner, two wagoners and horsemen, and one commissary."[8]

The unique circumstances of Zion's Camp afforded Joseph opportunities to give instructions on a variety of intriguing topics and to clarify earlier revelations. A few of those lessons have been preserved. Sadly, the journal of camp historian, Frederick G. Williams, was lost. However, Joseph's young cousin, George A. Smith, recorded many of the Prophet's singular teachings and insights. Towards the end of the second week of travel, shortly after the camp passed Springfield, Ohio, George noted,

> I got into the wagon to ride a short distance with Presidents Joseph and Hyrum Smith and Brother Ezra Thayer. We were traveling through a thicket of small timber of recent growth. Brother Joseph said, "I feel very much depressed in spirits; there has been a great deal of bloodshed here at some time. When a man of God passes through a place where much blood has been shed he will feel depressed in spirits and feel lonesome and uncomfortable." We soon came out of the timber where a large farm had been cleared and to the left of the road was a mound 60 feet high occupying about an acre of ground set all over with apple trees which were growing in a very thrifty manner. We went to that mound and found that holes had been dug in it which disclosed the fact that it was filled with human bones.[9]

Thus, Joseph exhibited spiritual sensitivity and received revelation along the way regarding unique items of concern as well as teaching those who traveled with him.

Another item of interesting discussion was the interaction with wildlife, in particular poisonous snakes. "In pitching our tent," recorded George A. Smith,

> we found three prairie rattlesnakes on the ground and were about to kill them. Brother Joseph prevented us, saying, "When will the lion lie down with the lamb and the venom of the serpent cease, while man seeks to destroy and waste the flesh of beasts, waging a continual war against reptiles. Let man first get rid of his destructive propensities and then we may look for a change in the serpent's disposition." We then carried the snakes across the creek on sticks.[10]

Speaking of this same incident, the Prophet Joseph Smith explained further that he "exhorted the brethren not to kill a serpent, bird, or an animal of any kind during our journey unless it became necessary in order to preserve ourselves from hunger."[11] During the return journey to Ohio, Joseph further instructed those with him on the use of meat during times of summer, addressed previously in the revelation known as the Word of Wisdom. He directed them to obtain as much dried cod as they could. "He said fish was much healthier for us to eat than meat, and the use of fish in warm weather was not prohibited in the Word of Wisdom."[12]

On another occasion,

> Martin Harris, who had boasted to the brethren that he could handle snakes with perfect safety, was, while fooling with a blacksnake with his bare feet, bitten on his left foot. The circumstance was communicated to Joseph, and he took occasion to reprove Martin and to exhort the brethren never to trifle with the promises of God. That it was presumption for any man to provoke a serpent to bite him, but if a man of God was accidentally bitten by a poisonous serpent, he might have faith, or his brethren have faith for him, so that the Lord would hear his prayer and he be healed. But when a man designedly provoked a serpent to bite him, the principle was the same as when a man drinks deadly poison knowing it to be such; in that case no man had any claim on the promises of God to be healed.[13]

Perhaps the greatest challenges of the journey were those in which Joseph dealt with the murmurings and complaints of a few of the camp members. The Prophet showed forth meekness and courage in resolving problems and rebuking the offenders. For example, after an exceptionally long and hot day, several members of the camp became upset about the barking of a large watchdog that eighty-year-old Brother Samuel Baker had given to the Prophet:

> [the dog] enraged Sylvester Smith to that extent that he used much abusive language to Joseph, threatening the dog's life. . . . Joseph quoting the proverb that "A soft answer turneth away wrath," said, "I will give you a specimen of the spirit that is manifesting itself in our Camp. If a dog bites me I will kill him—if any man insults me, I will kill him—if any man injures me I will injure him, and this spirit keeps up division and bloodshed throughout the world."[14]

Two weeks previous, after a day's march of forty miles,

> a difficulty [had arisen] between Sylvester Smith and some of the brethren which Joseph was called upon to decide. Sylvester manifested a rebellious spirit, which to some extent was participated in by others. Joseph told them they would meet misfortunes, difficulties and hindrances as the certain result of giving way to such a spirit and said, "You will know it before you leave this place." He exhorted them to humble themselves before the Lord and become united, that they might not be scourged.[15]

As camp members arose the next morning, they discovered that their horses were so badly foundered that they could scarcely lead them to water, a vivid lesson of the effects of discord in the camp. It is apparent that Joseph knew that the power to redeem Zion would come from God and not from the strength of man. The classroom to teach this lesson was the route of the nearly thousand-mile journey of Zion's Camp.

Joseph journeyed with sure confidence that heavenly beings accompanied his band of Saints. Before the expedition began, the Lord promised, "Mine angels shall go up before you" (D&C 103:20). Parley P. Pratt related to Joseph an occasion in which, while dozing off to sleep in exhaustion, he heard a distinct voice say, *"Parley, it is time to be up and on your journey."* Joseph "bore testimony that it was the angel of the Lord who went before the camp, who found me overpowered with sleep, and thus awoke me."[16]

It must have been instructive to the Prophet to walk the many miles across Ohio, Indiana, Illinois, and Missouri, knowing that he was not alone in his journey. One can identify with the spirit that must have buoyed up Joseph in the challenges of the trek, all the time knowing that God watched over them and had sent his angels to accompany them along the way. While traveling in Illinois, Joseph acknowledged the hand of the Lord: "Notwithstanding our enemies were continually breathing threats of violence, we did not fear, neither did we hesitate to prosecute our journey, for God was with us, and His angels went before us, and the faith of our little band was unwavering. We know that angels were our companions, for we saw them."[17]

Notwithstanding the witness that angels accompanied the camp, Joseph did not take for granted that God would protect the camp from mobs or from sickness. On 18 June, while traveling toward Richmond, Missouri, "Joseph's health was so poor he left the affairs of the Camp to the management of General Lyman Wight," explained George A. Smith.

> When Joseph arrived where the Camp had pitched their tents and viewed our unsafe location, considering the danger of an attack from our enemies, he almost forgot his sickness, went some distance in the brush and bowed down and prayed to our Heavenly Father to suffer no evil to come upon us, but keep us safe through the night. He obtained an assurance that we should be safe until morning, notwithstanding a company of the Jackson County mob crossed the Lexington Ferry that evening for the purpose of joining the Ray County mob, and of making an attack upon us.[18]

The next day five men armed with guns rode into camp and threatened with oaths that the Mormons would "see hell before morning."[19] Wilford Woodruff recorded that as the men left camp a "small cloud like a black dot appeared in the north west," which grew into a terrible storm of wind, rain, thunder, lightning, and hail. "We all fled into a Baptist meetinghouse," he continued. "As the Prophet Joseph came in shaking the water from his hat and clothing he said, 'Boys, there is some meaning to this. God is in this storm.'" One of the armed men said "it was a strange thing they could do nothing against the Mormons but what there must be some hail storm or some other thing to hinder their doing anything."[20]

Joseph knew that the most difficult challenges of the journey would come not from the threats of Missouri mobs but from the chastening hand of the Almighty. During a noonday stop, before the camp crossed the Mississippi River from Illinois into Missouri, Joseph stood on a wagon wheel and made a speech to the camp. He said that the Lord was displeased with them and that their murmuring, fault-finding, and want of humility had kindled the anger of the Lord against them. He warned that a severe scourge would come upon the camp and many would die like sheep with the rot. He explained, "I cannot stop it; it must come; but by repentance and humility and the prayer of faith, the chastisement may be alleviated but cannot be entirely turned away, for as the Lord lives this Camp must suffer a severe scourge for their wickedness and rebellion. I say it in the name of the Lord."[21]

Three weeks later, on 24 June, the dreaded disease of cholera broke out. Joseph attempted to confront the disease with the power and authority of the priesthood. "I quickly learned by painful experience," explained the Prophet, "that when the great Jehovah decrees destruction upon any people, and makes known His determination, man must not attempt to stay His hand."[22] Two days before the appearance of cholera, Joseph received the word of the Lord telling him to disband the camp. The Lord released the camp members from the mandate to redeem Zion, explaining, "My people must needs be chastened until they learn obedience, if it must needs be, by the things which they suffer. . . . In consequence of the transgressions of my people, it is expedient in me that mine elders should wait for a little season for the redemption of Zion" (D&C 105:6–9). Within a short time cholera attacked not only members of Zion's Camp but Church members residing in the locale as well. About sixty-eight Saints were stricken, of whom fifteen died. Among those who died were Sidney Gilbert, keeper of the Lord's storehouse in Jackson County before being driven out by mobs, and John Murdock's six-year-old daughter, Phebe, who was staying with the Gilberts. It is probable that from this and other similar experiences, Joseph later taught, "Many of the righteous shall fall prey to disease, to pestilence, etc., by reason of the weakness of the flesh, and yet be saved in the Kingdom of God."[23]

THE AFTERMATH OF ZION'S CAMP

The expedition did not yield the redemption of the Saints' land in Zion, but it did fulfill the Lord's purposes. True, many of the Saints did not prove faithful in tribulation. However, many did. Many of Zion's Camp participants returned with stronger convictions of the divine call of the Prophet Joseph Smith and were much wiser regarding their own need to prove themselves more faithful in all circumstances. For example, upon his return to Kirtland, Brigham Young was met by a man, who asked, "Well, what did you gain on this useless journey to Missouri with Joseph Smith?" Brigham replied, "All we went for. I would not exchange the *experience* I gained in that expedition for all the wealth of Geauga county,"[24] Ohio. Similarly, Wilford Woodruff explained, "We gained an experience that we never could have gained in any other way. We had the privilege of beholding the face of the prophet, and we had the privilege of travelling a thousand miles with him, and seeing the workings of the Spirit of God with him, and the revelations of Jesus Christ unto him and the fulfilment of those revelations."[25]

On 14 February 1835 the Prophet Joseph Smith called a meeting and asked that those who journeyed with him the previous summer in Zion's Camp be seated together in a separate part of the meeting-house.

> He then gave a relation of some of the circumstances attending us while journeying to Zion—our trials, sufferings: and said God had not designed all this for nothing, but He had it in remembrance yet; and it was the will of God that those who went to Zion, with a determination to lay down

their lives, if necessary, should be ordained to the ministry, and go forth to prune the vineyard for the last time.[26]

On that day the Quorum of the Twelve Apostles was organized with nine of its members coming from those who marched with Zion's Camp. Two weeks later the First Quorum of Seventy was organized. All members of the quorum were chosen from among those who had journeyed with Zion's Camp.

The following year the participants in Zion's Camp and the Saints who had faithfully endured tribulation in Zion were among the first to receive the endowment as administered in the Kirtland Temple. Regarding those who gave their lives in the experience, Elder Joseph Young related that the Prophet Joseph Smith explained, "'Brethren, I have seen those men who died of the cholera in our camp; and the Lord knows, if I get a mansion as bright as theirs, I ask no more.' At this relation he wept, and for some time could not speak."[27]

CONCLUSION

Joseph exhibited that the call of a prophet is not limited to receiving revelation to be published as scripture and conducting meetings but includes the whole man and the work of the kingdom, whatever it may be. The most important benefit that may have come to those who traveled with Joseph was to be with him in prayer, marching in the heat and conversing along the way, feeling the Spirit of God, and seeing how the Lord directed the journey in everyday situations. George A. Smith summarized Joseph's experience thus:

> The Prophet Joseph took a full share of the fatigues of the entire journey. In addition to the care of providing for the Camp and presiding over it, he walked most of the time and had a full proportion of blistered, bloody, and sore feet, which was the natural result of walking from 25 to 40 miles a day in a hot season of the year. But during the entire trip he never uttered a murmur or complaint . . . Joseph had to bear with us and tutor us, like children.[28]

Lastly, the participants of Zion's Camp were called and known by the Lord. All told, by means of the experiences of the journey and through the faithfulness of his servant, Joseph, the Lord was able to refine camp members and prepare them to be future leaders in his kingdom.

NOTES

1. Smith, *History of the Church,* 2:48.
2. Smith, *History of the Church,* 2:40.
3. George Smith, "My Journal," *Instructor* 81, no. 2 (February 1946): 77.
4. George Smith, "My Journal," *Instructor* 81, no. 3 (March 1946): 119.
5. See Smith, *History of the Church,* 2:80–81.
6. Jenson, *Historical Record,* 7:578.
7. Jessee, *Personal Writings of Joseph Smith,* 323.
8. Smith, *History of the Church,* 2:64.
9. Smith, *History of the Church,* 2:79. This mound is still visible and is from the Adena Indian culture. It is owned and maintained by the village of Enon, Ohio. Two weeks later the brethren explored other mounds in western Illinois, one which contained the skeleton of a man that Joseph identified as Zelph. That account is not referred to in this article as there appears to be many uncertainties regarding exactly what the Prophet Joseph Smith stated about Zelph on that occasion. See Kenneth W. Godfrey, "The Zelph Story," *BYU Studies* 29, no. 2 (Spring 1989): 31–56.
10. George Smith, "My Journal," *Instructor* 81, no. 3 (March 1946): 117.
11. Smith, *History of the Church,* 2:71–72.
12. George Smith, "My Journal," *Instructor* 81, no. 7 (July 1946): 323.
13. George Smith, "My Journal," *Instructor* 81, no. 5 (May 1946): 213–14.
14. George Smith, "My Journal," *Instructor* 81, no. 4 (April 1946): 187.
15. George Smith, "My Journal," *Instructor* 81, no. 3 (March 1946): 115–16.
16. Pratt, *Autobiography of Parley P. Pratt,* 94.
17. Smith, *History of the Church,* 2:73.
18. George Smith, "My Journal," *Instructor* 81, no. 5 (May 1946): 214–15.
19. Smith, *History of the Church,* 2:103.
20. Wilford Woodruff's note in *Manuscript History of the Church,* Book A, 332, noted in Smith, *History of the Church,* 2:104.
21. George Smith, "My Journal," *Instructor* 81, no. 4 (April 1946): 184.
22. Smith, *History of the Church,* 2:114.
23. Smith, *History of the Church,* 4:11.
24. B. H. Roberts, "Brigham Young: A Character Sketch," *Improvement Era,* June 1903, 567.
25. Woodruff, *Journal of Discourses,* 13:158.
26. Smith, *History of the Church,* 2:182.
27. Smith, *History of the Church,* 2:181n.
28. George Smith, "My Journal," *Instructor* 81, no. 5 (May 1946): 217.

CHAPTER TWENTY-THREE

THE CALLING OF THE TWELVE APOSTLES
AND THE SEVENTY IN 1835

Richard E. Turley Jr.

he Zion's Camp march of 1834 helped refine those who participated in it, providing them not only with experience that they could apply later in life but also proving to Church leaders which members were willing to "hearken . . . unto the counsel which . . . the Lord their God, shall give unto them."[1] Part of the revelation calling for the organization of Zion's Camp commanded, "Let no man be afraid to lay down his life for my sake; . . . And whoso is not willing to lay down his life for my sake is not my disciple" (D&C 103:27–28). Zion's Camp thus became an Abrahamic test of worthiness, and when that test was over, the Lord declared, "There has been a day of calling, but the time has come for a day of choosing; and let those be chosen that are worthy." The revelation designated Joseph Smith as the one through whom "the voice of the Spirit" would manifest those who "are chosen" (D&C 105:35–36).

On Sunday, 8 February 1835, the Prophet Joseph Smith invited Brigham Young and his brother Joseph Young to his home in Kirtland and "proceeded to relate a vision to these brethren, of the state and condition of those men who died in Zion's Camp, in Missouri." Some persons had worried about those who died on the march, and Joseph's vision responded to their concern, moving and comforting both him and those who accepted his testimony of it. "Brethren," he told his visitors tearfully, "I have seen those men who died of the

---

Richard E. Turley Jr. serves as managing director of the Family and Church History Department of The Church of Jesus Christ of Latter-day Saints.

cholera in our camp; and the Lord knows, if I get a mansion as bright as theirs, I ask no more."[2]

The Prophet wept for some time before turning to Brigham Young and directing, "I wish you to notify all the brethren living in the branches, within a reasonable distance from this place, to meet at a General Conference on Saturday next. I shall then and there appoint twelve special witnesses, to open the door of the gospel to foreign nations." Pointing to Brigham, he said, "And you . . . will be one of them." After further describing the responsibilities of the Twelve, the Prophet turned to Joseph Young and said, "Brother Joseph, the Lord has made you President of the Seventies."[3]

The Young brothers marveled at what they had been told. Joseph Young later recalled that "they had heard of Moses and seventy Elders of Israel, and of Jesus appointing other Seventies, but had never heard of Twelve Apostles and of Seventies being called in this Church before."[4]

Soon word went out to the branches of the Church in that area, announcing "a meeting of the brethren in General Conference" to be "held in Kirtland, in the new school house under the printing office" the next Saturday.[5] The meeting was open to Church members generally but was intended especially for "those who journeyed to Zion for the purpose of laying the foundation of its redemption."[6]

On Saturday, 14 February 1835, Joseph Smith opened the meeting by reading John 15 from the New Testament, a chapter that resounded with verses meaningful to the Zion's Camp members and pertinent to the meeting's purpose.[7] "After an appropriate and affecting prayer," Joseph spoke directly to the Zion's Camp veterans, telling them that the meeting was being held because "God had commanded it and it was made known to him by vision and by the Holy Spirit."[8]

After relating "some of the circumstances attending us while journeying to Zion, our trials, sufferings, &c.," Joseph "said God had not designed all this for nothing, but he had it in remembrance yet." Joseph revealed that it was God's will that "those who went to Zion, with a determination to lay down their lives, if necessary, . . . should be ordained to the ministry and go forth to prune the vineyard for the

The Twelve Apostles, *by Del Parson*

last time." Joseph said that "even the smallest and weakest among" them could accomplish "great things." He predicted, "From this hour . . . you shall begin to feel the whisperings of the Spirit of God, and the work of God shall begin to break forth from this time, you shall be endowed with power from on high." Joseph invited all Zion's Camp members who "agreed with him" to stand; they all rose to their feet. He asked the remaining members of the congregation "if they would sanction the movement. They all raised the right hand."[9]

After an intermission, Joseph declared the first order of business to be "for the three witnesses of the Book of Mormon, to pray each one and then proceed to choose twelve men from the Church as Apostles to go to all nations, kindred, to[ngue]s and people." The Three Witnesses prayed and "were then blessed by the laying on of the hands of the Presid[e]ncy." Having prepared their hearts and minds, "they then according to a former commandment, proceeded to make choice of the *twelve*."[10]

The "former commandment" was a revelation given in June 1829 before the Church was organized. In it, the Lord spoke to Oliver Cowdery and David Whitmer "even as unto Paul mine apostle," telling them that they were called "with that same calling with which he was called."[11] The revelation outlined qualifications for the Twelve and commanded Oliver and David to "search out the Twelve," who will "have the desires of which I have spoken," instructing the Witnesses that "by their desires and their works you shall know them."[12]

One of the Zion's Camp veterans attending the meeting of 14 February 1835, Heber C. Kimball, would cite this revelation and recall, "This was the day appointed for choosing." The Three Witnesses "proceeded to call forth those whom the Lord had manifested by his spirit to them, that they might make known their desires."[13] The names had earlier been reviewed by Joseph Smith.[14] Those called to the first Quorum of the Twelve in this dispensation were Lyman Johnson, Brigham Young, Heber C. Kimball, Orson Hyde, David W. Patten, Luke Johnson, William E. McLellin, John F. Boynton, Orson Pratt, William Smith, Thomas B. Marsh, and Parley P. Pratt.[15]

During that first meeting, Lyman Johnson, Brigham Young, and Heber C. Kimball were ordained by the Three Witnesses. The next day, a Sunday, Oliver "Cowdery called forwar[d] Orson Hyde, David W. Patten and Luke Johnson and proceeded to their ordination & blessing." William E. McLellin, John F. Boynton, and William Smith were ordained the same day. On Saturday, 21 February, "Parley P. Pratt was called to the stand and ordained as one of the Twelve" by Joseph Smith, David Whitmer, and Oliver Cowdery.[16]

Although each blessing was unique to the apostle who received it, Heber C. Kimball summed them all up when he wrote that they "predicted many things which should come to pass, that we should have power to heal the sick, cast out devils, raise the dead, give sight to the blind, have power to remove mountains, and all things should be subject to us through the name of Jesus Christ, and angels should minister unto us, and many more things too numerous to mention."[17]

While organizing the Twelve, the Prophet Joseph Smith prepared to organize the Seventy. On 28 February, Joseph Smith, Sidney Rigdon, and Oliver Cowdery began to ordain "certain individuals to be Seventies, from the number of those who went up to Zion." The next day, 1 March, the meeting reconvened, Joseph Smith spoke, and other Seventy were ordained.[18]

According to Elder Kimball, the ordained members of the Twelve "assembled from time to time as opportunity would permit, and received such instruction as the Lord would bestow upon us, and truly he blessed us with his spirit, and inspired his prophet to speak for our edification."[19] On 28 March 1835, the members of the Twelve who had been ordained to that point met in council. In a few weeks, they would leave together on a mission, and in preparation for that experience, they "unitedly asked God, our Heavenly Father to grant unto us through his Seer, a revelation of his mind and will concerning our duty this coming season."[20] Heber C. Kimball wrote that while they "were assembled to receive instructions, the revelation . . . on Priesthood was given to Brother Joseph as he was instructing us, and we praised the Lord."[21] The revelation declared, among other things, that "the twelve traveling councilors are called to be the Twelve Apostles, or special witnesses of the name of Christ in all the world— thus differing from other officers in the church in the duties of their calling. . . . The Seventy are also called to preach the gospel, and to be especial witnesses."[22] The Twelve were "to officiate . . . under the direction of the Presidency," and the Seventy "under the direction of the Twelve."[23]

The remaining two members called to the original Twelve in the last dispensation, Thomas B. Marsh and Orson Pratt, were away on a mission at the time and thus had not yet been ordained. Brother Marsh returned to Kirtland from his mission on 25 April.[24] On 26 April, the eleven new apostles met together, awaiting the arrival of Orson Pratt to complete their quorum.[25]

Twenty-three-year-old Orson had apparently known for years that he would be an apostle. Sometime after the 1829 revelation was received directing the Three Witnesses to select the Twelve, Joseph Smith had shown it to Orson, telling him he would "be one of this Twelve." Joseph's words startled him. "I looked upon the Twelve Apostles who lived in ancient days with a great deal of reverence—as being almost superhuman," Orson later said. "They were, indeed, great men—not by virtue of the flesh, nor their own natural capacities, but they were great because God called them." The idea that he might become an apostle awed Orson.[26]

Later, he had gone to Missouri with the Prophet in Zion's Camp and remained there for months on a mission before returning to Ohio. Reaching Columbus, he asked directions "of a man who was standing in the street" and was surprised to discover that he was a Church member. Orson followed the man home, where he saw the Latter-day Saint paper published in Kirtland.[27] In the paper there was a notice that Thomas B. Marsh and Orson Pratt were "desired to attend a meeting of the elders" in Kirtland on 26 April. "We hope that circumstances may render it convenient for them to attend," the paper continued, "as their presence is very desirable."[28] With assistance, he hurried by stage and foot to Kirtland, arriving at the meeting "valise in hand."[29] Orson was "invited to take [his] seat as one of the 12."[30]

The eleven members of the Twelve meeting in Kirtland on 26 April had waited expectantly for him. Orson would learn that during that meeting and in previous ones "it had been prophesied . . . [that] I would be there on that day. They had predicted this, although they had not heard of me for some time, and did not know where I was." Yet "the Lord poured out the spirit of prophecy upon them, and they predicted I would be there at that meeting." When Orson walked in, "many of the Saints could scarcely believe their own eyes, the prediction was fulfilled before them so perfectly."[31] "At this time while we were praying, and wishing for his arrival," Elder Kimball recalled, "while opening the meeting he entered the house, [and] we rejoiced at his presence, and thanked the Lord for it."[32] Thomas B. Marsh and Orson Pratt were ordained later that day by Oliver Cowdery and David Whitmer.[33]

Under the direction of Joseph Smith, Oliver Cowdery spoke to the Twelve and gave them an apostolic charge. He prefaced it by citing the revelation directing "that in process of time there should be Twelve chosen to preach his gospel to Jew & Gentile." During the intervening years, Cowdery reflected, "Our minds have been on a constant stretch to find who these Twelve were."[34] Those directed to select the Twelve did not know "when the time should come" but earnestly "sought the Lord by fasting and prayer to have our lives prolonged to see this day, to see you, and to take a retrospect of the difficulties through which we have passed." The day having come, he gave the Twelve a lengthy charge describing the importance of the calling, the sacrifices it would require, and the blessings that would flow through humble and obedient service to the Lord.[35]

Having delivered the charge, President Cowdery took each member of the Twelve "separately by the hand" and asked, "Do you with full purpose of heart take part in this ministry, to proclaim the gospel with all diligence with these your brethren, according to the tenor and intent of the charge you have received?" Each in turn committed to do so.[36] The Twelve was then fully organized, and its members prepared to set off on a mission together.[37]

On 2 May, a "grand council" of the Church's general authorities was held in Kirtland, at which Joseph Smith presided. The conference opened with a prayer by Brigham Young, and Joseph instructed the Twelve on how to organize for conducting business. The eldest was to preside in the first meeting, the second oldest in the second meeting, and so on until each had presided, then start over again.[38] This approach made sense at first when the Twelve had all been called and ordained at roughly the same time. Later, however, the system was changed, gradually developing into the current practice by which "the date . . . a person becomes a member of the Quorum (usually the date he is sustained as an apostle) establishes his position of seniority in the Quorum relative to other quorum members."[39]

The 2 May meeting also dealt with the question of the Twelve's jurisdiction, another feature that would change over time. Joseph Smith instructed the Twelve that they had "no right to go into Zion or any of its stakes and there undertake to regulate the affairs thereof where there is a standing High Council." Instead, their jurisdiction extended only to the areas outside Zion, the Church's center place in Missouri, "or any of its stakes."[40] The separate jurisdictions between the Twelve and the high councils in Zion and its stakes would raise questions of overall seniority in Church administration, and after the members of the Twelve returned from their second mission to Great Britain in the early 1840s, Joseph Smith broadened the Twelve's jurisdiction to cover the entire Church worldwide. The Quorum of the Twelve then stood second only to the First Presidency in overseeing Church affairs across the globe.[41]

At the 2 May meeting, Joseph also provided for the new system of Seventies to expand as necessary to meet the Church's growing needs. He explained that if the first Seventy were all employed in the Lord's work and more help was needed, the seven presidents had a duty "to call and ordain other Seventy and send them forth to labor in the vineyard." At the same time, although the Seventy as a quorum were considered in one sense "equal in authority" as a body to the Twelve, they were clearly subordinate in terms of day-to-day administration.[42] Joseph made it clear in the meeting, for example, that "the Seventy are not to attend the conferences of the Twelve unless they are called upon or requested to by the Twelve." After Joseph spoke, additional seventies were called forward and ordained, as were yet others after the conference adjourned and reconvened.[43]

After calling the Twelve and the Seventy, Joseph responded to elders in Kirtland who were disappointed when the men of Zion's Camp did not fight in Missouri.[44] "Let me tell you," Joseph said, "God did not want you to fight. He could not organize his kingdom with twelve men to open the gospel door to the nations of the earth, and with seventy men under their direction to follow in their tracks, unless he took them from a body of men who had offered their lives, and who had made as great a sacrifice as did Abraham." With apparent satisfaction, he added, "Now, the Lord has got his Twelve and his Seventy, and there will be other quorums of Seventies called, who will make the sacrifice, and those who have not made their sacrifices and their offerings now, will make them hereafter."[45] Although further changes would occur over time, Joseph Smith's organization of the Twelve and the Seventy in Kirtland in 1835 would provide the foundation for leading the Church in the generations that followed.

NOTES

1. D&C 103:5. See also Abraham 3:25. On the impact of Zion's Camp, see Roberts, *Comprehensive History of the Church,* 1:370–71; Young, *History of the Organization of the Seventies,* 14; Smith, *History of the Church,* 2:182 n; Brigham Young, October 23, 1853, in *Journal of Discourses,* 2:10; *Church History in the Fulness of Times,* 151; Esplin, "Emergence of Brigham Young and the Twelve," 122–25, 128.

2. Young, *History of the Organization of the Seventies,* 1; Smith, *History of the Church,* 2:180–81.

3. Young, *History of the Organization of the Seventies,* 1–2.

4. Young, *History of the Organization of the Seventies,* 2. Apostles had been mentioned in earlier revelations. For example, in June 1829, the Lord spoke to Oliver Cowdery and David Whitmer "as unto Paul mine apostle" because they were "called . . . with that same calling with which he was called." D&C 18:9. The Articles and Covenants of the Church described Joseph Smith and Oliver Cowdery each as "an apostle of Jesus Christ." D&C 20:2–3. On Moses and seventy elders of Israel, see Exodus 24:1, 9–11; Numbers 11:16–17, 24–25. On Christ's appointment of "other seventy," see Luke 10:1–20.

5. Young, *History of the Organization of the Seventies,* 2.

6. Kirtland High Council Minutes, 147, in Turley, ed., *Selected Collections from the Archives of the Church,* vol. 1, DVD 19; Smith, *History of the Church,* 2:181. Heber C. Kimball recalled that the "meeting was called for the camp of Zion to be assembled, to receive what was called a Zion's blessing." "Extracts from H. C. Kimball's Journal," *Times and Seasons* 6, no. 7 (April 15, 1845): 868.

7. Kirtland High Council Minutes, 147; Smith *History of the Church,* 2:181. Roberts, *Comprehensive History of the Church,* 1:373, writes: "The Prophet read at the opening of the conference the 15th chapter of *St. John;* the appropriateness of it is striking. In it is stressed the needed union with the Christ. So close that it must be as the branch to the vine, if it would have life; love so great that it will not withhold life as a sacrifice to friendship—'and greater love hath no man than this, that a man lay down his life for his friends'; the apostles are declared to be friends to the Christ. 'Ye have not chosen me but I have chosen you and ordained you that ye may bring forth much fruit.' 'Love one another'; and 'if the world hate you, ye know that it hated me before it hated you. . . . the servant is not greater

than his Lord. If they have persecuted me they will persecute you. . . . They hated me without a cause. . . . But when the Comforter is come . . . even the Spirit of Truth . . . he will testify of me; and ye also shall bear witness.' How fitting the scripture to the occasion!'"

8. Kirtland High Council Minutes, 147; Smith, *History of the Church,* 2:181–82. Because others were in attendance besides the Zion's Camp members, "the Brethren who went to Zion, were requested to take their seats together in one part of the house by themselves." Kirtland High Council Minutes, 147.

9. Kirtland High Council Minutes, 147–48; Smith, *History of the Church,* 2:182. Not all who were ordained participated in Zion's Camp, but most did, including nine of the Twelve and all of the original members of the First Quorum of Seventy. Backman, *Heavens Resound,* 199; *Church History in the Fulness of Times,* 151. The three apostles who did not participate were Thomas B. Marsh, John F. Boynton, and William E. McLellin. Esplin, "Emergence of Brigham Young and the Twelve," 129.

10. Kirtland High Council Minutes, 149, emphasis in original; Smith, *History of the Church,* 2:186–87.

11. D&C 18:9. According to Brigham Young, April 7, 1852, in *Journal of Discourses,* 6:320, "Joseph Smith, Oliver Cowdery, and David Whitmer were the first Apostles of this dispensation." Brigham Young, April 6, 1853, in *Journal of Discourses,* 1:134, clarified, "Joseph was ordained an Apostle." Heber C. Kimball, November 8, 1857, in *Journal of Discourses,* 6:29, said that Joseph ordained all three Book of Mormon witnesses as apostles. See D&C 27:12. Martin Harris's ordination as an apostle seems confirmed by D&C 19:8–9.

12. D&C 18:37–38. B. H. Roberts opined that "it was designed from the first that the Three Witnesses should choose the Twelve" but that "Martin Harris was out of favor with the Lord" when D&C 18 was given, "for which reason doubtless his name is not there associated with those of his fellow Witnesses when they were designated to choose the Twelve." Roberts suggested that Joseph was later inspired of the Lord to include Martin "in choosing the Apostles." Smith, *History of the Church,* 2:186–87 n.

13. "Extracts from H. C. Kimball's Journal," 868.

14. At least one substitution was made in the original list of those chosen. See Esplin, "Emergence of Brigham Young and the Twelve," 147–48 n. 108.

15. Kirtland High Council Minutes, 149; Smith, *History of the Church,* 2:187; "Extracts from H. C. Kimball's Journal," 868.

16. Kirtland High Council Minutes, 149, 151, 153–54; Smith, *History of the Church,* 2:187, 189–91. The record does not name who ordained each person. For B. H. Roberts's best guess on who ordained whom, see his *Comprehensive History of the Church,* 1:374–75 n. 13. After the

ordination, Oliver Cowdery gave Parley P. Pratt a charge, not to be confused with the one Cowdery gave to the Twelve later.

17. "Extracts from H. C. Kimball's Journal," 868. For the text of the blessings, see Kirtland High Council Minutes, 149–55; Smith, *History of the Church,* 2:188–92.

18. Smith, *History of the Church,* 2:201–4; Kirtland High Council Minutes, 164, 169, 172. Smith, *History of the Church,* 2:203, also lists the presidents and members of the newly called Seventy. Individual blessings of members of the Seventy can be found in the Kirtland High Council Minutes, 164–86.

19. "Extracts from H. C. Kimball's Journal," 868–69.

20. Kirtland High Council Minutes, 198; Woodford, "Historical Development of the Doctrine and Covenants," 3:1398.

21. "Extracts from H. C. Kimball's Journal," 869; Woodford, "Historical Development of the Doctrine and Covenants," 3:1399.

22. D&C 107:23, 25.

23. D&C 107:33–34.

24. Smith, *History of the Church,* 2:193.

25. "Extracts from H. C. Kimball's Journal," 869.

26. Orson Pratt, August 11, 1867, in *Journal of Discourses,* 12:85–86.

27. Orson Pratt Diary, vol. 2, April 20, 1835, Archives, The Church of Jesus Christ of Latter-day Saints, Salt Lake City, Utah; Pratt, August 11, 1867, in *Journal of Discourses,* 12:86.

28. *Messenger and Advocate* 1, no. 6 (March 1835): 90; Pratt Diary, vol. 2, April 20, 1835; Pratt, August 11, 1867, in *Journal of Discourses,* 12:86.

29. Pratt, August 11, 1867, in *Journal of Discourses,* 12:87.

30. Pratt Diary, vol. 2, April 26, 1835.

31. Pratt, August 11, 1867, in *Journal of Discourses,* 12:85–87.

32. "Extracts from H. C. Kimball's Journal," 869.

33. Pratt Diary, vol. 2, April 26, 1835.

34. Kirtland High Council Minutes, 158–64; Smith, *History of the Church,* 2:194–98; D&C 18. On October 26, 1831, Oliver Cowdery wrote that he and David Whitmer "had received this morning [directions] respecting the choice of the twelve . . . that they would be ordained & sent forth from the Land of Zion." Cannon and Cook, eds., *Far West Record,* 26. The Missouri persecutions, however, required changing the location from Zion to Kirtland.

35. Kirtland High Council Minutes, 159–64; Smith, *History of the Church,* 2:194–98.

36. Kirtland High Council Minutes, 164; Smith, *History of the Church,* 2:198. An apostolic charge would continue to be administered to new apostles in subsequent generations. See, e.g., Gibbons, *George Albert Smith,* 45; Gibbons, *Joseph Fielding Smith,* 152; Gibbons, *Harold B. Lee,* 155; Gibbons, *Spencer W. Kimball,* 149; Neal A. Maxwell, in Conference Report,

October 1981, 8, or *Ensign,* November 1981, 8; Jeffrey R. Holland, in Conference Report, October 1994, 40, or *Ensign,* November 1994, 32.

37. Pratt Diary, vol. 2, May 4, 1835; "Extracts from H. C. Kimball's Journal," 869; Esplin, "Emergence of Brigham Young and the Twelve," 157, 162, 163–66; Backman, *Heavens Resound,* 251; Jessee, ed., *Papers of Joseph Smith,* 2:143–49.

38. Kirtland High Council Minutes, 187; Smith, *History of the Church,* 2:219.

39. William O. Nelson, "Quorum of the Twelve Apostles," in *Encyclopedia of Mormonism,* 3:1188; Roberts, *Comprehensive History of the Church,* 5:519–24. This seniority, in turn, affects succession to the presidency of the Church. "There is no mystery about the choosing of the successor to the President of the Church," Joseph Fielding Smith wrote. "The Lord settled this a long time ago, and the *senior apostle automatically becomes the presiding officer of the Church,* and he is so sustained by the Council of the Twelve which becomes the presiding body of the Church when there is no First Presidency." *Doctrines of Salvation,* 3:156; emphasis in original. See also Gordon B. Hinckley, in Conference Report, April 1986, 61–62, or *Ensign,* May 1986, 46–47; James E. Faust, in Conference Report, October 1994, 94–95, or *Ensign,* November 1994, 72–73; Boyd K. Packer, in Conference Report, April 1995, 5–6, or *Ensign,* May 1995, 7; Brewster, *Prophets, Priesthood Keys, and Succession,* 111–17; Backman, *Heavens Resound,* 425 n. 63.

40. Kirtland High Council Minutes, 187; Smith, *History of the Church,* 2:220. See also D&C 107:36–37.

41. "Conference Minutes," *Times and Seasons* 2, no. 21 (September 1, 1841): 521–22; Smith, *History of the Church,* 4:403; Backman, *Heavens Resound,* 250, 426 n. 64; Durham and Heath, *Succession in the Church,* 47–54. See also Brewster, *Prophets, Priesthood Keys, and Succession,* 41–49; Roberts, *Comprehensive History of the Church,* 2:87–88, 368–71.

42. Kirtland High Council Minutes, 188; Smith, *History of the Church,* 2:221; D&C 107:26.

43. Kirtland High Council Minutes, 188–91; Smith, *History of the Church,* 2:221. For a list of Seventies called in Kirtland, see Young, *History of the Organization of the Seventies,* 2–4.

44. On the rumblings in Kirtland about Zion's Camp, see Joseph Smith to Lyman Wight and Others, August 16, 1834, in Jessee, ed., *Personal Writings of Joseph Smith,* 347–50; Backman, *Heavens Resound,* 196; Marvin S. Hill, "Cultural Crisis in the Mormon Kingdom: A Reconsideration of the Causes of Kirtland Dissent," *Church History* 49, no 3 (September 1980): 287–88.

45. Joseph Smith, address to the Elders assembled in Kirtland, in Young, *History of the Organization of the Seventies,* 14. In the revelation releasing the members of Zion's Camp, the Lord declared, "I have heard their

prayers, and will accept their offering; and it is expedient in me that they should be brought thus far for a trial of their faith." D&C 105:19. Wilford Woodruff testified, "God accepted our works as He did the works of Abraham" Woodruff, December 12, 1869, in *Journal of Discourses,* 13:158.

THE LORD'S "OLIVE LEAF"

Guy L. Dorius

Kirtland, Ohio, was a place of intense spiritual growth for the Saints in the 1830s. During the period from late 1831 to early 1834 almost one third of the revelations contained in the Doctrine and Covenants were given to Joseph Smith. These revelations contain instruction for the continued growth in the administration of the Church as well as new and revolutionary doctrine. Although this was a season of overflowing spiritual insight, it was also a period laden with many challenges for the Prophet. Trials came not only from the growing number of antagonists outside the young Church but also from an increasing number of Saints who did not have sufficient understanding of the laws of the kingdom or the role of God's prophet. In this Pentecostal, yet difficult, era, the Lord presented to Joseph an "olive leaf" in the form of a revelation—Doctrine and Covenants 88. A review of the historical context of this revelation and its lofty doctrine helps us understand why Joseph gave the title "Olive Leaf" to the revelation.[1]

Many of the early revelations given to Joseph had to do with organizing the presiding officers of the Church to deal with its expansion. The office of bishop was revealed, and Edward Partridge was ordained in February of 1831. Shortly thereafter, the first high priests were ordained, and by March of 1832, Joseph had begun to organize the First Presidency under the Lord's direction, by revelation establishing them as holding "the keys of the kingdom" (D&C 81:2). In the

---

Guy L. Dorius is an associate professor of Church history and doctrine at Brigham Young University.

process of directing the offices of the priesthood, the Lord revealed important doctrine to help the Saints understand the intended direction of the Church.

On a journey to Missouri in the summer of 1831, it was revealed to Joseph that Jackson County would be the place of Zion in the last days. Additional revelations about the placement of the temple in Zion only increased its importance (D&C 57; 58; 84). After the November 1831 conference, where a decision was made to publish the revelations, Oliver Cowdery and John Whitmer were sent with the revelations to Jackson County so that publishing could begin. Many of the early leaders were established there to manage the growth of the Church and maintain a stewardship over publications. With continual growth, the Church in Missouri was gaining strength and attracting attention. Persecution was beginning there as well as in Kirtland.

One concern for Joseph was that of administrative stewardship. Joseph's authority had been established by revelation in April 1830 when the Lord stated: "Wherefore, meaning the church, thou shalt give heed unto all his words and commandments which he shall give unto you as he receiveth them" (D&C 21:4). This commandment was reiterated when Oliver Cowdery was taught that "no one shall be appointed to receive commandments and revelations in this church excepting my servant Joseph Smith, Jun., for he receiveth them even as Moses" (D&C 28:2). Presiding officers of the Church in Missouri became necessary in order to care for the Church. Joseph called Oliver Cowdery, William W. Phelps, John Whitmer, Sidney Gilbert, Edward Partridge, Isaac Morley, and John Corrill to preside over the Saints in Zion. They, in turn, organized branches with presiding officers to direct the affairs.

As faithful as these early members were, contention arose not only on the smaller branch level but with the general officers as well. Joseph had to intervene on issues pertaining to the laws of consecration and stewardship (D&C 85). Of greater concern was the competitiveness he was sensing from the presiding officers in Zion. The Lord corrected them when he revealed to Joseph "that they shall repent of

Joseph Smith Standing in Front of the Kirtland Temple, *by Robert T. Barrett*

their former evil works; for they are to be upbraided for their evil hearts of unbelief, and your brethren in Zion for their rebellion against you at the time I sent you" (D&C 84:76). There was a feeling among some that Joseph was "seeking after monarchial power and authority."[2] Although Orson Hyde and Hyrum Smith corresponded with the leadership in Zion to correct the misconception, Joseph personally addressed the issue. On 14 January 1833, he wrote a letter to William W. Phelps, who was called as a presiding elder in Missouri in March 1833. Enclosed in the letter was a copy of Doctrine and Covenants 88, most of which Joseph received 27 December 1832:

> I send you the "olive leaf" which we have plucked from the Tree of Paradise, the Lord's message of peace to us; for though our brethren in Zion indulge in feelings towards us, which are not according to the requirements of the new covenant, yet, we have the satisfaction of knowing that the Lord approves of us, and has accepted us, and established His name in Kirtland for the salvation of the nations; for the Lord will have a place whence His word will go forth, in these last days, in purity; for if Zion will not purify herself, so as to be approved of in all things, in His sight, He will seek another people; for His work will go on until Israel is gathered, and they who will not hear His voice, must expect to feel His wrath. Let me say unto you, seek to purify yourselves, and also all the inhabitants of Zion, lest the Lord's anger be kindled to fierceness. Repent, repent, is the voice of God to Zion; and strange as it may appear, yet it is true, mankind will persist in self-justification until all their iniquity is exposed, and their character past being redeemed, and that which is treasured up in their hearts be exposed to the gaze of mankind. I say to you (and what I say to you I say to all,) hear the warning voice of God, lest Zion fall, and the Lord sware in His wrath the inhabitants of Zion shall not enter into His rest.
>
> The brethren in Kirtland pray for you unceasingly, for, knowing the terrors of the Lord, they greatly fear for you. You will see that the Lord commanded us, in Kirtland, to build a house of God, and establish a school for the Prophets, this is the word of the Lord to us, and we must, yea, the Lord helping us, we will obey: as on conditions of our obedience He has promised us great things; yea, even a visit from the heavens to honor us with His own presence.[3]

It appears that Joseph sent this revelation with the intent to affirm himself as the Prophet and let the Saints in Missouri see that the will of the Lord was still flowing to him and the Church in Kirtland. The Missouri Saints were also able to see that the Lord not only had plans for a temple in Zion, but it was necessary for them to build one in Kirtland.

What may not be immediately apparent is why Joseph considered Doctrine and Covenants 88 to be an "Olive Leaf," a "message of peace." Was it simply because it would stabilize the Church with its strong doctrinal content and reestablish him as the Lord's prophet? As noted, these seem to be reasons it was sent. Another event may have added to the impact of this important revelation. On Christmas Day 1832, Joseph received a revelation which must have been a stark reminder of the hazards of the last days. Section 87 of the Doctrine and Covenants revealed to the brethren the proliferation of wars which would accompany the second coming of the Savior. At the end of that revelation, the Lord declared:

> And thus, with the sword and by bloodshed the inhabitants of the earth shall mourn; and with famine, and plague, and earthquake, and the thunder of heaven, and the fierce and vivid lightning also, shall the inhabitants of the earth be made to feel the wrath, and indignation, and chastening hand of an Almighty God, until the consumption decreed hath made a full end of all nations;
>
> That the cry of the saints, and of the blood of the saints, shall cease to come up into the ears of the Lord of Sabaoth, from the earth, to be avenged of their enemies.
>
> Wherefore, stand ye in holy places, and be not moved, until the day of the Lord come; for behold, it cometh quickly, saith the Lord. Amen. (D&C 87:6–8)

Zion, a holy place, was being shaken by the previously discussed problems in leadership. This revelation must have been troubling for the Prophet Joseph. It was in this troubling season that the Lord revealed the sacred content of the "Olive Leaf" to Joseph Smith. In the minutes of the meeting in which the revelation was received, Frederick G. Williams recorded:

> A conference of High Priests assembled in the translating room in Kirtland Ohio on the 27th day of Dec A.D. 1832—Present—Joseph Smith,—Sidney Rigdon—Orson Hyde—Joseph Smith, Jr.—Hyrum

Smith—Samuel H. Smith—N. K. Whitney—F. G. Williams—Ezra Thayer—& John Murdock commenced by prayer, Then Bro. Joseph arose and said, to receive revelation and the blessings of heaven it was necessary to have our minds on god and exercise faith and become of one heart and of one mind therefore he recommended all present to pray seperately and vocally to the Lord for to receive his will unto us concerning the upbuilding of Zion, & for the benefit of the saints and for the duty and employment of the Elders—Accordingly we all bowed down before the Lord, after which each one arose and spoke in his turn his feelings, and determination to keep the commandments of God, And thus proceded to receive a revelation concerning the [not legible] above stated 9 o clock P.M. the revelation not being finished the conference adjourned till tomorrow morning 9 o clock A.M.—27th meet according adjournment and commenced by Prayer thus proceeded to receive the residue of the above revelation and it being finished and there being no further business before the conference closed the meeting by prayer in harmony with the brethren and gratitude to our heavenly Father for the great manifestations of his holy Spirit during the setting of the conference.

F. G. Williams clk of con.[4]

The great outpouring of the Spirit at this conference must have been both a relief and comfort to the brethren. To know that the Father would bless them in this way provided evidence that they had not lost his confidence. It is hard to know what specific parts of the revelation provided the feeling of peace, but there are portions that would lend themselves to be labeled the "Olive Leaf." It should be noted that the original revelation received in the above mentioned conference consisted of Doctrine and Covenants 88:1–126. Verses 127–37 were received by Joseph on 3 January 1833. The Prophet combined these two separate revelations along with verses 138–41 when the 1835 edition of the Doctrine and Covenants was published.[5]

In the opening verses of the revelation, the Lord issued a statement of comfort:

Verily, thus saith the Lord unto you who have assembled yourselves together to receive his will concerning you:

Behold, this is pleasing unto your Lord, and the angels rejoice over you; the alms of your prayers have come up into the ears of the Lord of

Sabaoth, and are recorded in the book of the names of the sanctified, even them of the celestial world. (D&C 88:1–2)

For Joseph to have a reaffirmation of his standing with God, knowing his prayers had been heard and his name was recorded with those of the sanctified, must have been a blessing in this time of conflict. The Lord used the title "Lord of Sabaoth," which is based on a Hebrew expression and means "Lord of Hosts" or "Lord of Armies." In the revelation given just two days earlier, which contained a devastating message of war, he used the same title as the avenger of the spilt blood of the Saints (D&C 87:7). His all-encompassing role was being laid out for the early Saints. He would not only protect them in battle but he would listen to their prayers and sanctify them. Later in revelation, he expanded the meaning of this title when he reminded the Prophet "that your fastings and your mourning might come up into the ears of the Lord of Sabaoth, which is by interpretation, the creator of the first day, the beginning and the end" (D&C 95:7).

In verses 3–4 of section 88, the "Olive Leaf" is further extended through the promise of "another Comforter" to the brethren whom he refers to as his "friends." The promised comforter was the Holy Spirit of Promise which would lead them to eternal life. Some have misunderstood this promise of another comforter to be the Second Comforter, which would be Christ himself. The clarifying hint given is "which other Comforter is the same that I promised unto my disciples, as is recorded in the testimony of John" (D&C 88:3). The promise made to the ancient disciples was that when Jesus left them, he would send another to abide with them, even the Holy Ghost (John 14:16). In addition, the term "friend" used by the Savior would have been a source of great peace for Joseph.

The Lord further expanded the Prophet's mind by revealing His all-encompassing role in the governance of all things through His light, even the Light of Christ (D&C 88:6–13). He taught Joseph of His omnipotence and omniscience. He reminded him that all things are governed by His Law, even the resurrection of the dead and the kingdoms of glory (D&C 88:17–38).

The Lord reaffirmed to Joseph and the brethren that he was still with them and in charge. He had promised them that when they journeyed from New York to Ohio that he would take care of them. Beyond that, the Lord promised that they would see him: "I am in your midst and ye cannot see me; But the day soon cometh that ye shall see me" (D&C 38:7–8). That promise appears again in section 88:

> The light shineth in darkness, and the darkness comprehendeth it not; nevertheless, the day shall come when you shall comprehend even God, being quickened in him and by him.
>
> Then shall ye know that ye have seen me, that I am, and that I am the true light that is in you, and that you are in me; otherwise ye could not abound. (D&C 88:49–50)

This promise was again put before the brethren. In sending this revelation to the Church leaders in Missouri, Joseph was reminding them of the goal they were working toward—to see God and to know Him. This was indeed a message of peace. Although there had been struggles, they were still on track and the opportunity had not passed.

In other parts of the revelation, the Saints were reminded of the need to teach and be taught "things both in heaven and in the earth" so that they could be prepared to go out to the world and teach the gospel (D&C 88:79). They were instructed to build the Kirtland Temple: "Organize yourselves; prepare every needful thing; and establish a house, even a house of prayer, a house of fasting, a house of faith, a house of learning, a house of glory, a house of order, a house of God" (D&C 88:119). This was to be not only a place of worship but a house of learning where they could fulfill the commission given them to teach each other. The learning was to be done "by study and also by faith" (D&C 88:118). In order to accomplish this charge, the Lord warned the brethren that they were to "cease from all your light speeches, from all laughter, from all your lustful desires, from all your pride and light-mindedness, and from all your wicked doings" (D&C 88:121). They were also cautioned about other behaviors: "See that ye love one another; cease to be covetous; learn to impart one to another as the gospel requires. Cease to be idle; cease to be unclean;

cease to find fault one with another; cease to sleep longer than is needful; retire to thy bed early, that ye may not be weary; arise early, that your bodies and your minds may be invigorated" (D&C 88:123–24).

This commission was designed for the circumstances that Joseph found himself in. In sending it to Zion, the Lord through his Prophet reminded the Missouri Saints that there was still work to be done in Kirtland. They were also indirectly cautioned about their own inappropriate behavior and invited to act differently so that they could become a part of the "school of the prophets" (D&C 88:127).

The "Olive Leaf" contains some of the most sublime and beautiful doctrine ever revealed to man. Beyond that, it suggested to the Saints things they could do to be better prepared to preach the gospel and ready themselves for the second coming of our Lord. It was a reminder that he had promised that they would see him if they were worthy. After receiving Doctrine and Covenants 88, along with the letter from Joseph, the brethren in Missouri repented for a season and the work went forward. Joseph must have found great peace in this gift from God—an "Olive Leaf." In times of trouble, he often received important and comforting doctrine from the heavens. Years later, while in Liberty Jail, Joseph would receive important revelations on principles of priesthood power which would have a similar impact on him. Joseph knew by revelation that God would not let him or the Saints down. The Lord would bless them in every time of need with sweet doctrines and important directions for their success.

NOTES
1. See Smith, *History of the Church,* 1:316.
2. Smith, *History of the Church,* 1:318.
3. Smith, *History of the Church,* 1:316.
4. Kirtland Council Minute Book, 3–4, LDS Church Archives, as cited in Robert J. Woodford, "How the Revelations in the Doctrine and Covenants Were Received and Compiled," *Ensign,* January 1985, 29.
5. See Woodford, "How the Revelations," 29.

CHAPTER TWENTY-FIVE

THE KIRTLAND TEMPLE

Richard O. Cowan

he School of the Prophets was a forerunner to temple worship. Two days after Christmas in 1832, a revelation from God instructed Joseph Smith to organize the school, whose meetings were termed a "solemn assembly." Only the worthy were to attend: "He that is found unworthy . . . shall not have place among you; for ye shall not suffer that mine house shall be polluted by him" (D&C 88:70, 134). Subsequent revelations would use almost identical language concerning who should or should not be permitted to enter the temple (D&C 97:15–17). Furthermore, compliance with the Word of Wisdom became a requirement for participation, and those attending accepted a commitment "not to wilfully divulge that which was discussed in the school."[1] Hence, several policies and procedures which would later be applied to temple service were anticipated in the functioning of the School of the Prophets.

To accommodate the school, the Lord commanded the brethren to "establish a house" (D&C 88:119). The Saints, eager to begin building the house, looked forward to further divine instructions. During the winter of 1833, Church leaders decided that the best location for the house or temple would be on the crest of the rise just south of the Kirtland village. From this site there was a magnificent view of Kirtland and the valley below. The blue waters of Lake Erie could be seen in the distance.[2]

On 1 June 1833, the Lord admonished the Saints to move

Richard O. Cowan is a professor of Church history and doctrine at Brigham Young University.

forward in building the temple in which "I design to endow those whom I have chosen with power from on high." He instructed them that this sacred structure should not be built "after the manner of the world" and promised to reveal a pattern to three brethren whom the Saints appoint (D&C 95:8, 13). Pursuant to this revelation, two days later a conference of high priests "appointed" three brethren—Joseph Smith, Sidney Rigdon, and Frederick G. Williams (who then constituted the First Presidency)—"to obtain a draft or construction" of the temple.[3]

The Lord fulfilled his promise to reveal the building's design. On an occasion when the three men were kneeling in prayer, "the building seemed to come right over us." This let them view its interior. While speaking in the completed temple, Frederick G. Williams testified that the hall in which they were convened coincided in every detail with the vision given to the Prophet.[4] "Joseph not only received a revelation and commandment to build a Temple," President Brigham Young affirmed, "but he received a *pattern* also, as did Moses for the Tabernacle, and Solomon for his Temple; for without a pattern, he could not know what was wanting, having never seen [a temple], and not having experienced its use."[5]

Some of the brethren favored constructing the temple of logs while others preferred a frame building. "Shall we, brethren, build a house for our God, of logs?" the Prophet challenged. "I have a better plan than that. I have a plan of the house of the Lord, given by himself; and you will soon see by this, the difference between our calculations and his idea." The Prophet then unfolded the "full pattern" for the temple, "with which the brethren were highly delighted."[6] In light of this revealed "pattern," the brethren promptly began developing plans for the Kirtland Temple as well as for a similar but larger building for Independence, Missouri.[7] On 25 June 1833, Joseph Smith sent to the brethren in Missouri his plat for the city of Zion together with plans for a temple.

The exterior may have looked something like the New England meetinghouses of the time, but it was the revealed design of the

Elijah Restores the Power to Seal Families for Eternity, *by Gary Kapp*

"inner court," or interior, that made the building plans truly unique. There would be two main rooms, one above the other.

Four levels of pulpits at both ends of the auditoriums were a unique feature of the Kirtland Temple. Those on the west end were for the Melchizedek Priesthood, while those on the east end were for the Aaronic. Initials on each pulpit represented the priesthood office held by the individual occupying it. Elder Orson Pratt affirmed that the Lord not only revealed to Joseph the size and purpose of the temple's two main rooms, but he also revealed "the order of the pulpits, and in fact everything pertaining to it was clearly pointed out by revelation."[8] Seating in the main part of these halls was reversible so the congregation could face either set of pulpits. Architect Truman O. Angell later recorded that "the leading mechanic" recommended that these seats be modified. The Prophet refused because "he had seen them in vision and insisted that the original plans be carried out."[9] Canvas partitions, or "veils," could be rolled down from the ceiling to divide the room into four quarters, enabling a separate meeting to be conducted in each area.

Actual construction on the Kirtland Temple began in June 1833. On the sixth of that month, a council of high priests directed the building committee to immediately procure materials so the work could begin. Joseph Smith, therefore, personally led a group in search of suitable stone for the temple. A source was found two miles south of the building site, and they immediately quarried a wagon load.

Eager to start, Hyrum Smith and Reynolds Cahoon began to dig by hand a trench for the foundation. The Saints were so impoverished at this time, an early member later recalled that "there was not a scraper and hardly a plow that could be obtained."[10] Nevertheless, the Prophet observed "our unity, harmony and charity abounded to strengthen us to do the commandments of God."[11] On Wednesday, 23 July 1833, Joseph Smith and other elders laid cornerstones for the Kirtland Temple "after the order of the Holy Priesthood," beginning with the southeast corner.[12]

A major interruption in temple construction occurred during the summer of 1834. At the time of the year when the weather was most favorable for construction, few workmen were available because many had joined Joseph Smith on the march of Zion's Camp to Missouri. Furthermore, funds that normally would have gone to the temple were sent to aid the distressed Saints in Zion. Following the return of Zion's Camp, work on the temple went forward more rapidly. In

October 1834, Joseph Smith recalled, "Great exertions were made to expedite the work of the Lord's house, and notwithstanding it was commenced almost with nothing, as to means, yet the way opened as we proceeded, and the Saints rejoiced."[13] At this time, the temple walls were four feet high.

The walls rose quickly during the winter of 1834–35. Almost all able-bodied men, except those away on missions, worked on the temple. Joseph Smith set the example, serving as foreman in the quarry. "Come, brethren," he admonished, "let us go into the stone-quarry and work for the Lord."[14] On Saturdays a number of men brought teams and wagons, quarried the rock, and hauled stone to the building site to keep the masons busy during the ensuing week.

Work on the temple went forward, but not without difficulty. Under the cover of darkness, vandals attempted to destroy the walls. Those who worked on the temple by day guarded it at night to protect what they had built from further mob violence. Night after night for many weeks, Heber C. Kimball recalled, "We . . . were not permitted to take off our clothes, and were obliged to lay with our fire locks in our arms."[15] President Sidney Rigdon later described how the Saints "had wet those walls with their tears, when, in the silent shades of the night, they were praying to the God of heaven to protect them, and stay the unhallowed hands of ruthless spoilers, who had uttered a prophecy . . . that the walls should never be erected."[16]

By November 1835, the exterior plastering had commenced. Crushed glassware (probably most discarded, but some, perhaps, contributed by Church members to the temple specifically for this purpose) was mixed with stucco to give the walls a glistening appearance. This covering included "weather-resistant natural cements that had recently been discovered and used in building the nearby Ohio Canal."[17] Under Brigham Young's direction, finishing touches were given to the temple interior in February 1836.

The women, under Emma Smith's direction, "made stockings, pantaloons and jackets" for the benefit of the temple workmen. "Our wives were all the time knitting, spinning and sewing," Heber C. Kimball recalled years later, and "were just as busy as any of us."[18]

They also made curtains and carpets for the Lord's house. Polly Angell, wife of the architect, recalled how Joseph Smith told the sisters: "Well, sisters, you are always on hand. The sisters are always first and foremost in all good works. Mary was first at the resurrection; and the sisters now are the first to work on the inside of the temple."[19]

During this building period, the Church faced financial distress. Funds were needed to support the temple workers. Saints in the United States and Canada were invited to make contributions as they could. Vienna Jacques, a single sister, was one of the first to donate, giving much of her material resources. John Tanner lent money to pay for the temple site, and then sold his 2,200-acre farm in New York State to give three thousand dollars to buy needed supplies. He continued to give "until he had sacrificed nearly everything he owned."[20] Others did likewise. The Saints gave or borrowed forty to sixty thousand dollars to complete the project.

Great spiritual blessings followed this period of sacrifice. The two months preceding the Kirtland Temple dedication were filled with remarkable spiritual manifestations to an unusual degree. Saints reported seeing heavenly messengers in at least ten different meetings. At five of these meetings, individuals testified that they had beheld the Savior himself. Many received visions, prophesied, and spoke in tongues.[21]

On Thursday afternoon, 21 January 1836, the First Presidency met in an upper room of the schoolhouse/printing office—a building immediately west of the temple—and were washed "in pure water." That evening "at early candle-light," the Presidency met with Patriarch Joseph Smith Sr. in the west room of the temple attic.[22] There in Joseph Smith's office, they anointed one another with consecrated olive oil and pronounced blessings and prophecies. Then "the heavens were opened," the Prophet recorded, and he "beheld the celestial kingdom of God, and the glory thereof." He saw "the blazing throne of God" and the "beautiful streets of that kingdom, which had the appearance of being paved with gold" (D&C 137:1, 3–4). Joseph also saw many prophets, both ancient and modern. When he saw his brother Alvin in the celestial kingdom, he "marveled" because Alvin had died before the gospel was restored and consequently had not been baptized by the proper authority. The Lord declared to his Prophet, "All who have died without a knowledge of this gospel, who would have received it if they had been permitted to tarry, shall be heirs of the celestial kingdom of God." Joseph was also shown that "all children who die before they arrive at the years of accountability are saved in the celestial kingdom of heaven" (D&C 137:6–7, 10).

Concerning this occasion, Joseph Smith testified,

> Many of my brethren who received the ordinance [of washing and anointing] with me saw glorious visions also. Angels ministered unto them as well as to myself, and the power of the Highest rested upon us, the house was filled with the glory of God, and we shouted Hosanna to God and the Lamb. . . . Some of them saw the face of the Savior, and . . . we all communed with the heavenly host.[23]

On 6 February, just two weeks later, various priesthood quorums met in small rooms in the temple attic and experienced yet another spiritual feast. The seventies "enjoyed a great flow of the Holy Spirit. Many arose and spoke, testifying that they were filled with the Holy Ghost, which was like fire in their bones, so that they could not hold their peace, but were constrained to cry hosanna to God and the Lamb, and glory in the highest." Others "were filled with the Spirit, and spake with tongues and prophesied." The *History of the Church* declares that "this was a time of rejoicing long to be remembered."[24] In later years, Elder Orson Pratt looked back with similar feelings on these sacred experiences in the temple:

> God was there, his angels were there, the Holy Ghost was in the midst of the people, the visions of the Almighty were opened to the minds of the servants of the living God; the vail was taken off from the minds of many; they saw the heavens opened; they beheld the angels of God; they heard the voice of the Lord; and they were filled from the crown of their heads to the soles of their feet with the power and inspiration of the Holy Ghost, and uttered forth prophecies in the midst of that congregation, which have been fulfilling from that day to the present time.[25]

Some of the most memorable spiritual experiences occurred on

Sunday, 27 March, the day of the temple dedication. Latter-day Saints from Missouri and other parts of North America crowded into Kirtland in anticipation of the great blessings the Lord had promised to bestow upon them, including a special gift or endowment of power from on high. Early that morning, hundreds stood outside the temple hoping to attend the dedicatory service. The temple doors were opened at 8:00 A.M. The First Presidency assisted in seating the congregation of nearly a thousand people, about double the building's usual capacity. With the leaders seated in the elevated pulpits and benches at each end of the hall and all the available seats in the temple filled, the massive doors were closed. Many still remained outside, including some who had sacrificed much for the temple construction and had come a long distance to attend the dedication. Sensing their disappointment, the Prophet directed them to hold an overflow meeting in the nearby schoolhouse. (The dedicatory service was repeated the following Thursday for their benefit.)

The service commenced at 9:00 A.M. A choir, seated in the four corners of the hall, provided the music. President Sidney Rigdon spoke eloquently for two and a half hours, declaring that the temple was unique among all the buildings erected for the worship of God, having been "built by divine revelation." After he concluded, the choir sang Elder W. W. Phelps's hymn "Now Let Us Rejoice." Following a twenty-minute intermission, the congregation sustained the officers of the Church, with the various priesthood quorums voting individually. Joseph Smith then prophesied that if the Saints would "uphold these men in their several stations, . . . the Lord would bless them; yea, in the name of Christ, the blessings of heaven should be theirs."[26]

The climax of the day was the dedicatory prayer, which had been given to the Prophet by revelation. After expressing gratitude for God's blessings, with tears flowing freely Joseph prayed that the Lord would accept the temple which had been built "through great tribulation . . . that the Son of Man might have a place to manifest himself to his people" (D&C 109:5). He petitioned that the blessings promised in the Lord's 1832 command to build the temple (D&C 88:117–20) might now be realized. The prayer also asked that Church leaders, members, and leaders of nations might be blessed and that the promised gathering of "the scattered remnants of Israel" might be accomplished (D&C 109:67; see also 6–9, 54–55, 68–72).

Following the prayer, the choir sang "The Spirit of God," a hymn written by Elder Phelps in anticipation of the temple's dedication. After the sacrament was administered and passed to the congregation, Joseph Smith and others testified that they saw heavenly messengers present during the service. The dedication concluded with the entire congregation standing and rendering the sacred Hosanna Shout: "Hosanna, hosanna, hosanna to God and the Lamb, amen, amen, and amen." Eliza R. Snow felt that the shout was given "with such power as seemed almost sufficient to raise the roof from the building."[27] After seven hours, the service ended at 4:00 P.M.

That evening more than four hundred priesthood bearers met in the temple. Joseph Smith instructed the brethren that they should be prepared to prophesy when directed by the Spirit. The Prophet recorded:

> Brother George A. Smith arose and began to prophesy, when a noise was heard like the sound of a rushing mighty wind, which filled the Temple, and all the congregation simultaneously arose, being moved upon by an invisible power; many began to speak in tongues and prophesy; others saw glorious visions; and I beheld the Temple was filled with angels, which fact I declared to the congregation.[28]

David Whitmer testified that "he saw three angels passing up the south aisle."[29] People living in the area heard "an unusual sound" coming from the Lord's house and saw "a bright light like a pillar of fire resting upon the Temple." Others reported seeing angels hovering over the temple and hearing heavenly singing.[30]

A transcendently important spiritual manifestation occurred on Sunday, 3 April, just one week following the temple's dedication. After the close of the afternoon worship service, Joseph Smith and Oliver Cowdery retired to the Melchizedek Priesthood pulpits at the west end of the lower room of the temple. Joseph Smith testified that "the veil was taken from our minds" and that he and Oliver beheld a series of remarkable visions. The Lord Jesus Christ himself appeared, accepted the temple, and promised to manifest himself therein "if my people will keep my commandments, and do not pollute this holy house." Moses then appeared and bestowed "the keys of the gathering of Israel from the four parts of the earth, and the leading of the ten tribes from the land of the north." Elias next conferred "the dispensation of the gospel of Abraham." Finally, in fulfillment of Malachi's prophecy, Elijah committed "the keys of this dispensation" in preparation for the "great and dreadful day of the Lord" (D&C 110: 1, 8, 11–12, 16; see also Malachi 4:5–6 and D&C 2). Through the sealing keys restored by Elijah, priesthood ordinances performed on earth can be "bound" or "sealed" in heaven; also, Latter-day Saints can perform saving priesthood ordinances in behalf of loved ones who died without the opportunity of accepting the gospel in this life. In this way, the hearts of the children are turning to their fathers. Reflecting on the significant events of 3 April, Elder Harold B. Lee concluded that restoration of these vital keys was "sufficient justification for the building of [this] temple."[31]

Less than two years after these glorious events, the forces of persecution and apostasy compelled Joseph Smith and other faithful Saints to turn their backs on their homes and the temple in Kirtland. But this was not the end of temples for Joseph Smith. Subsequent revelations called for the building of yet other temples. In Nauvoo sacred ordinances and the privilege of performing them for both the living and the dead were unfolded. In the twenty-first century, as temples increasingly dot the earth, we can be grateful for the foundations laid through the Prophet Joseph Smith at the Lord's house in Kirtland.

NOTES

1. Peterson, "History of the Schools," 24.
2. Cowan, *Temples to Dot the Earth,* 23.
3. Smith, *History of the Church,* 1:352.
4. Truman O. Angell, Autobiographical Sketch, MS, Harold B. Lee Library Special Collections, Brigham Young University, 3, cited in Marvin E. Smith, "The Builder," *Improvement Era,* October 1942, 630.

5. Brigham Young, *Journal of Discourses*, 2:31.

6. Smith, *History of Joseph Smith by His Mother,* ed. Nibley, 230.

7. T. Edgar Lyon, "The Sketches on the Papyri Backings," *Improvement Era,* May 1968, 19.

8. Orson Pratt, *Journal of Discourses*, 13:357; see also 14:273.

9. Truman O. Angell, Journal, Archives, The Church of Jesus Christ of Latter-day Saints, Salt Lake City, cited in Anderson, *Joseph Smith's Kirtland,* 157.

10. Johnson, *My Life's Review,* 16.

11. Smith, *History of the Church,* 1:349.

12. Smith, *History of the Church,* 1:400.

13. Smith, *History of the Church,* 2:167.

14. Quoted by Heber C. Kimball, *Journal of Discourses,* 10:165.

15. Smith, *History of the Church,* 2:2n.

16. Morgan, *Eliza R. Snow, an Immortal,* 59.

17. Robison, *First Mormon Temple,* 79.

18. Kimball, *Journal of Discourses,* 10:165.

19. Tullidge, *Women of Mormondom,* 76.

20. Backman, *Heavens Resound,* 153.

21. Backman, *Heavens Resound,* 285.

22. Smith, *History of the Church,* 2:379.

23. Smith, *History of the Church,* 2:381–82.

24. Smith, *History of the Church,* 2:392.

25. Pratt, *Journal of Discourses,* 18:132.

26. Smith, *History of the Church,* 2:415, 418.

27. Morgan, *Eliza R. Snow, an Immortal,* 62; see also Lael Woodbury, "Origin and Uses of the Sacred Hosanna Shout," in *Sperry Lecture Series 1975,* 18–22.

28. Smith, *History of the Church,* 2:428.

29. George A. Smith, *Journal of Discourses,* 11:10.

30. Smith, *History of the Church,* 2:428; Backman, *Heavens Resound,* 300.

31. Harold B. Lee, "Correlation and Priesthood Genealogy," address at Priesthood Genealogical Research Seminar, 1968 (Provo, Utah: Brigham Young University Press, 1969), 60, cited in Cowan, *Temples to Dot the Earth,* 33.

CHAPTER TWENTY-SIX

THE KIRTLAND SAFETY SOCIETY

Reid L. Neilson

n October of 1838, one year after Latter-day Saint apostates forced Joseph Smith to flee from Kirtland, Ohio, in the wake of the failed Kirtland Safety Society, the main body of the Latter-day Saints found themselves under siege in Far West, Missouri. Fearing a massacre and betrayed by their own military leader, the Saints surrendered their arms. They then endured the verbal abuse of their militia captors and earlier associates who had apostatized previously in Kirtland. Former apostle William E. McLellin sought out Elder Heber C. Kimball and snarled, "What do you think of the fallen prophet now? Has he not led you blindfolded long enough? Look and see yourself, poor, your family stripped and robbed, and your brethren in the same fix; are you satisfied with Joseph?" To McLellin's astonishment, Elder Kimball retorted: "Yes, I am more satisfied with him a hundred-fold than ever I was before, for I see you in the very position that [Joseph] foretold you would be in; a Judas to betray your brethren." He continued, "Where are *you?* What are you about?" Then the faithful apostle concluded: "Mormonism is true, and Joseph is a true prophet of the living God; and you with all others that turn therefrom will be damned and go to hell."[1]

"During all the lifetime of the Prophet Joseph," said Elder Francis M. Lyman, "men [including McLellin] who were associated with him in council were turning against him, warring upon him, questioning his authority, and holding that he was a fallen prophet."[2]

Reid L. Neilson is a Ph.D. candidate in religious studies at the University of North Carolina at Chapel Hill.

Elder Lyman's statement raises a number of questions. First, what did dissidents mean by the designation "fallen prophet"? None of the Lord's prophets in holy writ ever "fell" from their callings. "Some have talked of fallen prophets," one of Joseph's supporters contended. "Show me a man of this description and you show me a character of whom the Bible gives no account. I challenge the world to produce the history of a fallen prophet of God."[3] Second, why did Joseph's spiritual status decline—in the minds of apostates—because of the fall of a financial institution? Third, what do the varied 1837 Latter-day Saint responses to this crossroads suggest about the importance of Church members gaining a testimony of Joseph Smith's *entire* prophetic calling?

As I have reviewed the sources and literature on the Kirtland Safety Society, I have come to believe that this unfortunate temporal incident acted as the meridian of Joseph's spiritual career. Much as the Babe of Bethlehem cleaved the Western calendar into two distinct eras, so Joseph's involvement in Kirtland banking divided early Latter-day Saints into two opposing camps: those who still believed he was God's prophet and those who did not. As the latter's confidence in the anti-banking society fell, so did their belief in Joseph's prophetic calling. In their minds, the two issues were inextricably linked. This was a recurring theme in early Mormonism. "There were [some] during Joseph's day, who professed to have the authority which he possessed, or, as they said, which he had once possessed," President George Q. Cannon observed. "The doctrines which he had first taught were correct, they said, and the position which he first assumed was acceptable in the sight of God; but through some cause, he had strayed from the path and had become a fallen prophet."[4] As Elders Brigham Young and Willard Richards lamented in Nauvoo, "'Tis the same old story over again—'The doctrine is right, but Joseph is a fallen prophet.'"[5]

Kirtland Safety Society Bank Note

JOSEPH'S PROPHETIC AUTHORITY BEFORE THE KIRTLAND SAFETY SOCIETY, 1820–1836

Since the days of Adam, God, not man, has determined a prophet's real worth. The public's perception of a prophet has never been the final arbiter. In fact, there seems to be an inherently negative correlation between a prophet's perceived and actual authority: Prophets are rarely popular with the masses or treasured by them. Offsetting this bias, God endows his servants with spiritual resources that act as sacred signs to the honest in heart. In Joseph's case, the Lord provided him with at least six sources of prophetic authority.

Visions. Joseph Smith received an extraordinary number of visions, his first vision being received during his fifteenth year while praying for spiritual guidance.[6] Speaking from experience, he would later declare: "Could you gaze into heaven five minutes, you would know more than you would by reading all that ever was written on the subject," and he affirmed that "the best way to obtain truth and wisdom is not to ask it from books, but to go to God in prayer, and obtain divine teaching."[7] Historian Alexander Baugh has documented Joseph's recorded visions, carefully differentiating between visions and other forms of inspiration, including revelations. As he cataloged the Prophet's visionary experiences, Baugh was impressed by three factors: first, "the sheer number of visions the Prophet received";

second, that these visions "became almost commonplace experiences" for him; and third, that many of his family members and friends witnessed these visions.[8] According to Baugh, Joseph's early visions (1820–30) consisted of "personal visitations of deity, angels, and Satan," visions received through the Urim and Thummim, "and visions opened to the mind"; his later visions (1831–44) included "personal visitations from the Father and the Son together, the Son alone, other heavenly beings, and Satan."[9] The Prophet received fifty-five documented visions between the spring of 1820 and the fall of the Kirtland Safety Society in 1837.[10]

Sacred objects. Joseph's early prophetic authority was also connected to his possession of sacred objects. In 1822, two years after the First Vision, he discovered a small seer stone as he dug a well near his family's Palmyra farm. According to Lucy Mack Smith, her son could see things "invisible to the natural eye" with the aid of the stone.[11] Later, in September of 1823, the angel Moroni told Joseph about the golden plates and the Urim and Thummim (Joseph Smith–History 1:42). The Nephite interpreters were composed of "two stones which were fastened into the two rims of a bow" and "were prepared from the beginning, and were handed down from generation to generation, for the purpose of interpreting languages" by chosen seers (Mosiah 28:13–14, 16). Joseph saw the plates and the Urim and Thummim the next day but did not gain possession of them until four years had passed (Joseph Smith–History 1:52–59). He also saw other sacred objects buried in the Hill Cumorah, including a breastplate used in conjunction with the Nephite interpreters, the sword of Laban, and the Liahona, all of which were displayed to the Three Witnesses in 1829 (D&C 17:1). "From the time of the discovery of the seerstone through the completion of the [gold plates] translation," Smith biographer Richard Bushman writes, "Joseph's influence had always sprung from his followers' faith in his supernatural powers" associated with these sacred objects.[12]

The Book of Mormon. Joseph used his sacred objects—the Urim and Thummim and seerstone—to translate the ancient Nephite record—the golden plates. As a result, the Book of Mormon itself became an important indication of his prophetic authority. An April 1830 revelation states that the Lord gave Joseph "power from on high" to translate the golden plates. The Book of Mormon, then, "was given by inspiration, and is confirmed to others by the ministering of angels, and is declared unto the world by them—Proving to the world that the holy scriptures are true, and that God does inspire men and call them to his holy work in this age and generation, as well as in generations of old" (D&C 20:8–11). Book of Mormon scholar Terryl Givens argues that the translated New World scripture was the primary sacred sign of Joseph's prophetic calling. "In any assessment of Joseph's prophetic stature, the first and greatest evidence in his favor was the Book of Mormon he so miraculously obtained and translated. His role and authority as a prophet and seer rested firmly on the validity of those claims."[13]

Ancient translations. After translating the golden plates by "the gift and power of God," Joseph "seemed to embrace translation as a fixed element of his religious identity," writes Richard Bushman.[14] He began translating or revising the Old and New Testaments in June of 1830 and completed most of the translation work—known today as the Joseph Smith Translation—by June of 1833. In July of 1835, Joseph obtained Egyptian papyri and several mummies from Michael Chandler in Kirtland, Ohio, and eventually produced additional scriptures through his prophetic understanding of the Egyptian artifacts.

Revelations. Early Latter-day Saints valued Joseph's ability to receive revelations. They prized these celestial epistles and often clamored for more. "As American democracy necessarily distanced itself from direct revelation," historian Steven Harper argues, "Joseph Smith offered a satisfying alternative that appealed to people whose sole common characteristic, perhaps, was a willingness to believe that God spoke to Joseph Smith 'even as Moses'" (D&C 28:2). Latter-day Saint converts were seeking "power from on high," not "authority vested finally in the people."[15] And Joseph did not disappoint them. During his prophetic tenure, he received scores of revelations on myriads of topics including missionary work, Church organization, doctrine, temple building, gathering, and, most important, the reality of Jesus Christ. Today's Doctrine and Covenants contains more than 130 of Joseph's heavenly communications. Between September of 1823 and the spring of 1837, he recorded 111 of these published revelations.

Priesthood power. The Prophet was also blessed with priesthood power to bolster his prophetic authority and enable him to officiate in sacred ordinances. John the Baptist restored the Aaronic Priesthood to Joseph Smith and Oliver Cowdery on 15 May, 1829, near the Susquehanna River, in the area of Harmony, Pennsylvania, by the laying on of hands. Christ's chief apostles—Peter, James, and John—bestowed the Melchizedek Priesthood on both men in the same manner thereafter. In the years that followed, Joseph used his priesthood authority to baptize, heal the sick, ordain others to the priesthood, govern the church, set apart missionaries, officiate in temple ordinances, and, in general, build up Zion.

In summary, between the First Vision and the Kirtland Safety Society, Joseph's prophetic authority increased because of his visions, sacred objects, the Book of Mormon, ancient translations, revelations, and priesthood authority. By 1837 more than 13,000 North Americans had placed their trust in Joseph's religious claims and joined The Church of Jesus Christ of Latter-day Saints.[16]

JOSEPH'S PROPHETIC AUTHORITY AFTER THE KIRTLAND SAFETY SOCIETY, 1837–44

In January of 1837, Joseph and other LDS Church leaders formed the Kirtland Safety Society Anti-Banking Company to provide crucial banking services for the growing population of Latter-day Saints in northeastern Ohio. Designated as one of the early gathering places for the Latter-day Saints, Kirtland's need for capital and financial liquidity outstripped available frontier financing options. Soon Church leaders were unable to provide sufficient credit to newly arrived Church members in Kirtland, and they struggled to pay their own debts. Faced with a cash flow problem, they sought to establish a bank that "could convert long-term assets (land) into liquid assets (bank notes)." They envisioned their bank "serving the important purpose of providing credit and a circulating medium of exchange to the growing community."[17] However, during a national depression, the state legislature of Ohio in 1836 and 1837 denied the Saints, and many others, their sought-after bank charters.

To capitalize the Kirtland Safety Society, many Church members made deposits in specie, or coined money. Within a month, their anti-bank was issuing its own currency backed by limited reserves. By November 1837, their anti-bank had issued about one hundred thousand dollars in notes to the citizens of Kirtland and the surrounding communities. Unfortunately, it began losing its capacity to honor its financial obligations. The bank struggled to pay its depositors from existing cash balances. Not surprisingly, local residents began worrying about their deposits. As their confidence in the bank plummeted, so did the bank's supposed and real value. When investors finally made a run on the bank, its liabilities outstripped its assets: the Kirtland Safety Society was bankrupt.[18]

Many Latter-day Saint depositors blamed the Prophet for the loss of their money. Thereafter, they declared Joseph spiritually bankrupt and made a run on his prophetic authority. Elder Brigham Young recounted meeting in the upper room of the Kirtland Temple with several disaffected apostles and witnesses of the Book of Mormon who were plotting to replace Joseph with David Whitmer as Church president. "I rose up, and in a plain and forcible manner told them that Joseph was a Prophet, and I knew it," he recorded. And although "they might rail and slander him as much as they pleased, they could not destroy the appointment of the Prophet of God, they could only destroy their own authority, cut the thread that bound them to the Prophet and to God and sink themselves to hell."[19] Young asserted the supremacy of a prophet's true worth. It was God's confidence in Joseph that mattered, not the people's opinion. They could not destroy Joseph, but they would (and did) destroy themselves in the attempt. Moreover, no historical evidence suggests Joseph was spiritually insolvent after Kirtland.

Visions. Joseph continued to receive and record visionary

experiences subsequent to the fall of the Kirtland Safety Society. He received another twenty visions between April of 1837 and his martyrdom in June of 1844.[20] "It is my meditation all the day, and more than my meat and drink," he declared in 1843, "to know how I shall make the Saints of God comprehend the visions that roll like an overflowing surge before my mind."[21] This surge included visions of the future, heavenly beings, Zion, the organization of the Church, and temple patterns.

Sacred objects. The Prophet returned the golden plates, Urim and Thummim, breastplate, Liahona, and sword of Laban to Moroni in 1829, after he completed his translation of the Book of Mormon.[22] But he retained his seer stone, a tangible evidence of his early prophetic authority. Four years after fleeing Kirtland, Joseph displayed this stone to the Quorum of the Twelve Apostles gathered in Nauvoo. Brigham Young inherited the seer stone and showed it to Hosea Stout in 1856. Two decades later, Wilford Woodruff consecrated Joseph's seer stone on the Manti Temple altar.[23]

The Book of Mormon. All of the Three Witnesses—Oliver Cowdery, Martin Harris, and David Whitmer—left the Church in the aftermath of the Kirtland Safety Society. But not one ever recanted his testimony of the book's divine origin and content.[24] Even former apostle William E. McLellin, who accosted Heber C. Kimball in Far West, Missouri, rebuked detractors of the Book of Mormon as late as 1880. "I have set to my seal that the Book of Mormon is a true, divine record and it will require more evidence than I have ever seen to ever shake me relative to its purity," he wrote to one critic of the Church. "I have more confidence in the Book of Mormon than any book of this wide earth!"[25] As Givens points out, "If Joseph Smith turned traitor to God, it took nothing from the privileged status he once held as mouthpiece of a sacred revelation from the dust. Fallen prophets, like fallen angels, could not be denied their prior glory, even by the faithless."[26] During Joseph's lifetime, the Church printed five editions of the Book of Mormon, three of them after the fall of the Kirtland Safety Society.

Ancient translations. After fleeing from Kirtland, Joseph continued to work on his translations of the Egyptian papyri. He published his inspired translations, the writings of Abraham, in three issues of the Church's *Times and Seasons* newspaper in the spring of 1842. Church members read these writings as continuing proof of a prophet in their midst. He also continued to refine his translation of the Old and New Testaments and prepare it for print.

Revelations. From July 1837 until June 1844, Joseph received sections 112 through 132 of the Doctrine and Covenants. Many of these revelations are considered to be among his most important scriptural contributions. For example, he revealed doctrines describing the temple experience, baptism for the dead, and eternal marriage. Furthermore, several of his classic sermons, including his remarks at the funeral of King Follett, came forth in Nauvoo, not in Kirtland. On one occasion, Joseph rebuked Nauvoo Church members for being unable to receive even more revelations. "Some people say I am a fallen Prophet, because I do not bring forth more of the word of the Lord. Why do I not do it? Are we able to receive it? No! not one in this room." He then bemoaned: "a man would command his son to dig potatoes and saddle his horse, but before he had done either he would tell him to do something else. This is all considered right; but as soon as the Lord gives a commandment and revokes that decree and commands something else, then the Prophet is considered fallen."[27]

Priesthood power. Finally, Joseph continued to exercise his priesthood power in Missouri and Illinois. His dramatic healing of Elijah Fordham and several other Latter-day Saints on both sides of the Mississippi River in July of 1839 is evidence of his priesthood. He also officiated in priesthood ordinances and, while in Nauvoo, began to endow the Saints with the higher priesthood ordinances of the temple. Most important, Joseph passed vital priesthood keys to Brigham Young and the other apostles, which enabled the Restoration to continue after the martyrdom.

Sadly, some Ohio residents believed they could make a run on the Prophet Joseph just as they had on the Kirtland Safety Society. In their minds, when the bank fell, so did the Prophet. As a result, they plunged into spiritual bankruptcy. Yet Joseph, thanks to a merciful God, maintained the divine resources that buttressed his early prophetic authority. The historical record shows that God was still with his prophet after the Kirtland Safety Society and through Joseph's death.

CONCLUSION

Ninety years after the fall of the Kirtland Safety Society, Elder B. H. Roberts dismissed the weathered allegation that Joseph fell from prophetic grace. The year was 1926, and LDS Church membership now numbered over 623,000—an increase of 2,296 percent since dissenters drove Joseph from Kirtland.[28] "There are those who undertake to say that Joseph Smith was a fallen prophet, and that in the latter years of his life he marred his mission," Elder Roberts thundered.

> A fallen prophet! What? [Joseph] is no fallen prophet. His life ended *en crescendo.* It grew richer, it grew greater as it neared its close. His nearness to God was emphasized more in the closing years of his life than ever before. The revelations that he gave increased in power and magnificence. And so, too, in his discourses, they grew in magnificence and power as he proclaimed God's great and mighty truths in the last few months of his life. The Saints of God who witnessed the inspiration of God upon him, come to us with testimonies of his increasing power as a Prophet of God in the latter years of his life.[29]

In Elder Roberts's view, Joseph was martyred standing tall before God. He was no fallen prophet, as evidenced by "the great sermons that he delivered near the close of his life, such as the King Follett sermon."[30]

In conclusion, I echo the sentiments of Elder Roberts and the majority of the early Saints who held their spiritual prophet in greater esteem than their temporal profits. The sources of Joseph's prophetic intrinsic value—visions, sacred objects, the Book of Mormon, ancient translations, revelations, and priesthood power—remained constant before, during, and after the fall of the Kirtland Safety Society. As the faithful antebellum Latter-day Saints and their twenty-first century-counterparts realize, it is one thing to believe that Joseph was the Lord's prophet near Cumorah; it is quite another to know that he was still God's seer in Carthage. Yet this is the task that all Church members can and must complete: gaining a testimony that the Prophet of the Restoration lived his life in crescendo, not diminuendo. Joseph "lived great, and he died great in the eyes of God and his people" (D&C 135:3).

NOTES

1. Whitney, *Life of Heber C. Kimball*, 218.
2. Stuy, ed., *Collected Discourses*, 4:6.
3. "Conference Proceedings," *Times and Seasons* 4, no. 18 (August 1, 1843): 282.
4. Cannon, in *Journal of Discourses*, 13:45.
5. Smith, *History of the Church*, 6:354.
6. See Baugh, "Parting the Veil," 48.
7. Smith, *Teachings of the Prophet Joseph Smith*, 191, 324.
8. Baugh, "Parting the Veil," 24–25.
9. Baugh, "Parting the Veil," 25, 34.
10. Baugh, "Parting the Veil," 57–61.
11. Bushman, *Joseph Smith and the Beginnings of Mormonism*, 69.
12. Bushman, *Joseph Smith and the Beginnings of Mormonism*, 148.
13. Givens, *By the Hand of Mormon*, 84.
14. Richard Lyman Bushman, "Joseph Smith as Translator," in *Believing History*, ed. Neilson and Woodworth, 234.
15. Harper, "'Dictated by Christ,'" 3.
16. *Deseret Morning News 2004 Church Almanac*, 580.
17. Garr, Cannon, and Cowan, *Encyclopedia of Latter-day Saint History*, 622.
18. Garr, Cannon, and Cowan, *Encyclopedia of Latter-day Saint History*, 622.
19. Watson, ed., *Manuscript History of Brigham Young*, 15–16.
20. Baugh, "Parting the Veil," 61–63.
21. Smith, *Teachings of the Prophet Joseph Smith*, 296.
22. It is unclear how much access Joseph had to the breastplate, Liahona, and sword of Laban during this time.
23. Bushman, *Joseph Smith and the Beginnings of Mormonism*, 69.
24. See Anderson, *Investigating the Book of Mormon Witnesses*.
25. William E. McLellin to James T. Cobb, August 14, 1880, in Porter, "William E. McLellin's Testimony of the Book of Mormon," 486.
26. Givens, *By the Hand of Mormon*, 88.
27. Smith, *History of the Church*, 4:478.
28. *Church Almanac*, 581.
29. Roberts, Conference Report, October 1926, 127.
30. Roberts, Conference Report, October 1926, 127.

CHAPTER TWENTY-SEVEN

"LET THE CITY FAR WEST BE A HOLY AND CONSECRATED LAND"

Craig K. Manscill

"There is such a wide difference in the aspect and prospect of Far West, that I hardly know how to describe it to you," wrote William W. Phelps to his wife, Sally. "The inhabitants are gone. The sound of the hammer, and the bustle of business have ceased; The grass is growing in the streets, or where they were: The fences have disappeared, and nothing but empty houses, and the moaning of the Spring breeze, tell what was in Zion."[1] So wrote Phelps on 1 May 1839, four months after the exodus of the Latter-day Saints from Caldwell County, Missouri. The exiled Saints, still loyal to Mormonism and the Prophet Joseph Smith, were forced to leave Missouri by order of the governor. A small number of Mormons remained in Far West and vicinity; however, most had abandoned the faith, much like the Phelps family.[2]

From 14 March to 1 November 1838, less than eight months, Joseph Smith resided in Far West. There he received eight revelations, reorganized the leading quorums of the Church, directed the settlement of two counties, dedicated a temple site, called missionaries to labor locally and abroad, and cleansed the Church of dissidents. These events tested the leadership and prophetic role of Joseph Smith during the Far West period.

THE CHURCH SETTLES IN FAR WEST

As early as 1834, Latter-day Saint families began settling north and east of Clay County in sparsely populated Ray County. By March

Craig K. Manscill is an associate professor of Church history and doctrine at Brigham Young University.

1836, Church leaders were searching for a permanent site for these Saints in the less inhabited regions north of Ray County. After extensive exploration, leaders purchased a one-mile-square plot situated near Shoal Creek on 8 August 1836. The site was subsequently named Far West.

As Latter-day Saint numbers increased in this region, some believed that the Mormon problem might be solved if a county were created exclusively for them. Alexander Doniphan, a representative to the state legislature and a friend of the Mormons, spearheaded a bill in the legislature to create such a county. The passage of Doniphan's bill on 29 December 1836 created not just one county but two. The first, measuring 18 by 24 miles, was created for the Latter-day Saints and named in honor of Matthew Caldwell of Kentucky, an Indian scout and soldier in the Revolutionary War and a friend of Alexander's father, Joseph Doniphan. Far West was designated the county seat. It was assumed that Latter-day Saints would confine themselves to this county. The second county, Daviess, situated north of Caldwell, was nearly twenty-four miles square and named for Colonel Joseph H. Daviess, another friend of Alexander's father. He was killed in the 1811 Battle of Tippecanoe. Gallatin was selected as the county seat of Daviess.[3]

The prospects of northern Missouri becoming a permanent settlement for Latter-day Saints brought Joseph Smith to Far West in November 1837. After his arrival, he and several of the brethren held meetings for approximately ten days. At these meetings, it was concluded that there were enough resources and space in northern Missouri for the gathering of the Saints. A committee was formed to locate sites for new settlements. In addition, problems relating to the selling of land in Far West associated with the activities of the stake presidency in Missouri were temporarily resolved, and the presidency, W. W. Phelps, David Whitmer, and John Whitmer, were sustained once again in their callings. At a 7 November meeting, Frederick G. Williams was rejected as second counselor in the First Presidency due to his role in selling church lands in Jackson County; Hyrum Smith was sustained in his place.

From the decisions made at these March meetings, it was clear that Far West would function as the future headquarters of the Church. Thus, from 1834 to 1839 the Latter-day Saint population in and around Far West mushroomed to nearly 5,000 inhabitants, making it the largest community in northwestern Missouri. Conservative figures put the Caldwell County population at 8,000, although it may have been as high as 10,000. The large Mormon populace gave the Church political control of the county. By fall of 1838, the county clerk, two judges, thirteen magistrates, and the militia officers were all Mormon. According to the history of Caldwell County, the Saints built "150 homes, four dry goods stores, three family grocery stores, several blacksmith shops, two hotels, a printing shop, and a large schoolhouse that doubled as a church and courthouse."[4]

FAR WEST REVELATIONS AND TEACHINGS

In late April 1838, the Prophet received a revelation designating "The Church of Jesus Christ of Latter-day Saints" as the correct name for the Church (D&C 115:4). This settled a growing confusion, for the congregation of Saints had been referred to as the Church of Christ, the Church of the Latter Day Saints, and the Church of Christ of Latter Day Saints. In that revelation, the Lord also commanded the building of a temple: "Let the city, Far West, be a holy and consecrated land unto me; and it shall be called most holy, for the ground upon which thou standest is holy" (D&C 115:7). The First Presidency was instructed not to incur debt for the temple as had been done in Kirtland. The Lord also directed the brethren to establish stakes in the surrounding regions. This was to be done so "that the gathering together upon the land of Zion, and upon her stakes, may be for a defense, and for a refuge from the storm, and from wrath when it shall be poured out without mixture upon the whole earth" (D&C 115:6).

The Prophet spent the next three weeks visiting with and teaching the Saints in Caldwell County about the principles of the gospel. "The first time I saw the Prophet Joseph Smith," said James B. Bracken Sr., "was in June, 1838, in the town of Far West, Caldwell County,

Far West Honey, *by Al Rounds*

Missouri. I went to a meeting and he preached to the people, teaching them the principles of salvation."[5]

Soon after, with the assistance of Sidney Rigdon, the Prophet embarked on an ambitious project to write the history of the Church. John Whitmer, Church historian, had refused to turn over his brief history for publication. A letter to Whitmer from the Prophet dated 9 April stated:

> Sir. We were desireous of honouring you by giving publicity to your notes on the history of the Church of Latter day Saints, after such corrections as we thought would be necessary. . . . if you can be made to know your own interest and give up your notes, so that they can be corrected, and made fit for the press. But if not, we have all the materials for another, which we shall commence this week to write.
>
> Your humble Servents
>
> Joseph Smith Jr
>
> Sidney Rigdon[6]

The history of Joseph Smith and the early events of the Restoration in the Pearl of Great Price were the results of their labors begun in April 1838.

JOSEPH DIRECTS THE SETTLEMENTS IN CALDWELL AND DAVIESS COUNTIES

While Far West was the largest community in Caldwell County, additional settlements were established on or near Shoal, Log, Bush, Mill, Panther, Mud, and Plum Creeks, and Crooked River. Many of these settlements were named for their founders or prominent inhabitants. For example, the Allred settlement was named for William, William M., and Wiley Allred; the Curtis settlement was named for Jeremiah Curtis; the Carter settlement for Simeon and Orlando Carter; the Durfee settlement for James and Perry Durfee; the Free settlement for Absalom and Joseph Free; the Lyon settlement, called Salem, for Aaron C. Lyon; the Myers settlement for Jacob Myers; the Plumb settlement for Merlin Plumb; the Stevens settlement for Roswell Stevens; and the Haun's Mill settlement for Jacob Haun. These sites were abandoned when the Latter-day Saints were expelled from the state.

In 1837 Saints settled in Daviess County. One of the most prominent settlers was Lyman Wight. In February 1838, he purchased a farm and established a ferry on the Grand River in the area known as Spring Hill. On 19 May 1838, while visiting Elder Wight, the Prophet Joseph received a revelation disclosing that Spring Hill "is named by the Lord Adam-ondi-Ahman, because . . . it is the place where Adam shall come to visit his people" (D&C 116:1). Consequently, in the summer of 1838 a major settlement was established at Adam-ondi-Ahman (called Diahman). It became the most populated community in the county. On 28 June 1838, the Prophet Joseph Smith organized a stake in that community with John Smith, uncle to the Prophet, as president and Reynolds Cahoon and Lyman Wight as counselors. Vinson Knight was called to be acting bishop, and a temple site was dedicated by Brigham Young. Besides Diahman, Latter-day Saints resided in the Marrow-bone (also called Ambrosia), Honeycreek, Lickfork, and Grindstone Fork settlements. Hostilities, which began in August 1838, erupted in mid-October 1838, forcing many residing in these outlying areas to move to Diahman for safety and protection, swelling its population to 1,500. When Church leaders agreed to surrender and leave the state in November 1838, Latter-day Saints evacuated Daviess County and relocated temporarily in Caldwell before making their way out of the state in the winter of 1838–39. After the Saints left, Adam-ondi-Ahman became known as Cravensville, named after John Cravens. By the early 1870s, most of the remaining settlers, who were not Mormons, had abandoned the community.

JOSEPH CLEANSES THE CHURCH AND REORGANIZES THE PRIESTHOOD QUORUMS

The problems associated with dissenters that plagued the Church in Ohio were also evident in Missouri. Even before the Prophet arrived in Far West, leaders in Missouri were mishandling Church funds, challenging Joseph's authority, questioning his worthiness, and sowing seeds of dissent. During the winter of 1837–38, discord had erupted between the stake presidency and the high council. Oliver Cowdery and Frederick G. Williams, who had been out of harmony with the Prophet in Kirtland, had moved to Far West and, together with the stake presidency, sold Church lands in Jackson County held in their names. Selling lands in Zion violated the Lord's directive that the Saints continue to hold claim to their lands in Jackson County (D&C 101:99).

In early February 1838, the high council tried John Whitmer and W. W. Phelps for misuse of sacred funds and David Whitmer for willfully breaking the Word of Wisdom. Despite some feelings that the high council was not authorized to hold a court on the stake presidency, a majority voted to reject them, and a resolution to this effect was sent to the branches and accepted by the Saints. When the presidency claimed that the court trial was illegal and that they had not been present to defend themselves, the high council was convinced that they were "endeavoring to palm themselves off upon the Church, as her Presidents" after they had been properly removed.[7] Therefore, on 10 February the high council, with the assistance of two apostles, excommunicated W. W. Phelps and John Whitmer and sustained Thomas B. Marsh and David W. Patten as acting presidents until the arrival of Joseph Smith. Additional actions against David Whitmer, Oliver Cowdery, and Lyman Johnson were postponed pending the Prophet's return to Far West.

In a letter to Joseph, Elder Marsh explained,

> Had we not taken the above measures, we think that nothing could have prevented a rebellion against the whole high council and bishop; so great was the disaffection against the presidents, that the people began to be jealous, that the whole authorities were inclined to uphold these men in wickedness, and in a little time the church, undoubtedly, would have gone, every man to his own way, like sheep without a shepherd.[8]

Joseph concurred and removed the stake presidency upon his return to Far West.

At the April general conference, the Prophet called three senior members of the Quorum of the Twelve Apostles—Thomas B. Marsh, David W. Patten, and Brigham Young—as the new stake presidency in Missouri. After the conference, this presidency held court on other dissidents. Oliver Cowdery was charged with persecuting Church leaders with vexatious lawsuits, seeking to destroy the character of Joseph Smith, failing to abide ecclesiastical authority in temporal affairs, selling lands in Jackson County, and leaving his calling as Assistant President of the Church and turning to the practice of law. Oliver refused to appear before the council but asked that his fellowship in the Church be withdrawn. On 12 April 1838, he was excommunicated. The council also cut off David Whitmer on charges of usurping too much authority, writing letters of dissension to apostates, and breaking the Word of Wisdom. Lyman Johnson was cut off at the same time.

Even though excommunicating such former stalwarts was painful, the new stake presidency felt it necessary to cleanse the Church. By June 1838, with the exception of William E. McLellin, the excommunicated dissenters were still living in Far West and posing a threat to Church leaders. The five men who posed the greatest threat were Oliver Cowdery, David and John Whitmer, W. W. Phelps, and Lyman Johnson. An ultimatum was issued publicly and individually to these men informing them that they were no longer welcome in Far West. The ultimatum did not produce the desired results until Sidney Rigdon gave his infamous "Salt Sermon."⁹ While Rigdon did not name names in his speech, he clearly left the impression that the detractors were not welcome in Far West.

In the meantime, the Prophet turned to the important matter of filling vacancies in the Quorum of the Twelve Apostles. There was great sadness over the loss of four of the original Twelve to apostasy. Elizabeth Barlow reflected, "We felt more sorrowful at seeing Apostles leave the Church than we did over our trials and persecutions."¹⁰ Despite the grief felt by many, Joseph prayed, "Show unto us thy will O Lord concerning the Twelve."¹¹ In the revelation that followed, the Lord directed that "men be appointed to supply the place of those who are fallen" (D&C 118:1). John Taylor, John E. Page, Wilford Woodruff, and Willard Richards were called. Elders Taylor and Page were ordained on 19 December 1838 in Far West by Brigham Young and Heber C. Kimball. Elder Woodruff and Elder George A. Smith were ordained on 26 April 1839 in Far West (D&C 118:6). Elder Richards was ordained in April 1840 in Great Britain. The revelation concerning the Twelve also instructed Thomas B. Marsh to continue publishing the Lord's word (in the *Elders' Journal*) in Far West and directed others to preach "in all lowliness of heart, in meekness and humility, and long-suffering" (D&C 118:3). The Lord further charged the Twelve to prepare to depart on 26 April 1839 from Far West "to go over the great waters, and there promulgate my gospel" (D&C 118:4).

On the day this revelation was received, Joseph Smith read to the Saints two other revelations concerning Church revenues. With the Church deeply mired in economic difficulties, the Prophet sought clarification on how the law of consecration should be applied. The Lord modified the law given in 1831 when he said:

I require all their surplus property to be put into the hands of the bishop of my church in Zion,

For the building of mine house, and for the laying of the foundation of Zion and for the priesthood, and for the debts of the Presidency of my Church.

And this shall be the beginning of the tithing of my people.

And after that, those who have thus been tithed shall pay one-tenth of all their interest [income] annually; and this shall be a standing law unto them forever. (D&C 119:1–4)

The second revelation assigned a committee of general authorities with the responsibility of expending the tithes (D&C 120).

CELEBRATION IN FAR WEST ON 4 JULY 1838

By 4 July 1838, the Church in Far West had reached its zenith. The celebrations of that day gave evidence that the Latter-day Saints had become a permanent presence in northern Missouri. An oration by President Sidney Rigdon made that fact clear. Parley P. Pratt wrote of Sidney's speech and the activities of that day:

On the Fourth of July, 1838, many thousands of our people assembled at the city of Far West, the county seat of Caldwell, erected a liberty pole, and hoisted the bald eagle, with its stars and stripes, upon the top of the same. Under the colors of our count[r]y we laid the corner stone of a house of worship, and had an address delivered by Elder Rigdon, in which was painted, in lively colors, the oppression which we had long suffered from the hands of our enemies; and in this discourse we claimed and declared our constitutional rights, as American citizens, and manifested a determination to do our utmost endeavors, from that time forth, to resist all oppression, and to maintain our rights and freedom according to the holy principles of liberty, as guaranteed to every person by the constitution and laws of our government. This declaration was received with shouts of hosannah to God and the Lamb, and with many and long cheers by the assembled thousands, who were determined to yield their rights no more, except compelled by a superior power.

With the events that soon followed, the rights of the Saints were trampled by the power of the state. Elder Pratt wrote of the war clouds that gathered:

The thunder rolled in awful majesty over the city of Far West, and the arrows of lightning fell from the clouds and shivered the liberty pole from top to bottom; thus manifesting to many that there was an end to liberty and law in that state, and that our little city strove in vain to maintain the liberties of a country which was ruled by wickedness and rebellion. It seemed to portend the awful fate which awaited that devoted city.[12]

Far West, a "holy and consecrated land," was devastated by government sanctions. Yet the Lord's decree that Far West be a holy place has never been rescinded.

NOTES

1. Alexander L. Baugh, "A Community Abandoned: W. W. Phelps's 1839 Letter to Sally Waterman Phelps from Far West, Missouri," *Nauvoo Journal* 10 (Fall 1998): 26.

2. It should be noted that W. W. Phelps returned to the Church in 1840. He addressed the Prophet in a heartfelt letter asking for forgiveness and fellowship. See Joseph Smith's reply, 22 July 1840, in Smith, *History of the Church,* 4:164.

3. See Baugh, "Community Abandoned," 26.

4. Allen and Leonard, *Story of the Latter-day Saints,* 116–17.

5. *Juvenile Instructor* 27, no. 7 (April 1, 1892): 203.

6. Jessee, *Papers of Joseph Smith,* 226–27.

7. Smith, *History of the Church,* 3:7.

8. *Elders' Journal,* July 1838, 45.

9. Baugh, "Community Abandoned," 22.

10. Arrington and Madsen, *Sunbonnet Sisters,* 24.

11. Smith, *History of the Church,* 3:46.

12. "A History, of the Persecution, of the Church of Jesus Christ, of Latter Day Saints in Missouri," *Times and Seasons* 1, no. 5 (March 1840): 81–82.

CHAPTER TWENTY-EIGHT

"THE MORMONS MUST BE TREATED AS ENEMIES"

Alexander L. Baugh

ne of the most nefarious names in early Mormon history is that of Missouri governor Lilburn W. Boggs. His infamy among Latter-day Saints is primarily due to an executive directive issued by him on 27 October 1838 known as the Extermination Order which declared that "the Mormons must be treated as enemies, and must be exterminated or driven from the State if necessary for the public peace."[1] Within three days, 2,500 state militia were on the outskirts of the Mormon settlement of Far West calling for the surrender of the Mormons and demanding they comply with the governor's mandate. Faced with no alternative but to leave, during late 1838 and early 1839 some 5,000 to 6,000 Latter-day Saints made their way to Illinois, where they obtained refuge and sanctuary with the more hospitable citizens of that state.

The action taken by Boggs raises several questions. Why did he issue the order? What events led him to take such action? What did he mean that the Mormons "must be exterminated or driven from the State if necessary"? What were his intentions? Did the order authorize full-scale annihilation, or was it one of removal?

CAUSE NO. 1: JOSEPH SMITH TAKES UP PERMANENT RESIDENCE IN FAR WEST

During the latter part of 1837 the Mormon Church was fractured by internal dissension in Ohio. At the heart of the agitation was not

Alexander L. Baugh is an associate professor of Church history and doctrine at Brigham Young University.

so much Mormonism per se as it was dissatisfaction with Joseph Smith and the temporal policies he incorporated into the Church. The nationwide economic panic of 1837, inflated land prices, and the failure of the Church-backed Kirtland Safety Society Anti-Banking Company caused a sizeable number of Saints to question Joseph Smith's leadership and inspiration. Warren Parish, John F. Boynton, Luke S. Johnson, and Martin Harris were the leading and most influential detractors. By January 1838, the Kirtland dissenters had gained the upper hand, threatening the Mormon leader with legal battles and personal threats against his life. Seeing no other recourse, in January 1838, Joseph Smith fled Kirtland for Missouri. After a two-month journey, the Prophet arrived in Far West on 14 March 1838 where he took up permanent residence.

By the time of his arrival in Missouri, Mormons had lived and occupied various counties in the western part of the state for over seven years. Although Mormon occupation of the region had been fraught with turmoil, including the forced removal of the Mormon community from Jackson County in 1833, followed by a more voluntary removal of the Latter-day Saint population from Clay County to Caldwell County (a county created by the state legislature exclusively for the Mormons) in 1836, relative peace had prevailed for over a year. Significantly, during this time, the headquarters of the Church had remained in Ohio. However, the Prophet's move to Far West in 1838 signaled that the Mormon center was taking up a permanent position in Missouri once and for all. This did not set well with locals who believed that as long as the Prophet and the headquarters of the Church remained in Ohio, Mormonism in Missouri could probably be contained. Once Far West became the primary place of gathering, Missourians feared it would only be a matter of time before Mormons would dominate the region.

CAUSE NO. 2: MORMON EXPANSION OUTSIDE CALDWELL COUNTY

In December 1836, Alexander Doniphan, the chief legal counsel for the Mormons and Clay County's representative to the state

Leaving Missouri, *by C. C. A. Christensen.* © *Intellectual Reserve, Inc.*
Courtesy BYU Museum of Art

legislature, spearheaded a bill in the Missouri House to create a new
county exclusively for the Mormons. Passage of Doniphan's bill came
on 29 December. With the creation of Caldwell County, Missourians
believed that most of the state's problems with the Mormons had been
essentially resolved. However, by creating Caldwell for Mormon occupation, officials were actually setting up conditions for a potentially
greater conflict. With a county exclusively their own, Missouri
Mormons immediately began relocating in the area. Members and new
converts in the East, encouraged by the news that a region had been
designated exclusively for Latter-day Saint settlement also began
pouring in. Believing the Mormon migration to Far West and the rest
of Caldwell County would cause the county to be filled up or overrun,
Joseph Smith in late 1837 publicly declared the Church's proposition
that other of the "upper counties," with probable reference to Daviess
County, could support newcomers and that "other stakes" would be
created and organized "in the regions round about."[2] While Caldwell
remained the principal gathering place, with Daviess County second,
Mormons did not confine themselves to just these two counties. In

July 1838 Latter-day Saint emigrants began purchasing property in the community of De Witt, in Carroll County. In addition, Ray, Livingston, Clinton, and Chariton Counties had a share of Mormon occupants. Thus, with the expectation that an ever-growing number of Latter-day Saints would continue to emigrate and settle in Caldwell, and the fact that there were those of the faith who were beginning to colonize in the surrounding regions contrary to original agreements, Mormon phobia once again resurfaced. Wrote one Missouri reporter, "the Mormons . . . agreed to settle in, and confine themselves to . . . the county of Caldwell; but they have violated that agreement, and are spreading over Davies[s], Clinton, Livingston, and Carroll." He went on to say that so many Mormons had moved into Daviess County that it would not be long before the local settlers would be governed "by the Revelations of the great Prophet, Joe Smith, . . . hence their anxiety to rid themselves of [them]."[3]

CAUSE NO. 3: SIDNEY RIGDON'S SALT SERMON

Joseph Smith expected Missouri would bring a respite from the internal opposition he experienced in the Kirtland community. However, at the time of his arrival at Far West, the Missouri Church was in the middle of an apostasy crisis of its own. Between March and May of 1838, several leading elders, including Oliver Cowdery; David, John, and Jacob Whitmer; William E. McLellin; William W. Phelps; Frederick G. Williams; and Lyman Johnson, were the subject of Church discipline. While Brothers Phelps and Williams reconciled with the authorities, Cowdery, the Whitmer brothers, McLellin, and Johnson were formally cut off from the Church. Following their excommunication, the dissenters (with the exception of McLellin who had left and moved to Liberty) remained in Far West where they continued to stir up trouble. Fearing a repeat of Kirtland, an ultimatum was issued publicly and individually to the detractors that they were no longer welcome in Far West. On 17 June 1838, during a worship service of the Saints at the public square, Sidney Rigdon delivered a scathing sermon, using as his text the words of Jesus from

St. Matthew, "If the salt have lost its savour, it is thenceforth good for nothing, but to be cast out and trodden under the feet of men" (Matthew 5:13), making it explicitly clear that the men would be expected to move from the county. The rhetorical threats made against the dissenters produced the desired results, and within a few days, the men left, taking up permanent residence with their families in Richmond, Ray County. The episode involving the dissenters' expulsion opened the door for further troubles between Mormons and non-Mormons. Following their flight, these former Mormon leaders were quick to spread the news of their alleged mistreatment. Their reports of so-called abuse by the Mormon leadership were evidence to the Missourians that Joseph Smith and his associates could not be trusted. Furthermore, it reconfirmed in the minds of the Missourians that the Latter-day Saints posed a genuine threat to the peace and security of the region.

CAUSE NO. 4: SIDNEY RIGDON'S JULY 4TH SPEECH

The Mormon Independence Day celebration held at the public square of Far West on 4 July 1838 proved to be another defining moment in connection with the Mormon expulsion from Missouri. The order of the day included a military parade, music, prayers, a flag ceremony, and the dedication and laying of the four cornerstones for the proposed temple. However, these events were upstaged by an articulate and passionate oration given by Sidney Rigdon. Rigdon used the occasion to eloquently recount the principles of freedom by which the founders established the government and the rights to which religious societies are entitled under its provisions. Speaking in general terms he also spoke of the false reports circulated about Mormonism as well as the persecution and suffering experienced by the Church from its earliest beginnings. But in his closing statements, the speech took on a different tone. Buoyed by the relative peace which had existed in northern Missouri since 1836, and secure in the notion that continued emigration would result in a steady increase in

Mormon population, Rigdon announced that the Mormons would no longer suffer abuse at the hands of their enemies. "We have proved the world with kindness, we have suffered their abuse without cause, with patience, and have endured without resentment, until this day. . . . But from this day and this hour, we will suffer it no more." His final words were words of warning. "That mob that comes on us to disturb us; it shall be between us and them a war of extermination, for we will follow them, till the last drop of their blood is spilled, or else they will have to exterminate us; for we will carry the seat of war to their own houses, and their own families, and one party or the other shall be utterly destroyed."[4] Looking back six years later, Jedediah M. Grant believed Rigdon's speech reignited the fire of Missouri anti-Mormon opposition. "[The oration] was the main auxiliary that fanned into a flame the burning wrath of the mobocratic portion of the Missourians. They now had an excuse, their former threats were renewed, and soon executed, [and] we were then . . . all made accountable for the acts of one man."[5] Brigham Young's hindsight concerning the occasion was similar to that of Grant's. He noted, "Elder Rigdon was the prime cause of our troubles in Missouri, by his fourth of July oration."[6]

CONFLICTS BETWEEN THE MORMONS AND MISSOURIANS

Following Rigdon's speech, Missourians living in the counties bordering Caldwell prepared to strike out against the Mormons. Beginning on 6 August 1838 and continuing through 27 October (the date Boggs issued the Extermination Order), at least six conflicts broke out between the two groups. The first of these was the election-day skirmish in Gallatin, the county seat of Daviess County. In spite of the fact that Caldwell County had been created and designated for the Mormons, a significant number of Latter-day Saints lived in other Missouri counties, and the majority of those who lived outside Caldwell lived in Daviess, situated just to the north. On 6 August, a number of Mormon men turned out at Gallatin to exercise their right to vote in the state election. When the Mormons started for the polls, several Missourians put up some resistance and a bloody fight broke out. Being unarmed, the Mormon men used what means were available for their defense, including rocks, clubs, and an occasional butcher knife. The entire melee lasted only about two minutes, and fortunately no one on either side was killed, but there were plenty of cuts, bruises, and sore skulls. Although it is still unclear whether or not the Mormons ever voted, to the settlers living in the northern counties the incident was evidence they could not live compatibly with their Mormon neighbors.

The next major conflict occurred during the latter half of August and through September when vigilante forces from Daviess, Livingston, Carroll, and Saline Counties intimidated and harassed Mormon settlers living in Daviess and Livingston Counties. In order to be assured of greater protection from hostile bands, the majority of Mormon families living in outlying settlements in Daviess as well as the adjacent counties moved to Adam-ondi-Ahman and established temporary quarters. When news of the vigilante activities reached Missouri officials, the regional state militia, under the command of David R. Atchison, was called out to put down the disturbances. By mid-September, temporary order was restored.

Following the scene of conflict in Daviess, vigilante forces shifted their field of operations to De Witt, a small Mormon settlement in southeast Carroll County. Beginning 1 October, several hundred local citizens laid siege to the settlement. Local Mormon leaders dispatched A. L. Caldwell, a non-Mormon and sympathetic local citizen, to Jefferson City to meet with the governor and to request military intervention. Caldwell's trip was unsuccessful. Upon returning he indicated the governor was unsympathetic towards the Mormons and refused to intervene. "The quarrel was between the Mormons and the mob," Caldwell reported Boggs as saying, and "we might fight it out."[7] For several days, the Mormons succeeded in defending the community but finally capitulated on 10 October. Following the surrender, approximately four hundred Latter-day Saints abandoned their homes and property and moved to Caldwell County.

After the removal of the Saints from De Witt, vigilante members immediately set out to recommence operations in Daviess County in an attempt to bring about the wholesale removal of the Mormons from that region. The cry of the expulsionist forces was to drive the Mormons "from Daviess to Caldwell and from Caldwell to hell."[8] They also supposed they had little to fear, believing the Mormons would give them only moderate resistance and confident most civil officers and members of the state militia were actually on their side and would not intervene or attempt to check them in their activities. Knowing they could not afford to give up any of their claims in Daviess, Mormon leaders moved to oppose and halt additional incursions by vigilante groups. Hereafter, using what they considered to be state-authorized and sanctioned Mormon militias from both Caldwell and Daviess counties, Latter-day Saint officials and military officers initiated active, rather than passive, defensive warfare. Beginning on 18 October, Mormon troops marched against anti-Mormon antagonists in three settlement areas—Millport and Gallatin in Daviess County, and the Grindstone Fork region situated about eleven miles west of Adam-ondi-Ahman. The Mormons scored victories in each area before the troops returned to Caldwell. Following the raids, Mormon guards in Daviess County continued their patrols of the region searching for vigilante forces who roamed the area.

The standoff in Daviess County between the Mormons and the Missouri vigilantes shifted the seat of the conflict from Daviess County in the north to Ray County in the south. During the early morning hours of 25 October 1838, a contingent of Mormon militia from Caldwell County, engaged in armed conflict with a company of state militia from Ray County under the command of Captain Samuel Bogart at Crooked River in northern Ray County. The event was precipitated when word reached Far West that Bogart's men had taken three Mormon men prisoners and threatened to kill them. Elias Higbee, a Caldwell County judge, issued a call for volunteers to go rescue the prisoners, appointing David W. Patten, a Mormon apostle, to lead the company. Although the Caldwell militia succeeded in routing Bogart's troops and in rescuing the Mormon prisoners, a number of casualties resulted on both sides. Three members from the Caldwell company were killed (including Patten) and seven wounded. The Ray militia suffered one killed and half a dozen wounded.

EXTERMINATION ORDER ISSUED FOLLOWING THE BATTLE OF CROOKED RIVER

On 27 October 1838, word reached the governor in Jefferson City that the Mormons had attacked and completely annihilated the Ray County militia at Crooked River. Although the reports were spurious and greatly exaggerated, Boggs perceived that the Mormons had perpetrated the conflict and that they were coming out in open rebellion against the state of Missouri by deliberately attacking state militia. He viewed this act as treasonous: "The Mormons [are] in the attitude of an open and avowed defiance of the laws, and of having made war upon the people of this state."[9] Such actions on the part of the Latter-day Saints led him to justify his final solution to the Mormon problem—full scale expulsion. The governor immediately called out seven divisions to march to Caldwell County. No one could have known that the Mormons would give up so easily and that the conflict would be over less than a week after the governor issued his edict. In the end, 2,500 state troops moved against the Mormons in order to bring about their submission, and another 1,600 arrived after the capitulation to assist in carrying out the terms of the surrender. Another estimated 3,000 to 4,000 men were en route to Far West when peace was established, but because the conflict had come to an end, they were discharged and did not see duty.

INTERPRETATION OF *EXTERMINATED*

Contrary to the belief of many Latter-day Saints and even some Mormon historians, the governor's Extermination Order was not meant to give authorization to the state militia or its citizens to kill or eradicate the Latter-day Saint population. Boggs certainly did not like the Mormons, but in a report to the Missouri House of Representatives, he stated that the order and call-up of troops was issued "to prevent the effusion of blood."[10] Significantly, the first definition of the word *exterminate* as defined in Webster's 1828 dictionary reads, "to drive from within the limits or borders."[11] Given this definition, the order should probably be interpreted to read that "the Mormons must be exterminated or *[in other words]* driven from the State . . . for the public peace." Thus, Governor Boggs was calling for the removal of the Mormons by the militia, not their death.

MORMON LEADERS' LIBERTY JAIL IMPRISONMENT TIED TO THE EXTERMINATION ORDER

Sufficient historical evidence exists to show that Governor Boggs and Austin A. King (the circuit court judge who conducted the preliminary court hearing against Mormon leaders taken into custody after the surrender at Far West) never intended to prosecute Joseph Smith and the other Mormon prisoners. At the completion of the Richmond hearing in late November, as Joseph Smith and his companions were being taken to Liberty Jail, one of the men in charge of the prisoners informed them that "the Judge declared his intention to keep us in jail until all the 'Mormons' were driven out of state. He also said that the Judge had further declared that if he let us out before the 'Mormons' had left the state, . . . there would be another . . . fuss kicked up."[12] Some of the details of how this happened were given in the following statement by Hyrum Smith:

> The jailer [at Liberty Jail], Samuel Tillery, Esq., told us . . . that the whole plan was concocted by the governor down to the lowest judge in that upper country. . . . He also told us that the governor was now ashamed of the whole transaction and would be glad to set us at liberty if he dared do it. "But," said he, "you need not be concerned, for the governor has laid a plan for your release." He also said that Squire Birch . . . was appointed to be circuit judge on the circuit passing through Daviess county, and that he (Birch) was instructed to fix the papers, so that we would be sure to be clear from any incumbrance in a very short time.[13]

In short, Boggs and the lower court judges instigated a plan whereby once the main body of Mormons complied with the order to leave the state, the leaders would be released. That is indeed what took place. On 16 April 1839, following the Gallatin hearing, while en route with the prisoners to Columbia, Boone County, Sheriff William Morgan, the officer in charge of the transport, allowed the Mormon prisoners to escape. Morgan told the men that Judge Birch had instructed him to let them go.[14] Six days later, the escapees crossed the Mississippi River, where they joined the main body of Saints who had assembled in Quincy.[15]

EXTERMINATION ORDER RESCINDED

In the spirit of goodwill and reconciliation, on 25 June 1976, Missouri Governor Christopher S. Bond formally rescinded the executive order issued by his predecessor 138 years earlier. The document, in part, reads as follows:

> Whereas, on October 27, 1838, the Governor of the State of Missouri, Lilburn W. Boggs, issued an order calling for the extermination or expulsion of Mormons from the State of Missouri; and
>
> Whereas, Governor Boggs' order clearly contravened the rights to life, liberty, property and religious freedom as guaranteed by the Constitution of the United States, as well as the Constitution of the State of Missouri. . . .
>
> Now, therefore, I, Christopher S. Bond, Governor of the State of Missouri, by virtue of the authority vested in me by the Constitution and the laws of the State of Missouri, do hereby order as follows:
>
> Expressing on behalf of all Missourians our deep regret for the injustice and undue suffering which was caused by this 1838 order, I hereby rescind Executive Order Number 44 dated October 27, 1838, issued by Governor Lilburn W. Boggs.[16]

NOTES
1. Lilburn W. Boggs to John B. Clark, October 27, 1838, in *Document Containing the Correspondence, Orders, &C.,* 61.
2. *Elders' Journal* 1 (November 1837): 28.
3. "The Mormons," *Missouri Argus,* September 27, 1838. The article, dated September 14, first appeared in the *Western Star,* publication date unknown.
4. Rigdon, *Oration Delivered by Mr. S. Rigdon,* 12. The entire document has

subsequently been published in Peter Crawley, "Two Rare Missouri Documents," *BYU Studies* 14, no. 4 (Summer 1974): 517–27.

5. Grant, *Collection of Facts,* 10.

6. "Continuation of Elder Rigdon's Trial," *Times and Seasons* 5, no. 18 (1 October 1844): 667.

7. Joseph Smith, "Extract, from the Private Journal of Joseph Smith, Jr." *Times and Seasons* 1, no. 1 (November 1839): 3.

8. "The First Memorial," in Johnson, *Mormon Redress Petitions,* 118.

9. Lilburn W. Boggs to John B. Clark, October 27, 1838, in *Document,* 61.

10. Lilburn W. Boggs to the House of Representatives of the State of Missouri, December 5, 1838, in *Document,* 14; also in *Missouri Republican,* December 10, 1838.

11. See Webster, *American Dictionary,* s.v. "Exterminate."

12. Hyrum Smith affidavit in Johnson, *Mormon Redress Petitions,* 635; also Smith, "Testimony of Hyrum Smith," in *History of the Church,* 3:420.

13. Smith affidavit, in Johnson, *Mormon Redress Petitions,* 636; also Smith, "Testimony of Hyrum Smith," in *History of the Church,* 3:421. The Mormon prisoners later testified that "by order of the Governor of the State of Missouri, [they] were set at large, with directions to leave the State without delay" (Caleb Baldwin, et al., affidavit, in Johnson, *Mormon Redress Petitions,* 684–85). Hyrum Smith, Caleb Baldwin, Alexander McRae, and Lyman Wight's names appear on the affidavit, but Joseph Smith's does not. Parley P. Pratt, James Sloan, and Dimick B. Huntington's names also appear on the document.

14. Hyrum Smith testified that Morgan told them that Judge Birch instructed him "never to carry us to Boone County" (Smith affidavit, in Johnson, *Mormon Redress Petitions,* 638); see also Smith, "Testimony of Hyrum Smith," in *History of the Church,* 3:423.

15. For an account of the release of the Mormon prisoners by the Missouri authorities, see Alexander L. Baugh, "'We Took Our Change of Venue to the State of Illinois': The Gallatin Hearing and the Escape of Joseph Smith and the Mormon Prisoners from Missouri, April 1839," *Mormon Historical Studies* 2, no. 1 (Spring 2001): 59–82.

16. Interestingly, members belonging to the LDS Church assumed Bond rescinded Boggs's extermination order with the LDS Church in mind; in fact, he issued the announcement to a group of RLDS (now Community of Christ) Far West Stake members at Stewartsville, Missouri.

CHAPTER TWENTY-NINE

PRISONERS FOR CHRIST'S SAKE

Susan Easton Black

*T*he enemy was reinforced by about one thousand five hundred men today, and news of the destruction of property by the mob reached us from every quarter," penned the Prophet Joseph Smith of events transpiring on 31 October 1838 near Far West. In response to these harrowing events, inhabitants of Far West scurried to defend their families, homes, and improved properties from the ever encroaching enemy who outnumbered them "five to one." It was not until eight o'clock in the morning of October 31 that a "flag of truce" was raised, giving hope to Latter-day Saints that the extermination order forced upon the residents of Haun's Mill would not be enacted on their soil.[1]

Colonel George M. Hinkle, the highest ranking officer of the Mormon militia, met the "flag." Although Latter-day Saint leaders trusted that he was capable of negotiating a satisfactory truce, his chameleon-like character prevented such hope from being realized. Foremost among Hinkle's secret concessions to the enemy was "to give up their [the Church's] leaders to be tried and punished." Although years later, the colonel denied his role in the betrayal of Joseph Smith and other Mormon leaders, the Prophet affirmed that "towards evening I was waited upon by Colonel Hinkle, who stated that the officers of the militia desired to have an interview with me and some others, hoping that the difficulties might be settled without having occasion to carry into effect the exterminating orders."[2] The interview proved a

Susan Easton Black is a professor of Church history and doctrine at Brigham Young University.

sham, a ploy to lure Mormon leaders beyond the safety of Far West into the hands of their enemies so that they could be "taken as prisoners of war, and treated with the utmost contempt."[3]

This article will examine the events stemming from the actions of Colonel Hinkle. Although historians fall short of claiming that the colonel was solely to blame for the subsequent military tribunal that condemned Joseph to death, a prisoner's wagon that conveyed him to Independence Jail, the mock judicial hearing in Richmond, and the sufferings endured in Liberty Jail, most agree that his betrayal set such events in motion.

THE MILITARY TRIBUNAL

As word of the capture of Joseph Smith and other Latter-day Saints passed from man to man in the military encampment stationed outside of Far West, soldiers blatantly cast aside military decorum and yelled like lawless mobbers or as "so many bloodhounds let loose upon their prey . . . if the vision of the infernal regions could suddenly open to the mind, with thousands of malicious fiends, all clamoring, . . . raging and foaming like a troubled sea, then could some idea be formed of the hell which we had entered."[4]

"[We] could distinctly hear their horrid yellings," wrote Mother Smith of that late October night in 1838. "Not knowing the cause, we supposed they were murdering [Joseph]." Father Smith sobbed, "Oh, my God! my God! they have killed my son! they have murdered him! and I must die, for I cannot live without him!" He then "fell back upon [the bed] helpless as a child."[5] During the long evening hours that followed, military guards

> kept up a constant tirade of mockery, and the most obscene black-guardism and abuse. They blasphemed God; mocked Jesus Christ; swore the most dreadful oaths; taunted brother Joseph and others; demanded miracles; wanted signs, such as: "Come, Mr. Smith, show us an angel." "Give us one of your revelations." "Show us a miracle." . . . "Or, if you are Apostles or men of God, deliver yourselves, and then we will be Mormons."[6]

In answer to the mockery, Joseph and the other Mormon captives fell silent. The danger in which they now found themselves demanded their quiet attention, not verbal expressions of fear.

While the anxious prisoners awaited word of their fate, a military tribunal convened late in the afternoon of 1 November under the leadership of General Samuel Lucas of Independence. Fourteen officers, twenty local ministers including the notorious Presbyterian Sashiel Woods, and an assortment of self-proclaimed "qualified" judges demanded the prisoners' lives be forfeited. Only one man, Alexander Doniphan, expressed a contrary view. Doniphan elected to defend the Mormon prisoners for they "had never belonged to any lawful military organization and could not therefore have violated military law."[7] In spite of a plausible defense and his famed courtroom theatrics, Doniphan failed.

Surprisingly, within that failure there was a hint of victory. One of the guards said to another, "The damned Mormons would not be shot this time."[8] General Lucas did not share his view. He was confident an execution would follow the court proceedings. In a military directive to Doniphan, Lucas ordered:

> Sir: You will take Joseph Smith and the other prisoners into the public square of Far West, and shoot them at 9 o'clock to-morrow morning.
>
> Samuel D. Lucas
> Major-General Commanding.

In defiance, Doniphan wrote these words to his commanding officer:

> It is cold-blooded murder. I will not obey your order. My brigade shall march for Liberty tomorrow morning, at 8 o'clock; and if you execute these men, I will hold you responsible before an earthly tribunal, so help me God.
>
> A. W. Doniphan
> Brigadier-General[9]

Privately, Doniphan said to General Lucas, "You hurt one of these men if you dare and I will hold you personally responsible for it, and at some other time you and I will meet again when in mortal combat

Joseph Smith Looking out Liberty Jail Window, *by Robert T. Barrett*

and we will see who is the better man."[10] Fearing the retribution of the provoked officer, Lucas dared not execute the prisoners that morning. Instead he chose to "show off" the prisoners in his hometown of Independence.

THE ROAD TO INDEPENDENCE: LADEN WITH ABUSE

Reluctant Mormon captives were forced to climb inside what Lucas called "prisoner wagons" for the journey that lay ahead. When one wagon drew near Joseph's home in Far West, it stopped. A guard of six soldiers escorted the Prophet inside. "Father, is the mob going to kill you?" Joseph's young son asked. "You d— little brat, go back; you will see your father no more," was a guard's retort.[11] After obtaining necessary food and clothing, the Prophet was forced back into the wagon where a tarp was quickly affixed to prevent near neighbors, who now rushed toward the scene, from communicating with him. But not so for Mother Smith. "I am the mother of the Prophet—is there not a gentleman here, who will assist me to that wagon, that I may take a last look at my children, and speak to them once more before I die?" she asked. A man stepped forward and assisted her to the wagon. "Mr. Smith, your mother and sister are here, and wish to shake hands with you," spoke the man. Joseph responded by thrusting his hand through the cloth covering. "Joseph, do speak to your poor mother once more—I cannot bear to go till I hear your voice." The words "God bless you, mother!" were spoken.[12] The well-guarded wagons then rolled out of Far West.

Although Joseph had said, "Be of good cheer, brethren; the word of the Lord came to me last night that our lives should be given us, and that whatever we may suffer during this captivity, not one of our lives should be taken," the route to Independence was laden with mockery and abuse.[13] "Which of the prisoners [is] the Lord whom the 'Mormons' [worship]?" a woman sarcastically asked as the wagons passed through her town. A soldier pointed to Joseph. She turned to him and asked "whether [he] professed to be the Lord and Savior?" Joseph replied, "I [profess] to be nothing but a man, and a minister of salvation, sent by Jesus Christ to preach the Gospel."[14] He then taught her the basic doctrines of the kingdom—faith, repentance, and baptism. "All seemed surprised, and the lady, in tears, went her way, praising God for the truth, and praying aloud that the Lord would bless and deliver the prisoners."[15]

An immediate answer to her prayer was slow in coming. A jail in Independence awaited the prisoners on 3 November 1838. Under the scrutiny of watchful prison guards, "hundreds flocked to see us day after day," Parley P. Pratt recalled. "We spent most of our time in preaching and conversation, explanatory of our doctrines and practice. Much prejudice was removed, and the feelings of the populace began to be in our favor."[16]

THE RICHMOND HEARING:
"AN OCEAN OF TRIBULATION"

Such words could not be written of what lay ahead. Within days, General John B. Clark prevailed upon Governor Boggs to have the prisoners removed to Richmond. Clark's request was granted. Although only a few guards escorted the prisoners out of Independence, before the prisoner wagons reached Richmond, Colonel Sterling Price, a member of Clark's militia, with seventy-four guards took command of the captives. By 10 November 1838, they had incarcerated Joseph and other Mormon leaders in a ramshackle log cabin.[17]

They forced the prisoners to relinquish all pocket knives and submit to being chained together. "Brother Robison is chained next to me he has a true heart and a firm mind, Brother Whight, is next, Br. Rigdon, next, Hyram, next, Parely, next Amasa," wrote Joseph to his wife. He concluded, "And thus we are bound together in chains as well as the cords of everlasting love, we are in good spirits and rejoice that we are counted worthy to be persecuted for Christ['s] sake."[18] The captives' spirits remained high even when denied common courtesies like utensils for eating. They were able to look past the faults of unfeeling guards who ignored Joseph's distress over a toothache and mocked Sidney Rigdon's delirium, fainting spells, fits of uncontrollable laughter, and incoherent speech. Yet they could not and would not turn a deaf ear to recitations of atrocities committed in Far West under the guise of the Extermination Order. Boasts of rape, murder, and robbery provoked Parley P. Pratt, who later penned, "I had listened till I became so disgusted, shocked, horrified, and so filled with the spirit of indignant justice that I could scarcely refrain from rising upon my feet and rebuking the guards."

> On a sudden [Joseph] arose to his feet, and spoke in a voice of thunder, or as the roaring lion. . . . "SILENCE, ye fiends of the infernal pit. In the name of Jesus Christ I rebuke you, and command you to be still; I will not live another minute and hear such language. Cease such talk, or you or I die THIS INSTANT!"

There was such a tone of finality in Joseph's words, such an air of commanding authority in his bearing, that the "quailing guards, whose weapons were lowered or dropped to the ground; whose knees smote together, and who, shrinking into a corner, or crouching at his feet, begged his pardon, and remained quiet till a change of guards."[19]

As the guards were being changed, word arrived that Governor Boggs wanted Mormon "ring-leaders" delivered over to civil authorities for examination.[20] Although General Clark preferred a military court and had assured his men, "Gentlemen, you shall have the honor of shooting the Mormon leaders on Monday morning at eight o'clock!" he acquiesced to his superior.[21] The civil hearing, known as the "mock trial," began on 12 November 1838 and ended on 28 November. Austin A. King, judge of the fifth judicial circuit court, presided. William T. Wood and Thomas C. Burch served as prosecuting attorneys. Alexander Doniphan and Amos Rees were hired to represent the defendants. Of the latter's legal service, Joseph recorded, "We could [get] no others in time for the tryal, they are able men and will do well no doubt."[22]

As the hearing neared, the courtroom filled to capacity with Mormon haters. "There is a red hot Mormon, d-m him, I am acquainted with him," shouted one man. Another yelled, "Shoot your Mormon. I have shot mine." Yet another uttered, "That dam rascal was in the battle—or out to Davis—or to De Wit, such a one is a great preacher and leader amongst them, he ought to be hung, or sent to the penitentiary."[23] The hostile audience intimidated the witnesses and defendants throughout the hearing. Judge King did not stop their outbursts; in fact, it appeared that he was pleased.

The prosecution began by calling Dr. Sampson Avard as its first witness. The appearance of Avard surprised both Mormons and Missourians. Many expected him to be a prime suspect, not a key witness. Although his testimony was damaging to the Prophet, Joseph wrote of his confidence that he and fellow prisoners would be set free:

My Dear Emma,

We are prisoners in chains, and under strong guards, for Christ sake and for no other cause . . . but on examination, I think that the authorities, will discover our innocence, and set us free. . . . I am your husband and am in bands and tribulation &c—

Joseph Smith Jr[24]

As the days of the hearing extended to fourteen, his confidence waned. Apostate witnesses took the stand, swore under oath that they would tell the truth, and then perjured themselves in an attempt to prove old rumors and fabricate new ones. Of their disgrace, Joseph penned, "Renegade 'Mormon' dissenters are . . . spreading various foul and libelous reports against us, thinking thereby to gain the friendship of the world." Their actions caused the Prophet and his fellow prisoners to "[wade] through an ocean of tribulation and mean abuse." Yet Joseph knew their "cloak of hypocrisy was not sufficient to shield them or hold them up in the hour of trouble."[25]

Judge King viewed the dissenting Mormons not as renegades but as convincing witnesses. His prejudice against Mormons, stemming from the death of his brother-in-law in a conflict with Latter-day Saints five years earlier, was apparent in his cross-examinations. For example, after eliciting testimony about Joseph Smith's teachings of the prophecy in Daniel 7:27 about the kingdom of God rolling forth and destroying all earthly kingdoms, Judge King instructed the court clerk, "Write that down; it is a strong point for treason." Doniphan objected to the instruction but was overruled. "Judge, you had better make the Bible treason," he retorted.[26]

Following the examination of the prosecution witnesses, the defense attempted to introduce witnesses on behalf of the prisoners. Forty or fifty names of defense witnesses were submitted to Judge King, who promptly turned the names over to Captain Bogart for further arrests. A second attempt to introduce witnesses resulted in the same charade. Only seven witnesses, four men and three women, evaded Bogart's threats and intimidations of the court and testified in behalf of the prisoners. Their testimonies discredited statements made by the prosecution witnesses but had no apparent effect on the judge's decision.

Judge King found probable cause to order twenty-four defendants to stand trial on suspicion of committing arson, burglary, robbery, and larceny. Those so charged were allowed to post bail in amounts ranging from five hundred to one thousand dollars. In the absence of adequate jail facilities in the counties where the alleged crimes took place, King committed six prisoners to Richmond Jail on charges of murder for their supposed participation in the Battle at Crooked River in Ray County. The six remaining prisoners—Joseph Smith, Hyrum Smith, Sidney Rigdon, Lyman Wight, Caleb Baldwin, and Alexander McRae—were committed to Liberty Jail on charges of overt acts of treason in Daviess and Caldwell Counties. Because some of the alleged crimes were capital offenses, Judge King did not permit bail for the prisoners charged with treason and murder. Grand jury trials for the defendants were scheduled for March 1839. Judge King then gavelled the preliminary hearing to a close. Exasperated by the ruling, Doniphan exclaimed, "If a cohort of angels were to come down, and declare we were innocent, it would all be the same; for [King] had determined from the beginning to cast us [the Mormon leaders] into prison." The other twelve defendants were either released or admitted to bail.[27]

LIBERTY JAIL

On 29 November, the six prisoners ordered to Liberty Jail were chained, handcuffed, and driven from Richmond toward Liberty, Clay County, Missouri. Two days later, on 1 December, these men were incarcerated in Liberty Jail, "prisoners of hope, but not as sons of liberty."[28] Of their situation, Hyrum Smith recorded:

> Our place of lodging was the square side of a hewed white oak log, and our food was any thing but good and decent; poison was administered to us three or four times . . . it would inevitably have proved fatal, had not the power of Jehovah interposed in our behalf, to save us from their wicked purpose.[29]

Two petitions addressed to the highest court in Missouri requesting a writ of habeas corpus for the prisoners were denied. Unofficially, the reason given was that "there was no law for the Mormons in the state of Missouri."[30]

Why the constant abuse? Joseph believed it stemmed from hatred. "The soldiers and officers of every kind hated us, and the most profane blasphemers and drunkards & whoremongers hated us," he wrote. "They all hated us most cordially. And now what did they hate us for, purely because of the testimony of Jesus Christ."[31]

> O Columbia, Columbia! How thou art fallen! "The land of the free, the home of the brave!" "The asylum of the oppressed"—oppressing thy noblest sons, in a loathsome dungeon, without any provocation, only that they have claimed to worship the God of their fathers according to His own word, and the dictates of their own consciences.[32]

At the very time when hope seemed darkest, Joseph wrote optimistic letters to Emma and the Saints who had escaped from Missouri to Quincy, Adams County, Illinois. To Emma, he wrote:

> As to yourself if you want to know how much I want to see you, examine your feelings, how much you want to see me, and Judge for yourself, I would gladly walk from here to you barefoot, and bareheaded, and half naked, to see you and think it great pleasure, and never count it toil.[33]

To the Saints in Quincy, he wrote of his confidence in the Lord: "What power shall stay the heavens? As well might man stretch forth his puny arm to stop the Missouri river in its decreed course, or to turn it up stream, as to hinder the Almighty from pouring down knowledge from heaven upon the heads of the Latter-day Saints" (D&C 121:33). He also wrote of the Lord's promise: "My son, peace be unto thy soul; thine adversity and thine afflictions shall be but a small moment" (D&C 121:7). "Fear not what man can do, for God shall be with you forever and ever" (D&C 122:9).

CONCLUSION

Could such be said of Colonel George M. Hinkle, who assured the Prophet and other Mormon leaders on 31 October 1838 of peaceable arrangements with the enemy camped outside Far West? The Prophet, in a letter to his wife dated 4 November 1838, Independence, Missouri, answered that query: "Colonel Hinkle, proved to be a trator, to the Church, he is worse than a hull who betraid the army at detroit, he decoyed [us] unawares God reward him."[34] In a subsequent letter, Joseph recounted again the betrayal of Hinkle: "A wolf in sheep's clothing . . . After we were bartered away by Hinkle and were taken into the militia camp we had all the evidence we could have wished for that the world hated us."[35]

Hyrum Smith "endeavored to find out for what cause" he and fellow prisoners were subjected to such foul abuse that stemmed from the betrayal of Hinkle. "All we could learn was, that it was because we were 'Mormons,'" said Hyrum. Joseph lamented, "We have been driven time after time, and without cause; and smitten again and again, and that without provocation."[36] But this time, the abuse was unprecedented—a military court-martial and months of prison confinement. Of these difficulties, the Prophet wrote, "We have waded through an ocean of tribulation and mean abuse, practiced upon us by the ill bred and the ignorant." First and foremost on his list of those categorized as "ill bred and the ignorant" appears the name of "Hinkle." Of him and the other apostates, Joseph stated, "They cannot appear respectable in any decent and civilized society" nor are they respectable before God. For "if men sin wilfully after they have received the knowledge of the truth, there remaineth no more sacrifice for sin," said the Prophet. Awaiting them is "a certain fearful looking for of judgment and fiery indignation to come, which shall devour" the "adversaries." Of such men as Hinkle, Joseph prophesied, "Of how much more severe punishment suppose ye, shall he be thought worthy, who hath sold his brother."[37]

NOTES

1. Smith, *History of the Church,* 3:188.
2. Smith, *History of the Church,* 3:188; George Hinkle letter to W. W. Phelps, esq. dated 14 August 1844, Buffalo, Scott County, Indian Territory: "It has been the theme of many since I left Missouri, to calumniate and vilify me for the course which I, as the acting colonel of the militia of Caldwell, pursued in the surrender of the citizens of Far West, Caldwell, &c. To the authorities of Missouri. . . . all of which, before God, I declare to be as false as Satan himself." *Messenger and Advocate,* Pittsburgh, Pennsylvania, August 1, 1845.
3. Smith, *History of the Church,* 3:189.
4. Pratt, *Autobiography of Parley P. Pratt,* 187.
5. Smith, *History of Joseph Smith by His Mother,* ed. Nibley, 289.
6. Pratt, *Autobiography of Parley P. Pratt,* 187.
7. Sidney Rigdon affidavit, July 1, 1843.

8. "Truth Will Prevail," *Times and Seasons* 4, no. 16 (July 1, 1843): 251.

9. Smith, *History of the Church,* 3:190–91.

10. J. Wickliffe Rigdon, "I Never Knew a Time When I Did Not Know Joseph Smith," 36, as cited in Launius, *Alexander William Doniphan,* 64.

11. Smith, *History of the Church,* 3:447.

12. Smith, *History of Joseph Smith by His Mother,* ed. Nibley, 290–91.

13. Pratt, *Autobiography of Parley P. Pratt,* 192.

14. Smith, *History of the Church,* 3:200–201.

15. Pratt, *Autobiography of Parley P. Pratt,* 193.

16. Pratt, *Autobiography of Parley P. Pratt,* 195.

17. The exact location of the Richmond Jail is unknown. Tradition places it on the north side of the courthouse.

18. Joseph Smith letter to Emma Smith, November 12, 1838, as cited in Jessee, *Personal Writings of Joseph Smith,* 368.

19. Pratt, *Autobiography of Parley P. Pratt,* 210–11.

20. Excerpt from Boggs's communication to General Lucas, as cited in Smith, *History of the Church,* 3:192.

21. "The Testimony of Hyrum Smith," as cited in Smith, *History of the Church,* 3:417. During this confusing semantics of legal jurisdiction, Lyman Wight penned, "I was informed by one of the guards that, two nights previous to [our] arrival, General Clark held a court-martial, and the prisoners were again sentenced to be shot." "Testimony of Lyman Wight," as cited in Smith, *History of the Church,* 3:447.

22. Letter to Emma Smith, November 12, 1838, as cited in Jessee, *Personal Writings of Joseph Smith,* 368.

23. E. Robinson, "Items of Personal History," *Return* 2 (March 1890), as cited in LeSueur, *1838 Mormon War in Missouri,* 198.

24. Letter to Emma Smith, November 12, 1838, as cited in Jessee, *Personal Writings of Joseph Smith,* 367–68.

25. Smith, *History of the Church,* 3:230, 232.

26. Pratt, *Autobiography of Parley P. Pratt,* 212.

27. Smith, *History of the Church,* 3:212–13.

28. Smith, *History of the Church,* 3:245. Parley P. Pratt, King Follett, Darwin Chase, Norman Shearer, Luman Gibbs, and Morris Phelps remained in Richmond Jail.

29. "Truth Will Prevail," *Times and Seasons* 4, no. 16 (July 1, 1843): 254.

30. "Truth Will Prevail," 255.

31. Letter to the Church in Caldwell County, Missouri, December 16, 1838, as cited in Jessee, *Personal Writings of Joseph Smith,* 377.

32. Joseph Smith wrote these words on 1 January 1839 in Liberty Jail. Smith, *History of the Church,* 3:245.

33. Letter to Emma Smith, April 4, 1839, as cited in Jessee, *Personal Writings of Joseph Smith,* 426.

34. Letter to Emma Smith, November 4, 1838, as cited in Jessee, *Personal Writings of Joseph Smith,* 362.
35. Letter to the Church in Caldwell County, Missouri, December 16, 1838, as cited in Jessee, *Personal Writings of Joseph Smith,* 376–77.
36. Smith, *History of the Church,* 3:420, 67.
37. Smith, *History of the Church,* 3:212.

CHAPTER THIRTY

TEMPORARY SAFE HAVEN IN QUINCY

William G. Hartley

*I*n early 1839, the Mississippi River town of Quincy, Illinois, and nearby countryside served as a compassionate, temporary safe haven for Latter-day Saints forced from Missouri, including Joseph Smith's family. For a few weeks, Joseph himself sought refuge there, too, after six months in Missouri jails. Several developments important in Church history and for Joseph Smith transpired during the Saints' short stay in Quincy.[1]

Missouri governor Lilburn Boggs's October 1838 extermination order expelling the Saints from Missouri, as enforced, allowed them until spring 1839 to leave. Thousands of Joseph Smith's followers took part in that exodus.[2] Their two most pressing concerns were where to go, and how to get there. No place north, south, or west was an option. Only Illinois, bordering Missouri on the east, seemed adequate. Common sense, if not inspiration, caused leaders to instruct Saints to collect in or near Quincy, then the largest town on the upper Mississippi. As a result, a sizeable portion of the Missouri Saints moved en masse that way, while others individually scattered to St. Louis, to Lee County in Iowa Territory, to other parts of Illinois, or to other states.

Quincy is about 130 miles upriver from St. Louis and 45 miles directly south of Nauvoo. It hugs the east bank of the Mississippi on a limestone bluff, 125 feet above the river.[3] The county seat for Adams County, it and the county were named for United States president

---

William G. Hartley is an associate professor of history at Brigham Young University.

Of One Heart: Emma Crossing the Ice, *by Liz Lemon Swindle*

John Quincy Adams. In 1839, Quincy had about fifteen hundred residents.

THE SAINTS' WINTER EXODUS FROM MISSOURI

With the First Presidency in prison, leadership for the Saints' mass exodus from Missouri fell upon Brigham Young and Heber C. Kimball, members of the Twelve. They developed a Committee of Removal to assist those in need. The outflow of Saints primarily took place between January and April 1839.[4] Some reached Quincy by boat, but most went overland by wagon, horse, or on foot. From Far West, two primitive road networks extended to the shores opposite Quincy. By mid-January, Mormon refugees were leaving for Quincy daily. On 22 February, a man who arrived at Far West from Illinois said he counted 220 eastbound wagons along his route. Emily Partridge, age fifteen, recalled that in mid-February "the bank of the river was dotted with tents" and that the shore on the Quincy side "was lined with the inhabitants of that place, to witness the crossing over of the Mormon outcasts."[5] At the end of February, the Daniel Stillwell Thomas family found several hundred families camped opposite Quincy.[6]

In mid-March, Joseph Holbrook said a hundred men were along that west shoreline.[7] On 16 March Elder Wilford Woodruff looked across the river and "saw Saints, old and young, lying in the mud and water, in a rainstorm, without tents or covering. . . . The sight filled my eyes with tears, while my heart was made glad at the cheerfulness of the Saints in the midst of their afflictions."[8]

From January through March, river ice sometimes prevented ferry boats from operating, stranding Saints across from Quincy. Ferries, when running, were not free. Ebenezer Robinson, for example, crossed on 1 February, "having one dollar left, after paying our ferriage."[9]

TO GATHER OR TO SCATTER?

In February, priesthood bearers in Quincy, having been offered land to buy upriver, debated whether or not the Saints should gather to form a Mormon community again. Bishop Edward Partridge thought Saints should spread out in other communities. Joseph Smith's counselor Sidney Rigdon, recently escaped from Missouri, agreed.[10] However, Brigham Young wanted the Saints to gather in order to better help each other.[11] By letter, Joseph Smith advised the leaders to obtain enough property for the Saints to gather rather than scatter.[12]

QUINCY'S COMPASSION

Early in February, elders in Quincy selected an LDS committee of eleven to look after the poor. But Mormon residents in Quincy were too few to provide shelter, food, and jobs for so many refugees. Quincy's Democratic Association held meetings in late February in which they passed several resolutions and appointed a committee to help the Mormons. "The strangers recently arrived here from the state of Missouri, known by the name of 'Latter-day Saints' are entitled to our sympathy and kindest regard," Resolution One said; "we recommend to the citizens of Quincy to extend all the kindness in their power to bestow on the persons who are in affliction." Community leaders worked with the Mormon committee to gather information about destitute, sick, or houseless individuals, so they could "directly and promptly appeal" to Quincy residents to provide means for relief. The Quincy committee pledged to "use their utmost endeavors to obtain employment for all these people, who are able and willing to labor." They urged Quincyans to show the Saints "sympathy and commiseration."[13]

Elias Higbee, writing on behalf of a Church committee, thanked the Quincy Democratic Association for "the friendly feelings which have been manifested, and the benevolent hand which has been stretched out to a poor, oppressed, injured, and persecuted people." Immediate Mormon needs, he explained, were "beyond all calculation"—they having been robbed of their food, animals, clothing, and houses, and "all that renders life tolerable." Mormons were incapable of meeting the needs of their poor "who are daily crowding here and looking to us for relief." The best means to promote the Mormons' "permanent good," he said, would be "to give us employment, rent us farms, and allow us the protection and privileges of other citizens." Such help would "deliver us from the ruinous effects of persecution, despotism, and tyranny."[14]

Many Quincyans provided lodging and work. When Esaias Edwards found Mormons camped out in the snow, he was filled with compassion and let the Alexander Williams family live with him and farm eight of his acres.[15] A Quincy woman took in an old Mormon woman who was "expected to assist a little in light housework and sewing for her board."[16] The Heil Travis family gave William Cahoon employment and a place to live.[17] Mr. Travis also hired Truman O. Angell to frame a barn, gave the Angells lodging, treated them with kindness, and "minister[ed] to our wants."[18] A butcher moved tenants out of a dozen small houses he owned, let Mormons use them, and provided some with meat, all without charge. "It seemed a new thing to us to be treated with so much kindness," said John Lowe Butler, one of those assisted.[19]

Eliza R. Snow praised Quincyans' generous hearts in a poem published in the 11 May issue of the *Quincy Whig* newspaper.[20] Some lines of the poem read:

> Ye Sons and Daughters of Benevolence,
> Whose hearts are tun'd to notes of sympathy
> Who have put forth your liberal hand to meet
> The urgent wants of the oppress'd and poor!
>
> . . . .
>
> No laurel branch nor cypress bough will wave
> In graceful dignity about your heads, to tell
> In speechless eloquence what you have done.

CHURCH MATTERS

In a priesthood meeting on 17 March, formal action removed several men from membership who had become disaffected or acted against the interests of the Church, including Thomas B. Marsh, president of the Twelve; Frederick G. Williams, formerly in the First Presidency; and George M. Hinkle, Sampson Avard, John Corrill, Reed Peck, and Burr Riggs.[21]

JOSEPH SMITH'S FAMILY

Emma Smith and her children left Far West on 7 February 1839. Jonathan Holmes and Stephen Markham, friends of the family, drove them. "They loaded the wagon, hitched it to a pair of beautiful, matched black horses, and left." Weather turned bad during the trip. One horse died during the journey.[22] At the Mississippi River shore they found the river frozen over. Not trusting the ice, she walked instead of riding in the heavy wagon. She carried Alexander, eight months old, and Frederick, two. Julia, eight, and Joseph six, clung to her skirt. She had two cotton bags tied under her long skirt in which she carried some of Joseph Smith's valuable documents. Carefully, she and the children walked across the ice to the outskirts of Quincy, without mishap.[23]

Arriving in Quincy on 15 February,[24] Emma moved in with Judge John Cleveland and his wife, Sarah, four miles east of Quincy.[25] (Sarah Cleveland later became Emma Smith's first counselor in the Nauvoo Relief Society.) "I still live and am yet willing to suffer more if it is the will of kind Heaven, that I should for your sake," Emma wrote to Joseph on 9 March: "No one but God, knows the reflections of my mind and the feelings of my heart when I left our house and home . . . leaving you shut up in that lonesome prison."[26]

After Joseph Smith's parents reached Quincy in early March, mother Lucy was "seized with the cholera" and "suffered dreadfully." Learning of her sickness, "the ladies of Quincy sent us every delicacy which the city afforded; in fact, we were surrounded with the kindest of neighbours."[27]

PROPHECY FULFILLED AT FAR WEST

Back on 8 July 1838, at Far West, Joseph Smith had received a revelation instructing the Twelve to leave from the Far West Temple building site on 26 April 1839 to "go over the great waters" to "promulgate my gospel" (D&C 118:4). To fulfill that assignment, which anti-Mormons planned to block, in April 1839 members of the Twelve traveled clandestinely to Far West, and just after midnight on 26 April held a conference. Elders Brigham Young, Heber C. Kimball, Orson Pratt, John E. Page, and John Taylor ordained Wilford Woodruff and George A. Smith as new apostles. They laid a foundation stone at the temple site, prayed one by one, sang, and then took their leave to start on their mission. They took with them to Quincy "the last company of the poor."[28] With those departures, Governor Boggs's extermination order was basically fulfilled. When the group reached Quincy, to their delight they found Joseph Smith there.

THE PROPHET'S EIGHTEEN DAYS IN QUINCY

On 22 April, five days after members of the Twelve had left Quincy for Far West, Joseph Smith arrived unannounced in Quincy. His group had traveled day and night for ten days, covering 170 miles from Gallatin, Missouri, "suffering much fatigue and hunger." "He was drest in an old pair of boots full of holes," Dimick Huntington said, "pants torn, tucked inside of boots, blue cloak with collar turned up, wide brim black hat, rim sloped down, not been shaved for some time, looked pale & haggard." While Huntington and Joseph and others passed through "the back streets of Quincy," a number of men recognized him. "On arriving at the Clevelands', Emma saw him and met him halfway to the gate." Although fearful he might be arrested again, he enjoyed "the congratulations of my friends, and the embraces of my family."[29]

Joseph's flock urgently needed to relocate. It was mid-spring, and crops and gardens had to be planted and places obtained to pasture livestock. Sustained by a priesthood council vote on 24 April, Joseph inspected lands for sale upriver and made purchases. He returned to Quincy on 3 May , where the Twelve, just back from Far West, saw him for the first time since his escape from Missouri.[30] Six of the

Twelve rode to the Clevelands. "He greeted us with great Joy," Elder Woodruff said.[31] "It was one of the most joyful scenes of my life," Brigham Young said, "to once more strike hands with the Prophets, and behold them free from the hands of their enemies."[32]

On 4 and 5 May, Joseph presided at a Church general conference held at a Presbyterian campground two miles north of Quincy.[33] Joseph Young led the congregation in singing "with the spirit and meaning thereof" a hymn whose words included

> Glorious things of thee are spoken,
> Zion, city of our God!
> He whose word cannot be broken,
> Chose thee for his own abode.[34]

"Joseph was overcome," Wandle Mace said. "He arose to his feet to speak but it was with difficulty that he controlled his emotions." Being among the Saints after a long absence, knowing their recent hardships, and hearing them yet sing fervently about Zion, "he could scarcely refrain from weeping."[35] Perrigrine Sessions said it "gave us much joy to see his [Joseph's] face among the Saints and here the voice of inspiration that floed from his lips this caused our drooping spirits to revive as we were like sheap with out a shepherd that had been scatered in a cloudy and dark day."[36] About this same time, Brigham Young was set apart as president of the Twelve.[37]

PETITIONS FOR REDRESS

From jail on 25 March 1839, Joseph Smith had written to the Saints in Quincy and elsewhere, instructing them to "take statements and affidavits" detailing their property, physical, and character damages suffered in Missouri and the names of their oppressors (D&C 123:4). "It is an imperative duty," he warned, "enjoined on us by our Heavenly Father" that such documentation be presented to heads of government and to the public (D&C 123:7, 6).[38] In response, Saints at Quincy and elsewhere commenced authenticating their affidavits before civil authorities.[39] Joseph Smith wrote his own bill of damages at Quincy on 4 June, seeking one hundred thousand dollars for lands, houses, horses, harnesses, hogs, cattle, books, store goods, expenses while in bonds, moving expenses, and damages for false imprisonments, threatenings, and exposures.[40] (Late in 1839 Joseph Smith and others presented the members' petitions for redress to the federal government but met with little success.)[41]

RELOCATING TO COMMERCE

Church leaders soon promoted twenty thousand acres of land at Commerce, Illinois, and across the river in Iowa as the new gathering place. On 10 May, Joseph Smith and his family moved into a small two-story log house there, "hoping that I and my friends may here find a resting place for a little season at least."[42] Saints moved onto the newly acquired lands, and, by summer 1839, their inundation of Quincy was over. By summer, Commerce was unofficially renamed Nauvoo, and the First Presidency established Church headquarters there.

In 1841, Joseph and Hyrum Smith and Sidney Rigdon, the First Presidency, issued a proclamation of appreciation to Quincy:

> It would be impossible to enumerate all those who in our time of deep distress, nobly came forward to our relief, and like the good Samaritan poured oil into our wounds, and contributed liberally to our necessities, as the citizens of Quincy *en masse* and the people of Illinois, generally, seemed to emulate each other in this labor of love.[43]

NOTES

1. For a collection of essays dealing with Quincy history, see Black and Bennett, *City of Refuge.*
2. "It has been judg'd, there were eight thousand of our people in the County," Eliza R. Snow to [Isaac] Streator, 22 February 1839, LDS Church Archives.
3. Roberts, *Comprehensive History of the Church,* 2:3.
4. William G. Hartley, "'Almost Too Intolerable a Burthen': The Winter Exodus from Missouri 1838–1839," *Journal of Mormon History* 18 (Fall 1992): 6–40.
5. "Emily Dow Partridge Smith, Autobiography," *Woman's Exponent* 14 (1885–86): 18.
6. Kirkham, "Daniel Stillwell Thomas and Martha Paine Jones Thomas," 13.
7. Holbrook, *Autobiography,* 58.

8. Wilford Woodruff, Journal History, 16 March 1839, 2.

9. Ebenezer Robinson, Autobiography, in *Return* 2 (April 1890): 243.

10. Smith, *History of the Church,* 3:260–61. President Rigdon "counseled Saints to scatter for the time being," said William H. Miller. Jenson, *Latter-day Saint Biographical Encyclopedia,* 1:482.

11. Smith, *History of the Church,* 3:283.

12. Joseph Smith and Others to Edward Partridge and the Church, March 25, 1839, published in *Times and Seasons* 1 (July 1840): 132; see Smith, *History of the Church,* 3:283.

13. Smith, *History of the Church,* 3:267–69.

14. Smith, *History of the Church,* 3:269–70.

15. Esaias Edwards Autobiography and Diary, Document 6, 11.

16. Flanders, *Nauvoo,* 13.

17. William Farrington Cahoon, Autobiography, 47.

18. Carter, *Our Pioneer Heritage,* 10:199–200.

19. Hartley, *My Best for the Kingdom,* 398.

20. Eliza R. Snow, "To the Citizens of Quincy," *Quincy Whig,* 11 May 1839, 1.

21. Smith, *History of the Church,* 3:284.

22. Launius, *Joseph Smith III,* 10.

23. See *Church History in the Fulness of Times,* 213.

24. Smith, *History of the Church,* 3:262.

25. Before making the trip from Far West, Emma had written to ask the Clevelands for lodging until the Smiths could secure a home of their own. Launius, *Joseph Smith III,* 11.

26. Emma to Joseph Smith, 9 March 1839, Joseph Smith Letterbooks, LDS Archives.

27. Anderson, *Lucy's Book,* 693, 695.

28. Woodruff, *Wilford Woodruff's Journal,* 27 April 1839, 329.

29. Dimick Baker Huntington, Autobiography.

30. Smith, *History of the Church,* 3:343.

31. Woodruff, *Wilford Woodruff's Journal,* 1:331.

32. Arrington, *Brigham Young,* 72.

33. Woodruff, *Wilford Woodruff's Journal,* 1:330.

34. *Hymns,* no. 46.

35. Autobiography of Wandle Mace, 28.

36. Smart, *Exemplary Elder,* 43.

37. Autobiography of Wandle Mace, 29.

38. Smith, *History of the Church,* 3:289–90, 302, 305.

39. Johnson, *Mormon Redress Petitions,* xix–xxvii.

40. Johnson, *Mormon Redress Petitions,* 346–50.

41. Johnson, *Mormon Redress Petitions,* xxi; Johnson, "Government Responses to Mormon Appeals, 1840–1846," in Garrett, *Illinois,* 185–89.

42. Smith, *History of the Church,* 3:342, 349.

43. "A Proclamation, to the Saints Scattered Abroad," *Times and Seasons* 2 (15 January 1841): 273. In 1989, the city of Quincy and the LDS Church joined in honoring Quincy for help given the Saints 150 years earlier. Then, on 5–6 November 1989, local historians joined with LDS historians in a day-long Quincy History Symposium. Several papers presented there are in Black and Bennett, *City of Refuge.*

CHAPTER THIRTY-ONE

MORMON COMMUNITIES IN ILLINOIS AND LEE COUNTY, IOWA

Donald Q. Cannon

We are accustomed to thinking of Brigham Young as a great colonizer, and indeed he was. What is lesser known is that Joseph Smith also played a role as a colonizer. During the 1840s, he directed the establishment of several Mormon communities on both sides of the Mississippi. Mormon settlements were founded in Lee County, Iowa, and in Hancock County, Illinois.

In March 1843, Joseph Smith said of the Mormon settlements, "There is a wheel; Nauvoo is the hub: we will drive the first spoke in Ramus, second in La Harpe, third Shokoquon, fourth in Lima: that is half the wheel. The other half is over the river."[1] Using a pioneer image of wagon wheels and spokes, the Mormon Prophet described the extent of Latter-day Saint settlements that would be founded on both sides of the Mississippi River.

HANCOCK COUNTY, ILLINOIS

The seventeen communities the Latter-day Saints either planned or established in Hancock County may be divided into various categories. Some towns may be appropriately called major colonies, such as Ramus (also known as Webster and Macedonia) and Lima. Other settlements may be designated minor colonies, including Plymouth, Green Plains, and Yelrome (Tioga). The Saints also lived among non-Mormons, in what we might call "missionary towns," hoping to

---

Donald Q. Cannon is a professor of Church history and doctrine at Brigham Young University.

convert them to the gospel: Carthage, Bear Creek, La Harpe, and Fountain Green. Several small settlements such as String Town and Davis Mound were on the outskirts of Nauvoo and might be called Nauvoo suburbs. The Saints even planned one settlement that never came into being. This town, which was to be called Warren, might be called a paper town. There were also non-Mormon towns, such as Warsaw and Pontoosuc.

String Town was located three miles east of Nauvoo on the old La Harpe Road (now Illinois Alternate 2). About 75 members, some five or six families, resided in this town. They were converts from England who had given all their money to the Church for the construction of the Nauvoo Temple in exchange for a few acres of land east of Nauvoo. Since they had no money, they lived on a shoestring—hence the name String Town for their settlement.

Davis Mound is located about five miles east of Nauvoo and one fifth of a mile east of String Town, also on Illinois Alternate 2. It is a landmark also called Big Mound or The Mound. It was named Davis Mound after Amos Davis, a Mormon resident who built a large home and barn atop the fifty-foot hill north of the road. Davis owned a store in Nauvoo and a hotel immediately south of the temple on Mulholland Street. Joseph Smith purchased the mound from Hiram Kimball on 16 June 1842. The Prophet recorded, "Rode to the big mound on the La Harpe Road, accompanied by Emma [Smith], Hiram Kimball, and Dr. [Willard] Richards, and purchased a three-quarter section of land [480 acres] of Kimball, including the mound."[2]

Pontoosuc is located on State Highway 96, which runs along the Mississippi River, thirteen miles northwest of Nauvoo and two miles west of present-day Dallas City. Four brethren, including Phineas H. Young and his son Brigham, Richard Ballantyne, and James Standing, were abducted by an anti-Mormon mob near Pontoosuc. They were forcibly taken into Pontoosuc, where they were met by fifty armed men.

La Harpe, a missionary town, is located twenty-five miles east of Nauvoo and eight miles north of Ramus on State Highway 9/94. The earliest Mormon settler in La Harpe was Erastus Bingham, who came in 1839. Bingham and other Mormons began doing missionary work, and the nucleus of a branch (local congregation) of the Church formed. Apparently, the most successful missionary in the town was Zenos H. Gurley, who reported baptizing fifty-two people in six days. The combination of immigration and missionary work led to the creation of a branch at La Harpe on 17 April 1841. This branch was part of the Ramus Stake.

Church leaders from Nauvoo frequently visited the La Harpe Branch. For instance, Charles C. Rich's group stopped at La Harpe on a return trip to Nauvoo in July 1843, and William Clayton and Stephen Markham stopped briefly at La Harpe on their way to Dixon to warn Joseph Smith of his impending arrest.

Fountain Green, a non-Mormon town, is located seven miles south of La Harpe on present-day Illinois Alternate 17. After visiting his brother Don Carlos in Macomb on 24 June 1839, Joseph Smith and his family went to see William Perkins, who lived near Fountain Green, and were invited to stay. This they did, and Joseph preached with considerable liberty to a large congregation the next day before he and his family continued their journey to Nauvoo.

Ramus (also called Crooked Creek, Macedonia, and Webster) is eight miles northeast of Carthage on Illinois Alternate 4. The town, established entirely by Latter-day Saints, was regarded as an important settlement in the plans developed by Joseph Smith. As a result of missionary work performed by Joel H. Johnson and others, several families along Crooked Creek joined the Church, and soon the Crooked Creek Branch was organized. A site for a town, chosen in the fall of 1840, was surveyed and platted under the direction of William Wightman. The residents of the area chose the name Ramus for their town. *Ramus* is a Latin word meaning "branch" and may indicate the strong interest of the Latter-day Saints in ancient languages.

The Ramus Stake was created in this beautiful farming area by Hyrum Smith on 15 July 1840, with Joel H. Johnson as stake president. A meetinghouse was built by the members of the Ramus Stake, an unusual practice in the early days when meetings were held in homes or out-of-doors. This was one of the first meetinghouses built

Colonizer, by Del Parson. *Joseph Smith was the architect of Nauvoo*

by the Latter-day Saints. A monument has been erected there to identify the site.

Joseph Smith visited Ramus frequently. He held Church conferences, convened courts, visited relatives, and received revelations, including Doctrine and Covenants, sections 130 and 131, in the community. The Saints in Ramus saw Joseph Smith not only in his prophetic role but also in an athletic role. On one visit, the Prophet pulled sticks with Justus A. Morse, the strongest man in Ramus, and beat him using only one hand. During the same visit, Joseph wrestled William Wall, the most expert wrestler in Ramus, and threw him.[3]

Carthage, the county seat of Hancock County since 1833, is located about thirteen miles southeast of Nauvoo (twenty-three miles via State Highway 96 and U.S. 136) in the geographic center of the county.

The Stephen Douglas prophecy was given in Carthage on 18 May 1843 as Joseph dined with Sheriff Jacob Backenstos and Judge Douglas. During the conversation that ensued, Joseph prophesied that the judge would aspire to the presidency of the United States and added that if he ever turned against the Latter-day Saints, he would feel the weight of the Almighty upon him. This exacting prophecy was printed in the *Deseret News* on 24 September 1856 and was fulfilled in the election of 1860.

Carthage Jail is located on the northeast corner of Fayette and Walnut Streets, with a parking lot on the south side of State Highway 36. The jail, a stone building thirty-four feet by twenty-eight feet and two stories high, was built between 1840 and 1842, with walls two and one-half feet thick. Part of the jail was occupied by the jailer as a residence. The martyrdom of the Prophet Joseph Smith took place in the jail on 27 June 1844.

Plymouth is located forty miles southeast of Nauvoo near the McDonough County line on State Highway 61. William Smith, Joseph Smith's brother and an apostle from 1835 to 1845, settled in Plymouth in 1839, where he farmed and kept a tavern (public house) after he was excommunicated from the Church. Catherine Smith Salisbury, sister of the Prophet, also lived there for a time before moving to Ramus.

Samuel H. Smith, another of the Prophet's brothers, moved to Plymouth in the fall of 1842 to manage William's tavern. The brothers lived under the same roof for a time. It was here that Joseph Smith stayed on 27 December 1842, as he was traveling to Springfield to stand trial before Judge Nathanial Pope on the charge of attempted assassination of Missouri governor Boggs. On 9 January 1843, Joseph, returning from his trial before Judge Pope, stopped at Plymouth again.

At his sister Catherine's home, Joseph talked of Alvin, his brother, who had died in 1823. Joseph said, "He [Alvin] was a very handsome man, surpassed by none but Adam and Seth, and of great strength." Joseph also visited his brother Samuel. The next day, January 10, Joseph received a royal welcome in Nauvoo.

Bear Creek, the present-day town of Basco, is located twenty-one miles southeast of Nauvoo on Illinois Alternate 11, ten miles east of State Highway 96. It was a missionary town with a few Mormon settlers. Joseph Smith stopped here on 5 June 1841, while returning to Nauvoo after a visit with Illinois governor Thomas Carlin in Quincy. He stayed at Heberlin's Hotel, and while there was arrested by a sheriff's posse under the direction of Thomas King, sheriff of Adams County, and Tomas Jasper, constable of Quincy. His arrest was on a requisition from Governor Carlin, who was going to deliver Joseph to Missouri authorities.

Yelrome (also known as Tioga and Morley's Settlement) is located twenty-five miles south of Nauvoo and two miles east of State Highway 96. Isaac Morley was the first Mormon settler in the area. "Yelrome" is "Morley" spelled backwards with an extra "e." The name may have originated from a Mormon penchant to spell words backwards. (For example, the Council of Fifty was called "Ytfif.") Yelrome resident Alpheus Cutler, who was from Tioga County, Pennsylvania, may have had something to do with the name Tioga.

The names of the Latter-day Saints (at least 424 members) who lived in Yelrome in the 1840s constitute a genealogical treasure chest. In addition to the Morleys and the Cutlers, there were the families of Thomas Hickenlooper, Lucy Morley Allen, Orville S. Cox, William Critchlow, Edward Whiting, Enos Curtis, Edmund Durfee, William Garner, Anna N. Gifford, and Solomon Hancock, just to name a few. Eliza R. Snow also lived in Yelrome from 1843 to 1844.

Latter-day Saints in Yelrome had many opportunities to hear the Prophet speak. On Sunday, 14 May 1843, for example, Joseph preached that "knowledge through our Lord and Savior Jesus Christ is the grand key that unlocks the glories and mysteries of the kingdom of heaven."[4] That night, Emma arrived with a carriage, and the next morning they rode home together.

Since Yelrome was located near anti-Mormon elements in Warsaw and Adams County, the Saints in that community were often the target of mob attacks. A total of 175 homes were burned, and on 15 November 1845, Edmund Durfee was killed.

Lima is located three miles south of Yelrome, just over the Adams County line on State Highway 96. A number of the Saints settled here after their explusion from Missouri in 1839. When the Lima Stake was organized on 22 October 1840, Isaac Morley, who lived in Yelrome, was appointed stake president.

Lorenzo Snow and Eliza R. Snow taught at the school in Lima before leaving the town in February 1844. Titus Billings, second counselor to Bishop Edward Partridge from 1837 to 1840, lived here until the "house burnings" in 1845. The Lima Cemetery is the burial site of several Saints.

Green Plains is located eight miles south of Hamilton on State Highway 96. John Smith, president of the Adam-ondi-Ahman Stake in Missouri (and later the Zarahemla Stake in Iowa and the Salt Lake Stake in Utah), settled in Green Plains in March 1839. Joseph Smith and his family stayed at his home on 9 May 1839, while on their way to Commerce. A branch of the Church called the Prairie Branch was established here with a membership of eighty individuals.

The house of Levi Williams, the notorious anti-Mormon mob leader, served as the post office for the area. Several of the mob expeditions organized to arrest the brethren or destroy the property of the Saints in Hancock County from 1844–46 originated in this area. A mob burned this farming settlement on 10 September 1845.

Warsaw, platted in 1834, is located on the Mississippi River sixteen miles south of Nauvoo and three miles west of State Highway 96. It was well-known in Joseph Smith's day as an anti-Mormon town.

Thomas Sharp, a bitter anti-Mormon and the founder of the Anti-Mormon political party in 1841, was editor of the *Warsaw Signal.* On the morning of 27 June 1844, a posse from Warsaw marched towards Carthage but were met by an order from Governor Thomas Ford to disband. Learning that Ford was not in Carthage, some two hundred of these men hastened there and participated in the attack on Carthage Jail that resulted in the deaths of Joseph and Hyrum Smith. After the martyrdom, the murderers met to celebrate in the Warsaw Hotel (Flemming's Tavern). When mob violence continued after the martyrdom, Governor Ford demanded a surrender of public arms at Warsaw in July 1844. The citizens of Warsaw refused to comply with his order.

Warren, named after one of Joseph Smith's lawyers, was a paper town located one mile south of Warsaw. Willard Richards settled in Warsaw in September 1841 to sell city lots in Warren, and Joseph Fielding brought a company of 204 British emigrants to Warren to settle on 24 November 1841, but because of the hostile feelings of the Warsaw residents, the community of Warren was never established. On 13 December 1841, the First Presidency of the Church asked the British emigrants to move to Nauvoo.

Let us turn now to a consideration of the settlements on the west bank of the Mississippi—Iowa Territory. This is the other half of the wheel described by the Prophet Joseph Smith.

LEE COUNTY, IOWA

The first Mormon contact with Iowa occurred in the winter of 1838–39 as the Mormons were being driven from the state of Missouri. Although most Mormon refugees fled into Illinois, a few found refuge in the territory of Iowa.[5]

In 1838 Israel Barlow and some other Mormons made contact with Isaac Galland, a land speculator with interests in both Iowa and Illinois. Latter-day Saints were especially interested in the abandoned barracks of Fort Des Moines, located in present-day Montrose, Iowa. Galland pointed out that he had land for sale in other parts of the so-called Half-Breed Tract,[6] which consisted of 119,000 acres in the area bounded by the Mississippi River, the Des Moines River, and Fort Madison. It was called *half-breed* because it was the area where Americans of mixed white and Indian blood who lived among the Sac and Fox Indians were located.[7] On 29 May and 26 June 1839, Isaac Galland sold 17,937 acres of land in the Half-Breed Tract for $49,662.26 to Oliver Granger and Vinson Knight, agents for the Church.[8] In July 1839, Joseph Smith and other Church leaders visited the Half-Breed Tract to see firsthand what they had purchased. During the visit, Joseph baptized Isaac Galland and ordained him to the office of an elder.[9]

Montrose, formerly Fort Des Moines,[10] was the residence of Latter-day Saint families. The earliest families to occupy the fort were that of Brigham Young, John Taylor, Wilford Woodruff, Orson Pratt, John Smith, Elijah Fordham, and Joseph B. Nobles.[11]

In Fort Des Moines, one of the best-documented cases of faith healing in Mormon history occurred. The healing of Elijah Fordham is especially noteworthy because Elijah believed he was too far gone— too sick to be restored to health. After receiving a blessing from the Prophet, he immediately arose and accompanied Joseph Smith in ministering to others who had fallen ill.[12]

Montrose became not only the first but also one of the largest and most important Mormon settlements in Lee County, Iowa. The Zarahemla Stake was organized there in October 1839, and John Smith was called as the stake president.[13] The branches of the Church in the Iowa Stake included Zarahemla, Ambrosia, Nashville, and Keokuk in Lee County. There were also branches in Van Buren and Des Moines counties.[14]

In 1843 Joseph participated in the installation of masonic officers of the Rising Sun Lodge in Montrose. In August 1842, he prophesied that the Latter-day Saints would become a mighty people in the midst of the Rocky Mountains.[15] In the fall of 1842 and in June 1844, Montrose served as a hiding place for the Prophet.[16]

Zarahemla is the name of a city in the Book of Mormon. During his visit in Iowa in 1839, Joseph Smith designated an area about one mile west of Montrose as Zarahemla and urged Church members to settle there. Eventually Zarahemla became the largest Mormon settlement in Lee County. At one time there were 326 members in Zarahemla. Those who lived there built about thirty small houses.

In January 1842, the Zarahemla Stake, formerly the Iowa Stake, was discontinued or reduced to branch status because of insufficient growth. Consequently, the first Mormon stake in Iowa had a short history—only twenty-seven months.[17]

Ambrosia, located two miles west of Zarahemla, listed 109 members under the direction of George W. Gee.[18]

Nashville had a branch of ninety members, who were presided over by Elias Smith.[19]

Keokuk had only thirteen Church members in the 1840s, but it has since grown in size and importance as a community and a congregation of Saints.[20]

Potter's Slough (now under water) was about two miles north of present-day Montrose. During the exodus to the West, one famous event took place here on 9 October 1846: the so-called Miracle of the Quail. The final group of Mormons evacuating Nauvoo had very little food with them. Their hunger was alleviated by the following miraculous event:

> This morning we had a direct manifestation of the mercy and goodness of God, in a miracle being performed in the camp. A large, or rather several large flocks of quails flew into camp—some fell on the wagons, some under, some on the breakfast tables. The boys and brethren ran about after them and caught them alive with their hands. Men who were not in the Church marveled at the sight. The brethren and sisters praised God and glorified his name, that what was showered down upon the children of Israel in the wilderness is manifested unto us in our persecution. The boys caught about 20 alive, and as to the number that were killed, every man, woman, and child had quails to eat for their dinner. After dinner the flocks increased in size. Captain [Orville] Allen ordered the brethren not to kill when they had eaten and were satisfied.[21]

Returning to Joseph Smith's metaphor of the wheel, it is now apparent that, indeed, as Nauvoo was the hub, so the settlements in Hancock County, Illinois, and in Lee County, Iowa, were the spokes of the wheel. These spokes, or satellite settlements, played a significant role in the experience of the Mormons who lived in and around Nauvoo in the 1840s. They also witnessed Joseph Smith's role as a colonizer.

NOTES

1. Smith, *History of the Church,* 5:296.
2. Smith, *History of the Church,* 5:25.
3. See Rugh, *Our Common Country,* 35–36, 51–52.
4. Smith, *History of the Church,* 5:389.
5. Brown, Cannon, and Jackson, *Historical Atlas of Mormonism,* 48–49.
6. Cook, "Isaac Galland," 264, 267.
7. Kimball, "Nauvoo West," 135.
8. Cook, "Isaac Galland," 271–74.
9. Cook, "Isaac Galland," 274–76.
10. Foley, "Lee County: Montrose" in Black and Hartley, ed., *Iowa Mormon Trail,* 193–98.
11. Kimball, "Nauvoo West," 137.
12. Garrett, ed., *Illinois,* 178.
13. Kimball, "Nauvoo West," 137.
14. Kimball, "Nauvoo West," 139.
15. Kimball, "Nauvoo West," 141.
16. Kimball, "Nauvoo West," 141–42.
17. Kimball, "Nauvoo West," 139, 141.
18. Kimball, "Nauvoo West," 139.
19. Kimball, "Nauvoo West," 139.
20. Kimball, "Nauvoo West," 139.
21. "Journal of Thomas Bullock," October 9, 1846.

CHAPTER THIRTY-TWO

THE GATHERING OF THE BRITISH SAINTS

Fred E. Woods

hree years following the First Vision, Joseph Smith began an annual four-year tutorial with Moroni, commencing with the first instruction late into the night of 21 September 1823. During their initial meeting, Joseph was told by this ancient Book of Mormon prophet that God had a work for him to do and that his name "should be had for good and evil among all nations" (Joseph Smith–History 1:33). Joseph was also told about the coming forth of the Book of Mormon, the ancient breastplate, and the Urim and Thummim (Joseph Smith–History 1:34–35). Finally, Moroni quoted a number of scriptures from both the Old and the New Testaments, several of which focused on the gathering of Israel in the last days (Joseph Smith–History 1:36–41).

Such references included a citation of the eleventh chapter of Isaiah (Joseph Smith–History 1:40), which noted that in the last days, "the Lord shall set his hand again the second time to recover [gather] the remnant of his people" (Isaiah 11:11). Moroni also "quoted many other passages of scripture" not recorded in the Joseph Smith History (Joseph Smith–History 1:41). However, Oliver Cowdery published a number of such passages in the *Messenger and Advocate* in 1835, which included Isaiah chapters 2, 28, 29; Jeremiah 16, 30, 31, as well as John 10:16, all of which focused on the restoration of the gospel and the gathering of Israel in the last days.[1]

Fred E. Woods is a professor of Church history and doctrine at Brigham Young University and currently occupies the Richard L. Evans chair of Religious Understanding.

Gathering to Zion, *by Joseph Brickey*

Joseph would have been continually reminded of this important doctrine as he translated the Book of Mormon and would have known through this prophetic process that the coming forth of the Book of Mormon was the sign that the Lord had commenced to gather Israel in the last days (3 Nephi 21:1; 29:1).[2] Thus, by the time the Church was organized, Joseph had already had a heavy dosage of the doctrine of the gathering.

During the second conference of the restored Church, less than six months after the Church was officially established,[3] Joseph received the following revelation:

> And ye are called to bring to pass the gathering of mine elect; for mine elect hear my voice and harden not their hearts;
>
> Wherefore the decree hath gone forth from the Father that they shall be gathered in unto one place upon the face of this land, to prepare their hearts and be prepared in all things against the day when tribulation and desolation are sent forth upon the wicked. (D&C 29:7–8)

The call to gather was not a new concept to a covenant people. "The gathering of the people of God has been a subject of great importance in all ages of the world," the LDS British periodical *The Latter-day Saints Millennial Star* wrote in 1841.[4] Just two months later the *Millennial Star* added, "The spirit of emigration [the gathering] has actuated the children of men from the time our first parents were expelled from the garden until now."[5]

The latter-day gathering came largely as a result of the doctrine preached by the Prophet of the Restoration, who ingrained in the Saints a desire to gather with the people of the Most High God. The Prophet Joseph Smith once asked rhetorically, "What was the object of gathering the Jews, or the people of God in any age of the world?" He answered, "The main object was to build unto the Lord a house whereby He could reveal unto His people the ordinances of His house and the glories of His kingdom, and teach the people the way of salvation."[6]

During much of the first decade of the restored Church of Jesus Christ, the call to gather did not extend beyond the boundaries of North America, and Church members did not enter into temple covenants until the construction of the Kirtland Temple. Furthermore, foreign proselyting did not commence until the necessary priesthood keys were restored to the earth, on 3 April 1836, just one week after the dedication of the Kirtland Temple (D&C 110). In this holy temple, the ancient prophet Moses appeared and restored to Joseph Smith and Oliver Cowdery "the keys of the gathering of Israel from the four parts of the earth" (D&C 110:11).

The restoration of such priesthood keys was the culmination of a rich Pentecostal season in Kirtland (January to April 1836), soon followed by a period of apostasy precipitated by the crisis of the Kirtland Safety Society. Unfortunately, several Church members began borrowing money from the society to purchase land, only to sell it quickly to fellow Church members for a profit.[7] These disturbing events led many Latter-day Saints to apostatize.[8] Many members were left spiritually weak and ailing.

A CALL TO GATHER THE BRITISH SAINTS

An infusion of fresh new converts, not yet soured on the rancid greed and human failings of straying members, was needed to heal the ailing Church.[9] In the Kirtland Temple on 4 June 1837, Joseph Smith approached one of his trusted associates, apostle Heber C. Kimball, and confided in him, "Brother Heber, the Spirit of the Lord has whispered to me: 'Let my servant Heber go to England and proclaim my Gospel, and open the door of salvation to that nation.'"[10] A short time later, Elder Kimball, with fellow apostle Orson Hyde, prepared to lead a small group of missionaries across the Atlantic to England to gather converts from afar. The members of this group included Willard Richards, Joseph Fielding, Isaac Russell, John Snyder, and John Goodson. Before their departure, Joseph warned Heber to "remain silent concerning the gathering . . . until such time as the work was fully established, and it should be clearly made manifest by the Spirit to do otherwise."[11]

During the space of just nine months, these early missionaries to the British Isles brought more than fifteen hundred converts into the fold and organized many branches. At the conclusion of this nine-month period, apostles Kimball and Hyde returned to America while Fielding, Richards, and English convert William Clayton served as an interim British Mission presidency.[12] This initial success was bolstered less than two years later when eight members of the Twelve embarked on another mission to Great Britain (January 1840 to April 1841). Their call was to expand the missionary work and to revive the lethargic spirit that had crept in among some of the British converts.

The Twelve found great success, and by the spring of 1840, the desired foothold had been secured. Following a motion to allow these foreign converts to emigrate,[13] the British Saints began their gathering to Nauvoo with the launching of the sailing vessel *Britannia,* on 6 June 1840. This "Mayflower" company consisted of 41 Saints, led by British convert John Moon. It was the beginning of nearly 5,000 British Saints who gathered to Nauvoo between June 1840 and January 1846 on thirty-four voyages chartered by the Church. By the time the Saints began their forced exile from Nauvoo (4 February 1846), over one-fourth of the city was made up of British converts.[14]

A CALL TO BUILD THE NAUVOO TEMPLE

The call to build the Nauvoo Temple seems to have been the greatest stimulus for these converts from afar to gather to Nauvoo. Just two months after the first British proselytes left Liverpool to gather to Nauvoo, the First Presidency issued an official call to erect the temple:

> Believing the time has now come, when it is necessary to erect a house of prayer, a house of order, a house for the worship of our God, where the ordinances can be attended to agreeably to His divine will, in this region of country—to accomplish which, considerable exertion must be made, and means will be required—and as the work must be hastened in righteousness, it behooves the Saints to weigh the importance of these things, in their minds, in all their bearings, and then take such steps as are necessary to carry them into operation.[15]

Just a few months later, on 19 January 1841, the Lord revealed to the Prophet Joseph a scriptural mandate that augmented the initial call to build the Nauvoo Temple: "And again, verily I say unto you, let all my saints come from afar . . . and build a house to my name, for the Most High to dwell therein" (D&C 124:25, 27).

THE ROUTE UP THE MISSISSIPPI AND THE NAUVOO RECEPTION

Such inspired words touched the hearts of thousands of British converts, who soon reached the shores of North America. With the exception of a few early ships that landed in New York or Quebec, the remaining ships, all of which were launched from Liverpool, disembarked at New Orleans.[16] Apparently the decision to use this southern United States port (commencing in December 1840), rather than New York or Quebec, came as a result of a letter Joseph sent to the Twelve in England in October 1840. In it he mentioned, "I think that those who came here this fall, did not take the best possible route, or the least expensive."[17] Six months later the *Millennial Star* reported an "Epistle of the Twelve," wherein counsel was given regarding when and how British converts should immigrate to Nauvoo: "It is much cheaper going by New Orleans than by New York. But it will never do for emigrants to go by New Orleans in the Summer on account of the heat and sickness of the climate. It is, therefore, advisable for the Saints to emigrate in Autumn, Winter, or Spring."[18]

Not only did this route up the Mississippi prove cheaper, but it also allowed the Prophet Joseph to be aware when groups of British converts were coming upriver from St. Louis. Here on the banks of the Mississippi, Joseph met the foreign Saints who had gathered to receive instruction from their prophet, to help build the temple, and receive their endowment. A number of accounts demonstrate how the Prophet Joseph led the way in welcoming the eager converts who had come from afar.

For example, in a letter to the *Millennial Star,* Heber C. Kimball described the welcome the Twelve and over a hundred immigrating Saints received the summer of 1841: "We landed in Nauvoo on the 1st of July, and when we struck the dock I think there were about three hundred Saints there to meet us, and a greater manifestation of love and gladness I never saw before. President Smith was the first one that caught us by the hand."[19]

To new converts of a religion which claimed to be a restoration of God's ancient covenant church, complete with apostles and prophets, the thrill of being greeted by the Prophet Joseph Smith must have been overwhelming. Robert Crookston testified, "As we approached the landing place to our great joy we saw the Prophet Joseph Smith there to welcome his people who had come so far. We were all so glad to see him and set our feet upon the promised land so to speak. It was the most thrilling experience of my life for I know that he was a Prophet of the Lord."[20]

The Prophet himself described what it was like for him to greet a boatload of Saints who had crossed the Atlantic on the *Emerald* and come upriver on the Church-owned steamboat, the *Maid of Iowa:*[21]

> About five P.M. the steamer *Maid of Iowa* hauled up at the Nauvoo House landing, and disembarked about two hundred Saints. . . . I was present at the landing and the first on board the steamer, when I met Sister Mary Ann Pratt (who had been to England with Brother Parley,) and her little

daughter, only three or four days old. I could not refrain from shedding tears.

So many of my friends and acqaintances arriving in one day kept me very busy receiving their congratulations and answering their questions. I was rejoiced to meet them in such good health and fine spirits; for they were equal to any that had ever come to Nauvoo.[22]

The *Maid of Iowa* also ferried other Saints who had crossed the Atlantic on the *Fanny* in 1844. When this group of British converts reached the shores of Nauvoo, many also recorded their endearing first encounters with the Prophet Joseph Smith. Priscilla Staines felt that notwithstanding the masses who had assembled to greet the incoming Saints, she would be able to recognize the Prophet Joseph Smith. She remembered: "I felt impressed by the spirit that I should know him. As we neared the pier the prophet was standing among the crowd. At the moment, however, I recognized him according to the impression, and pointed him out."[23] Thomas Steed said he recognized the prophet by his "noble expression": "The Prophet Joseph Smith was at the pier. At first glance I could tell it was him. . . . He came on board to shake hands and welcome us by many encouraging words, and express his thankfulness that we had arrived in safety."[24] The absence of published photographs of the Prophet available to these converts makes these experiences all the more significant. British convert Christopher Layton remembered the day as one of rejoicing: "There stood our Prophet on the banks of the river to welcome us! As he heartily grasped our hands, the fervently spoken words 'God bless you,' sank deep into our hearts, giving us a feeling of peace such as we had never known before."[25]

After being torn from kindred and homeland, having sailed thousands of watery miles, British Saints saw the Prophet for the first time. There he stood, before their faces, the noble embodiment of their faith. The Spirit bore witness to his holy calling as God's prophet and seer to all the world. Joseph Smith succored these weary Saints and greeted them with the warmest possible affections. Their faith now strengthened and the desire of their hearts realized, they were ready to meet the challenges that would confront them as they began to build Zion in a new land. The same prophet who first issued the call to gather was he who stood to welcome the Lord's chosen people who had crossed the awesome Atlantic to erect a temple of the Lord and to receive the sacred endowment. With this divine power, the Saints not only had strength to establish another Zion in the west, but they were also equipped to obtain a far greater land of promise.

NOTES

1. Peterson, *Moroni Ancient Prophet,* 143–45. Jackson, *From Apostasy to Restoration,* 114, lists thirty passages used by Moroni in tutoring Joseph according to Oliver Cowdery's accounts. In his book on pages 108–9, Jackson also lists a number of such passages that relate to the theme of "the gathering and restoration of Israel."

2. The chapter heading to 3 Nephi 21 reads, "Israel shall be gathered when the Book of Mormon comes forth"; and the heading to 3 Nephi chapter 29 reads, "The coming forth of the Book of Mormon is a sign that the Lord has commenced to gather Israel and fulfill his covenants."

3. The date of this conference was 26 September 1830.

4. "Important from America: Interesting Letter from Elder Moon who lately emigrated from England to America," *Millennial Star* 1 (February 1841): 252.

5. "Epistle of the Twelve," *Millennial Star* 1 (April 1841): 310.

6. Smith, *Teachings of the Prophet Joseph Smith,* 307–08.

7. *Church History in the Fulness of Times,* 171–72.

8. Milton V. Backman Jr., "A Warning from Kirtland," *Ensign,* April 1989, 30, estimates that about 13 percent, or 50 out of 475 families, left the Church at this time in the Kirtland region. Yet he also notes that about 40 percent of this number later returned to the Church.

9. Smith, *History of the Church,* 2:489, notes that during this turbulent era, the Prophet Joseph Smith received a revelation that "something new must be done for the salvation" of the Church.

10. Whitney, *Life of Heber C. Kimball,* 103–4. The uneducated Kimball was initially overwhelmed by the thought of going to the learned country of England to preach the gospel. Nevertheless, he was determined to carry out what he knew to be the will of heaven.

11. Smith, *History of the Church,* 2:492. Apostles Kimball and Hyde left Kirtland for New York City with Willard Richards and Joseph Fielding. There they met Isaac Russell, John Snyder, and John Goodson who had journeyed from Toronto. See Bloxham, et al., *Truth Will Prevail,* 38–39.

12. Allen, et al., *Men with a Mission,* 52–53. Elders Kimball and Hyde left England on 20 April 1838.

13. Smith, *History of the Church,* 4:119 notes that on 14 April 1840, in a council

meeting of the Twelve in England, the following decision was made: "Moved by Elder Brigham Young, seconded by Elder Heber C. Kimball, that the Saints receive a recommend to the Church in America to move in small or large bodies, inasmuch as they desire to emigrate to that new country."

14. For a complete listing of each chartered voyage, see Appendix A of Woods, *Gathering to Nauvoo,* 153–54.

15. Smith, *History of the Church,* 4:186.

16. Of the thirty-four chartered LDS voyages noted above, thirty-one of thirty-four were launched from Liverpool; three set off from Bristol. All three of the Bristol voyages disembarked at Quebec. The main reason Liverpool was the primary port of embarkation was that this was where the British Mission was located during most of the years the British Saints emigrated to Nauvoo. Woods, *Gathering to Nauvoo,* 153–54.

17. Smith, *History of the Church,* 4:230.

18. "Epistle of the Twelve," *Millennial Star* 1 (April 1841): 311.

19. Whitney, *Life of Heber C. Kimball,* 313.

20. Robert Crookston, Autobiography of Robert Crookston, typescript, 6, LDS Church Archives.

21. For an excellent article on the *Maid of Iowa,* see Donald L. Enders, "The Steamboat *Maid of Iowa:* Mormon Mistress of the Mississippi," *BYU Studies* 19, no. 3 (Spring 1979): 321–35.

22. Smith, *History of the Church,* 5:354.

23. Tullidge, *Women of Mormondom,* 291.

24. Steed, *Life of Thomas Steed,* 8.

25. Woods, *Gathering to Nauvoo,* 87.

CHAPTER THIRTY-THREE

JOSEPH SMITH MEETS PRESIDENT VAN BUREN

Arnold K. Garr

*O*n 23 June 2004 President George W. Bush presented the Presidential Medal of Freedom, the nation's most prestigious civil award, to Gordon B. Hinckley, president of The Church of Jesus Christ of Latter-day Saints. The official citation stated: "As the president of the Church of Jesus Christ of Latter-day Saints, and throughout his nearly 70 years in church leadership, Gordon B. Hinckley has inspired millions. . . . His tireless efforts to spread the word of God and to promote good will have strengthened his faith, his community and our nation."[1] After the award ceremony President Hinckley met with reporters in the White House East Room. There he took the opportunity to comment on "how much the treatment of the Church has improved" over the past 165 years. He contrasted the kindness and honor that President Bush had shown him that day in 2004 with the disrespectful way President Martin Van Buren treated Joseph Smith when they first met in the president's home, later known as the White House, in 1839. President Hinckley explained that Joseph Smith and his companion had visited the nation's capital "to plead the case for our people who had been despoiled and persecuted and driven, and were turned down by President Van Buren."[2] The story of Joseph Smith's memorable journey to Washington, D.C. during the fall and winter of 1839–40 is an important one.

The tragic event that ultimately led to Joseph's journey to the nation's capital was Missouri governor Lilburn W. Boggs's signing of

---

Arnold K. Garr is a professor of Church history and doctrine at Brigham Young University.

the infamous extermination order on 27 October 1838. This shameful decree forced nearly the entire Mormon population to flee from that state during the winter and spring of 1838–39.[3]

In the midst of this heart-wrenching exodus, leaders of the Church discussed ways in which the Saints might obtain redress for the property lost and afflictions suffered during the Missouri persecutions. In March 1839, while imprisoned in Liberty Jail, Joseph received a revelation that said the Church should appeal its case to the United States government in order to get compensation for the mistreatment of the Saints. The revelation admonished members of the Church to "[gather] up a knowledge of all the facts, and sufferings and abuses put upon them by the people of this State [Missouri]" (D&C 123:1). These facts were recorded in the form of sworn affidavits known as petitions for redress.[4]

Seven months later, on 20 October 1839, the Nauvoo high council voted that Joseph Smith go as a delegate to Washington, D.C. and present the Church's grievances to the president of the United States and the Congress. By 28 October, Sidney Rigdon and Elias Higbee received appointments to accompany the Prophet.[5] In addition, Orrin Porter Rockwell served as a driver for the delegates.

These four men left Nauvoo, Illinois, in a two-horse carriage on Tuesday, 29 October 1839, and traveled to Quincy, Illinois, where Sidney Rigdon became ill. Between Quincy and Springfield, Illinois, Robert Foster, a medical doctor, joined them to care for the ailing President Rigdon.[6] The party arrived in Springfield, the state capital, on Monday, 4 November.

Joseph and his companions remained in Springfield for most of the week, and the Prophet preached on several occasions. One of his listeners was General James Adams, a county probate judge, who invited Joseph Smith to his home and reportedly treated the Prophet as if he were his own son.[7] Judge Adams also wrote a letter of recommendation to President Martin Van Buren in behalf of Joseph and the other delegates.[8]

While staying in Springfield, Joseph Smith wrote a touching letter to his wife Emma. The correspondence gives insight into the private life of the Prophet and his willingness to sacrifice time with his family to help the cause of the Church. In the letter Joseph spoke of his "constant anxiety" for his wife and children. It was especially painful for him to leave his three-year-old son, Frederick, who was sick at the time of his departure. The Prophet lamented, "It will be a long and lonesome time dureing my absence from you and nothing but a sense of humanity could have urged me on to so great a sacrafice but shall I see so many perish and [not] seek redress no I will try this once in the [name] of the Lord therefore be patient."[9]

Joseph Smith and his party left Springfield on, or shortly after, 8 November 1839. It took them about ten days to reach Columbus, Ohio. By this time, Sidney Rigdon had become too sick to travel any further. Under these circumstances the Prophet thought it best to leave President Rigdon in Columbus under the care of Dr. Foster until the former had regained his health. Orrin Porter Rockwell stayed with them. Joseph Smith and Elias Higbee continued their journey by stagecoach.[10]

During the last phase of their travels, the Prophet was involved in a thrilling act of bravery that was as exciting as any scene from an action-packed, old-time cowboy movie. As the stagecoach approached Washington, D.C., the driver stopped the stage and went into a "public house" to get a drink. While the coachman was having his "grog," the horses became frightened and "ran down the hill at full speed." As one might imagine, the passengers were terrified and some panicked. One woman became so hysterical that she attempted to throw her own baby out of the window. In this desperate moment, Joseph performed a remarkable act of courage. He opened the door of the stage and climbed up the side of the coach to the driver's seat. He grabbed the reins and brought the horses to a halt "after they had run some two or three miles." None of the passengers were injured. Of course they were most grateful, calling Joseph's deed "daring and heroic." Some of the passengers were members of Congress and set forth the idea of mentioning the Prophet's act of bravery in a session of that body, "believing they would reward such conduct by some public act." However, when the congressmen found out their heroic

The White House, *artist unknown*

rescuer was Joseph Smith, "the 'Mormon Prophet,'" their enthusiasm quickly diminished. Said the Prophet, "I heard no more of their praise, gratitude, or reward."[11]

Joseph and Elias Higbee arrived in the nation's capital on Thursday, 28 November 1839. They stayed in an inexpensive boarding house on the corner of Missouri and Third Street. Joseph said it was "as cheap boarding as can be had in this city."[12] The next morning they walked to the White House and requested an audience with President Martin Van Buren. They were ushered into the parlor, where they were introduced to the president. They gave Van Buren their letters of recommendation. After reading one of them, the president frowned and declared, "What can I do? I can do nothing for you! If I do anything, I shall come in contact with the whole state of Missouri."[13] After further discussion, however, Van Buren promised to reconsider his position. "He felt to sympathize with us, on account of our sufferings."[14]

During the course of the interview, they discussed religion. President Van Buren asked how Mormonism differed "from the other religions of the day." The Prophet replied that "we differed in mode of baptism, and the gift of the Holy Ghost by the laying on of hands. We deemed it unnecessary to make many words in preaching the Gospel to him. Suffice it to say he has got our testimony."[15]

After their visit with President Van Buren, the Prophet and Elias Higbee met with several senators and representatives to espouse their cause. On 6 December, they began a series of meetings with the congressional delegation from Illinois which proved especially helpful. After some discussion, it was decided that the congressmen from Illinois would draw up a memorial and a petition and that Richard P. Young, a senator from Illinois, would present it to the Senate.[16]

The lengthy petition, which is reproduced in the *History of the Church,* is fourteen single-spaced pages. It enumerates the persecutions that the Saints endured from the time they were expelled from Jackson County in 1833 to their exodus to Illinois. The document concludes with an impassioned plea: "For ourselves we see no redress, unless it is awarded by the Congress of the United States. And here we make our appeal as *American Citizens,* as *Christians,* and as *Men*—believing that the high sense of justice which exists in your honorable body, will not allow such oppression to be practiced upon any portion of the citizens of this vast republic with impunity."[17] Senator Young faithfully introduced the petition in the Senate which, in turn, referred it to the Judiciary Committee.[18]

In the meantime, Joseph and Elias Higbee wrote to the Saints in Illinois asking them to send as many sworn affidavits as possible which would specifically confirm their persecutions and property losses in Missouri.[19] Altogether the Mormon delegates submitted 491 individual petitions for redress to Congress. These petitions itemized claims against the state of Missouri that amounted to $1,381,044.00.[20]

While Joseph Smith was in the East, he also took the opportunity to do what he loved most—preach the gospel and visit branches of the Church. On 21 December 1839 he took a train to Philadelphia where he "spent several days preaching and visiting from house to house."[21] Parley P. Pratt, who was staying in Philadelphia at the time, wrote about his conversations with the Prophet: "It was at this time that I received from him the first idea of eternal family organization. . . . It was from him that I learned that the wife of my bosom might be secured to me for time and all eternity."[22] Elder Pratt also told of an occasion when Joseph Smith spoke to a crowd of three thousand people who had assembled in a large church in Philadelphia: "Joseph arose like a lion about to roar; and being full of the Holy Ghost, spoke in great power, bearing testimony of the visions he had seen, the ministering of angels which he had enjoyed; and how he had found the plates of the Book of Mormon, and translated them by the gift and power of God." After this event Elder Pratt wrote, "The entire congregation were astounded; electrified, as it were, and overwhelmed with the sense of the truth and power by which he spoke, and the wonders which he related. . . . Many souls were gathered into the fold."[23]

The Prophet returned to Washington, D.C. at the end of January 1840 where he continued to preach the gospel.[24] He gave a two-hour sermon on the evening of 5 February 1840 which was attended by Matthew S. Davis, a United States Congressman. Davis wrote a letter to his wife, Mary, describing the Prophet's sermon in some detail. The congressman explained that Mormonism "appears to be the religion of meekness, lowliness, and mild persuasion." He concluded his letter by writing, "*I have changed my opinion of the Mormons. They are an injured and much-abused people.*"[25]

Soon after Joseph Smith's return to the nation's capital, he had another interview with President Van Buren, who by this time had lost any sympathetic feelings he might have had for the Church.[26] According to the Prophet, Van Buren treated him rudely and declared, "Gentleman your cause is just, but I can do nothing for you. . . . If I take up for you I shall lose the vote of Missouri."[27]

Frustrated and disappointed with the president, Joseph complained that Van Buren's "whole course went to show that he was an office-seeker, that self-aggrandizement was his ruling passion, and that justice and righteousness were no part of his composition." The Prophet also felt that he could no longer "conscientiously support" such a man at the head of the government. Joseph now believed that it was no longer beneficial for him to stay in Washington, and he departed for Nauvoo on, or before, 20 February.[28]

The Prophet was so infuriated with the president that he declared: "On my way home I did not fail to proclaim the iniquity and insolence of Martin Van Buren, toward myself and an injured people

. . . and may he never be elected again to any office of trust or power, by which he may abuse the innocent and let the guilty go free." Joseph Smith's declaration came true. Martin Van Buren lost the election of 1840 to William Henry Harrison, the Whig candidate. In 1848, Van Buren ran again for president as the candidate of the Free Soil Party "and did not receive a single electoral vote."[29]

After the Prophet left for Nauvoo, Elias Higbee stayed behind to work with the Senate Judiciary Committee on the petition. Between 20 February and 24 March, Higbee wrote six letters to the Prophet informing him of the activities of the Senate.[30] On 4 March the Judiciary Committee submitted its formal report to the Twenty-sixth Congress of the United States. For all intents and purposes, the committee simply washed its hands of any jurisdiction or responsibility in the case: "The committee, under these circumstances, have not considered themselves justified in inquiring into the truth or falsehood of the facts charged in the petition." Later in the report, the committee had the audacity to recommend that the Church "apply to the justice and magnanimity of the state of Missouri." Finally it recommended "that the committee on the judiciary be discharged from the further consideration of the memorial in this case."[31]

On 24 March Elias Higbee sadly reported, "Our business is at last ended here. Yesterday a resolution passed the Senate, that the committee should be discharged; and that we might withdraw the accompanying papers, which I have done. I have also taken a copy of the memorial, and want to be off for the west immediately." Even though all their work ended in disappointment, Higbee seemed to be at peace with the fact that he gave it his best effort. He concluded, "But there is no need of crying for spilt milk. I have done all I could in this matter."[32]

On 7 April at the general conference of the Church in Nauvoo, Illinois, the Prophet Joseph Smith gave a report of their travels to Washington, D.C. The next day, the conference formally thanked the delegates for their efforts in seeking redress for the Saints from the national government. The conference encouraged the delegates to keep trying, but it was not to be. Joseph had always intended that their journey to the nation's capital would be their last attempt at redress.

The revelation that Joseph Smith had received in Liberty Jail, back in March 1839, commanding the Saints to gather facts to present "to the heads of the government," clearly stated that this would be the "last effort" (D&C 123:6). When Joseph wrote to Emma on his way to Washington, he said most definitely that he would *try this once*" in the name of the Lord.[33] This would be the final attempt. The Prophet was now resigned to leave the matter in the hands of Providence. This attitude was eloquently stated in the final charge given the delegates at the April 1840 general conference. They were told that after all else had failed, "they then appeal our case to the Court of Heaven, believing that the Great Jehovah, who rules over the destiny of nations, and who notices the falling sparrows, will undoubtedly redress our wrongs, and ere long avenge us of our adversaries."[34]

NOTES

1. Lee Davidson, "Medal of Freedom," *LDS Church News* (June 26, 2004): 3.
2. Davidson, "Medal of Freedom," 3.
3. Baugh, "Extermination Order,"in Garr, Cannon and Cowan, *Encyclopedia of Latter-day Saint History,* 351.
4. See Johnson, *Mormon Redress Petitions.*
5. Smith, *History of the Church,* 4:16, 18.
6. Smith, *History of the Church,* 4:19.
7. Roberts, *Comprehensive History of the Church,* 2:29.
8. West, *Papers of Martin Van Buren.* This is a letter from Judge Adams to Martin Van Buren written in Springfield, Illinois, on November 9.
9. Jessee, *Personal Writings of Joseph Smith,* 448.
10. Smith, *History of the Church,* 4:21.
11. Smith, *History of the Church,* 4:23–24.
12. Smith, *History of the Church,* 4:40.
13. Smith, *History of the Church,* 4:40.
14. Smith, *History of the Church,* 4:40.
15. Smith, *History of the Church,* 4:42.
16. Smith, *History of the Church,* 4:43–44.
17. Smith, *History of the Church,* 4:38.
18. Roberts, *Comprehensive History of the Church,* 2:32.
19. Smith, *History of the Church,* 4:44.
20. Smith, *History of the Church,* 4:74.
21. Smith, *History of the Church,* 4:47.

22. Pratt, *Autobiography of Parley P. Pratt,* 297.
23. Pratt, *Autobiography of Parley P. Pratt,* 298–99.
24. Smith, *History of the Church,* 4:77.
25. Smith, *History of the Church,* 4:79.
26. Some histories maintain that Joseph Smith's interview with Martin Van Buren on 29 November 1839 was the only one he had with the president. See *Church History in the Fulness of Times,* 221, and Roberts, *Comprehensive History of the Church,* 2:30. However, the *History of the Church* also has an entry on 6 February 1840 that talks about the Prophet visiting Van Buren. Historians disagree over whether this entry is simply a retelling of the visit on 29 November 1839 or the recording of a second visit on 6 February 1840. The present author believes the evidence in favor of two distinct visits is the most persuasive. In the November account the Prophet said that Van Buren "felt to sympathize" with the Mormons. In contrast, in the February account the Prophet calls Van Buren "insolent" and not worthy to be president. In this account Joseph Smith also said that he planned to leave Washington, D.C. "in but a few days." If Joseph would have departed in a few days after his visit in November, he would not have been in Washington, D.C. in February. The *History of the Church* makes clear that the Prophet was definitely in Washington, D.C., in the month of February.
27. Smith, *History of the Church,* 4:80.
28. On 6 February, Joseph Smith stated that he "stayed but a few days" before he left Washington, D.C. However, he might have stayed as late as 20 February. On that day he wrote, "Judge Higbee I left at Washington, and he wrote me as follows." Higbee's letter was dated 20 February. Smith, *History of the Church,* 4:80.
29. Smith, *History of the Church,* 4:89.
30. See Smith, *History of the Church,* 4:81, 83, 85, 88, 94, 98.
31. Smith, *History of the Church,* 4:91, 92.
32. Smith, *History of the Church,* 4:98, 99.
33. Jessee, *Personal Writings of Joseph Smith,* 448; emphasis added.
34. Smith, *History of the Church,* 4:108.

CHAPTER THIRTY-FOUR

THE NAUVOO TEMPLE

Richard O. Cowan

n Kirtland, Joseph Smith learned that those who died without an opportunity to accept the gospel might still qualify for the celestial kingdom (D&C 137:7–9). It was in Nauvoo, however, that he unfolded the practice of performing vicarious ordinances for the dead.

The Prophet taught the practice of baptism for the dead for the first time in this dispensation on 15 August 1840 at the funeral of Seymour Brunson, a faithful member of the Nauvoo high council.[1] Joseph noted that in the congregation there was a widow whose son had died without baptism. He read from 1 Corinthians 15:29 about New Testament Saints performing baptisms for the dead and "remarked that the Gospel of Jesus Christ brought glad tidings of great joy" to this widow and to all mankind. He explained that "the plan of salvation was calculated to save all who were willing to obey the requirements of the law of God."[2] Almost immediately, Church members eagerly began performing the ordinance of baptism in the Mississippi River in behalf of deceased loved ones, Joseph Smith's own family leading the way.

The Prophet continued to give emphasis to this principle. Preaching at a conference on 2 October 1841, he declared: "Suppose the case of two men, brothers, equally intelligent, learned, virtuous and lovely, walking in uprightness and in all good conscience . . . One dies and is buried, having never heard the Gospel of reconciliation; to the other the message of salvation is sent, he hears and embraces it

Richard O. Cowan is a professor of Church history and doctrine at Brigham Young University.

Joseph Smith and Joseph Knight Jr. Study the Temple Plans, *by Paul Mann*

and is made the heir of eternal life. Shall the one become the partaker of glory and the other be consigned to hopeless perdition? Is there no chance for his escape? Sectarianism answers 'none.'" The Prophet then acknowledged "the wisdom and mercy of God in preparing an ordinance for the salvation of the dead." Then, in the spirit of warning, he concluded: "Those Saints who neglect it in behalf of their deceased relatives, do it at the peril of their own salvation."[3]

With such encouragement and admonition, the Saints readily took advantage of the opportunity to make gospel ordinances and blessings available to their departed loved ones. By 1844, the year of the Prophet's martyrdom, some 15,722 baptisms would be performed in behalf of the dead. Typically these were for family members.[4]

Meanwhile, early in August 1840, the First Presidency declared that the time had come to build a temple, "where the ordinances can be attended to agreeably to His divine will."[5]

A revelation received 19 January 1841 specifically pointed to the need for the Saints to build the temple. "For there is not a place found on earth that he may come to and restore again that which was lost unto you, or which he hath taken away, even the fullness of the priesthood" (D&C 124:28). Specifically, the Lord declared that the ordinance of baptism for the dead "belongeth to my house" (D&C 124:30).

The Lord promised to show the Prophet "all things pertaining to this house," including "the place whereon it shall be built" (D&C 124:42). The site chosen for the temple was on elevated ground at the east edge of the city which commanded a striking view of the town and the Mississippi River below. At about this same time, the Prophet Joseph Smith invited interested individuals to submit designs for the proposed temple. Several were received, but none suited him. When William Weeks, a recent convert who was an architect and builder from New England, came in with his plans, "Joseph Smith grabbed him, hugged him and said 'You are the man I want.'"[6] Weeks became the general superintendent of temple construction.

As had been the case with the Kirtland Temple, Joseph testified that the temple's plan had been given to him by revelation. For example, when Weeks questioned the appropriateness of placing round windows on the side of the building, Joseph explained that small rooms in the temple could be illuminated with one light at the center of each of the windows and that "when the whole building was thus illuminated, the effect would be remarkably grand." The Prophet therefore insisted, "I wish you to carry out *my* designs. I have seen in vision the splendid appearance of that building illuminated, and will have it built according to the pattern shown me."[7] The Nauvoo Temple followed the general plan of the earlier temple in Kirtland with the addition of a baptismal font in the basement and facilities for other sacred ordinances on the attic level.

A stone quarry was located just north of the city, and in February of 1841 excavations for the temple's foundation began. On 6 April the southeast cornerstone was lowered into place under the direction of the First Presidency. On that occasion, Joseph Smith stated:

> This principal corner stone in representation of the First Presidency, is now duly laid in honor of the Great God; and may it there remain until the whole fabric is completed; and may the same be accomplished speedily; that the Saints may have a place to worship God, and the Son of Man have where to lay His head.[8]

During the summer and fall of that year, the Saints eagerly pushed the temple's construction. When there was only a temporary wooden font enclosed by frame walls, Joseph dedicated the facility on Monday, 8 November. The first baptisms were performed there two weeks later before a large congregation which had gathered to witness this event. Hereafter, the Prophet and members of the Twelve frequently officiated in the temple. On 28 December 1841, for example, Joseph Smith recorded, "I baptized Sidney Rigdon in the font, for and in behalf of his parents; also baptized Reynolds Cahoon and others."[9]

The Saints, who had received a preliminary or partial endowment in Kirtland, knew with the building of the Nauvoo Temple that the time had come to unfold these blessings more fully. The instructions they would receive needed to be given in a place of privacy because they were sacred and would make known "things which have been kept hid from before the foundation of the world" (D&C 124:41).

Such a facility became available before the completion of the temple when Joseph Smith opened his store early in 1842. The second story of this twenty-five-foot by forty-four-foot red brick structure included the Prophet's small office and a large area known as the "assembly room."[10] Here the Relief Society was organized on 17 March 1842, and the first endowments were given seven weeks later.

With the assistance of five or six workmen, the Prophet divided the main room to represent the various stages in man's eternal progress. "We . . . went to work making the necessary preparations" one of the workmen later recalled, "and everything was arranged representing the interior of a temple as much as the circumstances would permit, [the Prophet] being with us dictating everything."[11] These preparations were completed before noon on 4 May 1842, and later that same day the first endowments were given. Seven leading brethren received the instructions of the endowment, which unfolded as the group moved from one area to another in the assembly room. Concerning this significant event, Joseph Smith recorded:

I spent the day in the upper part of the store . . . in council with [seven brethren], instructing them in the principles and order of the Priesthood, attending to washings, anointings, endowments and the communication of keys pertaining to the Aaronic Priesthood, and so on to the highest order of the Melchisedek Priesthood, setting forth the order pertaining to the Ancient of Days, and all those plans and principles by which any one is enabled to secure the fullness of those blessings which have been prepared for the Church of the First Born, and come up and abide in the presence of the Eloheim in the eternal worlds. . . . And the communications I made to this council were of things spiritual, and to be received only by the spiritual minded: and there was nothing made known to these men but what will be made known to all the Saints of the last days, so soon as they are prepared to receive, and a proper place is prepared to communicate them, even to the weakest of the Saints; therefore let the Saints be diligent in building the Temple.[12]

After giving these first endowments, the Prophet turned to Brigham Young and remarked: "Brother Brigham, this is not arranged perfectly; however, we have done the best we could under the circumstances in which we are placed. I wish you to take this matter in hand: organize and systematize all these ceremonies."[13] By the time of the Prophet's martyrdom, about fifty individuals had received the blessings of the endowment, the instructions being given in the assembly room or in private homes.

Early in September 1842, a group of Missourians crossed the Mississippi River into Illinois threatening to seize Joseph Smith and carry him back into Missouri. Realizing that his life was in danger, Joseph went into hiding. Amid these stressful circumstances, his overriding concern was not for himself but for pushing forward construction on the temple. By means of two letters, the Prophet gave the Saints further instructions concerning work for the dead. He emphasized the importance of having a recorder present, not only to keep an accurate record but also to assure that each ordinance was done properly (D&C 127:6; 128:3). The Prophet linked the keeping of proper records with the power to bind or loose on earth and have this action recognized in heaven (D&C 128:8–9; compare Matthew 16:18–19). The power to "bind on earth" and in heaven was associated with the keys which Elijah had restored in 1836 just after the dedication of the Kirtland Temple. Because temple baptismal fonts symbolize the grave, the Prophet explained they should be located "underneath where the living are wont to assemble" (D&C 128:13). Finally, expanding on the writings of Paul, Joseph Smith declared that "they [the fathers] without us cannot be made perfect—neither can we without our dead be made perfect" and that "their salvation is necessary and essential to our salvation" (D&C 128:15). This is so because in the celestial kingdom we will be organized as God's family according to the patriarchal order. Hence, he taught that there must be "a welding link of some kind or other between the fathers and the children" (D&C 128:18). Vicarious ordinances for the dead, he concluded, were the means of establishing this link.

Among the other blessings unfolded during these years was eternal marriage. The Master stressed the sanctity of the family. An earlier revelation to Joseph Smith had affirmed that "marriage is ordained of God" as the means of providing earthly tabernacles for the spirits who had lived before the world was created (D&C 49:15).

In May 1843 the Prophet instructed the Saints that in order to attain the highest degree of the celestial kingdom, one must enter "the new and everlasting covenant of marriage" (D&C 131:2). Two months later he recorded a revelation that declared: "If a man marry him a wife in the world, and he marry her not by me nor by my word, and he covenant with her so long as he is in the world and she with him, their covenant and marriage are not of force when they are dead, and when they are out of the world" (D&C 132:15). After these instructions, a number of marriages for eternity were performed.

During the closing year of his life, the Prophet Joseph Smith made sure that the Twelve and others received the highest blessings available through temple ordinances so that the authority necessary to roll forth the Lord's work would remain on the earth. Elder Orson Hyde later recalled that Joseph "conducted us through every ordinance of the holy priesthood, and when he had gone through with all the ordinances he rejoiced very much, and says, now if they kill me you have got all the keys, and all the ordinances and you can confer them upon others, and the hosts of Satan will not be able to tear down the kingdom."[14]

President Wilford Woodruff later recalled the Prophet's instructions:

> He stood upon his feet some three hours. The room was filled as with consuming fire, his face was as clear as amber, and he was clothed upon by the power of God. . . . "I have had sealed upon my head every key, every power, every principle of life and salvation that God has ever given to any man who ever lived upon the face of the earth. . . . Now," said he addressing the Twelve, "I have sealed upon your heads every key, every power, and every principle which the Lord has sealed upon my head. . . . I tell you, the burden of this kingdom now rests upon your shoulders; you have got to bear it off in all the world, and if you don't do it you will be damned."[15]

The martyrdom of Joseph and Hyrum Smith on 27 June 1844 caused only a temporary lull in temple construction. Even though the Saints knew they would soon be forced to leave Nauvoo and lose access to the temple, they were willing to expend approximately a million dollars to fulfill their Prophet's dream of erecting a house of the Lord. By autumn of the following year, the temple was sufficiently completed so that ordinances could commence in its attic story. On 30 November 1845, Brigham Young and twenty others who had received their endowment from Joseph Smith gathered to dedicate this area. During the next nine weeks, over five thousand Latter-day Saints received their endowment, thus fulfilling Joseph Smith's profound desire to make these blessings available before the westward exodus.

The Nauvoo Temple was dedicated in a private service on 30 April 1846, after most of the Saints had left the area and in a public meeting the following day. Just two years later this magnificent structure was destroyed by fire, probably set by those determined to remove any tangible link that might tempt the "Mormons" to return to Nauvoo. But the Saints would return. In 1999 Church president Gordon B. Hinckley announced plans to rebuild the Nauvoo Temple. He explained that in addition to providing sacred temple ordinances, it would "stand as a memorial" to Joseph Smith and the early Latter-day Saints who had built the original temple "there on the banks of the Mississippi."[16]

NOTES
1. Smith, *History of the Church*, 4:179; see also D&C 124:132.
2. Ehat and Cook, *Words of Joseph Smith*, 49.
3. Smith, *History of the Church*, 4:425–26.
4. "A Most Glorious Principle," in *Children of the Covenant*, 129–30.
5. Smith, *History of the Church*, 4:186.
6. Cited in J. Earl Arrington, "William Weeks, Architect of the Nauvoo Temple," *BYU Studies* 19 (Spring 1979): 340.
7. Smith, *History of the Church*, 6:197; emphasis in original.
8. Smith, *History of the Church*, 4:329.
9. Smith, *History of the Church*, 4:486.
10. Lisle G. Brown, "The Sacred Departments for Temple Work in Nauvoo: The Assembly Room and the Council Chamber," *BYU Studies* 19 (Spring 1979): 363.
11. Lucius N. Scovil letter in *Deseret News Semi-Weekly*, February 15, 1884, 2, cited in Andrew F. Ehat, "'They Might Have Known That He Was Not a Fallen Prophet': The Journal of Joseph Fielding," *BYU Studies* 19, no. 2 (Winter 1979): 159 n.
12. Smith, *History of the Church*, 5:1–2.

13. L. John Nuttall diary, February 7, 1877, cited in Ehat, "They Might Have Known," 159 n.
14. *Times and Seasons* 5 (September 15, 1844): 651.
15. *Deseret News Weekly* 44 (March 19, 1892): 406.
16. Hinckley, Conference Report, April 1999, 117.

THE FEMALE RELIEF SOCIETY
OF NAUVOO

Cynthia Doxey

The organization of the Female Relief Society of Nauvoo shows the prophetic foresight of Joseph Smith in initiating the work of women in the Church. "The Church was never perfectly organized until the women were thus organized," said the Prophet of the society.[1] In 1992, during the sesquicentennial celebration of its organization, President Gordon B. Hinckley, first counselor in the First Presidency of the Church, recognized the Relief Society as "the largest and most effective organization of its kind in all the world."[2]

Although the Relief Society was not organized until 17 March 1842, before that time women of the Church combined their talents to give meaningful service. When the Kirtland Temple was being built, women donated money, materials, and labor to help clothe and feed workmen and beautify the temple. Heber C. Kimball recalled, "Our women were engaged in spinning and knitting in order to clothe those who were laboring at the building."[3] When Joseph Smith observed the women sewing veils for the temple, he said, "The sisters are always first and foremost in all good works. Mary was first at the resurrection; and the sisters now are the first to work on the inside of the temple."[4]

After the loss of homes, property, and lives in Kirtland and Missouri, these same women, joined by a host of others, settled on the banks of the Mississippi. There they helped build the famed city of Nauvoo. They played a key role in the success of that community

Cynthia Doxey is an associate professor of Church history and doctrine at Brigham Young University.

by using their resourcefulness and frugality as homemakers. Women, sometimes left on their own for long periods of time while their husbands served missions, not only kept their households going but accepted additional opportunities to work as schoolteachers, seamstresses, weavers, milliners, and laundresses.[5]

Although most women of Nauvoo had their share of work experiences within and without the home, they recognized the needs of near neighbors and wished to organize themselves to aid such neighbors and promote the work of the Church.

ORGANIZATION IN NAUVOO

Sarah Melissa Granger Kimball, the wife of Hiram Kimball, a prominent merchant in Nauvoo, expressed interest in helping the poor who worked in the temple quarries of Nauvoo. She later recalled that a Miss Cooke (Cook) was a "seamstress for me and the subject of combining our efforts for assisting the Temple hands came up in conversation." Miss Cooke did not have the means to buy fabric to clothe the workmen but was willing to sew shirts for the men. Sarah had the means, and so the two women combined their talents. After finding satisfaction in such an undertaking, Sarah concluded that "some of our neighbors might wish to combine means and efforts with ours."[6]

She and Miss Cooke invited a few neighborhood women to join with them in forming a ladies' society. Their first meeting took place at the Kimball home on 4 March 1842. At this meeting, the assembled women expressed the belief that it was necessary to have a constitution and bylaws for their organization. Eliza R. Snow was appointed to write these documents. After she had done so, she presented them to Joseph Smith for approval. The Prophet observed that what she had written was "the best he had ever seen" but assured Eliza that the Lord had something better for the women of Nauvoo. He invited selected women to meet in the upper room of his red brick store on Thursday afternoon, 17 March, for the purpose of organizing "the women under the priesthood after the pattern of the priesthood."[7]

On that date, twenty women came to that upper room. Joseph Smith, John Taylor, and Willard Richards, who was appointed as secretary of that first meeting, were there to greet them.[8] At the meeting, Joseph expressed his hope that "the Society of Sisters might provoke the brethren to good works in looking to the wants of the poor" and assist the brethren in "correcting the morals and strengthening the virtues of the community." He then organized the women after the pattern of the priesthood quorums, namely, with a presiding officer and two counselors to lead. Minutes of this first meeting also reveal that he told the women that "he would ordain them to preside over the Society—and let them preside just as the Presidency presides over the church; and if they need his instruction—ask him, he will give it from time to time."[9]

The Prophet evidently felt that in organizing the sisters, he was making a connection between the priesthood and the women of the Church which would be important for promoting the work of the Lord. In a Relief Society Conference in the Weber Stake in 1880, Franklin D. Richards recognized this relationship when he said, "The Relief Societies are organized in such perfect harmony with the order of the Church and of the priesthood that there is no occasion for any discord between the officers or members" of either the priesthood or the society.[10]

IMPORTANT ORGANIZATIONAL DECISIONS

At the first meeting, several items of business were discussed and voted upon, using the democratic order taught to the women by Joseph Smith.[11] The first order of business was to choose a president. Elizabeth Whitney motioned that Emma Smith be elected president. The motion was seconded by Sister Packard and unanimously accepted. Emma chose for her counselors Sarah M. Cleveland and Elizabeth Ann Whitney.[12] Following her selection, Joseph read from a revelation given to Emma Smith in 1830 (D&C 25), in which Emma was called "an elect lady," who was "ordained under [Joseph's] hand to expound scriptures, and to exhort the church, according as it shall

Organization of the Relief Society, *by Dale Kilbourn.* © *Intellectual Reserve, Inc. Courtesy of the Museum of Church History and Art*

be given thee by my Spirit" (D&C 25:3, 7). Joseph explained that when the Lord called her an elect lady (a phrase also found in 2 John 1:1), it was because she was "elected to preside." He also taught that at the time of the 1830 revelation, Emma was "ordained . . . to expound the Scriptures" and to "teach the female part of [the] community," implying that her calling as the president of the Relief Society was a fulfillment of that revelation.[13] The presidency was set apart by Elder John Taylor.[14]

The name of the society was then discussed. Sarah Cleveland and Elizabeth Whitney suggested that the organization be called the Nauvoo Female Relief Society. Elder John Taylor suggested that the word *Relief* be replaced with the word *Benevolent*. Joseph Smith agreed with Elder Taylor, reminding the sisters that *benevolent* was much more popular among societies of the day and that *relief* might be misconstrued to signify the liberation of criminals from punishment. Emma Smith viewed the very popularity of the word *benevolent* as "one great objection," as there were some benevolent societies that had become corrupt, and she did "not wish to have it called after other societies in the world." Eliza R. Snow concurred with Emma, saying that "the popular institutions of the day should not be our guide." Emma then remarked, "We are going to do something extraordinary."[15] The name "Female Relief Society of Nauvoo" was then presented. It was unanimously accepted.

This interchange shows the democratic process that occurred at the first meeting. In the process, Joseph taught the women about the voting procedure and how to make decisions. The women were seen as both intelligent and capable of making their own decisions, and Mormon leaders were willing to be taught by them, showing an equality among men and women that was not always present in nineteenth century American society. In remarking about this interchange, Emmeline B. Wells in 1880 observed that the organization of the Relief Society "presented the great woman-question to the Latter-day Saints, previous to the woman's rights organizations . . . in America, Great Britain and Europe." She then acknowledged that unlike other female organizations, the Relief Society was not pitting women against men but rather "as a co-worker and helpmeet in all that relates to the well-being . . . of both [men and women]." Because of this direction, members of the society had great opportunities to augment their capacities for intellectual and moral capacities and their "gift of faith."[16]

CHARITABLE PURPOSE OF THE SOCIETY

As the society pushed forward in helping near neighbors, Joseph and Emma took occasion to outline the purposes and expected work of the society. Joseph said, "All I shall have to give to the poor, I shall give to this Society." He "offered $5.00 in gold to commence the funds of the Institution." Emma Smith spoke of the continuing need to relieve the poor and distressed. She taught that "each member should be ambitious to do good" and that each should "watch over the morals and be very careful of the character and reputation of the members of the Institution." Joseph observed that "it is natural for females to have feelings of charity—you are now placed in a situation where you can act according to those sympathies which God has planted in your bosoms."[17]

Aiding those in the community with temporal concerns soon became of paramount importance to the society. Minutes of society meetings reveal discussions of the needs of local families and the collection of money, clothing, and food to help the families. It appears that the women of Relief Society enthusiastically went about their charitable work, not only providing goods and means but also giving of their time by spinning wool and flax, sewing clothing, and nursing the sick. Eliza R. Snow observed that in the winter of 1843 so many experienced hardship from exposure and sickness that "had it not been for the timely aid of the F. R. Society [they] would have suffered very much, and probably some would have perished."[18]

In order to facilitate the charitable work of the society in and around Nauvoo, the women began a visiting program. Four sisters from each of the Nauvoo wards were appointed to "search out the poor and suffering" and "to call on the rich for aid and thus as far as possible relieve the wants of all."[19] The visiting among the sisters that began in Nauvoo was the precursor of the current visiting teaching program of the society.

SPIRITUAL GROWTH AND SISTERHOOD

Although the stated purpose of the fledgling society was to aid the poor, Joseph saw the meetings of the society as an opportunity for the women to learn gospel principles together in a spirit of sisterhood. He often attended their meetings and addressed the women on their duties as followers of Jesus Christ. He exhorted them to support one another and help each other to become better. Said he, "Nothing is so much calculated to lead people to forsake sin as to take them by the hand and watch over them with tenderness." The Prophet also taught that the society was to receive instruction from those appointed to lead. He declared, "I now turn the key to you in the name of God and this Society shall rejoice and knowledge and intelligence shall flow down from this time—this is the beginning of better days to this Society."[20] While the temple blessings were not yet available to the Saints in general, Joseph Smith promised the women of the society that they would have an opportunity to be endowed with a gift from God and that the holy order of matrimony would extend into the eternities. Relief Society, therefore, was also to prepare righteous women to receive the promised blessings of temple ordinances.

Along with service, learning, and preparation to receive awaited blessings, it naturally followed that the women of the society began to care deeply for one another. Lucy Mack Smith commended such care and admonished: "We must cherish one another, watch over one another, comfort one another and gain instruction that we may all sit down in heaven together."[21] The spirit of sisterhood that grew with each meeting is viewed as one reason why so many women wanted to be a part of the society in Nauvoo.

GROWTH OF THE RELIEF SOCIETY

The popularity of the society is most evident by the number of women who joined. Eliza R. Snow recounted that within the first year of its organization, there were 1,158 members. Since there was not a facility in Nauvoo large enough to house such numbers, the society met in groves, the usual meeting place for summer Sabbath meetings. Later, the society was divided according to the wards in the city, and meetings were held alternately from week to week in the ward locales. In 1872, when Eliza R. Snow wrote a historical sketch of the Relief Society to that date, she indicated that there were strong societies in every ward in the Territory of Utah. Although she could have boasted of such strength, instead she acknowledged that "it has but little more than emerged from its embryo state in comparison to its great future."[22] Her thoughts proved prophetic as the Relief Society today numbers into the millions of active members.

In our present day, modern prophets recognize the importance of the work of women as started by the Prophet Joseph Smith. President Gordon B. Hinckley asks, "Who can gauge the miraculous effects upon the lives of millions of women . . . whose understanding of the things of God has been enriched by reason of countless lessons effectively taught and learned in meetings of the Relief Society?" He commended the society on the great charitable work it has accomplished, and prayed that the "spirit of love which has motivated [women] . . . continue to grow and be felt over the world."[23] Truly, Joseph Smith had a vision of the blessings that would come to women in a society established on the principles of the priesthood and gospel truths. To date, the Relief Society has surpassed the work of any other women's organization established in Joseph's day, and it continues to grow and bring opportunities for learning, service, and leadership to women throughout the world.

NOTES

1. This statement was recorded by Sarah M. Kimball in her "Autobiography," cited in *Woman's Exponent* 12 (1 September 1883): 51.
2. Gordon B. Hinckley, "Ambitious to Do Good," *Ensign*, March 1992, 4.
3. "Extracts from H. C. Kimball's Journal," *Times and Seasons* 7 (15 April 1845): 867.
4. Polly Angell recollection, as cited in Tullidge, *Women of Mormondom*, 76.
5. Derr, et al., *Women of Covenant*, 24.
6. Kimball, "Autobiography," 51.
7. Kimball, "Autobiography," 51.
8. "A Book of Records Containing the Proceedings of The Female Relief Society of Nauvoo, March 17, 1842 to March 16, 1844," 6, LDS Church Archives; hereafter cited as "Minutes." Although twenty women were present, the names of two women, Athalia Robinson and Nancy Rigdon, were lined out because they later left the society and the Church.
9. "Minutes," 17 March 1842, 7–8.
10. Relief Society Report of the Weber Stake Quarterly Conference of the Ladies Relief Society, as cited in *Woman's Exponent* 8 (15 April 1880): 174.
11. See "Minutes," 17 March 1842, 9–10.
12. "Minutes," 17 March 1842, 8. Sarah M. Cleveland, age fifty-three, was the oldest woman at the meeting. She was the wife of a non-Mormon merchant

in Nauvoo. Emma and her children had taken refuge with the Clevelands in Quincy after they had crossed into Illinois from Missouri. Elizabeth Ann Whitney, age forty-seven, was the wife of Bishop Newel K. Whitney. She had been a friend to the Smiths since the early Kirtland era. See Derr, et al., *Women of the Covenant,* 29–30.

13. "Minutes," 17 March 1842, 8.
14. Later in the meeting, Eliza R. Snow was elected secretary of the society. Phebe M. Wheeler was appointed to be her assistant, and Elvira R. Coles was elected treasurer.
15. "Minutes," 17 March 1842, 10–12.
16. Emmeline B. Wells, "Women's Organizations," *Woman's Exponent* 8 (15 January 1880): 122.
17. "Minutes," 17 March 1842, 12–13; "Minutes," April 28, 1842, 38.
18. Eliza R. Snow, "The Female Relief Society: A Brief Sketch of its Organization and Workings in the City of Nauvoo, Hancock Co. Ill.," *Woman's Exponent* 1 (1 June 1872): 10.
19. "Minutes," 28 July 1843, 101.
20. "Minutes," 9 June 1842, 62; "Minutes," 28 April 1842, 40.
21. "Minutes," 24 March 1842, as cited in Hinckley, "Ambitious to Do Good," 4.
22. Snow, "Female Relief Society," 10.
23. Hinckley, "Ambitious to Do Good," 4, 6.

CHAPTER THIRTY-SIX

THE PROPHET'S TEACHINGS IN NAUVOO

Kent P. Jackson

oseph Smith's Nauvoo period, from mid-1839 to mid-1844, was a remarkable time, perhaps unparalleled in the history of the world except when Jesus was physically present on earth. During those five years, the Prophet delivered public and private discourses that drew open the curtains of heaven, giving us glimpses backward to our premortal existence and forward to our postmortal possibilities. The Prophet had taught the gospel openly since the beginning of the Restoration, but prior to the Nauvoo period, his public discourses seemed to play a smaller role in his ministry than did some other aspects of his calling, such as translating and publishing sacred books and revelations, organizing the Church, administering the day-to-day affairs of the Church, building buildings, and establishing communities. The Prophet had delegated much of the public speaking to his counselor in the First Presidency, the gifted and experienced orator Sidney Rigdon, who had been called by revelation to be his spokesman (D&C 35:23; 100:9–11). But when Joseph emerged in the spring of 1839 from his imprisonment in Liberty Jail, he seemed to bring with him a new urgency to make known the things of God. During the Nauvoo years that followed, sharing his teachings with the Church was clearly one of his highest priorities.

We are indebted to scholars Andrew F. Ehat and Lyndon W. Cook for publishing in 1980 the collection *The Words of Joseph Smith*, which contains all of the then-known transcripts of the Prophet's

---

Kent P. Jackson is a professor of ancient scripture at Brigham Young University.

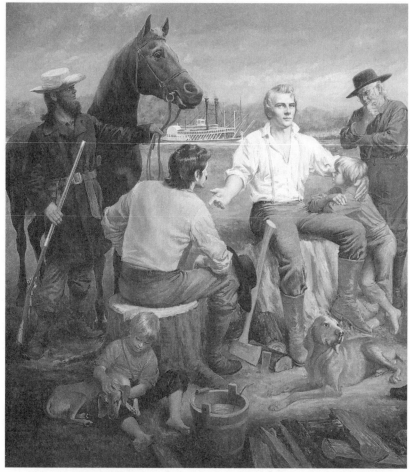

Joseph Smith at Nauvoo, *by Ted Gorka © Intellectual Reserve, Inc.*

Nauvoo discourses.[1] That book allowed readers access, for the first time, to the important primary sources that document the teachings of the Prophet Joseph Smith. Over 170 separate discourses of the Prophet are recorded in the Nauvoo period. Some were teaching sessions for small groups, but others were sermons in front of large public audiences. Many of the discourses were recorded by Church members without official assignment who loved Joseph Smith and wanted to document his teachings, such as Martha Jane Coray and James Burgess. But the Prophet also employed official recorders, such as Willard Richards, Thomas Bullock, and William Clayton, and their contributions in preserving his words are profound. Many of the transcriptions of the Prophet's discourses are fragmentary and incomplete, but in some instances we have extensive and relatively clear records. We are most fortunate when more than one scribe recorded a given sermon, providing important checks on the accuracy of the transcriptions and collaborative witnesses to the Prophet's teachings.

For the year 1843, fifty discourses are recorded, thus averaging about one per week. The heaviest concentrations were at the April and October general conferences. Fifty percent of the discourses in 1843 were on Sundays, and the rest were distributed more or less evenly throughout the other days of the week. Because many of the sermons were held out of doors, they were less frequent in the winter months. Outdoor sermons took place at the temple site, at more than one location called "the Grove," and elsewhere.[2] Much exertion was required of the Prophet for the outdoor speeches. There was no public address system, the crowds were huge—almost always in the thousands but sometimes as many as ten thousand—and the sermons were generally very long. In an 8 April 1843 address, the Prophet stated:

> I have three requests to make of the congregation. The first is that all who have faith will exercise it, that the Lord may be willing to calm the wind. The next is that I may have your prayers that the Lord may strengthen my lungs so that I may be able to make you all hear. And the next is that I may have the Holy Ghost to rest upon me so as to enable me to declare those things that are true.[3]

The next day, Willard Richards, who kept the Prophet's journal, recorded: "Joseph remarked that some might have expected him to preach, but his heart and lungs would not admit [i.e., permit it]."[4] One Church member recorded his feelings at one of the Prophet's sermons:

> As a matter of course we felt a desire to behold the Prophet Joseph—on the following day (Sunday) we proceeded to the Temple (then in an unfinished state) to hear him preach. We were gratified in seeing and hearing him on that occasion, and we soon felt and knew we were

listening to one that had not been taught of men—so different were all his thoughts and language.[5]

Another contemporary Latter-day Saint wrote: "I have listened to his clear and masterly explanations of deep and difficult questions. To him all things seemed simple and easy to be understood, and thus he could make them plain to others as no other man could."[6]

The subject matter in Joseph Smith's Nauvoo sermons varied based on the needs of members of the Church. Often he spoke of the current concerns of Latter-day Saints, such as the Missouri persecutions and their aftermath, the building of Nauvoo, persecutions in Illinois, and political developments as they affected the well-being of the Saints. But more than anything else, the Prophet taught doctrine, and he did it with a clearer understanding of doctrinal truth than any other man of modern times. He once said that he "understood the fullness of the gospel from beginning to end—and could teach it."[7] "When did I ever teach anything wrong from this stand?" he asked. "I never told you I was perfect—but there is no error in the revelations which I have taught."[8] "The doctrine I teach is true."[9] Joseph understood that it was his mission not only to receive God's word by revelation but also to teach it. "'Tis my duty to teach the doctrine," he stated,[10] and "it is my meditation all the day, and more than my meat and drink, to know how I shall make the Saints of God to comprehend the visions that roll like an overflowing surge before my mind."[11]

He taught doctrine primarily by quoting, paraphrasing, and reasoning out of the scriptures. In doing so, he was following the precedent of earlier doctrinal teachers. Moroni, Joseph Smith's early mentor, quoted and commented extensively on passages of scripture when he appeared to the young Prophet in September 1823. In the Joseph Smith–History account, the Prophet mentions five passages that Moroni quoted and discussed,[12] and he stated that the angel also "quoted many other passages of scripture" (Joseph Smith–History 1:41). Oliver Cowdery's *Messenger and Advocate* account of Moroni's coming, based undoubtedly on what Cowdery learned from Joseph, mentions some thirty passages that Moroni quoted or discussed.[13] The pattern of teaching doctrine by quoting and discussing scripture was also shown in Jesus' visit among the descendants of Lehi in the Book of Mormon. The account in 3 Nephi shows Jesus quoting the writings of previous prophets and applying and adapting them to the needs of his audience (3 Nephi 20–25). This is thus a model for good gospel teaching, and it was the model followed by Joseph Smith in many of his Nauvoo sermons.

It is interesting to note that although the Prophet bore testimony of the Book of Mormon and the revelations in the Doctrine and Covenants, he almost never incorporated passages from them into his sermons. Instead, he taught out of the Bible. The Bible was the book that early Latter-day Saint converts knew and turned to for revealed answers. Its chapter and verse divisions made access easy and provided a common referencing system regardless of what edition one used. In the early nineteenth century, Church members used the Doctrine and Covenants mainly as a source for Church government, and the Book of Mormon was used primarily as evidence that the heavens had been opened with new revelation. It was not until late in the century that those books had chapter and verse divisions that made them useable as references, and it was not until the twentieth century that Latter-day Saints in general began discovering that our richest sources for doctrine are not in the Bible but in the scriptures of the Restoration. But Joseph Smith's audiences both possessed and knew the Bible, and it was the source he chose to teach them from in his sermons and writings. Extant accounts list hundreds of verses from the Old and New Testaments that he used in his Nauvoo discourses.[14] A published collection of his commentary on the Bible shows that Joseph Smith most frequently discussed passages from the following books (total page numbers in parentheses): Matthew (41), Genesis (26), John (14), Revelation (14), 1 Corinthians (13), Hebrews (12), Isaiah (11), Acts (11), Luke (10), and Malachi (8).[15]

In the records of Joseph Smith's Nauvoo discourses, there is only one time where it appears that the Prophet used written notes for a sermon.[16] And with the hundreds of Bible verses that he alluded to, quoted, or paraphrased as he spoke, there is little to suggest that he took a Bible with him to the stand.[17] Joseph said "he was not like other men" when he spoke publicly. "He had to depend entirely upon the living God for every thing he said."[18] It is in this that the Nauvoo period was perhaps unparalleled in history except when Jesus was on earth. During the earlier years of the Prophet's ministry when most of the revelations in the Doctrine and Covenants were received, they were delivered in God's first-person words, and the Prophet's scribes recorded those words on paper as he dictated them. After the Prophet's ordeal in Liberty Jail and his arrival in Nauvoo, the revelations in God's words became less frequent, but the heavens were as open as ever and continued to pour forth new light to the Church.[19] Joseph Smith's sermons and other teaching sessions became the primary revelatory events and the major means by which the Lord brought new gospel light to the Church. Thus when the Prophet discussed Bible passages in his Nauvoo discourses, he was not simply using scripture to reinforce the teachings of earlier prophets and illustrate gospel principles. He was revealing new things, and he was bringing forth new gospel truth for the first time. In other words, Joseph Smith was not teaching out of the Bible, he was using Bible passages as the starting point to reveal new doctrine for the Church. Brigham Young was among those who recognized the unique blessing of witnessing Joseph Smith in such settings: "When I first heard him preach, he brought heaven and earth together. . . . he took heaven, figuratively speaking, and brought it down to earth; and he took the earth, brought it up, and opened up, in plainness and simplicity, the things of God."[20]

In his Nauvoo discourses, the Prophet was indeed opening up the things of God to the world, and the most important topic he discussed was God Himself. Along with the revelation of the temple and its purposes, it can be said that the most lasting doctrinal contribution during this period was Joseph Smith's teaching about the nature of God and man, continuing the process of revealing God that had begun with the First Vision. "But few understand the character of God," the Prophet stated. "They do not know, they do not understand their relationship to God. . . . What kind of a being is God?"[21] "If men do not comprehend the character of God, they do not comprehend themselves. What kind of a being is God? Eternal life [is] to know God. If man does not know God, [he] has not eternal life."[22] During the Nauvoo years, and especially during the last months of his life, an important part of Joseph's public teaching was dedicated to this topic. In the funeral sermon for Church member King Follett, delivered at general conference on 7 April 1844, and in the final public sermon of his life on 16 June 1844, Joseph unveiled to us the God of heaven and taught us of our true relationship to him.[23] The following are some of the things the Lord made known through his prophet about Deity and man, as recorded by scribes from Joseph's Nauvoo sermons and instructions:

1. *The Father, the Son, and the Holy Ghost are three separate beings.* "There are three personages in the heavens holding the keys of power."[24] "Every one [is] a different or separate person, and so [are] God and Jesus Christ and the Holy Ghost separate persons."[25] As one of the great truths made known in the First Vision, this doctrine's importance is enhanced because it stands in sharp contrast to the fundamental beliefs of most other Christians about the nature of God. "I have always declared God to be a distinct personage. Jesus Christ [is] a separate and distinct person from God the Father; the Holy Ghost is a distinct personage or spirit. And these three constitute three distinct personages and three Gods."[26]

2. *The Father and the Son have bodies of flesh and bones.* "The Father has a body of flesh and bones as tangible as man's; the Son also" (D&C 130:22). "There is no other God in heaven but that God who has flesh and bones."[27] This doctrine is another dramatic departure from traditional Christian doctrine.[28] Since God has a material body, then "the idea that the Father and the Son dwell in a man's heart is an old sectarian notion, and is false" (D&C 130:3).

3. *The Holy Ghost has a body of spirit.* "The Son has a tabernacle and so has the Father. But the Holy Ghost is a personage of spirit without tabernacle."[29] While "tabernacle" in this statement means *physical* body, the Holy Ghost is not without a body; he has a body

373

of spirit. Joseph Smith taught: "There is no such thing as immaterial matter. All spirit is matter, but it is more fine or pure, and can only be discerned by purer eyes; we cannot see it; but when our bodies are purified we shall see that it is all matter" (D&C 131:7–8).

4. *God is a man.* "God, that sits enthroned, is a man like one of yourselves. That is the great secret. If the veil were rent today and the great God, who holds this world in its sphere or its orbit, [and] the planets—if you were to see him today you would see him in all the person, image, [and] very form of man. For Adam was created in the very fashion of God."[30] For Latter-day Saints, this is a literal description.

5. *God was once as we are now.* "God [is] a man like one of us."[31] "I want you to understand God and how he comes to be God. We suppose that God was God from eternity. I will refute that idea, or I will do away or take away the veil so you may see. It is the first principle to know that we may converse with him and that he once was a man like us. . . . The Father was once on an earth like us."[32] We do not know exactly what this statement means, in part because the Prophet did not elaborate on the subject, and our scriptures are virtually silent on its implications. Thus we treat this issue and others like it with reverence and caution. As Joseph Smith said, this teaching draws back the veil so we can see as never before, and it should give us cause to ponder our own nature and our relationship with our Heavenly Father.

6. *There are other Gods.* Since God was once as we are, as Joseph Smith taught, it follows that there is much about the past ages of the universe that has not been revealed. Yet the Prophet taught that knowing who God is "sets one free to see all the beauty, holiness, and perfection of the Gods." He said, "All I want is to get the simple truth, [the] naked and the whole truth. . . . If Jesus Christ was the Son of God and . . . God the Father of Jesus Christ had a father, you may suppose that he had a father also. Where was there ever a son without a father? Where ever did [a] tree or anything spring into existence without a progenitor? And everything comes in this way. . . . Hence if Jesus had a father, can we not believe that he had a father also?"[33]

In some way still unrevealed to us and likely incomprehensible to us as well, a grand celestial process is at work and has been through the eons. But our Heavenly Father is still our only God. "I want to set it in a plain, simple manner," Joseph Smith said. "There is but one God pertaining to us, in all, through all."[34] The scriptures teach that our Heavenly Father is the only God, because the whole scope of our existence is under his divine government, and in all things we are dependent on him and subject to him.[35] We do not know all that there is to know, because not all reality in the universe pertains to us, and as the Lord told Moses, "Only an account of this earth, and the inhabitants thereof, give I unto you" (Moses 1:35).

7. *We are eternal beings.* "The spirit of man is not a created being. It existed from eternity and will exist to eternity."[36] Because all that we know has a beginning, it is difficult for us to comprehend an eternal past. Through the Prophet Joseph Smith, the Lord revealed much about our origin: "The soul, the immortal spirit,"[37] "the soul, the mind of man, where did it come from?"[38] "They say God created it in the beginning. The idea lessens man, in my estimation. [I] don't believe the doctrine [and] know better; God told me so. . . . We say that God was self-existent. . . . Who told you that man did not exist upon the same principle? . . . The mind of man, the intelligent part,"[39] "is as immortal as God himself."[40] Some part of us, described as "the spirit," "the soul," "the immortal spirit," "the mind of man," "the intelligent part," and "intelligence," is as eternal as God himself. According to Joseph Smith, God did not make it; it always existed: "Intelligence is eternal, and it is self-existing."[41] It is "a spirit from age to age, and [there is] no creation about it."[42]

8. *We are children of God.* Alluded to in these teachings of Joseph Smith and made clear by later prophets is the doctrine that in our pre-earth existence our "intelligence" was clothed in a spirit body, and we were born as spirit daughters and sons of God. President Joseph F. Smith and his counselors stated in 1909 that "man, as a spirit, was begotten and born of heavenly parents, and reared to maturity in the eternal mansions of the Father, prior to coming upon the earth in a temporal body."[43] As President Gordon B. Hinckley, his

counselors, and the Twelve announced in 1995, "All human beings—male and female—are created in the image of God. Each is a beloved spirit son or daughter of heavenly parents, and, as such, each has a divine nature and destiny. Gender is an essential characteristic of individual premortal, mortal, and eternal identity and purpose."[44] Thus God is not only our Creator, but he is our Father as well. Because we know that we are sons and daughters of Deity and that God is the Father of our spirits, we can understand the further revelation from Joseph Smith that was best articulated by Eliza R. Snow, who published it in a poem, "My Father in Heaven," not long after the Prophet's death:

> *I had learn'd to call thee father,*
> *Through thy spirit from on high;*
> *But until the key of knowledge*
> *Was restor'd, I knew not why.*
> *In the heav'ns are parents single?*
> *No, the thought makes reason stare;*
> *Truth is reason—truth eternal*
> *Tells me I've a mother there.*[45]

9. We may become as God is. "What was the design of the Almighty in making man? It was to exalt him to be as God."[46] That brief statement tells us why God created our spirit bodies, why he created our physical bodies, and what our ultimate purpose is for being on earth. Joseph Smith taught that "all the spirits that God ever sent into this world are susceptible of enlargement." "God himself, . . . because he was greater, saw proper to institute laws whereby the rest could have a privilege to advance like himself."[47] Through laws, ordinances, and covenants, the Father makes available to his children the opportunity to develop fully the divine qualities that we inherit from him. In an act of profound unselfishness, he offers us all that he has (D&C 76:55; 84:38), which is "to inherit the same power [and] exaltation, until you ascend the throne of eternal power, same as those who are gone before,"[48] "enjoying the same rise, exaltation, and glory, until you arrive at the station of a God."[49] We do this "by going from a small capacity to another, from grace to grace, until the resurrection, and sit in everlasting power as they who have gone before. . . . When you climb a ladder, you must begin at the bottom rung until you learn the last principle of the gospel. For it is a great thing to learn salvation beyond the grave."[50] Indeed, "it will take a long time after the grave to understand the whole."[51]

Again, a grand celestial process is at work in the universe. A loving God provides us countless opportunities for growth and progression if we are willing to trust his plan and submit ourselves to his kindness and wisdom. Through Joseph Smith, the Lord revealed that we, God's daughters and sons, have come to a world far from the celestial home of our origin to develop through life's experiences the qualities that will make us like our Heavenly Father.[52] It is only through our Father's plan of happiness—brought to pass through Jesus Christ, his Only Begotten Son in the flesh—that we can know who we really are. The Prophet taught that "through the atonement of Christ and the resurrection and obedience in the gospel, we shall again be conformed to the image of his Son Jesus Christ. Then we shall have attained to the image, glory, and character of God."[53]

In revealing God to us in his Nauvoo sermons and instructions, the Prophet Joseph was making known to us the answers to life's most universal questions: "Who am I?" "Where did I come from?" "Why am I here?" "Where am I going?" The restored gospel provides answers to those questions and many more. Through doctrines, priesthood, covenants, and keys restored by Joseph Smith, men and women are enabled to fulfill the purpose of their creation and assist those whom they love to do the same. The Prophet's Nauvoo teachings on these topics put all of the gospel blessings into perspective and let us know how they fit together in God's plan for our eternal happiness.

NOTES
1. See Ehat and Cook, *Words of Joseph Smith.* In some of the citations from this source, I have standardized capitalization, punctuation, or spelling to modern usage.

2. For the locations of the Grove and other meeting places, see LaMar C. Berrett, *Sacred Places: Ohio and Illinois,* 169–70, 174–75.

3. Ehat and Cook, *Words of Joseph Smith,* 183.

4. Ehat and Cook, *Words of Joseph Smith,* 190.

5. Ehat and Cook, *Words of Joseph Smith,* 258.

6. Cited in Ehat and Cook, *Words of Joseph Smith,* xx.

7. Ehat and Cook, *Words of Joseph Smith,* 215.

8. Ehat and Cook, *Words of Joseph Smith,* 369.

9. Jessee, *Papers of Joseph Smith,* 1:175.

10. Ehat and Cook, *Words of Joseph Smith,* 363.

11. Ehat and Cook, *Words of Joseph Smith,* 196.

12. See Joseph Smith–History 1:36–41; Malachi 3 ("part"); Malachi 4:1–6; Isaiah 11:1–16; Acts 3:22–23; Joel 2:28–32.

13. See Jackson, *From Apostasy to Restoration,* 103–4, 114–15 nn. 2–7.

14. See the list in Ehat and Cook, *Words of Joseph Smith,* 421–25. In the scripture index, most of the Book of Mormon and Doctrine and Covenants references are not in Joseph Smith's discourses but in the editors' notes.

15. Some of the Prophet's commentary comes from his letters and journal entries, but much more comes from his Nauvoo discourses. The individual passage he discussed most extensively was Malachi 4:5–6; see Smith, *Joseph Smith's Commentary on the Bible,* 69–74.

16. See Ehat and Cook, *Words of Joseph Smith,* 38–44, 50–51 n. 1.

17. This fact may point to the profound and lasting education he received during his three years of intense spiritual work on the Joseph Smith Translation of the Bible. As Robert J. Matthews pointed out, one of the great fruits of the New Translation was the education of the Prophet himself. See Matthews, *"Plainer Translation,"* 53; Matthews, "Using the Scriptures," *Brigham Young University 1981 Fireside and Devotional Speeches* (Provo, Utah: Brigham Young University Publications, 1981), 123.

18. Ehat and Cook, *Words of Joseph Smith,* 238.

19. After Liberty Jail, only Doctrine and Covenants sections 124–26 contain revelations presented in God's words. Sections 127 and 128 come from letters written by Joseph Smith, and sections 129–31 are excerpts from his teachings to groups of Latter-day Saints. Section 132 was revealed in the 1830s but was not recorded until 1843.

20. Young, *Journal of Discourses,* 5:332.

21. Ehat and Cook, *Words of Joseph Smith,* 343–44.

22. Ehat and Cook, *Words of Joseph Smith,* 340.

23. See Ehat and Cook, *Words of Joseph Smith,* 340–62, 378–83; Cannon and Dahl, *King Follett Discourse.* Edited amalgamations are found in Smith, *Teachings of the Prophet Joseph Smith,* 342–61, 369–76.

24. Ehat and Cook, *Words of Joseph Smith,* 214.

25. Ehat and Cook, *Words of Joseph Smith,* 382.

26. Ehat and Cook, *Words of Joseph Smith*, 378.
27. Ehat and Cook, *Words of Joseph Smith*, 60.
28. See, for example, "The Westminster Confession of Faith, 1647," 2.1, in Schaff, *Creeds of Christendom*, 3:606.
29. Ehat and Cook, *Words of Joseph Smith*, 64.
30. Ehat and Cook, *Words of Joseph Smith*, 357.
31. Ehat and Cook, *Words of Joseph Smith*, 361.
32. Ehat and Cook, *Words of Joseph Smith*, 344.
33. Ehat and Cook, *Words of Joseph Smith*, 380.
34. Ehat and Cook, *Words of Joseph Smith*, 378.
35. Elder Boyd K. Packer taught, "The Father *is* the one true God. *This* thing is certain: no one will ever ascend above Him; no one will ever replace Him. Nor will anything ever change the relationship that we, His literal offspring, have with Him." "The Pattern of Our Parentage," *Ensign*, November 1984, 69.
36. Ehat and Cook, *Words of Joseph Smith*, 9.
37. Ehat and Cook, *Words of Joseph Smith*, 351; Cannon and Dahl, *King Follett Discourse*, 49.
38. Ehat and Cook, *Words of Joseph Smith*, 345.
39. Ehat and Cook, *Words of Joseph Smith*, 359.
40. Ehat and Cook, *Words of Joseph Smith*, 352.
41. Ehat and Cook, *Words of Joseph Smith*, 346.
42. Ehat and Cook, *Words of Joseph Smith*, 360.
43. "The Origin of Man," in *Encyclopedia of Mormonism*, 1668.
44. First Presidency and Twelve Apostles, "The Family: A Proclamation to the World," *Ensign*, November 1995, 102.
45. *Times and Seasons* 6, no. 17 (November 15, 1845): 1039; "O My Father," verse 3, *Hymns*, no. 292.
46. Ehat and Cook, *Words of Joseph Smith*, 247.
47. Ehat and Cook, *Words of Joseph Smith*, 360.
48. Ehat and Cook, *Words of Joseph Smith*, 350.
49. Ehat and Cook, *Words of Joseph Smith*, 345.
50. Ehat and Cook, *Words of Joseph Smith*, 350.
51. Ehat and Cook, *Words of Joseph Smith*, 345.
52. As President Gordon B. Hinckley stated, "He is the greatest of all and will always be so. But just as any earthly father wishes for his sons and daughters every success in life, so I believe our Father in Heaven wishes for his children that they might approach him in stature and stand beside him resplendent in godly strength and wisdom." "Don't Drop the Ball," *Ensign*, November 1994, 48.
53. Ehat and Cook, *Words of Joseph Smith*, 231.

CHAPTER THIRTY-SEVEN

"LET THEM WORSHIP HOW, WHERE, OR WHAT THEY MAY"

Fred E. Woods

*I*t is one of the first principles of my life, and one that I have cultivated from my childhood, having been taught it by my father," wrote Joseph Smith, "to allow every one the liberty of conscience."[1] The same blood which coursed through the veins of America's founding fathers and the early patriots also pulsated through Joseph's New England ancestry. This heritage infused him with a deep regard for religious freedom and a love of liberty, not just for himself but for all.[2] This paradigm of religious tolerance, which began with heritage, was secured in the founding principles set forth in the Constitution of the United States of America. Joseph Smith became a man who could not separate the flag of his God from the flag of his country. His defense of the Constitution supported the liberality of conscience he espoused. He boldly declared, "I am the greatest advocate of the Constitution of the United States there is on earth."[3]

The Prophet Joseph also received direct tutelage from the Lord of the Constitution's divine sanction. One such occasion was on the eve of 6 August 1833 just as Latter-day Saints were being expelled from Jackson County, Missouri. Joseph was taught

> That law of the land which is constitutional, supporting that principle of freedom in maintaining rights and privileges, belongs to all mankind, and is justifiable before me. Therefore, I the Lord, justify you, and your

Fred E. Woods is a professor of Church history and doctrine at Brigham Young University and currently occupies the Richard L. Evans chair of Religious Understanding.

brethren of my church, in befriending that law which is the constitutional law of the land. (D&C 98:5–6)

Ironically, just four months later, after Mormon faithful had illegally been driven from their Missouri homes, the Lord reiterated to Joseph that the Constitution had been divinely established "and should be maintained for the rights and protection of all flesh, according to just and holy principles" (D&C 101:77). In the face of blatant disregard for and abuse of these principles, the Lord again affirmed to Joseph, "I established the Constitution of this land, by the hands of wise men whom I have raised up unto this very purpose" (D&C 101:80). These divine assurances must surely have helped Joseph maintain his loyalty to the tenets of the U.S. government—a government which failed to succor him and his followers. This loyalty was evidenced two years later in the dedicatory prayer in the Kirtland Temple: "May those principles, which were so honorably and nobly defended, namely, the Constitution of our land, by our fathers, be established forever" (D&C 109:54).

PROPHETIC WORDS OF RELIGIOUS LIBERTY

The Prophet's writings are consistent with his public declarations of religious freedom. After spending several months in a cold Missouri jail for his religious beliefs, Joseph wrote in spring 1839, "I have the most liberal sentiments, and feelings of charity towards all sects, parties, and denominations; and the rights and liberties of conscience, I hold most sacred and dear, and despise no man for differing with me in matters of opinion."[4] He wrote to Bishop Edward Partridge and the Saints abroad:

> We ought always to be aware of those prejudices which sometimes so strangely present themselves, and are so congenial to human nature, against our friends, neighbors, and brethren of the world, who choose to differ from us in opinion, and in matters of faith. Our religion is between us and our God. Their religion is between them and their God.[5]

After only a few months of freedom from the unjust confinement of Liberty Jail, Joseph wrote:

All persons are entitled to their agency, for God has so ordained it. He has constituted mankind moral agents, and given them power to choose good or evil; to seek after that which is good, by pursuing the pathway of holiness in this life, which brings peace of mind, and joy in the Holy Ghost here, and a fulness of joy and happiness at His right hand hereafter; or to pursue an evil course, going on in sin and rebellion against God, thereby bringing condemnation to their souls in this world, and an eternal loss in the world to come. Since the God of heaven has left these things optional with every individual, we do not wish to deprive them of it. We only wish to act the part of a faithful watchman, agreeably to the word of the Lord to Ezekiel the prophet, . . . and leave it for others to do as seemeth them good.[6]

The wording of Section One of the Nauvoo Charter written in 1840 shows again the Prophet's great concern for maintaining religious liberty:

Be it ordained by the city council of the city of Nauvoo that the Catholics, Presbyterians, Methodists, Baptists, Latter-day Saints, Quakers, Episcopalians, Universalists, Unitarians, Mohammedans, and all other religious sects and denominations, whatever, shall have free toleration and equal privileges in this city, and should any person be guilty of ridiculing and abusing, or otherwise deprecating another, in consequence of his religion, or of disturbing or interrupting any religious meeting within the limits of this city, he shall, on conviction before the mayor or municipal court, be considered a disturber of the public peace, and fined in any sum not exceeding five hundred dollars, or imprisoned not exceeding six months, or both, at the discretion of said mayor and court.[7]

In an 1842 letter, written at the request of *Chicago Democrat* editor John Wentworth, Joseph articulated the beliefs of the Latter-day Saints, later canonized as the "Articles of Faith."[8] In the eleventh article, he announced: "We claim the privilege of worshiping Almighty God according to the dictates of our own conscience, and allow all men the same privilege let them worship how, where, or what they may."[9] Later this same year, Joseph balanced the liberty doctrine with the responsibilities and restrictions that must accompany freedom. In a letter to James Arlington Bennett, he explained: "All men . . . ought to be free . . . to think, and act, and say as they please, while

Joseph Smith Writes the Wentworth Letter, *by Glen Hopkinson*

they maintain a due respect to the rights and privileges of all other creatures, infringing upon none. This doctrine I do most heartily subscribe to and practice."[10]

In an 1843 public discourse in Nauvoo, Joseph confirmed his universal regard for religious freedom:

> The Saints can testify whether I am willing to lay down my life for my brethren. If it has been demonstrated that I have been willing to die for a "Mormon," I am bold to declare before Heaven that I am just as ready to die in defending the rights of a Presbyterian, a Baptist, or a good man of any other denomination; for the same principle which would trample upon the rights of the Latter-day Saints would trample upon the rights of the Roman Catholics, or any other denomination who may be unpopular and too weak to defend themselves.
>
> It is a love of liberty which inspires my soul—civil and religious liberty to the whole of the human race. Love of liberty was diffused into my soul by my grandfathers while they dandled me on their knees.[11]

In this same discourse, Joseph explained the appropriate course to pursue when encountering differing beliefs: "If I esteem mankind to be in error, shall I bear them down? No. I will lift them up, and in their own way too, if I cannot persuade them my way is better; and I will not seek to compel any man to believe as I do, only by the force of reasoning, for truth will cut its own way."[12]

PROPHETIC WORDS OF RELIGIOUS FREEDOM PUT TO THE TEST

The Prophet had an opportunity to practice what he preached in the spring of 1843 when Samuel A. Prior, a Methodist preacher, spoke in Nauvoo.[13] Reverend Prior wrote of that experience:

> In the evening I was invited to preach, and did so.—The congregation was large and respectable—they paid the utmost attention. This surprised me a little, as I did not expect to find any such thing as a religious toleration among them.—After I had closed, Elder Smith, who had attended, arose and begged leave to differ from me in some few points of doctrine, and this he did mildly, politely, and affectingly; like one who was more desirous to disseminate truth and expose error, than to love the malicious triumph of debate over me. I was truly edified with his remarks, and felt less prejudiced against the Mormons than ever. He invited me to call upon him, and I promised to do so.[14]

The preaching of the reverend in the city of Nauvoo supported Joseph's doctrine that "one of the grand fundamental principles of Mormonism is to receive truth, let it come from whence it may."[15] Likewise, Joseph also stated that, "we should gather all the good and true principles in the world and treasure them up, or we shall not come out true 'Mormons.'"[16]

Joseph demonstrated kindness towards those who provided service in other faiths, as beautifully illustrated by the story of a local Catholic priest. In 1841, Father John Alleman, a priest from France, arrived at his assigned post in Fort Madison, Iowa Territory. From there he ministered to a number of Catholics residing in neighboring communities. During his labors, fellow believer Reverend Father John Larmer, noted:

> Strange to relate, Joseph Smith and the leading Mormons, at all times professed the greatest respect and friendship for the big French priest, as they called him. Father Alleman once related to the writer that

he had no means of getting across the Mississippi river, to attend a sick Catholic in McDonough county, but the Mormons, having made known to Joseph Smith that the priest wished to cross, the latter not only had him ferried over, but furnished him a conveyance [carriage] to the sick man.[17]

This act of service built a bridge of religious understanding and tolerance between the Latter-day Saints and their Catholic neighbors. This bridge of understanding was expanded by the Prophet:

> While one portion of the human race is judging and condemning the other without mercy, the Great Parent of the universe looks upon the whole of the human family with a fatherly care and paternal regard; He views them as His offspring, and without any of those contracted feelings that influence the children of men, causes "His sun to rise on the evil and on the good, and sendeth rain on the just and on the unjust." He holds the reins of judgment in His hands; He is a wise Lawgiver, and will judge all men, not according to the narrow, contracted notions of men, but "according to the deeds done in the body whether they be good or evil," in England, America, Spain, Turkey, or India.[18]

CONCLUSION

Principles of religious freedom were presented in word and deed by the Prophet Joseph Smith. He extended tolerance to those of other faiths, yet received so little tolerance of his beliefs in return. He was denied the very liberties he defended. To him, "the privilege of worshiping Almighty God according to the dictates of our own conscience, and allow all men the same privilege" was not mere rhetoric.[19] It was foundational in spite of how others treated him.

NOTES

1. Smith, *History of the Church*, 6:56. As reported by Willard Richards, Joseph gave this discourse in Nauvoo, Illinois, on 15 October 1843.
2. On the background of Joseph Smith's ancestors and their devotion to liberty, see Anderson, *Joseph Smith's New England Heritage*, 92; Bushman, *Joseph Smith and the Beginnings of Mormonism*, 12–15, 20.
3. Smith, *History of the Church*, 6:56–57.
4. Letter to Isaac Galland from Joseph Smith, 22 March 1839 from Liberty Jail, published in *Times and Seasons* 1, no. 4 (February 1840): 55–56.
5. Smith, *History of the Church*, 3:303–4, Letter to Edward Partridge and the

Church from Joseph Smith, 20 March 1839 from Liberty Jail. Five years earlier Joseph had taught, "We deem it a just principle, and it is one the force of which we believe ought to be duly considered by every individual, that all men are created equal, and that all have the privilege of thinking for themselves upon all matters relative to conscience. Consequently, then, we are not disposed, had we the power, to deprive any one of exercising that free independence of mind which heaven has so graciously bestowed upon the human family as one of its choicest gifts." See Smith, *History of the Church,* 2:6–7, taken from "The Elders of the Church in Kirtland to Their Brethren Abroad," *Evening and the Morning Star* (February 1834): 135.

6. Smith, *History of the Church,* 4:45 n, Letter to the Saints from the First Presidency and the Nauvoo High Council, November 1839, published in *Times and Seasons* (December 1839): 29. See Ezekiel 33:2–5 for Ezekiel's parable of the watchman on the tower.

7. Roberts, *Comprehensive History of the Church,* 2:55–56.

8. Allen and Leonard, *Story of the Latter-day Saints,* 181. The authors explain: "Statements, later extracted from the Wentworth letter, became known as the Articles of Faith. Intended for non-Mormons, these articles were never meant to be a complete summary of the gospel, for they included none of the more advanced doctrines first presented to the Church in Nauvoo, nor did they contain such obvious practices as prayer or the sacrament of the Lord's Supper. The Articles were simply a summary of some of the most basic LDS beliefs."

9. Articles of Faith 1:11, written at the request of John Wentworth, published in *Times and Seasons* (March 1, 1842): 710.

10. Smith, *History of the Church,* 5:156, Letter to James Arlington Bennett from Joseph Smith, 8 September 1842.

11. Smith, *History of the Church,* 5:498–99. This sermon was given in Nauvoo on 9 July 1843, as reported by Willard Richards.

12. Smith, *History of the Church,* 5:499. Letter to Joseph L. Heywood from Joseph Smith, 13 February 1844, Nauvoo, Illinois. Joseph stated, "Although I never feel to force my doctrine upon any person; I rejoice to see prejudice give way to truth, and the traditions of men dispersed by the pure principles of the Gospel of Jesus Christ." Smith, *History of the Church,* 6:213.

13. The diary of William Clayton notes, "In the evening we went to hear a Methodist preacher lecture," cited in Ehat and Cook, *Words of Joseph Smith,* 203.

14. Samuel A. Prior, *Times and Seasons* 4, no. 13 (May 15, 1843): 198. According to the diary of William Clayton, as cited in Ehat and Cook, *Words of Joseph Smith,* 203, the doctrinal corrections Joseph made had to do with an explanation of spirit matter. This doctrine is recorded in D&C 131:7–8: "There is no such thing as immaterial matter. All spirit is matter,

but it is more fine or pure, and can only be discerned by purer eyes. We cannot see it; but when our bodies are purified we shall see that it is all matter."

15. Smith, *History of the Church,* 5:499.
16. Smith, *History of the Church,* 5:517.
17. Father John Larmer, "Catholic Church McDonough County," 2, http://www.macomb.com/ilmcdono/church/cathch.html. This article points out that Father Alleman had a "practical sense of humor." It also notes that "Father Alleman died of apoplexy in the Sisters' hospital in St. Louis, September 10, 1866." However, Thomas Auge, "The Priest behind the Legends: Father John Alleman," *The Palimpsest, Iowa's Popular History Magazine* 74, no. 2 (Summer 1993): 86, 96, states that Alleman "was born on December 3, 1804, in the village of Attenschwiller in Alsace, France" and maintains that Alleman died on 24 July 1865, "the cause of death as 'Melancholia.'"
18. Smith, *History of the Church,* 4:595–96.
19. Articles of Faith 1:11.

CHAPTER THIRTY-EIGHT

THE NAUVOO LEGION

Richard E. Bennett

he colorful story of the Nauvoo Legion is far more than the mere history of just another mid-nineteenth century state militia.[1] Demonized by its critics as a symbol of Mormon militarism and empire-building and defended by its supporters as a means of self-defense, the Nauvoo Legion remains a controversial chapter in American and Latter-day Saint history. At issue is not so much the actions of the Legion, since indeed its colorful parades and ceremonial performances are hardly the stuff of debate; rather, the misunderstanding has centered in its chartered powers, its religious orientation, its eventual size, and its fearsome potential as an "army of Israel." Sanctioned by state statute in December 1840, then renounced by the same just over four years later, the Nauvoo Legion can never be accurately understood outside the maelstrom of misunderstanding and religious persecution that swallowed up in death the Mormon prophet, Joseph Smith Jr., and led to the eventual expulsion of the Latter-day Saints from Illinois. The challenge for responsible historians is to separate the rhetoric from the reality. Thus this short history will try to examine and explain as objectively as possible the origin, history, and demise of one of antebellum America's most popular, short-lived militias—the Nauvoo Legion.

The collective hurt from Missouri was still an open wound among the Latter-day Saints as they sought refuge in Illinois in 1839. Although not by nature a violent people, they had run headlong and

Richard E. Bennett is a professor of Church history and doctrine at Brigham Young University.

unprepared into a more militant, pro-slavery, Southern society. From their 1833 expulsion from Independence to the slaughter at Haun's Mill in 1838, the Mormon stay in Missouri is written in blood. Their dreams of Zion shattered, the Saints retreated eastward out of the state while their Prophet leader lay chained in Liberty Jail.

Little wonder, then, that as they reassembled in Illinois self-defense was an uppermost priority. As Joseph Smith affirmed in May 1841, "The Legion is . . . a body of citizen soldiers organized . . . for the public defense, the general good, and the preservation of law and order—to save the innocent, unoffending citizens from the iron grasp of the oppressor, and perpetuate and sustain our free institutions against misrule, anarchy, and mob violence."[2] And on a later occasion he said: "A burnt child dreads the fire, and when my old friends . . . look to me in the hour of danger for protection, . . . I am bound by my oath of office and by all laws human and divine to grant it."[3]

Yet there was more to its formation than self-defense. Upon settling in Nauvoo, the Latter-day Saints, like any other new settlers, were also legally obligated to serve in the Illinois state militia. It was the law—and had been so since the passage of the Military Act of 1792—that every able-bodied, white male between the ages of eighteen and forty-five had to enlist in a local militia. Failure to do so could result in heavy fines of up to a day's wages. In return, enlisted men would be provided arms by the state, no small consideration for a people who had surrendered almost everything in Missouri. Consequently, soon after their arrival in the state, scores of Latter-day Saints enlisted in the 59th Regiment of Hancock County while others across the river in Montrose joined local companies of the Iowa Territory militia.[4] And as their numbers grew, their representation far outpaced local regimental capacities. To accommodate the rapidly rising Mormon population and the demands of the law, either more county regiments or independent city companies would have to be organized.

Nauvoo's request to form a city militia could not have come at a more favorable time. The Illinois state militia, as with most other state militias in frontier America, was an acute embarrassment.

Joseph Smith Mustering the Nauvoo Legion, *by C. C. A. Christensen.*
© *Intellectual Reserve, Inc. Courtesy BYU Museum of Art*

Poorly provisioned, inadequately trained, and insufficiently staffed, it had failed to send in a single unit in the recent Black Hawk Indian War. Rather, crack volunteer companies from towns and cities across the state had fought side-by-side with regiments of the regular United States Army to win that conflict. In various pieces of legislation between 1834 and 1837, the state legislature encouraged local communities everywhere to form their own regiments or large independent battalions.[5] By encouraging local leadership and by promising to provide better arms and equipment, the state was signaling its intent to do whatever was necessary to improve the standing and performance of a disorganized and discouraged state militia. Thus the Latter-day Saints, in proposing a new city militia, were not only obeying the law but also fulfilling the encouragements of the state. Little wonder, then, that on purely military grounds, their petition for a Nauvoo militia passed the legislature virtually unanimously.

Learning from their mistakes in Missouri, Church leaders were intent on establishing Nauvoo on a firm legal basis. In fact, Joseph Smith would forever claim authorship of the Nauvoo Charter.[6] Yet just who was responsible for the Nauvoo Legion, really a separate charter, is debatable.[7] Unquestionably, as former quartermaster general of the Illinois state militia, John C. Bennett was highly instrumental in the legion's founding, if not its peculiar organizational makeup and design. An ambitious wanderlust, Bennett already had a hidden reputation of being a slick promoter of various community interests which put his own name in lights. His interests in medicine and in medical instruction had prompted him to petition several state legislatures for various schools and universities, often without the support or knowledge of local community leaders. When not pursuing his medical interests, he involved himself in his alternative passion—state militias, uniforms, and the trappings of military life. In 1835 he joined the 104th regiment of the Pennsylvania militia as surgeon. Two years later he tried to establish the Hocking Valley Dragoons in Buffalo, New York, and after removing to White County, Illinois, he took part in petitioning the legislature to create the "Invincible Dragoons and Flying Artillery" in February 1839.[8] Two months later Bennett became brigadier general of the Dragoons. He was also part of a failed effort to persuade Springfield to establish yet another, more grandiose military body called the "Illinois Legion," a combined force of various county militias.[9]

Whatever his faults and future embarrassments to the Church, Bennett possessed that needed mix of lobbying experience, talents, and contacts to aid the Mormon cause. And Joseph Smith, overwhelmed with other pressing needs and priorities, gave him the benefit of the doubt. "He has been one of the instruments in effecting our safety and deliverance, from the unjust persecutions and demands of the authorities of Missouri," Joseph wrote of his new ally, "a man of enterprise, extensive acquirements, and of independent mind."[10]

At the general conference of the Church in October 1840, Bennett was appointed to a blue-ribbon committee to draft a bill to incorporate the city of Nauvoo and be a "delegate, to urge the passage of said bill through the legislature."[11] Bennett soon joined lawyer Almon W. Babbitt in Springfield in time for the December convening of the Illinois legislature. Renewing his acquaintance with legislators on both sides of the aisle, including Stephen A. Douglas and Abraham Lincoln, Bennett saw the bill sail through both houses. Anxious to encourage new immigration and to court votes among the rapidly growing Latter-day Saint population, both Whig and Democratic politicians passed the measure with scant discussion and debate, despite Senator Sidney H. Little's reservations over the "extraordinary militia clause" which he nonetheless viewed as "harmless." As Robert Flanders has rightfully argued, "Its routine enactment seems natural considering the high optimism that prevailed in the state."[12]

The Nauvoo City charter, the Nauvoo Legion charter, and the University of Nauvoo charter—all three—were signed into law by Democratic governor Thomas Carlin on 16 December 1840 to take effect the following 1 February 1841. Two days later, on 3 February 1841, a grateful community elected Bennett Nauvoo's first mayor. The very next day, the new city council passed an ordinance organizing, according to law, the Nauvoo Legion with two cohorts, "the horse troops to constitute the first cohort, and the foot troops to constitute the second cohort"—all in six companies with a total of 250 men. Furthermore, Joseph Smith was duly elected lieutenant general with Bennett second in command as major general.[13]

As Nauvoo rapidly grew to become one of the largest cities in the state, its militia increased proportionately. Its ultimate size was simply the by-product of the city's mushrooming population. By late 1841 it counted 1,490 men in fourteen companies. Two years later, its numbers stood at near 3,000, and by June 1844, it boasted some 4,000 citizen-soldiers in five regiments, complete with a thirty-man Nauvoo Legion Band. While the Legion had the potential of 5,120 men, with each cohort totaling 2,560 men, it never reached maximum strength.[14]

Descriptions of the Legion's appearance and its military preparedness range from that of a "ragged, inefficient outfit, incapable of even standing at attention," to what one unidentified visitor said of them: "There are no troops in the states like them," the truth lying probably somewhere in between.[15] Called out for parades, practice drills, sham battles, musterings, and special occasions, Fourth of July celebrations, and more, the Legion—as was the case with so many other militias in America—never received its full complement of arms and equipment, and many men, especially the privates, were unable to afford uniforms. While some of its leaders, including Joseph Smith, may have looked exquisitely attired in full uniform (patterned after that of the U.S. Army), most regulars appeared in scruffy daily dress bandying about shovels and broom sticks in lieu of muskets and arms. Yet the Legion, with all its weaknesses, would have compared favorably with most other militias in Illinois. But not so to Thomas Sharp, editor of the *Warsaw Signal:*

> Why these weekly parades? Why all this strictness of discipline? We pause for reply. How military these people are becoming! Everything they say or do seems to breathe the spirit of military tactics. Their prophet appears, on all great occasions, in his splendid regimental dress, signs his name Lieutenant General, and more titles are to be found in the Nauvoo Legion than any one book on military tactics can produce . . . Truly fighting must be part of the creed of these saints. Are the Danites still separate or merged with the Nauvoo Legion?[16]

Fearful citizens wanted to know. Joseph Smith's rhetoric likely did little to help:

> If our enemies are determined to oppress us and deprive us of our rights and privileges as they have done and if the Authorities that be on earth will not assist us in our rights nor give us that protection which the Laws and Constitution of the United States and of this State guarantees unto us; then we will claim them from higher power from heaven and from God Almighty and the Constitution and I swear I will not deal so mildly with them again for the time has come when forbearance is no longer a virtue.[17]

Whatever the rhetoric from either side, the fact is the Nauvoo Legion never fought a battle or fired in anger upon its enemies. As Flanders rightly concluded: "The Legion was the product of a defensive rather than an aggressive psychology."[18] The feared invasion of Missouri and the expected attacks on nearby Illinois settlements never materialized. While some members of the legion did recapture Joseph Smith from arrest, and while others did obey city council directives to close a grog shop and demolish the press of the *Nauvoo Expositor*—the flashpoint that led to the murder of Joseph and Hyrum Smith in Carthage Jail in June 1844—the Legion acted always in a defensive mode and according to law. No better example of this can be found than when, at the behest of its commander-in-chief, Governor Thomas Ford, it surrendered its weapons and refrained from marching on the city of Carthage in retaliation for the death of its lieutenant general.

In retrospect and in light of continuing debate, how unique was the Legion? First of all, the concept of a legion was not new in military history. In 1792, during the Indian Wars of the Northwest campaign, the United States Army had been reorganized for a period of time into a legion complete with artillery, cavalry, and foot cohorts.[19] The famous New York Legion was probably the best known city militia in all of America in the 1840s. The memory of Napoleon's Grande Army of the Republic with its many legions was still fresh and vivid in many minds.[20] And research has shown that Bennett had tried to organize an Illinois legion in 1839. The legion concept was a popular one, even for county and city militias.

The phrase "a body of independent military men" in describing the Nauvoo Legion likewise begs for clarification. The Legion was not a volunteer company and was independent only in the sense that it, like so many other contemporary city militias across the country, was not a part of other nearby county regiments, like the Hancock 59th, or of city militias, like the Carthage Grays. It was not a "Mormon militia," as a separate and distinct body, but rather very much a part of the Illinois state militia and served at the ultimate command of the governor.

As for Joseph Smith's military appointment as lieutenant general, such has long been perceived by some as evidence of his interest in the military, if not an aspiration for power. Like his grandfathers before him, who had distinguished themselves in the Revolutionary War, Joseph Smith did have military interests. In 1834 he had led a paramilitary operation—Zion's Camp—from Ohio to Missouri in hopes of securing the legal rights and properties of those Saints who had been driven out of Jackson County. Yet his appointment in the Nauvoo Legion seems to be one he did not seek.

> As to the military station I hold, and the cause of my holding it is as follows: when we came here, the state required us to bear arms, and do military duty according to the law, and as the church had just been driven from the state of Missouri, and robbed of all their property and arms, they were poor and destitute of arms, [and] they were liable to be fined for not doing duty, when they had not arms to do it with. They came to me for advice and I advised them to organize themselves into independent companies and demand arms of the state: this they did . . . I then told the saints that though I was clear from military duty by law, in consequence of lameness in one of my legs, yet I would set the example, and would do duty myself, they said they were willing to do duty, if they would be formed into an independent company and I could be at their head; this is the origin of the Nauvoo Legion and of my holding office of lieutenant general.[21]

His military rank raised little or no comment at the office of the state adjutant general when the returns were submitted. Although by law most other regiments were commanded by a major general or lesser officer, in practice, militias were free to choose virtually whomever they wanted as leader and in what position. While it was unique and perhaps in the long run unwise for Joseph Smith to hold such a daunting ranking—one no other man in American military history had held since George Washington nor would again until Ulysses S. Grant of Civil War fame—militarily it meant little more than a ceremonial title for a local commander, in this case one held in such esteem as prophet, seer, and revelator by his followers. However, such a ranking, tantamount to that of major general elsewhere, certainly did not outrank any other unit's commanding officer. Indeed, the ultimate authority over the legion and every other local regiment, battalion, or legion was neither prophet nor priest, major nor mayor, but the governor of the state. Likewise, ever since controversies stemming from the War of 1812, it was well established in law and upheld by court ruling that no officer in any state militia from Massachusetts to Iowa could ever outrank an officer of the standing United States Army.

Yet some elements of the Legion do stand out as unique and potentially divisive, especially in the deteriorating social and political climate that engulfed Nauvoo. Those genuinely threatened by the rapid growth of the city and, with it, the raw size of the Legion, and those worried over the influx of so many new Mormon settlers and the sometimes impolitic statements of its leaders and their changing political commitments between Whig and Democratic candidates, became fearful. Others, animated by fear and prejudice, were quick to pounce on the political powers of the city as a threat to freedom and led efforts to rescind the city and its Legion as early as 1842. Whatever the case, perhaps the two most highly debatable provisions of the Legion Charter were 1) the granting of legislative authority, above those of mere judicial powers, to the Legion's courts-martial, and 2) the power of the mayor to call out the Legion "in executing the laws and ordinances of the City."

The legislative court-martial powers of the Legion were unlike those of any other Illinois militia yet found. Why its promoters sought such authority is unclear and they may not have anticipated its lightning rod ability to raise dissent. Nevertheless, it could only pass laws and ordinances that pertained to the regulation and conduct of the Legion and could not pass laws "repugnant to or inconsistent with" either the state or federal constitutions. In reality, such court-martial rulings were mundane and innocuous and pertained only to the everyday actions of the Legion—fines, appointments, elections, reprimand and dismissals, and other activities. It seems only to have been a formalization of the powers vested in every other militia.

Serving at the direction of the mayor is more problematic. Provisions of the city charter had indeed provided Nauvoo with its own municipal court, though even in this Nauvoo was not unlike some other communities. Likewise, as elsewhere, a police force had been authorized to help maintain law and order. That some members of the Legion, like Hosea Stout, wore both hats—that of the Legion and that of the police—is clear. When he and his deputies acted in one capacity and when in another is not always clear.

It was in the exercising of the writ of habeas corpus, wherein those arrested for crimes in other jurisdictions could be brought back to Nauvoo to stand trial in friendlier confines, that serious opposition developed. Among the many harassments that Joseph Smith experienced while in Nauvoo, trouble with Missouri and recurring attempts by Missouri law officials to retrieve the Prophet were some of the most vehement. And there is no question that small detachments of the Legion helped prevent such extradition efforts. Later fears that Joseph Smith and others intended to establish an "army of Israel" out of the Nauvoo Legion to aid in Mormon threats of empire-building, and accusations that a later discredited John C. Bennett made against his former friends, are unfounded.

Whatever the reality, the truth is that many perceived the Legion as a mounting threat. By late 1842, in his inaugural address, Governor Thomas Ford called for at least a modification of the Legion and of the Nauvoo City Charter. In January 1845, the state repealed the Nauvoo charter and the Legion ceased to be a legal entity. Nevertheless, Brigham Young, recognizing that their only hope was to quit the state and find a new home in the West, knew that his people needed both order and protection. After most of the Saints fled Nauvoo in 1846, remnants, including former members of the Legion, fought in the so-called Battle of Nauvoo, a sad and unsuccessful rearguard action that only forestalled the inevitable fall of the city. Brigham Young did call upon vestiges of the Legion for protection during the Mormon exodus, especially as a show of force against fearsome Indian tribes west of the Missouri. Many members of the Legion later served in the Mormon Battalion. With the establishment of the Territory of Utah in 1850 and the appointment of Brigham Young as territorial governor the Nauvoo Legion was again legally and officially reconstituted as a militia, seeing action in the Utah War of 1857 and in various Indian wars in the Territory, including the Black Hawk War. In 1862, during the Civil War, two units of the Nauvoo Legion protected overland mail and telegraph lines. Under terms of the Edwards-Tucker Act of 1887, the Nauvoo Legion was again disbanded. Once Utah became a state in 1896, the National Guard of Utah was organized as Utah's militia.

NOTES

1. I wish to acknowledge the kind and generous assistance of my colleagues Professors Susan Easton Black and Donald Q. Cannon in the preparation of this article. The three of us have co-authored a definitive study of the Nauvoo Legion which is soon to be published.

2. Roberts, *Rise and Fall of Nauvoo*, 98.

3. Jessee, *Personal Writings of Joseph Smith*, 563.

4. "Militia Regiments" Ledger, 1819–1835. See also "Commission Records, Ledger Book, 1835–1846," 12:368–71. Illinois State Archives, Springfield, Illinois. For evidence of Latter-day Saint militia service in Iowa, see the "Papers of Joseph B. Nobles", LDS Church Archives.

5. *Journal of the House of Representatives of Illinois, 1834–1835,* 9 December 1834; see also *Journal of the 10th Assembly, 1836,* 762.

6. Wrote the Prophet: "The City Charter of Nauvoo is of my own plan and device. I concocted it for the salvation of the Church and on principles so broad, that every honest man might dwell secure under its protection." Smith, *History of the Church,* 4:249.

7. Richard E. Bennett and Rachel Cope, "'A City on a Hill'—Chartering the City of Nauvoo," *John Whitmer Historical Association 2002 Nauvoo Conference Special Edition* (2002), 26–29.

8. Smith, *Saintly Scoundrel*. See especially pages 17, 25–32, and 47. Bennett had likely heard of the Latter-day Saints as early as 1832 when he lived near Kirtland, Ohio. See *Saintly Scoundrel,* 55–56.

9. See draft of House Bill #213, "A Bill for an Act to Incorporate the Illinois Legion." "Executive Papers, Governor's Correspondence, 1837–1839." See Journal of the House of Representatives of Illinois (1838), 5 February 1839 and 1 March 1839. See also Journal of the Senate of Illinois 1838, 6 January and 9 January 1839. The Senate rejected the bill on 1 March 1839.

10. Smith, *History of the Church,* 4:270. For a slightly more positive interpretation of Bennett, see Andrew C. Skinner, "John C. Bennett: For Prophet or Profit?" in Garrett, *Illinois,* 249–54.

11. Smith, *History of the Church,* 4 October 1840, 4:205. See also *Times and Seasons* 1, no. 12 (October 1840): 186.

12. Flanders, *Nauvoo, Kingdom on the Mississippi,* 97.

13. Smith, *History of the Church,* 4:293–94.

14. The composition of each company was made up of 32 to 64 militiamen. Four companies composed a battalion, totaling a possible 256 legionnaires. Two battalions formed a regiment of 512. Five regiments or a total of 2,560 citizen-soldiers formed a cohort and two cohorts formed the Nauvoo Legion. If every company, battalion, regiment, and cohort were filled to capacity, the total numbers would have been 5,120. Research has shown that the legion never exceeded 4,000. See the forthcoming book *Joseph*

Smith and the Nauvoo Legion, by Susan Easton Black, Richard E. Bennett, and Donald Q. Cannon.

15. Compare J. M. Field, editor of the *St. Louis Reveille,* as cited in the *Warsaw Signal,* 13 August 1845, to *New York Herald,* 8 May 1842 and reported in the *Millenial Star,* 1842.

16. *Warsaw Signal,* 9 July 1841; 21 July 1841.

17. See Cook, *Words of Joseph Smith,* 217. On another occasion, hounded by Missouri extradition efforts and threatened by kidnappers and persecutors, a harried Joseph Smith said: "I would welcome death rather than submit to this oppression; and it would be sweet, oh, sweet, to rest in the grave rather than submit to this oppression, agitation, annoyance, confusion, and alarm upon alarm, any longer. I have unsheathed my sword with a firm and unalterable decree that this people shall have their legal rights, and be protected from mob violence, or my blood shall be spilt upon the ground like water." Smith, *History of the Church,* 6:499–500.

18. Flanders, *Nauvoo, Kingdom on the Mississippi,* 101.

19. Weigley, *History of the United States Army,* 92. The term *legion* had come into renewed military use during the eighteenth century, especially in eastern Europe, to denote small mixed bodies of cavalry and infantry. As such it appeared in the American Revolution on both sides, as in Tarleton's Legion or Pulaski's Legion. "A more sentimental purpose of the legionary organization resided in the young American Republic's delight in drawing parallels between itself and the ancient Roman Republic." Weigley, *History of the United States Army,* 92.

20. John C. Bennett admitted: "I organized the military forces of this city [Nauvoo] like a Roman legion—a legion of cohorts." Bennett, *History of the Saints,* 211.

21. See Woodruff, *Wilford Woodruff's Journal,* 4 July 1843, 2:258.

CHAPTER THIRTY-NINE

THE MARTYRDOM

Donald Q. Cannon and Zachary L. Largey

here are few events, if any, in the Church's history as dramatic and memorable as the death of Joseph and Hyrum Smith. "I told Stephen Markham," the Prophet once wrote, "that if I and Hyrum were ever taken again, we should be massacred, or I was not a prophet of God."[1] True enough, on 27 June 1844, Joseph and Hyrum became the victims of nineteenth century mobocracy when roughly two hundred men surrounded Carthage Jail—some rushing the stairs, some firing from the outside. One of Joseph's prison mates, John Taylor, seriously wounded, crawled underneath the bed; Joseph and Hyrum both shot back with guns they had been given that day.[2] Finally, the mob finished the bloody deed when errant shots ripped Hyrum while he was defending the door, and two more caught Joseph as he tried to escape through the window. His last words were, "O Lord, my God!"[3]

Later, when the anger of a lawless and cowardly deed began to subside, fear, confusion, and grief set in. The Church had just been rendered prophet-less, leaving the Saints wary of the future. Benjamin Johnson described his feelings as "unutterable sorrow" and remembered to have cried out, "Oh God! what will thy orphan Church and people now do!"[4] Indeed, the question was more complex than this—it was, frankly, one that asked how and why the martyrdom

---

Donald Q. Cannon is a professor of Church history and doctrine at Brigham Young University. Zachary L. Largey is a graduate student and instructor in English at Brigham Young University.

occurred, what the tragic day meant for the veracity of the Church, and whether this solidified Joseph's place in the long history of sealed testimonies, or whether it was necessary at all. Of course, fully answering these questions requires a much larger venue, but one thing can be made certain—the martyrdom was a culmination of the Church's past persecutions, and its occurrence, in general, was not unthinkable.

A HISTORY OF PERSECUTION

Historical narratives of the events preceding the martyrdom often begin with the destruction of the *Nauvoo Expositor*. Joseph had faced increasing difficulty with apostasy and criticism within the Church, which, in the words of B. H. Roberts, were "more serious than all external opposition."[5] When former Church leaders William and Wilson Law along with Robert D. Foster and Chauncey Higbee established an anti-Mormon (and anti-Joseph Smith) newspaper, the Prophet, as mayor, ordered its destruction inasmuch as it was calculated to destroy the peace of the city.[6]

After the *Expositor* was demolished, criticism against Joseph engulfed newspapers such as the *Warsaw Signal,* whose editor, Thomas Sharp, responded by asking his readership the following: "Can you stand by and suffer such Infernal Devils! to rob men of their property and rights, without avenging them? We have no time to comment: every man will make his own. *Let it be made with powder and ball!!!*"[7]

On 12 June, rumors that mobs were gathering to attack reached Nauvoo, and on the 16th, Joseph wrote a letter informing Governor Ford of the growing mob's intent "to drive and exterminate 'the Saints' by force of arms."[8] He further indicated his decision to take a judge's advice to allow himself to be tried in court, and, the next day, Joseph appeared before Daniel H. Wells, a "friendly but non-Mormon justice of the peace."[9] After he was discharged, a mob, enraged that the Mormon leader was unlikely to face further trial from within

Nauvoo, adopted Sharp's sentiment and declared that if the "law could not reach [him]," then "powder and ball would."[10]

In the face of such opposition, Joseph empowered the Nauvoo police and the Legion to "see that no violent act is committed."[11] On the 18th, he made the following declaration:

> To the Marshal of the City of Nauvoo:
>
> From the newspapers around us, and the current reports as brought in from the surrounding country, I have good reason to fear that a mob is organizing to come upon this city, and plunder and destroy said city, as well as murder the citizens; and by virtue of the authority vested in me as Mayor, and to preserve the city and the lives of the citizens, I do hereby declare the said city, within the limits of its incorporation, under martial law. The officers, therefore, of the Nauvoo Legion, the police as well as all others, will strictly see that no persons or property pass in or out of the city without due orders.[12]

As with the destruction of the *Nauvoo Expositor,* Joseph's decision to put Nauvoo under martial law further outraged an already hostile mob, for which an official charge of "treason against the government and people of the State of Illinois"[13] was levied. In response, the Prophet spent some of his final days in Nauvoo preparing the city's defenses.

Of course, the situation in Nauvoo and Carthage did not go unnoticed. Governor Thomas Ford, who later called the *Expositor*'s destruction an "unlawful" and "unconstitutional" act that "hurt [the Mormons] more than ten presses could have injured them in ten years,"[14] arrived in Carthage on 21 June and wrote the following in a letter to Joseph:

> I think before any decisive measure shall be adopted, that I ought to hear the allegations and defenses of all parties. By adopting this course I have some hope that the evils of war may be averted, and, at any rate, I will be enabled by it to understand the true merits of the present difficulties, and shape my course with reference to law and justice.[15]

Ford then requested that delegations be sent from Nauvoo and Carthage, and, two days later, that Joseph give himself up for trial. Major events over the next couple of days included the Prophet's arrest by Ford's posse, his agreement to discharge the Nauvoo Legion,

Joseph Smith Era, *by Jerry Thompson.* © *Intellectual Reserve, Inc.*
Courtesy of the Museum of Church History and Art

and, under pressure from the governor, to surrender the arms that were owned by the state of Illinois. Then, between 25 and 27 June, Joseph and Hyrum Smith were placed under a minimal guard to await trial, scheduled two days later. Finally, around 5:16 P.M. on the 27th, the Prophet and his brother the Patriarch were killed.[16]

The details of Joseph's time in prison are well known. Much has been said of John Taylor's singing "A Poor Wayfaring Man of Grief," and of the miraculous escapes by both John Taylor and Willard Richards. Much has also been written about the injustice of an act that, according to the governor's promise to protect the prisoners, should not have otherwise happened. But one question that needs to be answered to understand the meaning of the martyrdom is one that revolves around Joseph's foreknowledge of it, as well as his resignation to it. Did it, in fact, need to happen?

When studying Church history, one quickly confronts its tribulations and trials, many of which involved the Prophet. When the Church was at Far West, Joseph was taken prisoner by a militia that threatened to execute him for treason. After a short battle near

Crooked River, where several Latter-day Saints tried to stem mobocratic persecution, then Missouri governor Lilburn W. Boggs issued
an order to expel them from the state and exterminate them if necessary. Once, while in Illinois, Joseph was taken prisoner by one Sheriff
Reynolds and his constable and endured several death threats while
responding himself, "Shoot away; I am not afraid of your pistols."[17]
Church history records various attempts to kill the Prophet, from
John C. Bennett's sham battle with the Nauvoo Legion[18] to Wilson and
William Law's promise of money to anyone who could successfully do
so. Joseph was also the target of numerous charges of treason, false
indictments, and months spent in prison. The best way, perhaps, to
sum up his experience is with his own words:

> Oh! I am so tired—so tired that I often feel to long for my day of rest.
> For what has there been in this life but tribulation for me? From a boy I
> have been persecuted by my enemies, and now even my friends are
> beginning to join with them, to hate and persecute me! Why should I not
> wish for my time of rest?[19]

From these experiences, Joseph's eventual murder seemed more than
possible, even probable, causing one to wonder whether his enemies
simply performed the inevitable; whether the martyrdom was nothing more than the mob finally succeeding. But to answer this question, we must also question Joseph's foreknowledge of the ensuing
event.

PROPHECIES AND PURPOSES

Without a doubt, the Prophet understood what lay before him.
Church history records several instances in which he spoke as though
he were already condemned to death. One of the more famous
instances occurred on the way to Carthage Jail. When Joseph and his
company saw a militia captain hurrying to retrieve Nauvoo Legion's
weapons, Joseph remarked, "I am going like a lamb to the slaughter;
but I am calm as a summer's morning."[20] A few days before, his
brother Hyrum told Reynolds Cahoon that "a company of men are
seeking to kill my brother . . . and the Lord has warned him to flee to

the Rocky Mountains."[21] Brigham Young later recalled how Joseph would often say, "I will not live until I am 40 years old."[22]

While in prison, Joseph wrote to his wife, Emma, the following postscript: "Dear Emma, I am very much resigned to my lot, knowing that I am justified, and have done the best that could be done."[23] Church historian Ronald K. Esplin has pointed out that by 1844, Joseph felt to hasten his work because of "some important Scene" that was to take place. In March 1844, Joseph conferred the keys of the priesthood upon the Twelve, saying, "It may be that my enemies will kill me, and in case they should, and the Keys and power which rest on me not be imparted to you, they will be lost from the Earth."[24] Even the Doctrine and Covenants hints at Joseph's fate: "And now I command you, my servant Joseph, to repent and walk more uprightly before me, and to yield to the persuasions of men no more . . . and if you do this, behold I grant unto you eternal life, *even if you should be slain*" (D&C 5:21–22; emphasis added).

Yet some documents claim that Joseph prophesied of his safety. One member wrote that his martyrdom had been inconceivable because she recalled a speech in which he defied earth and hell, saying that "he had received an unconditional promise from the Almighty concerning his days."[25] But Richard Lloyd Anderson has noted that such statements are taken out of context, for while Joseph often reaffirmed his mission on earth, he did so knowing that his martyrdom would eventually come. One particular quote illustrates this perfectly: "I know what I say; I understand my mission and business. God almighty is my shield, and what can man do if God is my friend. I shall not be sacrificed until my time comes—then I shall be offered freely."[26] Wilford Woodruff's journal records another such instance: "Some has supposed that Br. Joseph could not die but this is a mistake. It is true their has been times when I have had the promise of my life to accomplish such & such things, but having accomplish those things I . . . am as liable to die as other men."[27] Thus, it is easy to see that Joseph knew of his eventual fate and that even though he had suffered several brushes with death before, this one journey to Carthage would mark his last and fatal encounter with the mob.

Still, though, Joseph's liability to die should not have made his death necessary. Returning to Benjamin Johnson's quote, the Church was still in its embryonic stage, and the Prophet surely could have continued to serve the Church much like his successor, Brigham Young, had he lived to see the Saints cross the plains. And if Hyrum's comment that the Lord had warned Joseph was correct, why, then, would he be "offered freely" as a sacrifice? What did his martyrdom really mean?

Historically speaking, the Prophet may have understood the consequences surrounding his imprisonment. Had he tried to escape and succeeded, he might have only been able to do so for a short time. He, therefore, saw his martyrdom as the single way to appease the mob and rid himself of persecution completely—to find his "day of rest." Further, Joseph may have understood the consequences of calling out the Nauvoo Legion. As one historian writes, such an act could have caused severe bloodshed. Joseph clearly chose to shed his blood rather than bring harm upon his friends or enemies.[28] Yet, from a doctrinal perspective, there still seems to be a deeper reason—one that parallels the concluding lines of Joseph's favorite hymn: "My friendship's utmost zeal to try, He asked if I for him would die."[29]

SEALING THE TESTIMONY

In the Bible, the apostle Paul taught that the ultimate testimony—that which cannot be refuted—is one where the testator gives his or her life for the testament: "For where a testament is, there must also of necessity be the death of the testator. For a testament is of force after men are dead: otherwise it is of no strength at all while the testator liveth" (Hebrews 9:16–17). This concept was referred to as the sealing of one's testimony, thereby *sealing* a person's faith and obedience to God by performing the ultimate sacrifice; by making what was essentially mortal, immortal. When a testament was sealed by the testator's blood, it removed all doubt about the testator's willingness to stand firm in the gospel. And it was a concept that continued after the Restoration.

For example, when David W. Patten became the first apostolic martyr of the modern Church, Heber C. Kimball wrote in his journal: "It was indeed a painful circumstance to be deprived of the labors of this worthy servant of Christ . . . yet the glorious and *sealing testimony* which he bore of his acceptance with heaven, and the truth of the gospel, was a matter of joy and satisfaction."[30] During general conference in 1852, George Albert Smith referred to the sacrifices of past martyrs as a "sealing" of their testimonies,[31] and in 1857, Bishop Lorenzo D. Young reassured members that if they became modern-day martyrs, then they would "have the privilege and honour of sealing their testimony with their blood."[32] Such a "privilege," then, was Joseph's.

In 1868, Elder George A. Smith spoke on the various Christian sects and their refusal to accept the Prophet's revelations as genuine, or inspired. In this sermon, Elder Smith points out that as soon as Joseph testified of the truths that had been revealed to him, "a howl went up from all the world that he was an imposter, an ignorant fellow, a man without education."[33] If there was any title quickly adopted by anti-Mormons to describe Joseph Smith, it was that of imposter. But if he was such, one has to reconcile Joseph's willingness to die for the cause that he had given so much of his life for. Why would an imposter be willing to die for a cause that he knew to be false?

Joseph understood his mission in life. If he was not an imposter, then he would have to prove it, just as many of the Old and New Testament prophets did. And when Joseph and Hyrum's bodies were returned to Nauvoo, and the pain that spread through the city began to abate, the Church came to realize that Joseph's martyrdom held a much larger meaning than the death of one man. This, perhaps, is exactly what John Taylor understood when he wrote this poignant scripture: "He lived great, and he died great in the eyes of God and his people; and like most of the Lord's anointed in ancient times, has sealed his mission and his works with his own blood; and so has his brother Hyrum" (D&C 135:3). And such is the teaching of our current prophet, Gordon B. Hinckley: "To quote a truism uttered long ago and in different circumstances, 'the blood of the martyrs has become the seed of the Church.' The testimonies which were sealed here in these very precincts, that hot and sultry day 150 years ago now nurture the faith of people around the world."[34] In the end, this may be the best way to understand the martyrdom. It is true that the Church had undergone serious persecution in the past and that Joseph and Hyrum's deaths constituted the apex of their trials and tribulations, but it is also true that Joseph understood the need to make one final testimony to the world. And it is here, in the strength of a testimony marked with blood, that Joseph made his most valiant speech for what he believed and in whom he left his trust.

NOTES

1. Evans, *Joseph Smith, an American Prophet,* 200.
2. The official *History of The Church of Jesus Christ of Latter-day Saints* specifies that Joseph Smith was given two weapons: the first, a single barrel pistol from John S. Fullmer, and the second, a revolver from Cyrus H. Wheelock. These weapons, of course, were concealed by the Prophet and Wheelock. The history records the following conversation regarding their use: "Joseph then handed the single barrel pistol which had been given him by John S. Fullmer, to his brother Hyrum, and said, 'You may have use for this.' Brother Hyrum observed, 'I hate to use such things or to see them used.' 'So do I,' said Joseph, 'but we may have to, to defend ourselves'; upon this Hyrum took the pistol." Smith, *History of the Church,* 6:607–8.
3. Smith, *History of the Church,* 6:618.
4. Andrus and Andrus, *They Knew the Prophet,* 97.
5. Roberts, *Comprehensive History of the Church,* 2:221.
6. Smith, *History of the Church,* 6:432.
7. Roberts, *Comprehensive History of the Church,* 2:236.
8. Smith, *History of the Church,* 6:480.
9. Durham, *Joseph Smith, Prophet-Statesman,* 218.
10. Smith, *History of the Church,* 6:566.
11. Smith, *History of the Church,* 6:493.
12. Smith, *History of the Church,* 6:497.
13. Smith, *History of the Church,* 6:562.
14. Letter of Sarah Scott to her parents, printed in Partridge, *Death of a Mormon Dictator,* 17–18.
15. Smith, *History of the Church,* 6:521.
16. Conkling, *Joseph Smith Chronology,* 246–48.
17. Smith, *History of the Church,* 5:440.
18. The sham battle here is a reference to an activity where militia men in the

Nauvoo Legion would practice warlike activities. It was a fake "battle." See Cannon, *Life of Joseph Smith,* 397.

19. Andrus and Andrus, *They Knew the Prophet,* 97.
20. Littlefield, *Martyrs,* 63.
21. Smith, *History of the Church,* 6:547.
22. Wixom, *Truth and Travesty,* 66.
23. Smith, *History of the Church,* 6:605.
24. Ronald K. Esplin, "Joseph Smith's Mission and Timetable," in Porter and Black, *Prophet Joseph: Essays,* 309.
25. Partridge, *Death of a Mormon Dictator,* 17.
26. Anderson, "Joseph Smith's Prophecies of Martyrdom," 5. As printed in the proceedings of the 26 January 1980 Sidney B. Sperry Symposium, Brigham Young University. These proceedings can by found in *A Sesquicentennial Look at Church History,* Brigham Young University library.
27. Wilford Woodruff Journal, April 9, 1842, 168.
28. Anderson, "Joseph Smith's Prophecies of Martyrdom," 9.
29. See verse 6 of "A Poor Wayfaring Man of Grief," *Hymns,* no. 29.
30. *Times and Seasons,* 2:444; emphasis added.
31. Smith, *Journal of Discourses,* 1:43.
32. Young, *Journal of Discourses,* 6:223.
33. Smith, *Journal of Discourses,* 12:335.
34. Hinckley, *Teachings of Gordon B. Hinckley,* 513.

BIBLIOGRAPHY

BOOKS

Allen, James B., Ronald K. Esplin, and David J. Whittaker. *Men with a Mission, 1837–1841: The Quorum of the Twelve Apostles in the British Isles.* Salt Lake City: Deseret Book, 1992.

Allen, James B., and Glen M. Leonard. *The Story of the Latter-day Saints.* 2d ed. Salt Lake City: Deseret Book, 1992.

Anderson, Karl Ricks. *Joseph Smith's Kirtland: Eyewitness Accounts.* Salt Lake City: Deseret Book, 1989.

Anderson, Lavina Fielding, ed. *Lucy's Book: A Critical Edition of Lucy Mack Smith's Family Memoir.* Salt Lake City: Signature Books, 2001.

Anderson, Richard Lloyd. *Investigating the Book of Mormon Witnesses.* Salt Lake City: Deseret Book, 1981.

———. *Joseph Smith's New England Heritage.* Salt Lake City: Deseret Book, 1971.

Andrus, Hyrum, and Helen Mae Andrus. *They Knew the Prophet.* Salt Lake City: Deseret Book, 1999.

Arrington, Leonard J. *Brigham Young: American Moses.* Urbana and Chicago: University of Illinois Press, 1985.

———. *Charles C. Rich.* Provo, Utah: Brigham Young University Press, 1974.

Arrington, Leonard J., and Susan Arrington Madsen. *Sunbonnet Sisters: True Stories of Mormon Women and Frontier Life.* Salt Lake City: Bookcraft, 1984.

Backman, Milton V., Jr. *The Heavens Resound: A History of the Latter-day Saints in Ohio, 1830–1838.* Salt Lake City: Deseret Book, 1983.

———. *Joseph Smith's First Vision.* Salt Lake City: Bookcraft, 1980.

Backman, Milton V., Jr., and Richard Cowan. *Joseph Smith and the Doctrine and Covenants.* Salt Lake City: Deseret Book, 1992.

Backman, Milton V., Jr., Keith W. Perkins, and Susan Easton Black, comps.

A Profile of Latter-day Saints in Kirtland, Ohio and Members of Zion's Camp, 1830–1839. Provo, Utah: Department of Church History and Doctrine, Brigham Young University, 1982.

Bennett, John C. *A History of the Saints: An Expose of Joe Smith and the Mormons.* Boston: Leland and Whiting, 1842.

Benson, Ezra Taft. *A Witness and a Warning.* Salt Lake City: Deseret Book, 1988.

Berrett, LaMar C., ed. *Sacred Places: New York and Pennsylvania.* Vol. 1 of *Sacred Places* series. Salt Lake City: Deseret Book, 2000.

———., ed. *Sacred Places: Ohio and Illinois.* Vol. 2 of *Sacred Places* series. Salt Lake City: Deseret Book, 2002.

Black, Susan Easton, and Charles D. Tate, eds. *Joseph Smith: The Prophet, the Man.* Provo: Religious Studies Center, Brigham Young University, 1993.

Black, Susan Easton, and Richard E. Bennett, eds. *A City of Refuge: Quincy, Illinois.* Salt Lake City: Millennial Press, 2000.

Black, Susan Easton, and William G. Hartley, eds. *The Iowa Mormon Trail: Legacy of Faith and Courage.* Orem, Utah: Helix Publishing, 1997.

Bloxham, V. Ben, James R. Moss, and Larry C. Porter, eds. *Truth Will Prevail: The Rise of The Church of Jesus Christ of Latter-day Saints in the British Isles, 1837–1987.* Salt Lake City: Deseret Book, 1987.

Bradford, M. Gerald, and Alison V. P. Coutts. *Uncovering the Original Text of the Book of Mormon.* Provo, Utah: Foundation for Ancient Research and Mormon Studies (FARMS), 2002.

Brewster, Hoyt W., Jr. *Prophets, Priesthood Keys, and Succession.* Salt Lake City: Deseret Book, 1991.

Brown, Matthew B. *Plates of Gold: The Book of Mormon Comes Forth.* American Fork, Utah: Covenant Communications, 2003.

Brown, S. Kent, Donald Q. Cannon, and Richard H. Jackson, eds. *Historical Atlas of Mormonism.* New York: Simon & Schuster, 1994.

Bushman, Richard L. *Joseph Smith and the Beginnings of Mormonism.* Urbana and Chicago: University of Illinois Press, 1984.

Butler, Jon. *Awash in a Sea of Faith: Christianizing the American People.* Cambridge: Harvard University Press, 1990.

Cannon, Donald Q., and Lyndon W. Cook, eds. *Far West Record: Minutes of The Church of Jesus Christ of Latter-day Saints, 1830–1844.* Salt Lake City: Deseret Book, 1983.

Cannon, Donald Q., and Larry E. Dahl. *The Prophet Joseph Smith's King Follett Discourse.* Provo, Utah: BYU Printing Service, 1983.

Cannon, George Q. *Life of Joseph Smith, the Prophet.* Salt Lake City: Deseret Book, 1964.

Carter, Kate B. *Our Pioneer Heritage.* Salt Lake City: Daughters of Utah Pioneers, 1958–77.

Children of the Covenant. Salt Lake City: Genealogical Society of Utah, 1937.

Church History in the Fulness of Times: The History of The Church of Jesus Christ of Latter-day Saints. Salt Lake City: The Church of Jesus Christ of Latter-day Saints, 2000.

Clark, John A. *Gleanings by the Way.* Philadelphia: W. J. & J. K. Simon, 1842.

Conkling, Christopher J. *Joseph Smith Chronology.* Salt Lake City: Deseret Book, 1979.

Cook, Lyndon W. *David Whitmer Interviews: A Restoration Witness.* Orem, Utah: Grandin Book, 1991.

———. *Words of Joseph Smith: The Contemporary Accounts of the Nauvoo Discourses of the Prophet Joseph Smith.* Provo, Utah: Religious Studies Center, Brigham Young University, 1980.

Cook, Thomas L. *Palmyra and Vicinity.* Palmyra, New York: Palmyra Courier-Journal, 1930.

Cowan, Richard O. *Temples to Dot the Earth.* Springville, Utah: Cedar Fort, 1997.

Crawley, Peter. *A Descriptive Bibliography of the Mormon Church: Volume One, 1830–1847.* Provo, Utah: Religious Studies Center, Brigham Young University, 1997.

———. *The First Mormon Book: A Celebration of the 1830 Book of Mormon.* Salt Lake City: Benchmark Books, 2000.

Dahl, Larry E., and Charles D. Tate Jr., eds. *The Lectures on Faith in Historical Perspective.* Provo, Utah: Brigham Young University, 1990.

Delbanco, Andrew. *The Death of Satan: How Americans Have Lost the Sense of Evil.* New York: Farrar, Straus, Giroux, 1995.

Derr, Jill Mulvay, Janath Russell Cannon, and Maureen Ursenbach Beecher. *Women of Covenant: The Story of Relief Society.* Salt Lake City: Deseret Book, 1992.

Deseret Morning News 2004 Church Almanac. Salt Lake City: Deseret News, 2004.

Document Containing the Correspondence, Orders, &C. In Relation to the Disturbances with the Mormons. Fayette, Mo.: Boon's Lick Democrat, 1841.

Durham, G. Homer. *Joseph Smith: Prophet-Statesman.* Salt Lake City: Bookcraft, 1944.

Durham, Reed C., Jr., and Steven H. Heath. *Succession in the Church.* Salt Lake City: Bookcraft, 1970.

Ehat, Andrew F., and Lyndon W. Cook. *The Words of Joseph Smith.* Provo, Utah: Religious Studies Center, Brigham Young University, 1980.

Encyclopedia of Mormonism. Ed. Daniel H. Ludlow et al. 4 vols. New York: Macmillan, 1992.

Evans, John Henry. *Joseph Smith: An American Prophet.* New York: Macmillan, 1946.

Faulring, Scott H., Kent P. Jackson, and Robert J. Matthews. Joseph Smith's New Translation of the Bible: Original Manuscripts. Provo, Utah: Religious Studies Center, Brigham Young University, 2004.

Flanders, Robert Bruce. *Nauvoo: Kingdom on the Mississippi.* Urbana: University of Illinois Press, 1965.

Four Faith-Promoting Classics. Salt Lake City: Bookcraft, 1968.

Garr, Arnold K., Donald Q. Cannon, and Richard O. Cowan, eds. *Encyclopedia of Latter-day Saint History.* Salt Lake City: Deseret Book, 2000.

Garr, Arnold K., and Clark V. Johnson, eds. *Missouri.* Regional Studies in Latter-day Saint Church History series. Provo, Utah: Department of Church History and Doctrine, Brigham Young University, 1994.

Garrett, H. Dean, ed. *Illinois.* Regional Studies in Latter-day Saint Church History series. Provo, Utah: Department of Church History and Doctrine, Brigham Young University, 1995.

Gibbons, Francis M. *George Albert Smith: Kind and Caring Christian, Prophet of God.* Salt Lake City: Deseret Book, 1990.

———. *Harold B. Lee: Man of Vision, Prophet of God.* Salt Lake City: Deseret Book, 1993.

———. *Joseph Fielding Smith: Gospel Scholar, Prophet of God.* Salt Lake City: Deseret Book, 1992.

———. *Spencer W. Kimball: Resolute Disciple, Prophet of God.* Salt Lake City: Deseret Book, 1995.

Givens, Terryl L. *By the Hand of Mormon.* Oxford: Oxford University Press, 2002.

Godfrey, Kenneth W., Audrey M. Godfrey, and Jill Mulvay Derr. *Women's Voices.* Salt Lake City: Deseret Book, 1982.

Grant, Jedediah M. *Collection of Facts, Relative to the Course Taken by Elder Sidney Rigdon, in the States of Ohio, Missouri, Illinois, and Pennsylvania.* Philadelphia: Brown, Bicking & Gilbert, 1844.

Gunn, Stanley R. *Oliver Cowdery: Second Elder and Scribe.* Salt Lake City: Bookcraft, 1962.

Hartley, William G. *My Best for the Kingdom: History and Autobiography of John Lowe Butler, a Mormon Frontiersman.* Salt Lake City: Aspen Books, 2003.

———. *Stand by My Servant Joseph.* Salt Lake City: Deseret Book, 2003.

Hill, Donna. *Joseph Smith, the First Mormon.* Midvale, Utah: Signature, 1977.

Hinckley, Gordon B. *Teachings of Gordon B. Hinckley.* Salt Lake City: Deseret Book, 1997.

Holzapfel, Richard Neitzel, and Jeni Broberg Holzapfel. *Women of Nauvoo.* Salt Lake City: Bookcraft, 1992.

Howe, E. B. *Mormonism Unvailed.* Ann Arbor, Mich.: University Microfilms, 1975.

Hymns of The Church of Jesus Christ of Latter-day Saints. Salt Lake City: The Church of Jesus Christ of Latter-day Saints, 1985.

Jackson, Kent P. *From Apostasy to Restoration.* Salt Lake City: Deseret Book, 1996.

Jenson, Andrew. *Latter-day Saint Biographical Encyclopedia.* Salt Lake City: Andrew Jenson History Co., 1901–36.

———, ed. *The Historical Record.* Salt Lake City: Andrew Jenson, 1888.

Jessee, Dean C., ed. *Personal Writings of Joseph Smith.* Salt Lake City: Deseret Book, 1984.

———. *The Papers of Joseph Smith.* 2 vols. Salt Lake City: Deseret Book, 1989.

Johnson, Benjamin F. *My Life's Review.* Mesa, Ariz.: 21st Century Printing, 1992.

Johnson, Clark V. *Mormon Redress Petitions: Documents of the 1833–1838 Missouri Conflict.* Provo, Utah: Religious Studies Center, Brigham Young University, 1992.

Journal of Discourses. Liverpool: F. D. and S. W. Richards, 1854–86.

Kirkham, Francis W. *A New Witness for Christ in America: The Book of Mormon.* Salt Lake City: Utah Printing, 1959.

Largey, Dennis L., ed. *Book of Mormon Reference Companion.* Salt Lake City: Deseret Book, 2003.

Launius, Roger D. *Alexander William Doniphan: Portrait of a Missouri Moderate.* Columbia: University of Missouri Press, 1997.

———. *Joseph Smith III: Pragmatic Prophet.* Urbana: University of Illinois Press, 1988.

Laws of the State of New York. Albany, New York: H. C. Southwick & Co., 1813.

LeSueur, Stephen C. *The 1838 Mormon War in Missouri.* Columbia: University of Missouri Press, 1987.

Littlefield, Lyman O. *The Martyrs: A Sketch of the Lives and a Full Account of the Martyrdom of Joseph and Hyrum Smith.* Salt Lake City: Juvenile Instructor Office, 1882.

Mansfield, Harvey C., and Delba Winthrop, trans. and edss. *Democracy in America by Alexis de Tocqueville.* Chicago: University of Chicago Press, 2000.

Matthews, Robert J. *A Bible! A Bible!* Salt Lake City: Bookcraft, 1990.

———. *"A Plainer Translation": Joseph Smith's Translation of the Bible: A History and Commentary.* Provo, Utah: Brigham Young University Press, 1975.

McConkie, Bruce R. *Doctrinal New Testament Commentary.* 3 vols. Salt Lake City: Bookcraft, 1965.

———. *Mormon Doctrine.* 2d ed. Salt Lake City: Bookcraft, 1993.

McConkie, Joseph Fielding, and Craig J. Ostler. *Revelations of the Restoration: A Commentary on the Doctrine and Covenants and Other Modern Revelations.* Salt Lake City: Deseret Book, 2000.

Mehling, Mary Bryant Alverson. *Cowdrey-Cowdery-Cowdray Genealogy: William Cowdery of Lynn, Massachusetts, 1630, and His Descendants.* New York: Frank Allaben Genealogical Co., [1911].

Morgan, Nicolas G., comp. *Eliza R. Snow, an Immortal.* Salt Lake City: Nicholas G. Morgan Foundation, 1957.

Neilson, Reid L., and Jed Woodworth, eds. *Believing History.* New York: Columbia University Press, 2004.

Nichols, Beach. *Atlas of Ontario County, New York.* Philadelphia: Pomeroy, Whitman, 1874.

Partridge, George F. *Death of a Mormon Dictator: Letters of Massachusetts Mormons, 1843–1848.* Provo, Utah: Brigham Young University, 1956.

Peterson, H. Donl. *Moroni: Ancient Prophet, Modern Messenger.* Bountiful, Utah: Horizon Publishers and Distributors, 1983.

Porter, Larry C., and Susan Easton Black, eds. *The Prophet Joseph: Essays on the Life and Mission of Joseph Smith.* Salt Lake City: Deseret Book, 1988.

Porter, Larry C., Milton V. Backman Jr., and Susan Easton Black, eds. *New York.* Regional Studies in Latter-day Saint History series. Provo, Utah: Department of Church History and Doctrine, Brigham Young University, 1992.

Pratt, Parley P. *Autobiography of Parley P. Pratt.* Salt Lake City: Deseret Book, 1985.

Reynolds, Noel B., ed. *Book of Mormon Authorship Revisited: The Evidence for Ancient Origins.* Provo, Utah: Foundation for Ancient Research and Mormon Studies, 1997.

Ricks, Stephen D., Donald W. Parry, and Andrew H. Hedges, eds. *The Disciple as Witness: Essays on Latter-day Saint History and Doctrine in Honor of Richard Lloyd Anderson.* Provo, Utah: Foundation for Ancient Research and Mormon Studies, 2000.

Rigdon, Sidney. *Oration Delivered by Mr. S. Rigdon, on the 4th of July, 1838, at Far West, Caldwell County, Missouri.* Far West, Mo.: Printed at the Journal Office, 1838.

Roberts, B. H. *A Comprehensive History of The Church of Jesus Christ of Latter-day Saints.* Salt Lake City: Deseret News Press, 1930.

———. *The Missouri Persecutions.* Provo, Utah: Masai Publishers, 2001.

———. *The Rise and Fall of Nauvoo.* Provo, Utah: Masai Publishers, Inc., 2001.

Robinson, David M., ed. *The Spiritual Emerson.* Boston: Beacon Press, 2003.

Robison, Elwin Clark. *The First Mormon Temple.* Provo, Utah: Brigham Young University Press, 1997.

Rothman, Norman. *The Unauthorized Biography of Joseph Smith, Mormon Prophet.* Salt Lake City: Norman Rothman Foundation, 1997.

Rugh, Susan Sessions. *Our Common Country: Family Farming, Culture, and Community in the Nineteenth Century Midwest.* Bloomington: Indiana University Press, 2001.

Schaff, Philip. *The Creeds of Christendom.* 3 vols. 4th ed. 3 vols. New York: Harper, 1919.

Scraps of Biography: Designed for the Instruction and Encouragement of Young Latter-day Saints. Faith Promoting Series, Book 10. Salt Lake City: Juvenile Instructor Office, 1883.

A Sesquicentennial Look at Church History. Sidney B. Sperry Symposium Series. Provo, Utah: Religious Instruction, Brigham Young University, 1980.

Skousen, Royal, ed. *The Original Manuscript of the Book of Mormon: Typographical Facsimile of the Extant Text.* Provo, Utah: Foundation for Ancient Research and Mormon Studies (FARMS), 2001.

———, ed. *The Printer's Manuscript of the Book of Mormon: Typographical Facsimile of the Entire Text in Two Parts.* 2 vols. Provo, Utah: Foundation for Ancient Research and Mormon Studies (FARMS), 2001.

Smart, Donna Toland. *Exemplary Elder: The Life and Missionary Diaries of Perrigrine Sessions, 1814–1893.* Provo, Utah: BYU Studies and Joseph Fielding Smith Institute for Latter-day Saint History, 2002.

Smith, Andrew F. *The Saintly Scoundrel: The Life and Times of Dr. John Cook Bennett.* Urbana: University of Illinois Press, 1997.

Smith, Joseph. *History of the Church of Jesus Christ of Latter-day Saints.* Ed. B. H. Roberts. 2d ed., rev. 7 vols. Salt Lake City: The Church of Jesus Christ of Latter-day Saints, 1932–51.

———. *Joseph Smith's Commentary on the Bible.* Comp. and ed. by Kent. P. Jackson. Salt Lake City: Deseret Book, 1994.

———. *Teachings of the Prophet Joseph Smith.* Sel. Joseph Fielding Smith. Salt Lake City: Deseret Book, 1976.

Smith, Joseph F. *Gospel Doctrine.* Salt Lake City: Deseret Book, 1986.

Smith, Joseph Fielding. *Doctrines of Salvation.* 3 vols. Salt Lake City: Bookcraft, 1954–56.

Smith, Lucy Mack. *Biographical Sketches of Joseph Smith, the Prophet, and His Progenitors for Many Generations.* Liverpool: S. W. Richards, 1853. Reprint, Orem, Utah: Grandin Book, 1995.

———. *History of Joseph Smith by His Mother.* Ed. Preston Nibley. Salt Lake City: Bookcraft, 1958.

———. *The History of Joseph Smith by His Mother.* Ed. George A. Smith and Elias Smith. American Fork, Utah: Covenant Communications, 2000.

———. *Joseph Smith and His Progenitors.* Independence, Mo.: Herald Publishing House, 1969.

———. *The Revised and Enhanced History of Joseph Smith by His Mother.* Ed. Scott Facer Proctor and Maurine Jensen Proctor. Salt Lake City: Bookcraft, 1996.

Smith, William. *William Smith on Mormonism.* Lamoni, Iowa: Herald Steam Book and Job Office, 1883.

Steed, Thomas. *The Life of Thomas Steed from His Own Diary, 1826–1910.* N.p., 1935.

Studies in Scripture. Ed. Kent P. Jackson and Robert L. Millet. 8 vols. Salt Lake City: Deseret Book, 1984–88.

Stuy, Brian H., ed. *Collected Discourses.* 5 vols. Burbank, Calif., and Woodland Hills, Utah: B.H.S. Publishing, 1987–92.

Tullidge, Edward W. *The Women of Mormondom.* New York: Tullidge and Crandall, 1877.

Turley, Richard E., Jr., ed. *Selected Collections from the Archives of The Church of Jesus Christ of Latter-day Saints.* Provo, Utah: Brigham Young University Press, 2002, DVD.

Watson, Elden J., ed. *Manuscript History of Brigham Young, 1801–1844.* Salt Lake City: Smith Secretarial Service, 1968.

Webster, Noah. *An American Dictionary of the English Language.* New York:

S. Converse, 1828. Facsimile reprint, San Francisco: Foundation for American Christian Education, 1980.

Weigley, Russell F. *History of the United States Army.* Bloomington: Indiana University Press, 1984.

Weslager, Clinton A. *The Delaware Indian Westward Migration.* Wallingford, Pa.: Middle Atlantic Press, 1978.

———. *The Delaware Indians: A History.* New Jersey: Rutgers University Press, 1990.

West, Lucy Fish, ed. *The Papers of Martin Van Buren.* Alexandria, Va.: Chadwick-Healey, 1989.

Westergren, Bruce N., ed. *From Historian to Dissident: The Book of John Whitmer.* Salt Lake City: Signature Books, 1995.

Whitmer, John. *An Early Latter Day Saint History: The Book of John Whitmer.* Ed. F. Mark McKiernan and Roger D. Launius. Independence, Mo.: Herald Publishing House, 1980.

Whitney, Orson F. *Life of Heber C. Kimball, an Apostle, the Father and Founder of the British Mission.* 3d ed. Salt Lake City: Bookcraft, 1967.

Wigger, John H. *Taking Heaven by Storm.* Oxford: Oxford University Press, 1998.

Wixom, Hart. *Truth and Travesty: Critiquing the Critics of Joseph Smith.* Provo, Utah: SageCrest Publications, 2003.

Woodruff, Wilford. *Wilford Woodruff's Journal, 1833–1989.* Ed. Scott G. Kenney. 9 vols. Midvale, Utah: Signature, Books, 1983.

Woods, Fred E. *Gathering to Nauvoo.* American Fork, Utah: Covenant Communications, 2002.

Woods, Fred E., Steven C. Harper, and Andrew H. Hedges, eds. *Prelude to the Restoration: From Apostasy to the Restored Church.* Salt Lake City: Deseret Book, 2004.

Young, Brigham. *Discourses of Brigham Young.* Comp. John A. Widtsoe. Salt Lake City: Deseret Book, 1971.

Young, Joseph, Sr. *History of the Organization of the Seventies.* Salt Lake City: Deseret News Steam Printing Establishment, 1878.

Youngreen, Buddy. *Reflections of Emma: Joseph Smith's Wife.* Provo, Utah: Maasai Publishers, 2001.

ARTICLES AND PERIODICALS

Allen, James B. "Eight Contemporary Accounts of Joseph Smith's First Vision." *Improvement Era,* April 1970, 4–13.

———. "Historian's Corner." *BYU Studies* 10, no. 4 (Summer 1970): 479–90.

Anderson, Richard Lloyd. "'By the Gift and Power of God.'" *Ensign,* September 1977, 78–85.

———. "Circumstantial Confirmation of the First Vision through Reminiscences." *BYU Studies* 9, no. 3 (Spring 1969): 373–404.

———. "Confirming Records of Moroni's Coming." *Improvement Era,* September 1970, 4–8.

———. "Gold Plates and Printer's Ink." *Ensign,* September 1976, 71–76.

———. "Joseph Smith's Testimony of the First Vision." *Ensign,* April 1996, 10–21.

Arrington, J. Earl. "William Weeks, Architect of the Nauvoo Temple." *BYU Studies* 19, no. 3 (Spring 1979): 337–59.

Atkinson, Eleanor. "The Winter of Deep Snow." *Transactions of the Illinois State Historical Society* 13 (1909): 47–62.

Auge, Thomas. "The Priest behind the Legends: Father John Alleman." *Palimpsest* 74, no. 2 (Summer 1993): 86, 96.

Backman, Milton V., Jr. "Awakenings in the Burned-Over District: New Light on the Historical Setting of the First Vision." *BYU Studies* 9, no. 3 (Spring 1969): 301–20.

———. "A Warning from Kirtland." *Ensign,* April 1989, 26–30.

Baugh, Alexander L. "A Community Abandoned: W. W. Phelps' 1839 Letter to Sally Waterman Phelps from Far West, Missouri." *Nauvoo Journal* 10, no. 2 (Fall 1998): 19–32.

———. "Parting the Veil: The Visions of Joseph Smith." *BYU Studies* 38, no. 1 (1999): 22–69.

———. "'We Took Our Change of Venue to the State of Illinois': The Gallatin Hearing and the Escape of Joseph Smith and the Mormon Prisoners from Missouri, 1839." *Mormon Historical Studies* 2, no. 1 (Spring 2001): 59–82.

Benjamin, Alice E. "History of Palmyra." *Palmyra 175th Anniversary Celebration Program* (1964): 1.

Bennett, Richard E., and Rachel Cope. "'A City on a Hill'—Chartering the City of Nauvoo." *John Whitmer Historical Association 2002 Nauvoo Conference Special Edition* (2002): 26–29.

Brown, Kent. "Lehi's Personal Record: Quest for a Missing Source." *BYU Studies* 24, no. 1 (Winter 1984): 19–42.

Brown, Lisle G. "The Sacred Departments for Temple Work in Nauvoo: The Assembly Room and the Council Chamber." *BYU Studies* 19, no. 3 (Spring 1979): 361–88.

Bushman, Richard L. "The Character of Joseph Smith," *BYU Studies* 42, no. 2 (2003): 22–34.

Cannon, Donald Q. "The King Follett Discourse: Joseph Smith's Greatest Sermon in Historical Perspective." *BYU Studies* 18, no. 2 (Winter 1978): 179–92.

———. "Spokes on the Wheel: Early Latter-day Saint Settlements in Hancock County, Illinois." *Ensign*, February 1986, 62–68.

Carmack, John K. "Fayette: The Place Where the Church Was Organized." *Ensign*, February 1989, 14–19.

Cook, Lyndon W. "Isaac Galland: Mormon Benefactor." *BYU Studies* 19, no. 3 (Spring 1979): 261–84.

Crawley, Peter. "Two Rare Missouri Documents." *BYU Studies* 14, no. 4 (Summer 1974): 502–27.

Ehat, Andrew F. "'They Might Have Known That He Was Not a Fallen Prophet': The Journal of Joseph Fielding." *BYU Studies* 19, no. 2 (Winter 1979): 133–66.

Enders, Donald L. "The Steamboat *Maid of Iowa:* Mormon Mistress of the Mississippi." *BYU Studies* 19, no. 3 (Spring 1979): 321–35.

Faust, James E. "The Keys That Never Rust." *Ensign*, November 1994, 72–74; or Conference Report, October 1994, 94–98.

———. Conference Report, April 1984, 92–93.

First Presidency and Twelve Apostles of The Church of Jesus Christ of Latter-day Saints. "The Family: A Proclamation to the World." *Ensign*, November 1995, 102.

Gentry, Leland H. "Light on the 'Mission to the Lamanites.'" *BYU Studies* 36, no. 2 (1996–97): 226–34.

Godfrey, Kenneth W. "The Zelph Story." *BYU Studies* 29, no. 2 (Winter 1989): 31–56.

Hartley, William G. "'Almost Too Intolerable a Burthen': The Winter Exodus from Missouri 1838–1839." *Journal of Mormon History* 18 (Fall 1992): 6–40.

Hill, Marvin S. "Cultural Crisis in the Mormon Kingdom: A Reconsideration of the Causes of Kirtland Dissent." *Church History* 49, no. 3 (September 1980): 287–88.

Hinckley, Gordon B. "Ambitious to Do Good." *Ensign*, March 1992, 2–6.

———. "Come and Partake." *Ensign*, May 1986, 46–49; or Conference Report, April 1986, 61–65.

———. Conference Report, April 1999, 117.

———. "Don't Drop the Ball." *Ensign*, November 1994, 46–49.

Holland, Jeffrey R. "Like a Watered Garden." *Ensign*, November 2001, 33–35.

———. "Miracles of the Restoration." *Ensign*, November 1994, 31–34; or Conference Report, October 1994, 39–43.

Jessee, Dean C. "Joseph Knight's Recollection of Early Mormon History." *BYU Studies* 17, no. 1 (Autumn 1976): 29–39.

———. "The Original Book of Mormon Manuscript." *BYU Studies* 10, no. 3 (Spring 1970): 259–78.

———, ed. "The Early Accounts of Joseph Smith's First Vision." *BYU Studies* 9, no. 3 (Spring 1969): 275–94.

The Juvenile Instructor. Salt Lake City: Deseret Sunday School Sunday Union, 1866–1929.

Kimball, Stanley B. "Nauvoo." *Improvement Era,* July 1962, 516–17, 548–51.

———. "Nauvoo West: The Mormons of the Iowa Shore." *BYU Studies* 18, no. 2 (Winter 1978): 132–42.

Lyon, T. Edgar. "Independence, Missouri, and the Mormons, 1827–1833." *BYU Studies* 13, no. 1 (Autumn 1972): 10–19.

———. "The Sketches on the Papyri Backings." *Improvement Era,* May 1968, 18–23.

Matthews, Robert J. "Joseph Smith's Efforts to Publish His Bible Translation." *Ensign,* January 1983, 57–64.

———. "Using the Scriptures." *Brigham Young University 1981 Fireside and Devotional Speeches.* Provo, Utah: Brigham Young University Publications, 1981, 118–26.

Maxwell, Neal A. "A Choice Seer." *BYU Speeches Online,* Brigham Young University, Provo, Utah, 30 March 1986.

———. "Consecrate Thy Performance." *Ensign,* May 2002, 36–38.

———. "Encircled in the Arms of His Love." *Ensign,* November 2002: 16–18.

———. "'O, Divine Redeemer.'" *Ensign,* November 1981, 8–10; or Conference Report, October 1981, 8–12.

———. "Settle This in Your Hearts." *Ensign,* November 1992, 65–67.

Oaks, Dallin H. "Recent Events Involving Church History and Forged Documents." *Ensign,* October 1987, 67–69.

Packer, Boyd K. "The Cloven Tongues of Fire." *Ensign,* May 2000, 7–9.

———. "The Pattern of Our Parentage." *Ensign,* November 1984, 66–69.

———. "The Shield of Faith." *Ensign,* May 1995, 7–9; or Conference Report, April 1995, 5–9.

Porter, Larry C. "Joseph Smith's Susquehanna Years." *Ensign,* February 2001, 42.

———. "Reverend George Lane—Good 'Gifts,' Much 'Grace,' and Marked 'Usefulness.'" *BYU Studies* 9, no. 3 (Spring 1969): 321–40.

Roberts, B. H. "Brigham Young: A Character Sketch." *Improvement Era,* June 1903, 561–74.

———. Conference Report, October 1926, 121–27.

Romig, Ronald E. "The Lamanite Mission." *John Whitmer Historical Association Journal* 14 (Spring 1994): 30–32.

Skousen, Royal. "Piecing Together the Original Manuscript." *BYU Today* 46, no. 3 (May 1992): 18–24.

Smith, George. "My Journal." *Instructor* 81, no. 2 (February 1946): 74–79.

———. "My Journal." *Instructor* 81, no 3 (March 1946): 115–19.

———. "My Journal." *Instructor* 81, no. 4 (April 1946): 182–87.

———. "My Journal." *Instructor* 81, no. 5 (May 1946): 212–18.

———. "My Journal." *Instructor* 81, no. 7 (July 1946): 320–23.

Smith, Marvin E. "The Builder." *Improvement Era,* October 1942, 630–31, 648.

Stommel, Henry, and Elizabeth Stommel. "The Year without a Summer." *Scientific American* 240, no. 6 (June 1979): 176.

Walker, Ronald W. "Seeking the 'Remnant.'" *Journal of Mormon History* 19, no. 1 (Spring 1993): 1–33.

Woodbury, Lael J. "The Origin and Uses of the Sacred Hosanna Shout." Sperry Lecture Series. Provo, Utah: Brigham Young University, 1975.

Woodford, Robert J. "How the Revelations in the Doctrine and Covenants Were Received and Compiled." *Ensign,* January 1985, 26–33.

JOURNALS, DIARIES, AND AUTOBIOGRAPHIES

Bullock, Thomas. Journal of Thomas Bullock, October 9, 1846. Archives of The Church of Jesus Christ of Latter-day Saints, Salt Lake City, Utah.

Cahoon, William Farrington. Autobiography of William Farrington Cahoon. Archives of The Church of Jesus Christ of Latter-day Saints, Salt Lake City, Utah.

Crookston, Robert. Autobiography of Robert Crookston. Typescript. Archives of The Church of Jesus Christ of Latter-day Saints, Salt Lake City, Utah.

Edwards, Esaias. Autobiography and Diary of Esaias Edwards, 1856–1882. Typescript. L. Tom Perry Special Collections, Harold B. Lee Library, Brigham Young University, Provo, Utah.

Gilbert, John H. "Memorandum, made by John H. Gilbert Esq, Sept 8th. 1892." Typescript original is in the King's Daughters' Library, Palmyra, New York.

Grandin, Egbert B. Diary of Egbert B. Grandin. Archives of The Church of Jesus Christ of Latter-day Saints, Salt Lake City, Utah.

Huntington, Dimick Baker. Autobiography of Dimick Baker Huntington. Archives of The Church of Jesus Christ of Latter-day Saints, Salt Lake City, Utah.

Knight, Newel. "Newel Knight Autobiography." Harold B. Lee Library Special Collections, Brigham Young University, Provo, Utah.

———. Newel Knight's Journal, 1800–1847. L. Tom Perry Special Collections, Harold B. Lee Library, Brigham Young University, Provo, Utah.

Mace, Wandle. Autobiography of Wandle Mace. L. Tom Perry Special Collections, Harold B. Lee Library, Brigham Young University, Provo, Utah.

Miller, Reuben. Reuben Miller Journal, October 21, 1848. Archives of The Church of Jesus Christ of Latter-day Saints, Salt Lake City, Utah.

Murdock, John. John Murdock Journal. Typescript. L. Tom Perry Special Collections, Harold B. Lee Library, Brigham Young University, Provo, Utah.

Pratt, Orson. Diary of Orson Pratt. Archives of The Church of Jesus Christ of Latter-day Saints, Salt Lake City, Utah.

Smith, Joseph. Joseph Smith's 1832 Autobiographical Sketch. Joseph Smith Letter Book, Joseph Smith Collection. Archives of The Church of Jesus Christ of Latter-day Saints, Salt Lake City, Utah.

———. Joseph Smith Letterbooks. Archives of The Church of Jesus Christ of Latter-day Saints, Salt Lake City, Utah.

Whitmer, Peter, Jr. Peter Whitmer Jr. Journal. Archives of The Church of Jesus Christ of Latter-day Saints, Salt Lake City, Utah.

THESES AND DISSERTATIONS

Esplin, Ronald K. "The Emergence of Brigham Young and the Twelve to Mormon Leadership, 1830–1841." Ph.D. dissertation. Provo, Utah: Brigham Young University, 1981.

Gunnell, Wayne C. "Martin Harris—Witness and Benefactor to the Book of Mormon." M.A. thesis. Provo, Utah: Brigham Young University, 1955.

Parkin, Max H. "The Nature and Cause of Internal and External Conflict of the Mormons in Ohio between 1830–1838." M.A. thesis. Brigham Young University, 1966.

Peterson, Orlen Curtis. "A History of the Schools and Educational Programs of the Church of Jesus Christ of Latter-day Saints in Ohio and Missouri, 1831–1839." M.A. thesis. Provo, Utah: Brigham Young University, 1972.

Porter, Larry C. "A Study of the Origins of the Church of Jesus Christ of Latter-day Saints in the States of New York and Pennsylvania, 1816–1831." Ph.D. dissertation. Provo, Utah: Brigham Young University, 1971.

Woodford, Robert J. "The Historical Development of the Doctrine and Covenants." Ph.D. dissertation. Provo, Utah: Brigham Young University, 1974.

UNPUBLISHED MANUSCRIPTS

"A Book of Records Containing the Proceedings of The Female Relief Society of Nauvoo, March 17, 1842 to March 16, 1844." Archives of The Church of Jesus Christ of Latter-day Saints, Salt Lake City, Utah.

Coltrin, Zebedee. "High Priest Minutes, Spanish Fork, February 5, 1870." Archives of The Church of Jesus Christ of Latter-day Saints, Salt Lake City, Utah.

"Commission Records, Ledger Book, 1835–1846." Illinois State Archives, Springfield, Illinois.

Far West Record Book. Archives of The Church of Jesus Christ of Latter-day Saints, Salt Lake City, Utah.

Harper, Steven C. "'He Said There Was a Book Deposited': The Probation of a Teenage Seer, 1821–1927." N.p., n.d. In author's possession.

———. "'Dictated by Christ': Joseph Smith & the Politics of Revelation." N.p., n.d. In author's possession.

House Bill No. 213 (draft). "A Bill for an Act to Incorporate the Illinois Legion." Executive Papers, Governor's Correspondence, 1837–1839. Illinois State Archives, Springfield, Illinois.

Journal of the House of Representatives of Illinois, 1834–1835, December 9, 1834. Illinois State Archives, Springfield, Illinois.

Journal of the House of Representatives of Illinois, 1838. Illinois State Archives, Springfield, Illinois.

Journal of the Senate of Illinois, 1838. Illinois State Archives, Springfield, Illinois.

Journal of the 10th Assembly, 1836. Illinois State Archives, Springfield, Illinois.

Kirkham, Earl Kay. "Daniel Stillwell Thomas and Martha Paine Jones Thomas: Early Members of the LDS Church and Utah Pioneers of 1849." N.p.: E. Kay Kirkham, 1985.

"Kirtland Council Minute Book." Archives of The Church of Jesus Christ of Latter-day Saints, Salt Lake City, Utah.

"Kirtland High Council Minutes." Archives of The Church of Jesus Christ of Latter-day Saints, Salt Lake City, Utah.

"Kirtland Revelation Book." MS 4583, Fd 1. Archives of The Church of Jesus Christ of Latter-day Saints, Salt Lake City, Utah.

Bibliography

"Kirtland Township Trustees' Minutes and Poll Book, 1817–1838." Lake County Historical Society, Ohio.

Land Purchase Agreement between Isaac Hale and Joseph Smith Jr., 6 April, 1829. Joseph Smith Collection. Archives of The Church of Jesus Christ of Latter-day Saints, Salt Lake City, Utah.

Letter of Eliza R. Snow to [Isaac] Streator, 22 February 1939. Archives of The Church of Jesus Christ of Latter-day Saints, Salt Lake City, Utah.

Letter of Joseph Smith Jr. to Hyrum Smith, 3 March, 1831, MSS 155, Bx 2, Fd 3. Archives of The Church of Jesus Christ of Latter-day Saints, Salt Lake City, Utah.

Letter of Lucy Cowdery Young to Brigham H. Young, 17 March, 1887. Archives of The Church of Jesus Christ of Latter-day Saints, Salt Lake City, Utah.

Letter of Oliver Cowdery to Dearly Beloved Brethren, 7 May, 1831, Joseph Smith Letterbook 1:12–13, MSS 155, Bx 2, Fd 1. Archives of The Church of Jesus Christ of Latter-day Saints, Salt Lake City, Utah.

Letter of Oliver Cowdery to Dearly Beloved Brethren & Sisters, 8 April, 1831, Joseph Smith Letterbook 1:10–12, MSS 155, Bx 2, Fd 1. Archives of The Church of Jesus Christ of Latter-day Saints, Salt Lake City, Utah.

Letter of W. W. Phelps to Brigham Young, 12 August, 1861, MS 4583, Fd 78. Archives of The Church of Jesus Christ of Latter-day Saints, Salt Lake City, Utah.

"Militia Regiments Ledger, 1819–1835." Archives of The Church of Jesus Christ of Latter-day Saints, Salt Lake City, Utah.

Minutes, Salt Lake City School of the Prophets, 3 October 1883. Archives of The Church of Jesus Christ of Latter-day Saints, Salt Lake City, Utah.

Nobles, Joseph B. "Papers of Joseph B. Nobles." Archives of The Church of Jesus Christ of Latter-day Saints, Salt Lake City, Utah.

Old Testament (OT) Manuscript 2.

Revelation of 12 January 1838. Archives of The Church of Jesus Christ of Latter-day Saints, Salt Lake City, Utah.

Van Buren Papers. Library of Congress, reel 33, Harold B. Lee Library, Brigham Young University.

ARTICLES IN NEWSPAPERS

Deseret News (Semi-Weekly). Salt Lake City, Utah, 1865–89.
Deseret News Weekly. Salt Lake City, Utah, 1850–.
Deseret Evening News. Great Salt Lake City: G. Q. Cannon, 1867–1920.

Elders' Journal of the Church of Latter Day Saints. Kirtland, Ohio: Thomas B. Marsh, 1837–38.

The Evening and the Morning Star. Independence, Mo.: W. W. Phelps, Kirtland, Ohio: F. G. Williams, June 1832 to September 1834.

Kansas City Journal. Kansas City, Mo.: Robert T. Van Horn, 1856–1942.

Kansas City Times. Kansas City, Mo.: 1895 (started in 1865).

Latter Day Saints' Messenger and Advocate. Kirtland, Ohio: F. G. Williams, 1834–37.

The Latter-day Saints Millennial Star. Manchester, England: P. P. Pratt, 1840–1937.

LDS Church News: News of The Church of Jesus Christ of Latter-day Saints. Salt Lake City: 1981 to present.

Missouri Argus. St. Louis, Mo.: 1835–1841.

Missouri Republican. St. Louis, Mo.

Painesville Telegraph. Painesville, Ohio: E. D. Howe, 1822–1986.

Quincy Whig. Quincy, Ill.: H. V. Sullivan, 1838–56.

The Return. Davis City, Iowa: 1889–1900.

Tiffany's Monthly: Devoted to the Investigation of Spiritual Science. New York: Joel Tiffany, 1856–1859.

Times and Seasons. Nauvoo, Ill.: 1839–46.

The Warsaw Signal. Warsaw, Ill.: Sharp & Gamble, 1841–43.

Wayne Sentinel. Palmyra, N.Y.: P. Tucker, 1823–53.

Western Spectator & Wayne Advertiser. Palmyra, N.Y.: 1830–31.

Woman's Exponent. Salt Lake City: 1872–1914.

REPORTS

Ricks, Stephen. "Joseph Smith's Means and Methods of Translating the Book of Mormon." Report WRR-86. Foundation for Ancient Research and Mormon Studies (FARMS), Provo, Utah, 1984.

Welch, John W., and Tim Rathbone. "The Translation of the Book of Mormon: Basic Historical Information." Report WRR-86. Foundation for Ancient Research and Mormon Studies (FARMS), Provo, Utah, 1986.

WEBSITES

www.byu.edu
www.familysearch.com
www.waynecountyny.org

INDEX

source of JS's authority, 267; on
status of "fallen prophets," 270
Glories of Heaven, The, by Gary
Ernest Smith, *187*
Glory, kingdoms of, 188–92
God: and the First Vision, 42;
knowledge of us, 42, 49;
character of, 43, 190–91;
knowing, 43–44; as our father,
44, 375–76, 379 n. 52; at School
of the Prophets, 170–71;
standing before, 248–49; as
ruler, 249; nature of, 372–73,
379 n. 35, 385; physical body,
373–74; knowledge gained from
the First Vision, 373
Godhead, 42, 191–92, 373
Go into the Wilderness, by Robert T.
Barrett, *147*
Gold plates: temptation of wealth, 49,
54; announced by Moroni, 51,
68; waiting period, 54, 67–68;
obtaining, 58, 60–61, 63, 64–65,
70; box for, 69; attempts to steal,
70–73; hiding places, 71–75;
delivery to messenger, 74; plates
of Nephi, 82; rumors, 86; Three
Witnesses, 95–105; and
prophetic authority, 266. *See
also* Book of Mormon; Three
Witnesses; Translation of Book
of Mormon
Gorka, Ted, *Joseph Smith at Nauvoo,*
368
Grammar School, 173
Grandin, Egbert B., 96–97, 98,
107–8, 113–14, 114–15 nn. 5–6
Grandin building, 114
Granger, Oliver, 328
Grant, Jedediah M., on Sidney
Rigdon's Fourth of July speech,
289
Green Plains, Illinois, 326
Gurley, Zenos H., 322

Hale, Alva, 72–73
Hale, Emma. *See* Smith, Emma Hale

Hale, Isaac, 64, 91
Half-Breed Tract, 327–28
Harlin, Greg, *A Year After the
Eruption, 20*
Harmony, Pennsylvania, 62, 72–74,
89–92
Harper, Steven, on revelations as a
source of JS's prophetic
authority, 267
Harris, Lucy, 80–81
Harris, Martin, *97;* on JS money
digging, 62; knowledge of gold
plates, 69; and money diggers,
71; translation of Book of
Mormon, 72, 76–79; financial
help for JS, 72–73, 77–78, 83 n.
3, 97–99; testimony of the
restoration, 77–78; and Book of
Mormon copyright, 92; one of
Three Witnesses, 95–105, 270;
character of, 96–97; funding for
Book of Mormon printing, 98,
108, 112–13; proofreader for
Book of Mormon, 110; baptism,
122; June 1830 conference, 126;
gathering to the Ohio, 138;
snakebite, 223; detractor of JS,
285
Healings, 271, 328
Hebrew School, 173
Hell, 191
Higbee, Elias, 291, 312–13, 341–44,
346
High council trial of stake
presidency, 279–80
Hill Cumorah visits, 61
Hinckley, Gordon B., 340; on success
of Relief Society, 365; on being
spirit children of God, 376; on
God as our father, 379 n. 52; on
JS's martyrdom, 407–8
Hinkle, George M., 296–97, 305–6,
306 n. 2, 314
Hiram, Ohio, 195–205; publication of
Book of Commandments,
198–99; persecution, 200–205;
missionary work, 203

403–4, 406, 408; weapons, 408 n. 2

Masonic lodges, 328

Materialism, 137, 142 n. 14

Matter, 374, 386–87 n. 14

Matthews, Robert J.: on introduction of Church institutions, 122; on JS learning from translation of the Bible, 378 n. 17

Maxwell, Neal A.: on weaknesses being turned to strengths, 55; on law of consecration, 142 n. 11, 142 n. 13

McConkie, Bruce R.: on knowing God, 44; on the nature of the Church, 117; on Jesus Christ, 194 n. 4

McIntyre, Dr., 73

McLellin, William E.: School of the Elders, 172; Grammar School, 173; on JS's written revelations, 197–98; attempt to write a revelation, 198–99; called to be an apostle, 233; apostasy, 263; testimony of the Book of Mormon, 270; dissent, 287

McRae, Alexander, 304

Meetinghouses, 322–23

Melchizedek Priesthood pulpits, 254–55, 260

Melchizedek Priesthood restoration, 91

Methodist Church, 29, 135, 150

Military guard, behavior toward JS, 297–98

Military tribunal, 297–99

Militias: Jackson County, Missouri, 213–14; weapons, 213–14, 389; Caldwell County, Missouri, 291; Daviess County, Missouri, 291; Nauvoo Legion, 388–99; Illinois, 389–90, 391; legions, 394; Utah, 397

Miracles: for David Whitmer, 101, 102; clearing of the ice, 139; healing Alice Johnson, 196; and faith, 202–3; quail, 329

"Missionary towns," 320–21; La Harpe, Illinois, 321–22; Fountain Green, Illinois, 322; Carthage, Illinois, 324; Bear Creek, Illinois, 325

Missionary training, 168, 171, 172

Missionary work: to the Lamanites, 130, 131, 144–54, *147,* 158; emphasis on, 131; Lucy Mack Smith's, 139; covenant, 146; permits, 150–53, 154 n. 14; complaints about, 202; keys of gathering of Israel, 333; British mission, 334

Missouri: missionaries traveling through, 148; JS's visit in April 1832, 162–63; Church membership growth, 163; fears about Mormons, 284–89, 393–94; extermination order, 284–95; conflicts with Mormons, 289–92, 388–89; petitions for redress, 316–17, 344; attempts to extradite JS, 397. *See also* Zion

Mobs, *196,* 200; and gold plates, 71–73; in Harmony, 91; in Missouri, 163; destruction of printing press, 199; in Hiram, Ohio, 203–5; in Jackson County, 207–16, *209;* religious motivations, 208; and slavery, 208–9; Manifesto of the Mob, 210; Church printing office, 211; Church response, 212; and Church finances, 219; and Zion's Camp, 225–26; and Kirtland Temple, 256; and Fourth of July speech, 288–89; in Pontoosuc, 321; Green Plains, Illinois, 326; in Yelrome, Illinois, 326; JS's martyrdom, 326–27, 400; and the Nauvoo Legion, 388–89; after destruction of the *Nauvoo Expositor,* 401–2

Money digging, 61–63

Montrose, Iowa, 328